Latin American Cinema

The publisher gratefully acknowledges the generous support of the Eric Papenfuse and Catherine Lawrence Endowment Fund in Film and Media Studies of the University of California Press Foundation.

Latin American Cinema

A Comparative History

Paul A. Schroeder Rodríguez

UNIVERSITY OF CALIFORNIA PRESS

University of California Press, one of the most distinguished
university presses in the United States, enriches lives around the
world by advancing scholarship in the humanities, social sciences,
and natural sciences. Its activities are supported by the UC Press
Foundation and by philanthropic contributions from individuals
and institutions. For more information, visit www.ucpress.edu.

University of California Press
Oakland, California

Library of Congress Cataloging-in-Publication Data

Schroeder, Paul A., author.
    Latin American cinema : a comparative history /
Paul A. Schroeder Rodríguez.
        pages   cm
    Includes bibliographical references and index.
    ISBN 978-0-520-28863-8 (pbk. : alk. paper) —
    ISBN 978-0-520-96353-5 (ebook)
    1. Motion pictures—Latin America—History.
2. Motion picture industry—Latin America—History.
I. Title.
    PN1993.5.L3S28   2016
    791.43098—dc23

                                        2015029741

Manufactured in China

25   24   23   22   21   20   19   18   17   16
10   9   8   7   6   5   4   3   2   1

The paper used in this publication meets the minimum requirements
of ANSI/NISO Z39.48-1992 (R 2002) (Permanence of Paper).

Contents

Acknowledgments

My deepest appreciation goes to my wife, María Monasterios, and to our daughter, Uma Schroeder-Monasterios, for their patience and understanding during the ten years I worked on this project. I dedicate this book to them.

At my home institution, Northeastern Illinois University, I am grateful to my colleagues in the Department of World Languages and Cultures and in the College of Arts and Sciences' Dean's Office for their support and encouragement over the past seven years; to the Office of Academic Affairs for a semester-long leave that allowed me to finish a first draft of this book; and to the interlibrary loan staff for reliably finding the hundreds of materials I requested.

Finally, I am especially thankful to Michael Predmore for the opportunity to spend a year as a visiting associate professor at Stanford University, during which time I began research for this book in earnest; to Kris Lane and the anonymous readers for their constructive feedback on a first draft of the book; to the editors and anonymous readers in the journals where portions of the book were first published (*Latin American Research Review, Chasqui: Revista de Literatura Latinoamericana, Rethinking Marxism, Revista de Crítica Literaria Latinoamericana, Cinema Journal, Valenciana,* and *Camera Obscura*); to Mary Francis and her editorial team at the University of California Press for their enthusiastic support throughout the entire editing and publication process; and to the following individuals and institutions for providing stills as noted in the relevant captions: Marcela Cassinelli at Cinemateca Argentina, Fernando Fortes at Cinemateca Brasileira, Elizabeth Carrasco at Cinemateca Boliviana, and Marco Audrá of Maristela Films.

Introduction

This book charts a comparative history of Latin America's national cinemas from the silent period to the digital age. It differs from previous histories in that it privileges neither a national perspective nor a single period. Instead, it develops what the film historian Paulo Antonio Paranaguá calls a new history of the region's cinema: "A new history implies changes in focus and methodology, new objects and sources, new articulations and interpretations. Far from reducing options, a comparative perspective widens them. National differences should not be confused, but we do not consider it pertinent to isolate the national framework. Similarly, we do not privilege auteur theory because even though it has inspired notable interpretations and studies, it curtails historical research."[1]

In a series of brilliant essays collected in *Tradición y modernidad en el cine de América Latina* (Tradition and Modernity in the Cinema of Latin America, 2003), Paranaguá demonstrated just how much new light a comparative approach can shed on lesser-known periods of Latin American cinema such as silent cinema and neorealism. The model proved strong enough for me to set aside a national history I had been writing in favor of this comparative one. Crucially, despite the considerable differences between our perspectives—most notably, whereas Paranaguá defines modernity in the singular, my theoretical framework is that of multiple modernities—this book amply confirms Paranaguá's thesis that if what we call Latin American cinema exists at all, it does so only from a comparative perspective that sees the region's national cinemas as part of a century-long, triangular flow of moving images between Hollywood, Europe, and Latin America.[2]

Another major characteristic of *Latin American Cinema: A Comparative History* is that it focuses on narrative cinema. Why narrative cinema? On a practical level, narrative cinema is much more accessible than other types of media narratives such as documentaries, films made for television, animation, and indigenous or grassroots video. Readers will therefore readily find most of the films I discuss on DVD or via streaming. More importantly, a focus on narrative cinema enables the kind of diachronic study that only a study of the documentary can approximate, for only narrative feature films and documentaries have enjoyed continuous production since the early twentieth century.[3] And while the book does discuss a handful of documentaries, as well as documentary modes of production at key junctures in the history of the medium, the literature on narrative cinema is much denser, a reflection of the enduring hold that narrative fiction has had, and continues to have, on our collective imagination. By consolidating the major lines of inquiry that make up this otherwise fragmented body of knowledge, this book offers readers who are not familiar with Latin American narrative cinema a useful introduction that balances breadth, because it covers all the major periods, and depth, via close readings of paradigmatic films. Readers who are already familiar with Latin American narrative cinema and its critical literature will find novel readings throughout, sometimes in dialogue with previous or ongoing debates, or taking these debates in altogether new directions.[4]

Of the approximately twenty countries in Latin America, the combined output of just three—Mexico, Brazil, and Argentina—accounts for more than 80 percent of the region's narrative film production. Venezuela, Colombia, Cuba, Peru, Chile, and Bolivia constitute a second-tier group of countries with intermittent periods of production, and the rest of the countries constitute a third group characterized by long periods with very little or no production.[5] Throughout this book, close readings of approximately fifty films illustrate the major aesthetic, economic, and technological trends that define each major period and the transitions between them. The selection of films reflects the tripartite division of film production in the region: 75 percent are from Brazil, Mexico, and Argentina, and fully 25 percent are from countries other than the big three. Together, these films serve as signposts on a continental journey; I discuss some in greater depth than others, but all are

Major, second-tier, and intermittent film-producing nations in Latin America. Map by
Bill Nelson.

important in the conceptual mapping of what is an exceedingly diverse landscape characterized by aesthetic and ideological heterogeneity over space and over time.

Reading Latin American films comparatively within contexts that are simultaneously national, regional, and global reveals that, notwithstanding the very important differences between national contexts, many of the factors that influence modes of production and representation in Brazil, Mexico, and Argentina are similar to the factors that influence modes of production and representation in other countries in the region. One factor in particular, reception, provides a striking illustration of the shared cultural experience that is cinema in Latin America. Other than the two decades prior to World War I, when European cinema dominated screens throughout the region, and another, much briefer period in the 1940s when Mexican cinema competed head to head with Hollywood for screen time, Latin Americans are not very familiar with their own national cinemas or that of their neighbors. But they are intimately familiar with Hollywood cinema, as Hollywood's share of Latin American screen time since World War I has consistently exceeded 80 percent, oftentimes even surpassing 90 percent. From this perspective alone, all of Latin America's national cinemas share having developed in the shadow of Hollywood. Nevertheless, this book is not about how Hollywood achieved and continues to maintain its near monopoly in the arenas of distribution and exhibition, nor is it about Hollywood's stereotyped representations of Latin America and its peoples. Instead, Hollywood is in this book like a secondary character in the far richer story of how Latin American filmmakers have represented a multiplicity of Latin Americas, and their corresponding modernities, through narrative cinema.

ORGANIZATION OF THE BOOK

The book is divided into five parts, each one corresponding to a major period: silent cinema, studio cinema, Neorealism/Art Cinema, the New Latin American Cinema, and contemporary cinema. Part I, "Silent Cinema," consists of two chapters. Chapter 1, "Conventional Silent Cinema," combines a diachronic examination of major trends during the first thirty years of the medium with synchronic close readings of paradigmatic films. Chief among these are *Nobleza gaucha* (Gaucho Nobility; Eduardo Martínez de la Pera, Ernesto Gunche, and Humberto Cairo, Argentina, 1915), *Tepeyac* (José Manuel Ramos, Carlos E. González, and Fernando Sáyago, Mexico, 1917), *El último malón* (The Last Indian Uprising; Alcides Greco, Argentina, 1916), *El automóvil gris* (The Gray Automobile; Enrique Rosas, Joaquín Coss, and Juan Canals de Homs, Mexico, 1919), *Perdón, viejita* (Forgive Me, Mother; José Agustín Ferreyra, Argentina, 1927), *Sangue Mineiro* (Mineiro Blood; Humberto Mauro, Brazil, 1929), and *Wara Wara* (José María Velasco Maidana, Bolivia, 1930). I conclude that the most important legacy of this cinema on subsequent filmmaking in the region is not so much the elaboration of a *criollo* aesthetics tied to the project of Euro-liberal modernity (an aesthetics that would not survive beyond the silent period), but rather the development of a strategy of triangulation whereby Latin American filmmakers navigated a global cinematic land-scape—and modernity—from a position of marginality. Chapter 2, "Avant-Garde Silent Cinema," focuses on four films made at the very end of the silent period whose formal experimentation breaks with the conventions established over the previous thirty years: *São Paulo, A Sinfonia da Metrópole* (São Paulo, a Metropolitan Symphony; Rodolfo Rex Lustig and Adalberto Kemeny, Brazil, 1929), *Ganga Bruta* (Raw Gangue; Humberto Mauro, Brazil, 1933), *Limite* (Limit; Mário Peixoto, Brazil, 1929), and *¡Que viva México!* (Sergei Eisenstein, Mexico–United States, 1931). I argue that whereas *São Paulo, A Sinfonia da Metrópole* and *Ganga Bruta* identify modernity with the material and technological progress spearheaded by an emerging national bourgeoi-sie as part of a broader project for a rational and liberal utopia, *Limite* and *¡Que viva México!* represent the possibility of radically transform-ing the social structures and cultural values associated with peripheral capitalism.

Part II, "Studio Cinema," charts the emergence, development, and subsequent decline of a corporatist discourse of modernity in Latin American cinema's studio era through three chapters: chapter 3, "Tran-sition to Sound," chapter 4, "Birth and Growth of an Industry," and chapter 5, "Crisis and Decline of Studio Cinema." Throughout this period, and in response to the prohibitive costs associated with indus-trial modes of production, many private studios sought support from corporatist states, who saw this as an opportunity for them to control representation by countering Hollywood's stereotypes with positive representations of their own. As befits any major industry, production was standardized, both in the documentary, which experienced a boon thanks to direct state production of newsreels and educational films, and in fiction, through the consolidation of a few genres (musicals, melodramas, and comedies) and the creation of a star system (featuring, among many others, María Félix, Dolores del Río, Pedro Infante, Jorge Negrete, Cantinflas, Grande Otelo, and Libertad Lamarque). Ideologically, the discourse of liberalism is still evident in the films of the early 1930s, but the corporatist discourse of modernity becomes dominant after *Allá en el Rancho Grande* (*Out on the Big Ranch*; Fernando de Fuentes, Mexico, 1936) and continues to be dominant throughout the 1940s in films such as *Puerta cerrada* (*Closed Door*; Luis Saslavsky, Argentina, 1939), *María Candelaria* (Emilio Fernández, Mexico, 1943), *Río Escondido* (Emilio Fernández, Mexico, 1947), and *Dios se lo pague* (*God Bless You*; Luis César Amadori, Argentina, 1948).

Part III, "Neorealism and Art Cinema," examines in a single chapter the two major responses to the decline of the industrial model of production in the 1950s—neorealism and art cinema—when the rise of a sophisticated audience and the availability of lightweight portable cameras led a group of filmmakers to push the limits of studio cinema beyond the formulas required by that system, or else to work outside that system altogether. In the process, these filmmakers laid the foundations for Latin American cinema during the second half of the twentieth century by resurrecting artisanal modes of production that could be easily adapted to changing circumstances and (just as important) by radically questioning the discourse of corporatist modernity that had been dominant during the studio era. The three paradigmatic films of this period are *Los olvidados* (The Forgotten Ones; Luis Buñuel, Mexico, 1950), *Rio, Zona Norte* (Rio, North Zone; Nelson Pereira dos Santos, Brazil, 1957), and *La mano en la trampa* (*The Hand in the Trap*; Leopoldo Torre Nilsson, Argentina, 1961).

Part IV, "New Latin American Cinema," charts the development of the New Latin American Cinema in two phases. Chapter 7, "New Latin American Cinema's Militant Phase," covers the first phase, when films respond directly to the heady political environment created by the triumph of the Cuban Revolution, while chapter 8, "New Latin American Cinema's Neobaroque Phase," covers the subsequent phase, when filmmakers adopt baroque representational strategies in order to explore radical alternatives to dominant discourses of modernity. The militant phase of the New Latin American Cinema coincided with the appearance in the market of mass-produced portable cameras with synchronized sound, a technology that proved instrumental in the creation of a documentarist mode of representation where cameras were conceived as tools to record, re-present, and even help usher in socialism. The idea of cinema as a tool of socialist revolution, famously summarized in Fernando Solanas and Octavio Getino's guerrilla-inspired metaphor of the camera as a gun that shoots twenty-four frames per second, is most evident in their documentary *La hora de los hornos* (*The Hour of the Furnaces*; Argentina, 1968) and in the documentaries and newsreels of Santiago Álvarez, and less directly in films such as *Deus e o Diabo na Terra do Sol* (*Black God, White Devil*; Glauber Rocha, Brazil, 1963) and *La batalla de Chile* (*The Battle of Chile*; Patricio Guzmán, Chile-Cuba, 1975–79). Toward the end of the militant phase, in the late 1960s, films such as *Lucía* (Humberto Solás, Cuba, 1968), *Memorias del subdesarrollo* (*Memories of Underdevelopment*; Tomás Gutiérrez Alea, Cuba, 1968), and *De cierta manera* (*One Way or Another*; Sara Gómez, Cuba, 1974) begin to register a shift away from a realist epistemology toward an epistemology that highlights the rift between signifier and signified in order to call attention to the constructed nature not only of films, but, critically, of social relations as well. The result of this shift is a visually complex and intellectually challenging cinema in the 1970s and 1980s that uses baroque tropes (doubles, reflections, hyperbole) as well as baroque strategies of representation (alternate narrative threads, superimposed discourses, intertextuality, parody) to subvert the populist truth claims and monologism of the authoritarian regimes that were ruling throughout Latin America. This is evident in films as varied as *Macunaíma* (Joaquim Pedro de Andrade, Brazil, 1969), *La última cena* (*The Last Supper*; Tomás Gutiérrez Alea, Cuba, 1976), *Frida, naturaleza viva* (*Frida Still Life*; Paul Leduc, Mexico, 1983), and *La nación clandestina* (The Clandestine Nation; Jorge Sanjinés, Bolivia, 1989).

Finally, Part V, "Contemporary Cinema," argues that after the monumental collapse in film production that took place in the early 1990s, a new generation of filmmakers has succeeded in reinserting Latin American cinema into the global cinematic marketplace through the reactivation of traditional genres and identification techniques, and by redirecting the New Latin American Cinema's emphasis on societies or extraordinary individuals in upheaval to focus instead on the micropolitics of emotion. No longer epic, spectacular, or revolutionary, but rather intimate, realistic, and, ultimately, reformist, contemporary cinema mobilizes affect and emotion to explore memory and identity, first via nostalgic films such as *Central do Brasil* (*Central Station*; Walter Salles, Brazil-France, 1998) and *Fresa y chocolate* (*Strawberry and Chocolate*; Tomás Gutiérrez Alea and Juan Carlos Tabío, Cuba-Spain,

1993) (chapter 9, "Collapse and Rebirth of an Industry"), and more recently via suspenseful films such as *La mujer sin cabeza* (*The Headless Woman*; Lucrecia Martel, Argentina, 2008) and *La teta asustada* (*The Milk of Sorrow*; Claudia Llosa, Peru-Spain, 2009) (chapter 10, "Latin American Cinema in the Twenty-First Century").[6]

LATIN AMERICA'S MULTIPLE MODERNITIES

Modernity and *modernism* mean different things in English, Spanish, and Portuguese, and so it is crucial to be attentive to these differences in a book written in English that addresses the multiple discourses of modernity in Latin American narrative cinema. Both *modernity* and *modernism* share a common root in *modernus*, a Latin adjective that combines the adverb *modo* (mode, measured) with the suffix *-ernus* (today). When it first appeared in the fifth century, *modernus* simply meant "contemporary." In the early Renaissance, *modern* and its cognates in several European languages began to be used to describe contemporary society in opposition to Roman and Greek antiquity (with antiquity valued over contemporary society), but especially in opposition to non-European cultures and landscapes that Europeans conquered and colonized starting in the late fifteenth century. This second definition of *modern*, because it is tied to the imperial fortunes of specific European nation-states, has generated different understandings of modernity in different languages.

In Spanish historiography, for example, *modernidad* is linked to a project that began in the late fifteenth century, after Queen Isabella of Castile and King Ferdinand of Aragon combined their respective kingdoms in order to more effectively finish the Reconquista and impose territorial, linguistic, and religious unity over the multiplicity of religions, languages, and fiefdoms that characterized the Iberian peninsula at the time. The practice of territorial conquest and religious conversion that characterized the Reconquista was then extended to the Americas, where modernity as a Eurocentric project resulted in the genocide and enslavement of indigenous and African populations. In French historiography, on the other hand, *modernité* crystallizes in the eighteenth century, during the height of the French Enlightenment and French hegemony in Europe. Because of this, the French term *modernité* is sometimes linked to the Enlightenment's project of emancipation, summarized in the three principles of the French Revolution—freedom, equality, and fraternity—and linked at other times to the French empire's (instrumental) reasons of state, whether under the Bourbons or the Bonapartes. In Anglophone historiography, finally, the origins of modernity are frequently located in the nineteenth century, during Britain's industrialization, so that modernity is understood as a process of economic modernization based on technological progress and economic liberalism.

The multiple meanings and variants of the term *modern* carry over to the historiography of art, as evidenced by the fact that the English term *modernism* and its cognates in Spanish, Portuguese, and French are false cognates. In English and French, *modernism* and *modernisme* are used very broadly to refer to the experimental art produced since the late nineteenth century. In Spanish, Modernismo refers very specifically to the Parnassian-influenced literature written by the likes of Rubén Darío and Leopoldo Lugones from the late 1880s to the 1910s. And in Brazilian Portuguese, Modernismo is reserved for the work by artists associated with the Semana de Arte Moderna in São Paulo in 1922. Because these are false cognates, I will not use them in this book, so as to avoid any potential confusion. Instead, I will use *experimental* to describe specific films that are aesthetically innovative, *avant-garde* to refer to films that belong to a movement (or moment) of intensive experimentation, and additional terms such as *surrealism* and *agitprop* to refer to specific kinds of experimentalism and the avant-garde.

An equally important reason for avoiding the category "modernism" is that aesthetic modernism and political modernism do not always go together. It is true that the kind of self-conscious formal experimentation that defines aesthetic modernism has normally been linked to the kinds of projects of progressive social change one associates with political modernism, but there are many examples to the contrary, from the use of an aesthetically innovative mise-en-scène to celebrate Fascism in *Triumph des Willens* (*Triumph of the Will*; Leni Riefenstahl, Germany, 1935) to the use of unconventional cinematography in *Ganga Bruta* to celebrate the social status quo. Conversely, while the conventions of realism have historically been used in classical cinema to represent conservative values, there are many examples to the contrary, from Sergei Eisenstein's use of socialist realism to advocate for social change in the epilogue of *¡Que viva México!* to Nelson Pereira dos Santos's use of neorealism in *Rio, 40 Graus* (Rio, 100 Degrees F; Brazil, 1955) to give a voice and a face to the urban poor in Brazil.

Similar objections can be raised against the use of *postmodernism*. In fact, the objections to using the category "postmodernism" to study

Latin America art and culture have been better articulated than the objections to using the category "modernism." As John Beverly and José Oviedo noted in their introduction to *The Postmodernism Debate in Latin America* (1995):

> *Postmodern* seems a particularly inappropriate term for nation-states and social formations that are usually thought of as not yet having gone through the stage of modernity, in Weber's sense of the term, or, perhaps more exactly, that display an "uneven modernity" (what society does not, however?). To compound the problem, the words *modernismo* and *posmodernismo* designate in Latin American Spanish early-twentieth-century literary movements that have no direct correspondence to what are generally understood as modernism and postmodernism in English. Noting the anachronism, Octavio Paz has argued that postmodernism is yet another imported *grand récit* (like liberalism?) that does not fit Latin America, which needs to produce its own forms of cultural periodization.[7]

Paz is not alone in calling for categories of thought that grow organically out of the Latin American experience. From an altogether different perspective than the liberalism advocated by Paz, Latin American critics such as Irlemar Chiampi, Bolívar Echeverría, and Gonzalo Celorio have taken up this challenge by theorizing the Latin American neobaroque not only as a set of aesthetic practices, but also as a radical political project that Monika Kaup has perceptively called "Latin America's alternative modernity."[8] Unlike postmodernism, whose prefix underscores the idea of rupture, the Latin American neobaroque bespeaks of continuities and recyclings, in this case between the colonial period—when a few artists, such as José Kondori and Aleijadinho, appropriated and adapted baroque strategies of representation to affirm a local culture characterized by heterogeneity (instead of affirming imperial monologisms like one God, one king, and one language)—and the twentieth century, when writers such as Alejo Carpentier, José Lezama Lima, and Severo Sarduy recycled baroque strategies of representation to likewise affirm a project of cultural heterogeneity, this time on a pan–Latin American scale.

Ideologically, it is true that postmodernism and the neobaroque are similar insofar as both critique European modernity's instrumental reason through a set of similar representational strategies, including fragmentation, ironic repetition, parody, and the mixing of popular and elite cultures. However, while metropolitan postmodernism tends to stop at what Jean-François Lyotard calls an incredulity toward master narratives,[9] the Latin American neobaroque goes beyond a critique of these master narratives to actually affirm an alternative project of modernity based on a practice, widespread in Latin America, of selectively recovering and reconfiguring fragments from European, indigenous, and African traditions of modernity. This understanding of modernity—not as a temporal passage from premodern traditions to modernity and postmodernity, but rather as the spatialized reconfiguration of multiple discourses and practices, all of which are modern— allows us to see European, indigenous, and African cultures as active co-participants in the construction of global modernities. It is a well-known fact that indigenous and African cultures have played a central role in the construction of Eurocentric projects of modernity in the Americas through the process of othering. What is seldom considered is that indigenous and African cultures (in the Americas and elsewhere) have generated original discourses of modernity not subsumed under master narratives of European progress and cultural superiority. The Latin American neobaroque recovers fragments of these African and indigenous discourses of modernity and reconfigures them with fragments of European discourses of modernity in a dialogic praxis predicated on liberation. I elaborate on the historical roots and contemporary meanings of this neobaroque recovery and reconfiguration in the appendix, "Discourses of Modernity in Latin America," and in chapter 8, "New Latin American Cinema's Neobaroque Phase."

In terms of theory, this book builds on comparative modernity studies, an interdisciplinary field that approaches modernity in the plural as the crystallization of economic, political, and cultural institutions into different configurations. Comparative modernity studies emerged after the Second World War in response to growing evidence that contradicted the narrative, widespread in the North Atlantic, that one single model of modernity, culturally European and economically liberal, would naturally spread to all societies undergoing modernization.[10] Instead of privileging one (Euro-liberal) modernity, comparative modernity studies has emphasized the need to speak of multiple modernities: liberal modernity in the North Atlantic, socialist modernity in the Soviet sphere of influence and in China, and corporatist modernity in Japan. Also known as the "three ways," liberalism, socialism, and corporatism are normally understood as political discourses, with liberalism advocating private capitalism, socialism advocating state capitalism, and corporatism advocating state management of capital and labor for the "common good."

However, because these discourses grew out of and evolved within a broader context of historically determined cultural practices and values, it is also possible to conceive of them, as I do throughout the book, as cultural discourses of modernity, each with its own distinct narrative, recurring tropes, and values. This is especially evident if we consider the narratives of progress of each discourse. In Latin American liberalism, for example, progress has historically been defined in terms of Europeanization and privatization, and so this discourse has been used to justify the elimination of communal lands during Benito Juárez's Reforma (1861–72), the genocide of indigenous tribes in the pampas under Domingo Faustino Sarmiento, and the systematic selling off of state enterprises during the neoliberal 1980s and 1990s. In Latin American socialism, which advocates for state capitalism as a necessary step on the long road toward stateless communism, progress is defined in terms of collectivization, and so this discourse has been used to justify the elimination of private property as well as the restriction of individual rights of expression and assembly, as in Cuba under Fidel Castro. Finally, in Latin American corporatism, progress is defined as the advancement of the "common good" through an organic relationship between labor and capital, and so this discourse has been used to justify extensive state controls over labor unions and capital (both private and state owned), as happened in Mexico under Lázaro Cárdenas, in Argentina under Juan Perón's first presidency, and in Colombia under Laureano Gómez. Despite their differences, it is important to keep two things in mind: that in practice, discourses of modernity in Latin America, on screen and off, have always been mixed, even during periods when one discourse clearly prevailed over the others; and that regardless of whether they are on the left, the right, or the center of the political spectrum, "actually existing" liberalism, socialism, and corporatism all share a common grounding in instrumental reason, or the subjugation of reason to power. For more detailed definitions of these discourses, see the appendix ("Discourses of Modernity in Latin America").

Latin American narrative cinema is especially well suited for a study of multiple modernities because liberalism is hegemonic on the big screen throughout the silent period, corporatism during much of studio cinema, and socialism during the militant phase of the New Latin American Cinema. This does not mean, however, that only films with a liberal discourse were made during the silent period, that only films with a corporatist discourse were made during studio cinema, or that only films with a socialist discourse were made during the militant phase of the NLAC. *Juan sin ropa* (Juan Without Clothes; Georges Benoît and Héctor Quiroga, Argentina, 1919), for example, is an anarchist film from the silent period; *Distinto amanecer* (*Another Dawn*; Julio Bracho, Mexico, 1943) wields a critique of corporatist syndicalism from within the studio system;[11] and dozens of sexploitation films known as *pornochanchadas* in Brazil and *cine de ficheras* in Mexico were made in tandem with the militant phase of the NLAC. To speak of silent cinema as liberal, studio cinema as corporatist, and the militant phase of the NLAC as socialist therefore means that these respective discourses prevail during these respective periods, not that other discourses are absent. Just as important, while it is true that there is a clear preference for one discourse of modernity over others in the three aforementioned periods, this is not the case during the other periods covered in the book: the first avant-garde, the transition to sound, the crisis of studio cinema, Neorealism/Art Cinema, the neobaroque phase of the NLAC, the nostalgic cinema of the 1990s, and the suspenseful cinema since the 2000s. During these periods and transitions, no single discourse of modernity prevails, and what one finds instead is a contentious coexistence of discourses between and sometimes even within films.

This approach to Latin America's modernity, in the plural, goes against a common premise in comparative modernity studies, whereby different world regions are seen as having had more or less uniform experiences of modernity. In Latin America, no single form or discourse of modernity has ever become dominant, and this has meant that the region has experienced modernity in the plural, as both sequence and simultaneity.[12] As a sequence, Latin America experienced early modernity (roughly the sixteenth and seventeenth centuries) and classical modernity (roughly the eighteenth century) as part and parcel of the Spanish and Portuguese projects of imperial expansion and colonialism, a major legacy of which has been what Aníbal Quijano calls coloniality of power, or the prevalence of Eurocentric myths such as white racial superiority and Western progress in everyday relations.[13] By contrast, late modernity (roughly the twentieth century) has been experienced as a succession of projects: first a liberal project undertaken by the triumphant criollo elites after independence and into the 1920s; then as a developmentalist project undertaken by corporatist states beginning in the 1930s; then as a socialist project inaugurated by the Cuban Revolution and further developed by the Chilean government of Salvador Allende; and more recently as a neoliberal (e.g., Carlos Menem), neosocialist (e.g., Hugo Chávez), or neocorporatist (e.g., Evo Morales) project, depending on the country in question. At the same time, modernity in Latin America has also been experienced as a simultaneity, for just as successive invasions and migrations do not altogether displace previously existing cultures, successive discourses of modernity do not altogether displace previously existing discourses.[14] Rather, each successive discourse is added on top of previously existing ones, like porous layers that filter, warp, detach, overlap, or fuse with one another, depending on the circumstances.[15] This book is also an attempt to give a comparative and diachronic account of this discursive diversity in a cinematic tradition that is as rich and complex as any other cinematic tradition in the world.

I began this study with a seemingly simple question: how does Latin American cinema represent modernity for local audiences? The answer, however, is far from simple, not only because modernity is both a constructed narrative and a historical reality, but also because cinema moves back and forth between representation (thanks to the camera's ability to record what our eyes and ears perceive) and mediation (thanks to artists' ability to transform these recordings through artistic choices during shooting and in postproduction). As the research advanced, it became clear that I had to address cinema's dual ability to represent and mediate modernity by combining a historian's approach to cinema's technological, economic, and aesthetic evolution with a theoretician's approach to modernity as both a historical reality and a narrative of progress. Hence the book's method: to anchor ever-changing aesthetic, technological, economic, and ideological trends in the history of the medium to concrete historical realities that also vary over the course of time and across the region. In the end, what this method reveals is that the cinematic invention of Latin America is an ongoing project, with each succeeding generation of filmmakers reinventing what "Latin America" means through a succession of cinematic languages as varied as the region itself.

PART ONE

Silent Cinema

1

Conventional Silent Cinema

A CINEMA BY AND FOR CRIOLLOS

Latin American silent cinema was a cinema by and for *criollos*. The term *criollo* comes from the Portuguese *crioulo,* which was first applied in the fifteenth century to Portuguese peoples born in Africa, and soon afterward to African slaves born in Brazil.[1] In Spanish America, the earliest use of *criollo* kept its root meaning (from *criar,* which means "to raise") but was applied first to Africans born in the Americas, and only afterward to Spaniards born there as well.[2] By the seventeenth century, the term's meaning in Spanish had narrowed to refer only to the descendants of Spaniards in the Americas, but after independence it broadened to refer to a Eurocentric understanding of national histories and identities. In effect, by the middle of the nineteenth century, *criollo* was widely used as a stand-in for national hegemonic cultures through-out Spanish America. In Brazil, on the other hand, *crioulo* devolved, among other things, into a racial slur for descendants of Africans, while the French term *créole* came to refer to the African-inflected cultures and languages that emerged throughout the Francophone Caribbean Basin.[3]

Given the confusion that can arise from the polysemy of *criollo* and its cognates, I will limit my use of the term to refer to Europeanized cultures throughout Latin America, including Brazil. Such use is widely accepted to this day in music, where *criollo* is applied to local variants of European forms popular throughout the nineteenth century, for example the Peruvian *vals* or the Puerto Rican *danza*. In theater, *criollo* is also widely used to describe dramas that use Spanish or Portuguese forms, such as the *sainete* or the *autos sacramentales,* but are infused with local inflections of language, gesture, costume, and customs. Finally, in literature, the term was in wide circulation during the second half of the nineteenth century and the beginning of the twentieth to describe a heterogeneous body of regionalist narratives that combined elements of realism, naturalism, *costumbrismo,* and romanticism, and that set the action in very local, usually rural, contexts. The best-known example of such usage is the literature of the gaucho in Argentina and Uruguay. At the dawn of cinema, then, a criollo sensibility in Latin America did not negate non-European cultures or their role in the construction of the national imaginary, but rather grafted them (to use José Martí's organic metaphor) into a privileged, Eurocentric trunk. In the silent cinema of Latin America, then, a criollo aesthetic is one whose visual language and narrative structures are metropolitan but whose atmospheres, concerns, and characters are local, national, or regional.

The silent period in Latin American cinema coincided with the height of the region's export-import growth and its political expression, oligarchic liberalism (1870–1930). This was a period of exponential economic growth and political stability, when Latin America's economic and political elites belonged to the same socioeconomic group: a Europeanized, criollo oligarchy that became fabulously wealthy by exporting raw materials such as beef, wheat, coffee, sugar, tobacco, henequen, copper, nitrates, rubber, and bananas, and in turn imported manufactured goods such as textiles, machines, and luxury items. At a basic level, then, film in Latin America began as another imported manufactured good, for not only were the cameras and film stock produced in Europe and the United States, but the first to film and screen moving pictures in the region were representatives of the Lumière and Edison companies.[4]

Silent cinema in Latin America was not defined, however, by national oligarchies but by middle- and upper-middle-class politicians and businesspeople who set out to maximize film's huge potential for profits and propaganda. In particular, professional politicians were responsible for financing the official national and regional newsreels that thrived into the 1950s, while the criollo petit-bourgeoisie that emerged to support the expanding export economies adapted to cinema the artisanal and mercantile business model it was already familiar with. From this perspective, then, Latin American narrative silent cinema was predominantly a cinema made by an emerging criollo bourgeoisie using a small-scale, artisanal approach to production, distribution, and exhibition, and espousing a Eurocentric worldview with correspondingly Europeanized aesthetics. This sensibility applied to national filmmakers as well as to European itinerant and immigrant filmmakers who played a leading role in the development of silent cinema in Latin America. Thus, the Italian Pedro Sambarino was active in Bolivia and Peru filming and/or directing features with criollo themes, while another Italian, Gilberto Rossi, had a successful career in Brazil as a producer of official newsreels (Rossi Actualidades, 1921–31) and as a producer for José Medina, the most commercially successful silent feature director in São Paulo.

The criollo sensibility of the time was not only Eurocentric but also thoroughly patriarchal. This explains why all of the films of the period are androcentric and oftentimes misogynistic, and why, outside of acting, only two women ventured into film production and direction, and only after stints as actresses: Carmen Santos in Brazil and Mimí Derba in Mexico. Finally, in terms of political economy, criollos during the first decades of the twentieth century believed wholeheartedly in Positivism. This aspect of criollo ideology, however, would be shaken by the Mexican Revolution and especially by the world economic collapse of 1929, and helps to explain the qualitative difference between silent cinema and subsequent studio cinema in Latin America.

Significantly, two of the major social players of the previous century—the landed elite and the rural proletariat—did not leave their mark on silent cinema: the landed elite because they considered film a lowbrow form of entertainment, and the rural masses because they lacked the resources to make films. However, the third key social actor during the nineteenth century—the Catholic Church—did get involved with filmmaking during the silent period, and its participation is particularly evident in the regional cycles of the second half of the 1920s.

The class origins of these early producers and filmmakers may explain why there are only a handful of filmic narratives told from the perspective of the growing urban working classes: for example *Juan sin ropa* (Juan Without Clothes; Georges Benoît and Héctor Quiroga, Argentina, 1919), about the government repression of the anarchist insurrection in Buenos Aires in 1919, an event known as "The Tragic Week"; *A Vida de João Cândido* (The Life of João Cândido; dir. unknown, Brazil, 1912), about the Chibata Revolt, a 1910 mutiny led by a black corporal aboard a Brazilian navy ship; and the silent films of José Agustín Ferreyra, which grew out of and reflected life in the working-class suburbs south of Buenos Aires.

PERIODIZATION

Our knowledge of the early cinema in Latin America is literally full of silences. To begin with, many films have burned through spontaneous combustion or on purpose, whether as a form of censorship or to recycle them as combs.[5] Many others have been forgotten, and only sometimes rediscovered in a dusty basement or trunk.[6] Other silences persist beyond the silent cinema period, imposed by a market and distribution system that privileges North-to-South consumption at the expense of South-to-North and South-to-South exchanges. Notwithstanding these limitations, we can still make some broad claims about early Latin American cinema, beginning with the general observation that silent film production developed in three distinct stages: (1) actualities (roughly 1897–1907), proto-narrative cinema (1908–15), and feature narrative cinema (1915–30). Actualities consisted of one or at most two reels (at one to fifteen minutes per reel) of unstaged events, with little editing and narration, and hardly any thought to mise-en-scène. This was followed by a period (1908–15) of short- and medium-length films that sought to attract larger and more differentiated audiences with entertainment in various forms: reconstructed crimes, comedies, skits, plays, filmed songs (with live or recorded accompaniment), and literary adaptations, among others. These films are not so much cinematographic as theatrical, in that there is little use of filmic devices such as close-ups, crosscutting, or subjective points of view. Instead, cameras tend to remain in place, as one would in a theater, while the acting and mise-en-scène also reveal a strong theatrical influence. Finally, beginning in 1915 and lasting for a few years beyond the introduction of sound, silent cinema acquired the outlines of today's films, sans sound: Aristotelian narrative form, feature lengths of sixty to ninety minutes (in a few cases surpassing two hours), and the elaboration of genres and techniques that were first developed during the previous period of proto-narrative cinema.

Significantly, this periodization mirrors the evolution of silent film in Europe and North America, evidence that Latin American cinema was a triangulated practice from its very beginnings,[7] the result of what Paulo Antonio Paranaguá calls Latin America's "permanent tripolar circulation" with Europe and the United States.[8] This tripolar circulation has never been one of free-flowing exchanges of influences and products between equals, but more like an active process of triangulation whereby Latin American filmmakers navigate a global cinematic landscape from a position of marginality. The best-known application of triangulation is in the surveying of land, whereby angles and distances on the ground are measured to accurately plot positions on a map. In this book, however, I will use triangulation in a way that is closer to how it is understood and practiced in the sport of orienteering, where the objective is to physically reach as many points marked on a map as possible, using only a map and a compass. Here, triangulation is the process of locating one's position when at least two prominent landmarks are visible. The more landmarks and the farther apart they are, the better, as this increases the chances of accurately plotting one's location on the map and ultimately one's chances of navigating toward the desired objective.

Like orienteers, Latin American filmmakers have always been adventurous spirits who seek out audiences, financing, and success as artists and businesspeople by navigating a cinematic landscape whose three most prominent referents, at the level of visual and narrative practices, are European cinema, Hollywood cinema, and Latin American documentary practices. The weight that any of these three reference points carries in a filmmaker's calculations varies according to specifics such as the filmmaker's interests and objectives, historical circumstances, the country or region of production, and audiences' knowledge of said referents, among others. But what is relatively stable is the simultaneous presence of all three referents, to a greater or lesser degree, throughout the silent period, and indeed throughout the history of Latin American cinema. Therefore, when speaking of triangulation in this context, I refer to a filmmaker's self-positioning (metaphorically speaking) somewhere in between these three prominent referents, and in response to the factors just outlined. Individually, the resultant films will be visibly closer to one of these three referents than to the others, but as a group, the characterizing feature of Latin American cinema, regardless of this or that particular film's aesthetic proximity to any one referent, is the incorporation (to a greater or lesser degree) of elements from all three referents. A singular benefit of comparing Latin American filmmakers to orienteers is that it overcomes the tendency to reduce Latin American cinema to watered-down versions or reflections of foreign models, and instead reveals Latin American filmmakers as active constructors of their own representations who adjusted their sights as the contours of the cinematic and ideological landscape shifted over time. From this perspective, the question is not whether Latin American filmmakers adopt and adapt global as well as local models and practices, but how they do so and for what purposes.

ACTUALITIES (1897–1907)

For its first ten years, film in Latin America did not evolve beyond *vistas* (literally, "views"). These were very short actualities of mostly unedited shots of unstaged action that sought to present rather than represent, and show rather than narrate. These *vistas* were shot with early movie cameras that were lightweight and relatively inexpensive, which allowed for a lot of experimentation by artists not yet beholden to any overdetermination in their choice of genre, acting style, or sometimes even subject matter. In effect, what characterizes early Latin American silent cinema is how transparently it reflects the air of self-sufficiency of the early pioneers, as if they were looking at themselves and liked what they saw. The titles of that first decade speak for themselves: *Un célebre especialista sacando muelas en el Gran Hotel Europa* (A Celebrated Specialist Pulling Molars at the Gran Hotel Europa; Guillermo and Manuel Trujillo Durán, Venezuela, 1897), *Carrera de bicicletas en el velódromo de Arroyo Seco* (Bicycle Race at the Arroyo Seco Cycle Track; Félix Oliver, Uruguay, 1898), or *Fiestas presidenciales en Mérida* (Presidential Festivities in Mérida; Enrique Rosas, Mexico, 1906). The fascination with technology and movement that explains the production and reception of films such as *L'Arrivée d'un train en gare de La Ciotat* (Arrival of a Train at La Ciotat; Auguste and Louis Lumière, France, 1895) also explains the production and reception of these earliest nonnarrative films in Latin America. As in many a Lumière film, the important thing was to astonish an impressionable audience by recording movement in what amounted to moving photographs: sports events, people leaving a factory or a church, national leaders in official functions and travels (fig. 1.1), and panning shots of the vast rural landscapes of the interior.

Shortly thereafter, actualities evolved into newsreels and short entertainments in the form of songs, in which case audiences would see a performer on-screen and hear the song either from a live person or a phonograph recording, and attractions, a form of actualities that were staged and edited for effect.[9] The production and exhibition of these early one-reelers was usually done by the same person, oftentimes an itinerant European who in many cases also imported and exhibited films from Europe and to a lesser extent from the United States. As Paranaguá has noted, the introduction of film in Latin American is a story of mimetism (especially of the Lumière model) and of who did what first.[10]

FIGURE 1.1 Porfirio Díaz arrives in the Yucatán in the documentary *Fiestas presenciales en Mérida* (Presidential Festivities in Mérida; Enrique Rosas, Mexico, 1906)

TRANSITION (1908–15)

The emergence around 1908 of profitable short- and medium-length spectacles is linked to the creation of large, stable, and differentiated audiences. This is the period, for example, when the first permanent "movie palaces" were built in major cities such as Buenos Aires, Rio de Janeiro, São Paulo, Mexico City, and Havana, and when the marketing of films through radio and newspapers became an industry. It is also the period when exhibition expanded beyond urban centers to include rural areas, a development that would have repercussions in the representation of the dichotomy between city and countryside. In terms of production, Brazil, Argentina, and Mexico experienced what some historians retrospectively call the belle époque, or golden age, of their respective silent film histories. In Brazil, for example, production went from an average of twelve films (mostly documentaries) per year until 1907, to suddenly an average of 169 films (again, mostly documentaries) per year between 1908 and 1911. Similar bursts of production occurred in Argentina between 1916 and 1919, and in Mexico between 1918 and

1923, a delay that can be attributed to the disruption in production caused by the Revolution. In terms of aesthetics, the term *belle époque* is also a fitting qualifier of the films of this period, as they often emulate what Giorgio Bertellini calls, in reference to the extremely popular Italian films of the time, a "symbolist film culture that relied on melodramatic acting styles, archaic settings, decadent *mise-en-scène,* and liberty-style art decorations."[11]

Compared to the films of the first period, the films of the second period were longer (full reels or in some cases two reels) and had more extensive use of editing. For example, songs became staged operettas, while actualities and attractions were absorbed into staged re-creations of newsworthy events or sensational crimes. The language of cinema, moreover, was still very limited in that there was little use of editing within scenes (in the case of filmed plays or operettas) or within sequences (in the case of narrative films). Most of the films produced during the second period were documentaries, as was the case in the previous period, but what sets them and the fictions apart from earlier ones is that now we see the beginnings of representation, with all its attendant politics. For example, *La Revolución de Mayo* (The May Revolution; Mario Gallo, Argentina, 1910) uses theatrical sets and acting to re-create the 1810 removal of the viceroy of Buenos Aires by local criollos, and their subsequent establishment of a local government, all from an official (that is, nationalist and romantic) point of view (fig. 1.2). In Brazil, the most popular film of this period was *Paz e Amor* (Peace and Love; Alberto Botelho, 1910), a political satire that poked fun at then-president Nilo Peçanha, who had campaigned under the slogan "a government of peace and love."[12] Two years later, an even more controversial film was made, the aforementioned *A Vida de João Cândido*. The film was based on the Revolta da Chibata (literally, the Whip Revolt), in which a large number of sailors, let by a black corporal by the name of João Cândido, took possession of the principal navy vessels after one of their own was almost whipped to death. After five days of tense negotiations during which the mutinous sailors pointed the guns of their vessels toward Rio de Janeiro, the president kept true to his slogan of peace and love by granting them amnesty and by abolishing the use of whips as a form of punishment in the navy. Cândido and many of his followers were later imprisoned or sent to internal exile in the Amazon, however, and the film made about his feats became the first film to be censored in Brazil.

FIGURE 1.2 Theatricality in *La Revolución de Mayo* (The May Revolution; Mario Gallo, Argentina, 1910). Courtesy Cinemateca Argentina

Finally, in Mexico, the Revolution had shaken official certitudes to the point that a documentary such as *Revolución orozquista* (The Orozco Revolution; Salvador, Guillermo, and Eduardo Alva, Mexico, 1912) espoused a radical relativism. The first part intercuts between the advancing troops of two warring factions—those under Victoriano Huerta and those under Pascual Orozco—and culminates with battle scenes from the point of view of each faction.[13] Gone is the single privileged point of view, as evidenced in figure 1.3, where a visual of the heavy artillery used by the federal army follows an intertitle that speaks of the rebels' perspective: "85-millimeter cannon used by the federal army, baptized by the rebels as 'the kid.'" Just as important, a narrative outcome is omitted, as if the Positivist ideology that presumes only one scientifically predetermined path to the future had been thoroughly undermined by the outbreak of the Revolution—or at the very least, as if narrative closure were impossible in a period of frequent and dramatic reversals of fortune. The narrative complexity and ideological ambiguity evidenced in this documentary did not take hold, as Mexican

FIGURE 1.3 Ideological ambiguity in *Revolución orozquista* (The Orozco Revolution; Salvador, Guillermo, and Eduardo Alva, Mexico, 1912)

filmmakers increasingly and decisively reflected the interests of the victorious criollo bourgeoisie.

FEATURE NARRATIVE CINEMA (1915–30)

Around 1915, feature-length films with higher production values became a global standard in narrative cinema, and Latin American audiences became enthusiastic consumers of Italian superspectacles and French *films d'art*. For example, the first French blockbuster—*La reine Élisabeth* (*Queen Elizabeth*; Henri Desfontaines and Louis Marcanton, 1912), starring Sarah Bernhardt—made a splash throughout Latin America, while the Italians began a streak of blockbusters and very popular melodramas with *Quo vadis?* (Enrico Guazzoni, 1913) and *Cabiria* (Giovanni Pastrone, a.k.a. Piero Fosco, 1914). Hollywood's influence was more pronounced in the areas of exhibition and distribution. Already in 1914, European film imports began to decline because of the war, and beginning in 1916, Hollywood's major studios implemented the practice of block booking (selling multiple films to a theater as a unit) and of underselling their own film production in Latin America. These "dumped" films were initially distributed and exhibited by local entrepreneurs, who in many cases had abandoned production after having realized they could make more money by simply distributing and exhibiting European and U.S. films.[14] As if adding insult to injury, by the end of the silent period Hollywood had succeeded in virtually monopolizing even the distribution market through their own local representatives, leaving the less lucrative and riskier business of exhibition to local entrepreneurs.

Notwithstanding the intensity of this first Hollywood invasion, production in Latin America continued, in part due to the introduction of economical cameras for the amateur film market. Many of these cameras served both as recording devices and as projectors, a technological innovation that made possible the emergence of regional cycles in the late 1920s and the continuation of an artisanal cinema produced by studios and amateurs everywhere. Regional cycles also emerged to fill a void created by the limits of film distribution in Latin America, which privileged major cities. Some of the more important regional cycles include Orizaba, in the Mexican state of Veracruz; Barquisimeto, in the state of Lara, Venezuela; Recife, Brazil; and Cataguases, in the state of Minas Gerais, Brazil. Noteworthy titles include, in Orizaba, *El tren fantasma* (The Ghost Train; Gabriel García Moreno, 1927); in Barquisimeto, *Los milagros de la Divina Pastora* (The Miracles of the Divine Shepherdess; Amábilis Cordero, 1928); in Recife, *Aitaré da Praia* (Aitaré of the Beach; Gentil Roiz, 1925), and *A Filha do Advogado* (The Lawyer's Daughter; Jota Soares, 1926); and in Catagueses, the early films of Humberto Mauro, Brazil's most important filmmaker of the first half of the twentieth century: *Thesouro Perdido* (Lost Treasure; 1927), *Braza Dormida* (Sleeping Ember; 1928), and *Sangue Mineiro* (Mineiro Blood; 1929). Despite the quality of these films, the distribution and exhibition structures were such that regional films were almost never seen outside their country of origin, and sometimes not even beyond their region of origin.

Production in Latin America also continued thanks to the practice of projecting local newsreels before feature presentations. As a result, newsreel production provided the only schooling for many budding filmmakers and the only form of continuous practice for experienced ones. Given the important ideological role played by newsreels in promoting official versions of reality, it is not surprising that it alone received the kind of state support needed for stable and continuous output. The price for this stability and continuity was, according to Paulo Antonio Paranaguá, a double submission: "formally, to the *Pathé Journal* model [i.e., short news reports based on a single subject and told from a single perspective], and ideologically, to the dominant interests [i.e., oligarchic liberalism]."[15] The prevalence of the *Pathé Journal* as a formal model helps to explain the European accent of Latin American film production throughout the second half of the silent period. And yet Latin American cinema developed, from very early on, as a triangulated cinema in simultaneous dialogue with North America, Europe, and an autochthonous film production that was primarily documentary but not always indebted to the *Pathé* model, as the examples *Revolución orozquista* and *La Revolución de Mayo* demonstrate. The nature and intensity of this "trialogue" changed depending on historical circumstances, but it never ceased. This is especially evident when one considers the three major forms of narrative film production between 1915 and 1930: *films d'art*, religious films, and popular entertainment films.

Film d'art

As in France, where *film d'art* began, *film d'art* in Latin America sought to raise the status of film from lowbrow entertainment to a respectable seventh art through filmed plays and adaptations of literary classics, especially national romances such as José Mármol's *Amalia* (Enrique

García Velloso, Argentina, 1914), José de Alencar's *Iracema* (Vittorio Capellaro, Brazil, 1917), Federico Gamboa's *Santa* (Luis G. Peredo, Mexico, 1918), and Jorge Isaacs's *María* (Máximo Calvo and Alfredo del Diestro, Colombia, 1922).[16] The conservatism inherent in the hierarchical outcomes of these foundational narratives was oftentimes mitigated by the romantic convention that love conquers all, including racial, class, and ethnic differences between the lovers in question.[17] From this perspective, art films were part of a broader liberal project that sought to create, through allegory, Europeanized national identities in what were still very young and culturally heterodox republics.

Wara Wara (1930)

One of the most interesting examples in film of these national allegories is *Wara Wara* (José María Velasco Maidana, Bolivia, 1930), based on Antonio Díaz Villamil's play *La voz de la quena* (The Voice of the Quena Flute, 1922). Recently restored by the Cinemateca Boliviana, *Wara Wara* tells the story of frustrated love between an Aymara princess and a Spanish conqueror (fig. 1.4). Alfonso Gumucio Dagron, the foremost historian of Bolivian cinema, has written of the film:

> [Velasco Maidana] embarked on the country's first "superproduction," initially entitled *El ocaso de la tierra del sol* but eventually exhibited as *Wara Wara*, which means "star" in the native language of Aymara and is the name of the female lead in the film. The result was a monumental work, a sort of *Intolerance,* only one set in one of the poorest countries in Latin America. . . . With *Wara Wara* special sets were designed for a film's production for the first time in Bolivia. Artists and architects themselves built a recreation of the Aymara palace. Velasco Maidana's home in La Paz was filled with women sewing costumes for the actors. In a makeshift laboratory, Raúl Montalvo and José Jiménez developed the film by hand while Velasco Maidana played violin in the next room to entertain the crew. The only modern equipment used in the production was the Ernemans [*sic*] camera Velasco Maidana had brought from Buenos Aires. Editing was done by the naked eye with a small [M]oviola and a pair of scissors. . . . By the time it premiered in January 1930 at the Teatro Princesa in La Paz, accompanied by live music composed by César Garcés B., it was already famous.[18]

Besides the beautiful evocation of what must have been a very creative atmosphere, this passage also reveals the precariousness and improvisation that characterized silent film production in Latin America. At the same time, although *Wara Wara* doubtless had a more colorful production history than most other literary adaptations, it shares with all of

FIGURE 1.4 Juanita Taillansier as the Inca princess in *Wara Wara* (José María Velasco Maidana, Bolivia, 1930)

them the foundational impulse of their models—that is, the desire (and in the case of Bolivia in the 1920s, the audacity) to imagine a national identity that included the non-criollo "other" even as it continued to espouse a Eurocentric, aristocratic, and patriarchal order.

Religious Films

As noted earlier, of all the major social actors in the nineteenth century, only the Church participated in film production during the silent period. Today, when asked about the Catholic Church in the history of film, most people think of its role as a censor, as when it participated in the implementation of the Hays Code in the United States in 1934. But the Church has been involved in film production since the beginning of cinema, and in Latin America it has continued to play an active role in media production through institutions such as Chile's Channel 13, run by that country's Catholic University. Religious films during the silent period celebrate the role of the Church in maintaining an idealized patriarchal order, using as a model medieval mystery and morality plays, set invariably in a pastoral countryside that in many ways represents the *locus amoenus* of the criollo nation. Films that fit this description include the aforementioned *Los milagros de la Divina Pastora*, about a young boy who decides to become a priest in a town saved from

FIGURE 1.5 The Virgin of Guadalupe (Beatriz de Córdova) appears to Juan Diego (Gabriel Montiel) in *Tepeyac* (José Manuel Ramos, Carlos E. González, and Fernando Sáyago, Mexico, 1917)

flooding by the Virgin's intercession; *La Virgen de la Caridad* (Our Lady of Charity; Ramón Peón, Cuba, 1930), a family melodrama that relies on the Virgin's intercession for ethical guidance and narrative closure; and *Canção de Primavera* (Spring Song; Cyprien Ségur and Igino Bonfioli, Brazil, 1923), another family melodrama, where a priest serves as a saintly intercessor between a tyrannical patriarch and his two young daughters.

Tepeyac (1917)

The most important of these religious films, at least in terms of its impact on subsequent filmmaking, may be *Tepeyac* (José Manuel Ramos, Carlos E. González, and Fernando Sáyago, Mexico, 1917). The film, ostensibly framed by the First World War as opposed to the Mexican Revolution, tells the story of a young criollo couple that is reunited through the intervention of the Virgin of Guadalupe, whose apparition to the Indian Juan Diego in 1531 is told in a long, didactic flashback (fig. 1.5). As Paranaguá has noted, the film embodies many of the contradictions that would define Mexican cinema during the studio era: "*Tepeyac* is a kind of primitive scene of Mexican cinema: here we find the Mexican Revolution put in parenthesis, domestic matriarchy counterbalanced with institutional paternalism, the poor rewarded for their resignation . . ., the trinkets of modernity in no contradiction with the perpetuation of tradition, the evolution of customs without a change in mentalities, mimetic cosmopolitanism at the service of official nationalism, and the fine arts, filled with public solemnity, opposed to a popular culture that is reduced to private decor."[19]

With its theatrical mise-en-scènes, primitive editing, and narrative simplicity, *Tepeyac* is not of great consequence in terms of the evolution of cinematic form in Latin America. Nevertheless, it and other religious films of the period are very revealing of how a major institution co-opted a thoroughly modern medium for very conservative ends, namely, the celebration of traditional family, gender, race, and class values. This practice would flourish during the studio era under the aegis of the state and in many cases in conjunction with the Church.

Popular Entertainment Films

Popular entertainment films of the second half of the silent period included comedies, musicals (with musicians and/or singers live in the theater), action dramas, re-creations of crimes (known as *posados* in Brazil), and melodramas; the melodrama already showed signs of becoming the meta-genre it would in fact become during the studio period. Irrespective of their genre, popular entertainment films tended to be explorations of urban life, both middle- and working class, in the present and the recent past, a reflection no doubt of the audience sector for which these films were made. Because of this emphasis on contemporary urban life, with its variety of characters and lifestyles, they have the feel of the literature of customs and manners (*costumbrismo*), with which they also share the ideology of reformism and its attendant didacticism by teaching viewers how to navigate the new social and urban landscapes emerging at the time throughout Latin America. Compared to religious films, however, popular entertainment films show a more complex sense of morality, and the question of what is being taught is not as self-evident as in religious films. On the other hand, compared to *films d'art*, which very clearly reveal the filmmakers' quest to identify their own work and class with the interests of the national aristocracies, popular entertainment films reveal the contradictory aspirations and desires of an emerging bourgeoisie, most notably in the ambiguity with which they represent workers, immigrants, and indigenous populations.

After documentaries, popular entertainment films were the most watched form of locally produced films in Latin America. Some often-cited examples of comedy are *Don Leandro el inefable* (Don Leandro the Ineffable; Lucas Manzano, Venezuela, 1918) and *La borrachera del tango* (The Tango Drunken Spree; Edmo Cominetti, Argentina, 1929); of action dramas, *Nobleza gaucha* (Gaucho Nobility; Eduardo Martínez de la Pera, Ernesto Gunche, and Humberto Cairo, Argentina, 1915), *El último malón* (The Last Indian Uprising; Alcides Greco, Argentina, 1916), *El húsar de la muerte* (The Hussar of the Death; Pedro Sienna, Chile, 1924), *El tren fantasma* (The Ghost Train; Gabriel García Moreno, Mexico, 1927), and *Thesouro Perdido* (Lost Treasure; Humberto Mauro, Brazil, 1927); of crime re-creations, *El automóvil gris* (The Gray Automobile; Enrique Rosas, Joaquín Coss, and Juan Canals de Homs, Mexico, 1919) and *El pequeño héroe del Arroyo de Oro* (The Small Hero of Golden Creek; Carlos Alonso, Uruguay, 1930); and of melodramas, *Perdón, viejita* (Forgive Me, Mother; José Agustín Ferreyra, Argentina, 1927) and *Sangue Mineiro* (Mineiro Blood; Humberto Mauro, Brazil, 1929). Of these I will discuss five that have stood the test of time better than most: *Nobleza gaucha*; *El último malón*; *El automóvil gris*; *Perdón, viejita*; and *Sangue Mineiro*.

Nobleza gaucha (1915)

Nobleza gaucha was the first Latin American feature film to achieve box-office success outside its country of origin,[20] and so marked the feasibility of making films locally for a transnational market. Its popularity can be attributed to the film's skillful incorporation of comedic and melodramatic elements typically associated with Italian commedia dell'arte and melodrama into an action-driven plot structure typically associated with Hollywood productions. The film tells the story of the kidnapping (by a vulgar landowner) and subsequent rescue (by a noble gaucho) of a young country maid (fig. 1.6). At first the gaucho fails in his rescue attempt because his horse is too slow for the landowner's automobile. The gaucho then decides to enlist his neighbor, an Italian peasant who provides comic relief through his representation as a country bumpkin. After they arrive at the gates of the mansion where the landowner has imprisoned the young woman, however, the immigrant backs out and returns to the countryside. The gaucho, alone but

FIGURE 1.6 The gaucho Juan (Julio Scarcella) saves La Criollita (María Padín) in the Western *Nobleza gaucha* (Gaucho Nobility; Eduardo Martínez de la Pera, Ernesto Gunche, and Humberto Cairo, Argentina, 1915)

determined to free the object of his desire, succeeds in this second rescue attempt. The landowner retaliates by falsely accusing the gaucho of stealing cattle, but in a final chase on horseback, the landowner dies at the hands of the gaucho.[21]

Given the centrality of the conflict between landowner and peasant, and the film's emphasis on the contrast between city and countryside, it is not surprising that many critics have focused on these two interrelated themes. But the film revisited the theme of the gaucho and its associated discourse of civilization versus barbarism at a time when (1) class struggle was no longer rural but urban, (2) poor European immigrants were loathed as the new barbarians, and (3) gauchos survived as a social force only in the popular imagination. If we take these anachronisms into account, the reading of *Nobleza gaucha* changes dramatically from that of a progressive redemption of the gaucho against tyrannical landowners to that of a reactionary update of nineteenth-century criollo nationalism, particularly with its distrust of new urban sectors born of immigration, represented in the film by the unreliable immigrant who abandons the gaucho in his hour of need.[22] In its divergent readings, then, *Nobleza gaucha* is a perfect example of the contradictory impulses of the emerging criollo bourgeoisie in Argentina, torn as it was between reaping the economic rewards of a growing export-import economy that benefited principally the landowning elite, and claiming political power away from this elite through the Radical Party headed by Hipólito Yrigoyen.[23]

El último malón (1916)

El último malón (The Last Indian Uprising; Alcides Greco, Argentina, 1916) tried to generate, with some success, the audience response and box-office revenue of *Nobleza gaucha* through an action-filled plot that in the main follows the outlines of a Hollywood Western (a central conflict between Native Americans and Euro-Americans set in the borderlands, with the eventual triumph of European culture over indigenous ones), but is bracketed in the beginning by an ethnographic documentary of indigenous life and in the end by a melodramatic happy ending for the two indigenous leads. The film is about the last *malón*, or uprising, of native peoples in Argentina, which took place near Santa Fe in 1904. The film's prologue, "Civilization and the Indian," begins with a man pointing to the location of the uprising on a map of Argentina, continues with shots of newspaper clippings of stories about the uprising, and proclaims that what is to follow is a "historical reconstruction." What follows, however, is an ethnographic documentary on contemporary Mocovi life that begins with establishing shots of the community and introductions to four of its real-life noteworthy members: the old cacique Mariano López, his wife Petrona with their offspring, the rebel cacique Salvador López (the only one not to stay put for the camera), and the tribe's fool, Juan Saldón. The documentary continues with a survey of native customs—fishing, hunting, cattle herding, drinking—and an intertitle even explains that "the whites teach them to drink" in order to subdue them (fig. 1.7).

Suddenly, the film transforms Petrona, Mariano López, and Salvador López into fictional characters caught in a love triangle: Rosa, played by a white actress in brownface; the old cacique, renamed Bernardo López; and his rebellious young brother, renamed Jesús Salvador (fig. 1.8). Rosa, who has publicly supported Jesús Salvador's plans for an uprising, is held captive by the old cacique. After the uprising fails, Jesús Salvador frees her, and they both successfully escape to the jungles of northern Argentina. The film ends with the two lovers kissing, followed by an intertitle that explains how they learned this custom from the

FIGURE 1.7 *El último malón* (The Last Indian Uprising; Alcides Greco, Argentina, 1916) as an ethnographic documentary

FIGURE 1.8 *El último malón* as a fictional love triangle between the Mocoví cacique Mariano López (as himself), Rosa (Rosa Volpe), and the rebel Jesús Salvador (Salvador López, as himself)

whites. Such melodramatic excess, whereby a complex social and economic reality is reduced to an emotional narrative between two love-
birds, may very well explain the popularity of the film at the time of its
release, but it nevertheless undermines the film's thesis, elaborated
through the ethnographic introduction, that the Mocovis are the victims of the Euro-Argentineans' civilizing mission. Moreover, the melodramatic imperative that impels the narrative toward a return to the
status quo ante, coupled with the Western's inherent Manichaeism and
Eurocentric liberalism, effectively cancels any claims that the introduction may have made for the film as an objective and even sympathetic
representation of the plight of the Mocovis. Despite these limitations, *El
último malón* is so out of the ordinary in its dialectical incorporation of
documentary footage into a fictional narrative that Fernando Birri, the
acknowledged father of the New Latin American Cinema, regularly
screened it at his documentary film school in Santa Fe in the late 1950s.[24]

El automóvil gris (1919)

In contrast to the ambivalent progressiveness of *Nobleza gaucha* and *El
último malón*, *El automóvil gris* (The Gray Automobile; Enrique Rosas,
Joaquín Coss, and Juan Canals de Homs, Mexico, 1919) is openly reactionary. The twelve-episode film fictionalizes a string of high-profile
robberies that targeted Mexico City's upper classes in 1915, and efforts
by the police to capture the robbers who disguised themselves as federal
soldiers, all in the tradition of the French *Fantômas* series (fig. 1.9). In an
uncanny attempt to document as well as rewrite history, the film cast Juan
Manuel Cabrera, the police detective responsible for the capture of the
gang, as himself, but with the name of Pablo González, the name of a Carrancista general with presidential ambitions and close ties to the film's
producers. A subplot has the leader of the gang (Higinio Granda, played by
codirector Juan Canals de Homs) and two of his accomplices fall in love
with beautiful women, possibly prostitutes, and in the end Granda is the
only one to escape capture. The other members of the gang are sentenced
to death, but at the last minute, Pablo González pardons four of the ten.[25]

Charles Ramírez Berg has noted how the film blames the brief Emiliano Zapata regime of early 1915 for the gang's initial impunity by setting the action during Zapata's rule, by blaming the gang's initial escape
from prison on the ineptitude of Zapatista soldiers, and by glossing over
the crimes of the subsequent Carrancista regime, all of which helped
to polish the public image of the just-declared presidential candidate

FIGURE 1.9   A gang of robbers, dressed as federal soldiers, loads a stolen safe into their car in *El automóvil gris* (The Gray Automobile; Enrique Rosas, Joaquín Coss, and Juan Canals de Homs, Mexico, 1919)

General Pablo González.[26] More ominously, the film plays on criollo fears of the Mexican Revolution as an out-of-control struggle against their racial and class privileges. The film achieves this in two steps. First, it aligns spectators' identification with the bandits because they are at the center of a narrative trajectory, and also because they are all young, good-looking, and in love with beautiful women. Then, after most of the bandits are finally caught and jailed, the film closes with documentary footage of the real bandits being shot by a firing squad. These real-life bandits, however, do not look anything like the ones played by European-looking actors in European-looking clothes, but rather like indigenous and mestizo Zapatistas in their signature wide-rim hats and tight pants. In addition, they are dehumanized by the way the execution is filmed and edited to show only the moment of death from a full-shot perspective. Viewers are thus positioned to see not the likable individuals who robbed for love and glory, but a faceless, indistinct mass of falling bodies. The effect of this closing montage is that the spectatorial alignment with the fictionalized bandits is severed, criollo fears of losing their privileges and properties are allayed, and revolutionary activity is subliminally equated with banditry.

While *El automóvil gris* is local in its politics, it is very cosmopolitan in its aesthetics, and a good example of the kind of triangulated dialogue that Latin American films have continuously had with European and Hollywood cinemas. As Ramírez Berg notes, the film's references and influences include: "(1) Mexico's rich documentary tradition, [which] thrived for twenty years by feeding its audience's appetite for Mexican images; (2) Italian cinema, known for its attention to period detail and its mobile camera; (3) French cinema, especially . . . the crime serials . . . with their extensive use of location shooting, their fast-paced cops-and-robbers narratives, and their characters' reliance on disguises; and (4) the emerging Hollywood paradigm, with its goal-driven protagonist, its causally linked narrative, and its rules of editing, lighting, and shooting based on character psychology."[27]

Ideologically, *El automóvil gris* is also important for popularizing an understanding of the Mexican Revolution as necessary yet futile.[28] This take on the Revolution did in fact become one of the two major themes of Mexican cinema during the studio period, the other being the sanctity of the nuclear family foreshadowed by *Tepeyac*.[29]

Any discussion of *El automóvil gris,* and of Mexican cinema in general at the time, must address the effect of Hollywood's negative stereotyping of Mexicans on national productions. In Hollywood silent cinema, the most persistent Latino stereotype was that of the Mexican bandit. The stereotype turned vicious after the Mexican Revolution, with bandits who robbed, murdered, pillaged, raped, cheated, gambled, and lied with an intensity never seen before, and seldom since.[30] In 1922, the government of Álvaro Obregón reacted to Hollywood's constant negative stereotyping of Mexicans as bandits by threatening to ban all films from any company that perpetuated that stereotype. Hollywood responded by changing Mexican settings to thinly veiled stand-ins like "Costa Roja" or "El Dorado." This did not end the stereotyping, and ten years later, the Mexican government, under General Plutarco Calles, renewed its threat, this time with the backing of several Latin American countries. The new international censorship strategy worked, if only temporarily, and a convenient substitute for the bandit was found in another stereotype, the Latin Lover.[31]

Parallel to their governments' censorship strategy, Latin American filmmakers developed a strategy of countering Hollywood's negative stereotypes with positive stereotypes of their own. This quote from the founders of the longest-running film magazine in Brazil (*Cinearte*, 1926–42) exemplifies an attitude shared by many Latin American filmmakers of the second half of the silent period: "The making of films in Brazil should be an act of purification of our reality through the selection of things that deserve to be portrayed on screen: our progress, the work of modern genius, our beautiful whites, our nature."[32] Needless to say, this racist prescription led to "sanitized," yet equally shallow, misrepresentations, such as the whitewashing (*Wara Wara*) or brown-facing (*El último malón*) of indigenous cultures. In the case of blacks, misrepresentation took the form of absence. As Robert Stam has noted, "While blacks were a frequently (if much abused) presence in North American silent cinema, they form a kind of 'structuring absence' within silent Brazilian cinema, the exceptions being an adaptation of *Uncle Tom's Cabin* (1910), of Azevedo's *Mulato* (1917), and of *A Escrava Isaura* (*The Slave Isaura*, 1919)."[33] In other Latin American countries with important black and mulatto populations, such as those in the Caribbean basin, exceptions to this "structuring absence" are even harder to find.

To my knowledge, the only film of this period that did not base its positive stereotyping of Latin Americans on Eurocentric liberal values is *La venganza de Pancho Villa* (*The Vengeance of Pancho Villa*; Edmundo Padilla, United States, 1936). It is what we would today call a found-footage film. It takes fragments from North American films such as *The Life of General Villa* (William Christy Cabanné, 1914) and *Liberty, A Daughter of the U.S.A.* (Jacques Jaccard, 1916), which represent Mexicans in a negative light, and combines them with fragments of the Mexican documentary *Historia de la Revolución Mexicana* (History of the Mexican Revolution; Julio Lamadrid, 1928) and dramatic sequences of Pancho Villa's life re-created by the El Paso–based Padilla family. The result is a positive rendering of Pancho Villa's struggles for social justice on both sides of the U.S.-Mexico border. The film was made by the Padilla family to complement the offerings of Mexican and North American films that they screened throughout the border region as part of their itinerant film exhibition business, and is calculated to have been seen by more than twelve thousand spectators, sometimes to the cries of "*¡Viva Villa! ¡Mueran los gringos!*"[34]

Perdón, viejita (1927)

In the late 1920s, silent cinema in Latin America saw a shift away from action-based plots such as those of *Nobleza gaucha* and *El automóvil gris* to plots that explored, however superficially and externally, psychological conflict. Among the best directors who participated in this shift were José Agustín Ferreyra (1889–1943) and Humberto Mauro (1897–1983). Ferreyra was the most consistently productive director of the silent period in Latin America, and one of only a handful who succeeded in making the transition to sound after 1930. Nicknamed "el Negro," he grew up in the working-class suburb of Buenos Aires called Constitución, in a household made up of himself, his Afro-Argentine mother, his itinerant Euro-Argentine father, and his mother's extended family in nearby homes. It is this world, where economic necessity joins with the kind of longing, passion, and pain that the tango expresses so well, that Ferreyra brought to life in the vast majority of his films, twenty-five of which were silent, two hybrid, and fifteen with synchronous sound. Of his silent films, *Perdón, viejita* (Forgive Me, Mother; 1927) is both his last, and, according to Jorge Miguel Couselo, his most representative: "Historical perspective redeems the film's candor and veracity. In its overall unity nothing is out of place, and even though characters are superficially sketched, they ooze authenticity. . . . [The street is] both their backdrop and their atmosphere. In a short scene, the uniform facades of the homes in the train-depot neighborhood of Nueva Pompeya create a sense of humble enchantment, with kids playing in the background while grown-ups in the foreground talk about their problems."[35]

Perdón, viejita tells the story of Carlos (Ermete Meliante) and Nora (played by María Turgenova, Ferreyra's wife between 1924 and 1931), two wayward young adults who decide to bury their criminal past and begin a new life together with Doña Camila (Floricel Vidal), Carlos's mother, and Elena (Stella Maris), his younger sister. Everything seems to be going well until Elena is seduced by a pimp named El Gavilán, and whose gift of a stolen ring serves first as bait for the impressionable Elena, then as incriminatory evidence against Nora (who had forced Elena to give her the ring in order to protect her), and finally as incriminatory evidence against El Gavilán, whereupon Nora's name is cleared and everyone lives happily ever after. This happy ending, however, is very different from the happy endings of Hollywood, for what prevails is a sense of precariousness, of living in a world where luck is fleeting and tragedy is not. In this and in other films by Ferreyra, we are firmly in the world of the tango, where melodrama and tragedy support each other to "keep alive the illusion of happiness while knowing that happiness is an illusion."[36] The title of the film, in fact, came from a famous tango recorded by a group that included Carlos Gardel, and its use here foreshadows the central role that music (and its privileged medium, radio) would play in the development of Latin American cinema during the studio period. After *Perdón, viejita*, Ferreyra traveled throughout Latin America, Europe, and the United States to promote his films. He returned without having succeeded, yet energized by the possibility of filming with synchronous sound. In this new ballgame, Ferreyra, like many of the protagonists in his films, charged ahead in the face of daunting odds, fueled by the hope of material success as much as by circumstance. To his credit, he succeeded in breaking the silence that the advent of sound momentarily created among Argentinean filmmakers.

Sangue Mineiro (1929)

A native of the state of Minas Gerais, Humberto Mauro directed more than ninety films, including six silent features (five in Cataguases and one in Rio), six features with sound (all in Rio, between 1933 and 1952), and more than three hundred documentary shorts for INCE, Brazil's National Institute of Educational Cinema, between 1936 and 1964.[37] *Sangue Mineiro* (Mineiro Blood; 1929), the most critically acclaimed of Mauro's Cataguases regional cycle and among the best of all of Brazilian silent cinema, plays with narrative conventions by replacing an initial love triangle between a man and two sisters with another love triangle between one of those sisters (Carmem, played by Carmen Santos) and two male cousins. In the end, the man in the first triangle chooses the legitimate daughter over Carmem (who is adopted and therefore will not likely inherit any of her industrialist father's fortune), while in the second triangle, Carmem chooses the rich and European-looking cousin over the indebted mestizo one (fig. 1.10). The film's melodramatic closure therefore reinforces social hierarchies of gender, class, and race without hinting at any possibility of change.

Having said that, it breaks new ground in several areas. For one, it beautifully captures the region's natural splendor, not only as a backdrop to the action, but as a telluric presence that facilitates the expression of feelings such as lust and envy, and, ultimately, of love, redemption, and forgiveness, all between sharply dressed characters with plenty of money to spare. Another is the quality of the acting, which is no longer theatrical but cinematic, in that characters' emotions and intentions are explored through nuanced facial expressions shot in close-up. In addition, the editing is rhythmic, successfully interposing action sequences with more introspective ones. Finally, Edgar Brasil's camera-

FIGURE 1.10   Carmem (Carmen Santos) chooses the rich white suitor over the poor mestizo one in the melodrama *Sangue Mineiro* (Mineiro Blood; Humberto Mauro, Brazil, 1929). Courtesy Cinemateca Brasileira

work poeticizes the play of light and shadow in a way that few other Latin American films of the silent period achieve, while here and there, metonymic shots of hands, feet, and furniture prefigure his work in the avant-garde films *Limite* (Limit; Mário Peixoto, Brazil, 1929) and *Ganga Bruta* (Raw Gangue; Humberto Mauro, Brazil, 1933).

In José Agustín Ferreyra and Humberto Mauro one finds the most sustained attempts to create a popular cinema in Latin America during the silent period. Their relative success was in part due to their mastery of the language and syntax of cinema, but also to their search, at the narrative and ideological levels, for solutions to social and political problems through the conventions of the family melodrama, a genre inflected in Ferreyra's case by the reversals and ruptures typical of the tango, and in Mauro's case by the desire for the continuity of a rural lifestyle.

The Legacy of the Silent Period

Just as the filmmakers of the silent period adjusted their modes of production and representation according to the specifics of both local and global forces, filmmakers in Latin America today continue to appropriate dominant forms from the metropolis for their own ends. The forms have changed, as have the ends of that appropriation, but the strategy itself has not, and may very well characterize all of Latin American cultural production, not as separate from or opposed to metropolitan production, but as marginal to and sometimes subversive of that production. Robert Stam suggests as much when he writes that "cultural discourse in Latin America and the Caribbean has been fecund in neologistic aesthetics, both literary and cinematic: 'lo real maravilloso americano' (Alejo Carpentier), the 'aesthetics of hunger' (Glauber Rocha), 'Cine imperfecto' (Julio García Espinosa), 'the creative incapacity for copying' (Paulo Emilio Salles Gomes), the 'aesthetics of garbage' (Rogério Sganzerla), the 'salamander' (as opposed to the Hollywood dinosaur) aesthetic (Paul Leduc), 'termite terrorism' (Guillermo del Toro), 'anthropophagy' (the Brazilian modernists), 'Tropicalia' (Gilberto Gil and Caetano Veloso), 'rasquachismo' (Tomás Ybarra-Frausto), and santería aesthetics (Arturo Lindsay)."[38]

Stam goes on to note that "most of these alternative aesthetics revalorize by inversion what had formerly been seen as negative, especially within colonialist discourse."[39] Clearly, this is not the case with Latin American silent cinema, whose Eurocentric criollo aesthetics extended the valorization of colonialist discourse into the new medium that was then cinema. Notwithstanding these ideological limits, Latin American silent cinema nevertheless succeeded in establishing national cinematic landscapes characterized by repeated attempts to transform their subordination to dominant centers of production and distribution by recourse to (1) local modes of production that were artisanal in nature, (2) distribution networks that focused on the regional and national audiences not served by the global cinematic industries of Europe and Hollywood, and (3) modes of representation closely linked to documentary practices. The elaboration of triangulation as a conscious or unconscious strategy during Latin American cinema's formative silent period is arguably its most important legacy for subsequent filmmaking practices in the region. It also explains the successful attempts made by a small number of filmmakers to break with the criollo sensibility of Latin America's silent cinema by closely calibrating their sights with that of the global cinematic avant-gardes. The next chapter takes a close look at their films.

2

Avant-Garde Silent Cinema

A CINEMA AGAINST THE GRAIN

During the 1920s and 1930s, several important and well-documented avant-gardes emerged throughout Latin America: the Modernismo movement launched by Modern Art Week in São Paulo in 1922, the texts and art associated with *revista de avance* in Cuba, and the many and varied avant-garde *isms* in literature, from *ultraísmo* and *estridentismo* to the lesser known *noísmo* and *euforismo*.[1] In cinema, at least four Latin American avant-garde films from this period have survived: *São Paulo, A Sinfonia da Metrópole* (São Paulo, a Metropolitan Symphony; Rodolfo Rex Lustig and Adalberto Kemeny, Brazil, 1929), *Limite* (Limit; Mário Peixoto, Brazil, 1929), *¡Que viva México!* (Sergei Eisenstein, Mexico–United States, 1931), and *Ganga Bruta* (Raw Gangue; Humberto Mauro, Brazil, 1933).[2] They are not many, especially when compared to the thousands of films made during the preceding silent period and the subsequent studio era, yet their unique contributions to the development of Latin American cinema justify a separate chapter.

In contrast to the conventionalism of criollo cinema, these four avant-garde films experiment with non-Aristotelian narratives, and with a nonrealist cinematography that includes extreme angle shots, the fragmentation of the projected image, and even shots made with a camera tied to a rope and thrown up in the air. This kind of formal experimentation was not new in cinema; many avant-garde filmmakers in Europe and North America had already experimented with narrative form and cinematography in the early 1920s and even before. Yet while necessary, metropolitan precursors are not sufficient to account for the emergence of a cinematic avant-garde in Latin America. Just as important, metropolitan precursors do not account for the original contributions made by Latin American cinema's first avant-garde to the subsequent evolution of cinema in the region and beyond.

Consider for example how these films represent machines, the metaphor par excellence of modernity at the time, in one of two ways. On the one hand, *São Paulo* and *Ganga Bruta* represent machines as lyrical instruments that harmonize with the emerging national bourgeoisie's project of a rational and liberal utopia; on the other, *Limite* and *¡Que viva México!* represent machines as tools that can help transform the social structures and cultural values associated with peripheral capitalism. These two representations of the machine are in turn linked to two very different temporalities. In *São Paulo* and *Ganga Bruta,* machines reinforce a linear understanding of time where progress is defined as incremental steps toward the consolidation of vertical social relations, and where the national bourgeoisie (and its exemplar, the white, heterosexual male) is clearly at the helm. In *Limite* and *¡Que viva México!,* machines are tied to alternative temporalities punctuated by qualitative jumps (in *¡Que viva México!*) or multidirectional flows (in *Limite*) linked to the representation of horizontal social relations. These radically different representations of the machine speak to the highly contested nature of modernity in Latin America during the few pivotal years in the late 1920s and early 1930s when the region was transitioning from oligarchic liberalism to corporatism, and when socialism as a discourse of modernity made significant gains in the region's political economy.

São Paulo, A Sinfonia da Metrópole (1929)

São Paulo, A Sinfonia da Metrópole (São Paulo, a Metropolitan Symphony; Rodolfo Rex Lustig and Adalberto Kemeny, Brazil, 1929) belongs to a genre of lyrical city portraits that includes films such as *Manhatta* (Paul Strand and Charles Sheeler, United States, 1921), *Berlin, die Sinfonie der Großstadt* (*Berlin, Symphony of a City*; Walter Ruttman, Germany, 1927), *Chelovek s kino-apparatom* (*Man with a Movie Camera*; Dziga Vertov, USSR, 1927), and *Rien que les heures* (Nothing but the Hours; Alberto Cavalcanti, France, 1926) (fig. 2.1). Ideologically, this is a varied group of films: Vertov's film represents Kiev, Moscow, and

FIGURE 2.1 Poster for *São Paulo, A Sinfonia da Metrópole* (São Paulo, a Metropolitan Symphony; Rodolfo Rex Lustig and Adalberto Kemeny, Brazil, 1929). Courtesy Cinemateca Brasileira

Odessa as centers of a socialist modernity where workers own the means of production; Cavalcanti's film critiques the social inequalities that economic liberalism generates in Paris; and *Manhatta* and *Berlin, Symphony of a City* offer the spectator a vision of their respective cities that is at once technologically modernizing and socially conservative. *São Paulo* clearly belongs with the latter group. It is also a representation of Brazil's industrial and financial center as a hub of global capitalism, an idea that is summarized in a short sequence where the screen is split into five parts: São Paulo's skyline occupies the center of the screen, and iconic images of Paris, New York, Berlin, and Chicago surround it. The film therefore reflects the aspiration of its directors and the class they represent to be considered subjects of a nation that is Western (because it is conspicuously devoid of indigenous and African elements), and liberal (because it renders organized labor invisible). More specifically, the film represents the virtues of Positivism. For example, it celebrates how the city's visibly productive bourgeoisie is capable of providing order and progress—the Positivist ideals that had only recently (1889) been emblazoned on the national flag by the founding fathers of the Republic[3]—through new industrial machines. These machines produce mass-consumption products such as food, clothing, and housing; provide modern transportation through trams, bicycles, and automobiles; and deliver information through newspapers and radio, all in an orderly fashion. To be fair, there is a short sequence where a disembodied hand gives alms to a hungry street beggar, and then a fistful of bills to a wealthy businessman. But because the sequence is framed as a dream, its critique of corruption and social inequality is reduced to the discursive equivalent of almsgiving within the film's grander, positive narrative of material and technological progress.

Ganga Bruta (1933)

Ganga Bruta (Raw Gangue; Humberto Mauro, Brazil, 1933) also represents machines as a trope of Positivist modernity, but within a melodramatic narrative set in the countryside. Marcos (Durval Bellini) is a rich engineer who murders his wife (Lu Marival) on their wedding night because he suspects her of infidelity. After being acquitted under a law that protects a man's right to defend his honor, Marcos leaves the city and its web of intrigues to seek refuge in the pristine countryside. Once there, he supervises the construction of a factory represented lyrically as a concert of straight lines and sharp angles, in symphonic counterpoint to the natural curves of the rural setting (fig. 2.2). In this uncommon scenario, where the rural landscape, modern technology, and bourgeois social relations harmonize, Marcos meets Sônia (Déa Selva), accidentally kills her fiancé Décio (Décio Murillo), and redeems himself by marrying her.

FIGURE 2.2 Exuberant tropical flora as metonymic of healthy sexual desire in the melodrama *Ganga Bruta* (Raw Gangue; Humberto Mauro, Brazil, 1933)

Glauber Rocha, the *enfant terrible* of Brazilian Cinema Novo (see chapters 7 and 8) and Brazil's most important filmmaker of the second half of the twentieth century, wrote the film's most cited description:

> In *Ganga Bruta,* Mauro creates an anthology that seems to encompass the best of Renoir's impressionism, of Griffith's audacity, of Eisenstein's strength, of Chaplin's humor, of Murnau's compositions in light and shadow.... Expressionist in its first five minutes (the wedding night and the wife's murder by the husband), it is a realist documentary in the second sequence (the liberty of the assassin and his tram rides through the city). The film then evolves toward the Western (the brawl in the bar, with the main fight in the best John Ford style) and grows with the strength of the classical Russian cinema (the possession of the woman, the erotic Freudian connotations of the metaphoric montage at the steel factory). And while the mise-en-scène during the discussion between Sônia's boyfriend and the criminal husband ... reminds us again of German Expressionism, all of the final sequences are impregnated with an air of adventure melodramas.... Mauro's politics, while ideologically diffuse, are nevertheless devoid of demagoguery.[4]

Rocha is correct in noting that the film is not demagogic, yet it clearly responds to a conservative social impulse that favors the landed elite (represented by Marcos) over the rising middle class (represented by Décio). The reason why Rocha celebrated the film may therefore have less to do with its content than with an aesthetics that served as a kind of national precedent to the type of heterogeneity and expressive liberty Rocha was beginning to develop in his own filmmaking. It would be more accurate to say that in spite of the formal heterogeneity one sees in *Ganga Bruta,* the film is far from ideologically heterodox, because it naturalizes the superiority of Brazil's privileged landowning class through a protagonist, Marcos, whose class standing, European pheno-type, and traditional values are reason enough for him to transform unfavorable circumstances to his favor, as evidenced by his ability to escape murder charges in one episode, design and construct a steel fac-tory in the middle of the countryside in the next, and get the girl in the end. The film's title openly supports this reading, for if the meaning of *gangue* is "the worthless rock or vein matter in which valuable metals or minerals occur,"[5] then Sônia's boyfriend and Marcos's first wife are like society's gangue, disposable and left to accumulate in the form of colluviums, so that Marcos, patriarchy's valuable ore, can maintain his privileged position in a rapidly changing world. Something quite differ-ent happens in *Limite* and *¡Que viva México!,* both of which offer a coherent critique of the interconnected ideologies and practices of rac-ism, heteronormativity, androcentrism, and capitalism; and the two films where the artistic and the political avant-gardes come together for the first time in the history of Latin American cinema.

¡Que viva México! (1931)

In December 1930, the Soviet film director Sergei Eisenstein, accompa-nied by his longtime assistant Grigori Alexandrov and the cinematogra-pher Eduard Tisse, arrived in Mexico to work on what turned out to be an unfinished film—*¡Que viva México!* (Mexico–United States, 1931)— known today primarily for the impact its cinematography had on the development of a Mexican filmic aesthetic, especially evident in the work of Gabriel Figueroa in the 1940s. The film's innovative narrative structure, while often overlooked, also left a profound mark on subse-quent filmmaking, in particular the militant phase of the New Latin American Cinema, thanks to the availability of the script and Eisen-stein's many notes on the subject. For these reasons alone, it is worth considering *¡Que viva México!* as a Latin American film even though it was not made by Latin Americans.

FIGURE 2.3 Dialectical montage within the shot in the prologue of *¡Que viva México!*
(Sergei Eisenstein, Mexico–United States, 1931)

In his script, Eisenstein organized *¡Que viva México!* into four main narratives—"Sandunga," "Maguey," "Fiesta," and "Soldadera"—bracketed by a prologue and an epilogue. The prologue, according to Eisenstein, functions as a baseline where time is eternal, and therefore not yet part of history as Marx understood it (fig. 2.3). In "Sandunga," Eisenstein introduces narrative but time is still pre-historical. In this "novella," as Eisenstein called the four central narratives of the film, Concepción, a young maiden in a matriarchal society in Tehuantepec, must save enough money for a dowry. When she does, the elder women meet to discuss whether to approve Concepción's choice of a husband. They do, a wedding and festivities ensue, and "Sandunga" ends with an image of the happy couple "satisfied, and a child that smiles" (fig. 2.4).[6]

For "Maguey," Eisenstein sets the action in the major pulque-producing region of the country, the central highlands of Mexico near Hidalgo. Unlike the previous episode, where Concepción sold produce, Sebastián and his friends in "Maguey" can only sell their labor. This decisively Marxist premise led the Mexican censors, as Eisenstein claims, to "mitigate the argument and even to suspend it when we were filming the liveliest lines of the reality back then. . . . In response to our thesis that only an exact demonstration of the class struggle in the

FIGURE 2.4   The archetypal family in "Sandunga," *¡Que viva México!*

haciendas could explain and make comprehensible the Revolution against Porfirio Díaz in 1910, we were told that 'the landowners are as Mexican as the peasants, and it is not necessary to underline the antagonism between the different groups in the nation.'"[7]

Official protestations did not stop Eisenstein from framing Sebastián's narrative trajectory of avenging the rape of his fiancée by a guest of the landowner as a struggle with both class and ethnic dimensions. Indeed, Eisenstein was able to film most of what he wanted for this episode, including an intense play of gazes to represent Sebastián's heightened awareness and pride after being captured, and the climactic sequence where the landowner and his guests gallop repeatedly over Sebastián and two fellow workers who have been buried chest-deep after their unsuccessful revolt and subsequent capture (fig. 2.5).

The tone in "Fiesta," the next episode, is melodramatic, and according to Eisenstein, it was to center around the triangular plot of an upper-class woman, her husband, and a young picador (fig. 2.6). The climactic sequence was to have the husband surprise his wife and the young picador in a moment of supreme ecstasy, as they kissed in front of a huge crucifix on top of an isolated mountain. Just then, as the husband pulls out a gun, "the woman falls on her knees and pleads to Our Lord of

FIGURE 2.5 A Mexican pietà in "Maguey," *¡Que viva México!*

FIGURE 2.6 Baroque excess as celebration of life in "Fiesta," *¡Que viva México!*

Chalma to intercede. And a miracle takes place. The lover is transformed . . . into an altar, over which appears God. The vengeful and hurried husband has no other choice but to kneel down and pray in front of the altar."[8]

For the fourth and last narrative, Eisenstein developed several versions of the story of Pancha, a *soldadera* whose husband dies at the height of the Mexican Revolution and is then given to another soldier. As in "Maguey," the female in "Soldadera" is an object of exchange between men. Eisenstein was aware that this could strike the viewer as ironic, especially in a narrative intended to celebrate the proactive role of peasant women in the Mexican Revolution, and justified it as follows:

> [This final] version did not seem to us to constitute evidence of a lack of political awareness, or as evidence of the indifference of the Mexican woman. On the contrary. Her first husband belonged to the army of Pancho Villa. The second to the forces of Emiliano Zapata. In fact, in the intricate reversals of the Mexican Revolution there existed a moment in which the soldiers of Villa and Zapata fought each other, at the same time that both were fighting against the central government of Venustiano Carranza. . . . In the definitive version of the plot, the development of Pancha represents that of Mexico, which, passing as it did from hand to hand, gradually realizes that strength resides not in discord, but in the unity of the people against the reactionary nuclei.[9]

Finally, the epilogue represents contemporary Mexico City and was the part that most excited Eisenstein. It includes many of the social types from the previous episodes plus additional working-class subjects, and closes with a final montage where different subjects/types remove their skeleton masks to reveal either a skeleton or a flesh-and-blood person (fig. 2.7). For example, when a masked subject dressed in the style of the Porfirian-era elite removes his mask, the fact that behind the mask there is a skeleton visually signals that this social class is dead. On the other hand, when adults dressed in middle-class and working-class clothes take off their masks, what we see are always smiling faces. Most suggestively, when children remove their masks, we see the smiling faces of a working class in full control of its very bright future.

¡Que viva México! thus narrates the history of Mexico as an epic struggle spanning at least four centuries, from the preconquest times represented in the prologue and "Sandunga" to contemporary Mexico as represented in the epilogue. These episodes are linked neither narratively nor aesthetically, as in Aristotelian narratives. Instead, they are

FIGURE 2.7 A bright future for the working class in the epilogue of *¡Que viva México!*

distinctive parts of a dialectical metanarrative where each part represents a different mode of production in Mexico's history, for example
primitive communalism in "Sandunga," feudalism in "Maguey," and
socialism in the epilogue.

In order to represent this centuries-long epic, Eisenstein considered
the diachronic narrative model that D. W. Griffith developed for *Intoler-
ance* (United States, 1916), where different historical periods are contrasted. Eisenstein rejected this, however, because the film's "metaphysi-
cal philosophy of the eternal origins of Good and Evil"[10] was far removed
from the materialism that informed all of his theoretical and directorial
work, and because its "quantitative accumulation [i.e., parallel montage]
was not enough: we sought for and found in juxtapositions more than
that: a qualitative jump."[11] Eisenstein would later call this qualitative
jump "ideological montage," and it can be seen in *Stachka* (*Strike*; USSR,
1924), *Oktyabr* (*October*; USSR, 1927), and most famously in the lion
sequence in *Bronenosets Potyomkin* (*Battleship Potemkin*; USSR, 1925).
But it was in Mexico where Eisenstein was able, for the first time, to put
the theory and practice of ideological montage to work in a dialectical
metanarrative where conflict is no longer limited to a single historical
period, as happens in *Strike, October,* and *Battleship Potemkin,* but is

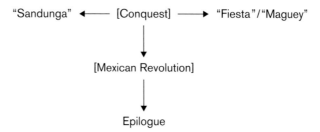

FIGURE 2.8 Dialectical structure of *¡Que viva México!*

now expanded diachronically, to include oppositions between modes of production across time.

Given that Eisenstein died before the reels were finally sent to Moscow in 1972, I should note that the rest of this analysis is based on two primary sources: Grigori Alexandrov's 1979 edition from the footage that made it to Moscow, and a Spanish-language version of Eisenstein's script published in Mexico in 1964.[12] In Alexandrov's edition, the prologue, the epilogue, "Sandunga," and "Maguey" closely reflect what Eisenstein penned in his script. "Fiesta," however, is placed before rather than after "Maguey," and it is missing the principal narrative plot of a love triangle because that part was never filmed. Finally, in lieu of the unfilmed "Soldadera," Alexandrov inserts himself in the film to explain what that episode was going to narrate and why it was never finished. Notwithstanding these differences, Alexandrov's version still manages to convey Eisenstein's conceptualization of the film as a dialectical metanarrative in three parts. For even though there are four central episodes, Eisenstein thought of "Fiesta" and "Maguey" as "intimately linked by their color and their character,"[13] by which he may have meant that both are melodramatic plots of love and revenge set before the Revolution. The resulting three parts ("Sandunga," "Fiesta" / "Maguey," and "Soldadera") represent, according to Eisenstein, "the three historical stages of the conception of life: from biological submission to death to the overcoming of death's principle through the power of the collectivity of the people" (fig. 2.8).[14] Seen in this way, the prologue functions as an abstraction of Death, the frozen face of the smiling boy at the end of the epilogue functions as an abstraction of Life, and everything in between reinterprets Mexican history as the dialectical succession of different historical epochs, each one identified with a dominant mode of production.

Thus, *¡Que viva México!* interprets Mexico's economic history as having developed from

1. an initial thesis in the episode of "Sandunga," which would correspond to an undeveloped mode of production based on simple sustenance, and which Marx called primitive communalism; through

2. a subsequent antithesis in the twin episodes of "Fiesta" and "Maguey," which would correspond respectively to the periods of colonialism and republican liberalism (roughly, the fifteenth, sixteenth, seventeenth, eighteenth, and nineteenth centuries), when the previous primitive communalism was transformed into a system that sutured different modes of production such as capitalism, feudalism, and slavery; and finally

3. a synthesis post-Revolution, when relations between social actors are transformed once again and are now based on solidarity, freedom, and workers' control of the means of production. In short, a synthesis not as the end of history or its dialectics, but as an idealized socialist modernity where social classes have been eliminated, and where contradictions and conflicts that will inevitably arise are not yet visible.

In addition, the connections between the thesis ("Sandunga"), antithesis ("Fiesta" and "Maguey"), and synthesis (the epilogue) are, as one would expect in a Marxist narrative, moments of transformative violence: between the thesis and antithesis, that moment is a short sequence that represents the conquest as an economic invasion followed by the construction of a new social order (fig. 2.9); while between the antithesis and the synthesis, the moment of transformative violence is the unfinished episode of "Soldadera," which was to represent the Mexican Revolution.

Eisenstein had been exploring the idea of a dialectical metanarrative since before his arrival in Mexico, as part of an ambitious attempt to adapt into film Marx's *Capital* and its thesis of historical materialism. For instance, on March 17, 1928, he wrote: "On the level of 'historical materialism,' current equivalents of historical turning points with a contemporary orientation must be sought. In *Capital,* for example, the themes of textile machines and machine-wreckers should collide: electric streetcar in Shanghai and thousands of coolies thereby deprived of bread, lying down on the tracks—to die. . . . An economic invasion and construction of new cities."[15]

As Eisenstein and his team scouted for shooting locations in early 1931—sometimes accompanied by Diego Rivera, Gabriel Figueroa, and

FIGURE 2.9 Franciscan asceticism as adoration of death in conquest, *¡Que viva México!*

other Mexican artists and government officials—he noted that the different modes of production described in *Capital* coexisted in Mexico: from primitive communalism in Tehuantepec, to feudalism in the maguey plantations near Hidalgo, to an industrial economy in Mexico City.[16] He was overjoyed, for he had found living examples of all the different modes of production described in *Capital*. He immediately set to work to try to figure out a way to represent these different modes of production diachronically, and as linked by historical turning points. *¡Que viva México!* is, from this perspective, Eisenstein's unfinished attempt to adapt Marx's magnum opus to the medium of film.

Besides Marx's *Capital*, another major source of inspiration for Eisenstein's shift away from a synchronic to a diachronic representation of history is *The History of Mexico*, the famous mural at the National Palace that Diego Rivera painted between 1928 and 1936, precisely when Eisenstein worked in Mexico. Specifically, Eisenstein adopts the mural's representation of Mexican history in three parts, whereby a side panel represents an idealized Aztec society before the arrival of the Spaniards, a massive central mural depicts key episodes from the conquest all the way to the Revolution,[17] and a second side panel on the opposite end portrays contemporary Mexico. In a progress report

Eisenstein sent to the government of Mexico in August 1931, he explicitly acknowledged this influence by stating that his intention was to create "a cinematographic symphony, a symphony that takes as its starting point a meaning comparable to that created through composition and arrangement in Diego Rivera's murals in the National Palace. Like those paintings, our film will show the political evolution of Mexico from antiquity to the present, when it emerges as a progressive and modern country, a land of liberty and opportunity."[18]

There is, however, a major difference in the representation of history in these two epic works of art. *Mexico Today and Tomorrow*, the third part of Diego Rivera's mural, explicitly denounces the authoritarianism of the post-Revolutionary governments. The mural, for example, shows government police in gas masks beating and firing upon striking workers in front of tanks with crosses that morph into swastikas. Immediately below this scene, faceless government soldiers aim firearms at indigenous farmers who stand below a banner that reads "Comunidades Agrarias" (Agrarian Communities), and to the right, two rebels hang dead from poles, a practice used by the Plutarco Elias Calles regime against political dissidents and especially against Christians who refused to renounce their religion during the Cristero War. By contrast, Eisenstein's epilogue depicts the working class free from state oppression and in full control of its destiny, to the point that machines such as the Ferris wheel now serve as entertainment. Notwithstanding the positive outlook for the working classes with which the film ends, Eisenstein was not naive enough to think that the contemporary situation in Mexico, at the tail end of the state violence that Calles unleashed during the Cristero War of 1926–29, matched the synthesis represented in the film's epilogue, or that the dialectical unfolding of History had come to an end in Mexico. In his script, for example, Eisenstein qualifies the epilogue's optimism by directly addressing the gap between the epilogue-as-synthesis and the bureaucratic authoritarianism that already plagued Mexico when he visited to make the film in 1930–32:

> In the definitive version of the film, the "apotheosis" of the epilogue clearly was not intended to reiterate, in that particular way, the triumph of "progress" nor the "paradise" of industrialization. We know very well that when the bourgeois states commence their expansion, the primitive forms of patriarchal exploitation are transformed in more advanced forms of labor. It is therefore not our intent to limit the ending of the film to a sampling of how Mexico has conquered contemporary civilization. . . . [T]he social principle of life, which is affirmation, will have to keep on fighting for a very long time against the forces of obscurantism, of reaction and of death, before the ideal of those who suffer underneath the boot of the oppressors becomes a reality.[19]

Eisenstein's implicit denunciation of Calles's authoritarian presidency is also conveyed through the film's use of neobaroque aesthetics, whereby contrasting elements and episodes do not cancel one another out, but rather coexist in a tensile relationship. From this perspective, the film's Marxism and its religiosity are not incompatible. Instead, their combination constitutes a heterodox Marxism that rejects the facile narrative synthesis advocated by socialist realism (which would justify the crushing of the Cristero rebellion), and instead suggests a more complex understanding of the Cristero War as part of the Mexican Revolution broadly defined. For example, "Maguey" clearly privileges the overthrow of the oppressor by the oppressed, and in this sense it is an orthodox Marxist take on Mexican history. Symbolically, however, the episode develops a parallel, spiritual argument in favor of the overthrow of the oppressor through the representation of the aptly named Sebastián as a warrior figure (Saint Sebastian is the patron saint of warriors). This is not to say that the film champions the Catholic Church, for the images of Franciscan friars holding skulls are a clear indictment of the historical role of the Church in the oppression of indigenous groups. Instead, the film champions the kind of popular Christianity embodied by Sebastián, a popular Christianity that struggles for the right of a people to express its aspirations and beliefs without intervention, censorship, or oppression from the outside, including the state.

"Fate found it convenient," Eisenstein wrote in 1931, "that I immerse myself very deeply—with my whole head—in the study of the dialectic in the surroundings of Central Mexico. . . . It was precisely here, in these circumstances, that I . . . experienced the basic dynamics of its (dialectical) principle—becoming."[20] Properly contextualized, these otherwise cryptic lines provide evidence that Eisenstein saw the Cristero War, which had recently ended in Central Mexico, as a legitimate rebellion against an authoritarian and monologistic state. Equally important, they also provide a key to interpreting ¡Que viva México! as a project whose unfinished production and partial reconstructions paradoxically support Eisenstein's ultimate goal to make a new kind of revolutionary art: an art of becoming, where struggles for liberation are as much a thing of the present as of the past.

Limite (1929)

Mário Peixoto (1908–1992) was the reclusive heir to a large fortune based on coffee (on his mother's side) and sugar (on his father's). As a young adult he studied in England and traveled to Paris, where he became acquainted with Soviet cinema, German Expressionism, French impressionist films, and other expressions of the European avant-garde. Upon returning to Brazil, he and a group of friends established the Chaplin Club as a space to discuss and promote cinema, and as part of that effort, the club published a journal titled *O Fan* between 1928 and 1930. It was during this time that Peixoto conceived and filmed *Limite* (Limit; Brazil, 1929), a beautifully evocative film that premiered in 1931 in Rio de Janeiro but failed to find a distributor. For the next three decades it was shown to selected audiences, until the film itself began to decompose. Plínio Süsekind Rocha, founder of the Chaplin Club, and his student, Saulo Pereira de Mello, began a first restoration that took up most of the 1960s and 1970s. A second restoration was finished in 2011, to worldwide acclaim.

Limite opens with a series of enigmatic shots: birds of prey atop a cliff, a woman framed by handcuffed arms, the handcuffs by themselves, a close-up of the woman's eyes, and finally a glistening sea (fig. 2.10). The next sequence is equally enigmatic: three adult characters in a small boat floating aimlessly in the middle of the sea: Woman 1 (Olga Breno), Woman 2 (Taciana Rei), and Man 1 (Raul Schnoor). They are without water or food, and tension fills the air as they each take turns telling their backstories in the form of extended and very loosely narrated flashbacks. Woman 1, for example, had escaped prison only to find herself imprisoned by a menial job; Woman 2 had abandoned an alcoholic husband only to find herself alone and adrift; and Man 1 had recently become engaged only to find that he was not in love with his fiancée. Soon after Man 1 finishes his story he jumps from the boat and drowns, and then a storm destroys the boat. The last sequence is composed of various shots of Woman 1 as she clings precariously to scraps of floating wood, juxtaposed with shots from the opening sequence: her face framed by handcuffs, the glistening sea, and the birds of prey feasting on an unseen carcass.

On first viewing, *Limite* appears to be, as Glauber Rocha famously wrote, "a film of images, with no social preoccupations . . . a film made for art's sake."[21] After all, it does feature Euro-Brazilian characters with what seem to be strictly psychological anxieties, and the hauntingly beautiful cinematography by Edgar Brasil recalls French impressionist films such as *La roue* (*The Wheel*; Abel Gance, France, 1922) and *La souriante Madame Beudet* (*The Smiling Madame Beudet*; Germaine Dulac, France, 1922). But this does not mean that it is devoid of social preoccupations, or that it is a film made for art's sake. On the contrary,

FIGURE 2.10   Handcuffs as a metaphor of Woman 1's (Olga Breno) marriage in *Limite* (Limit; Mário Peixoto, Brazil, 1929). Courtesy Cinemateca Brasileira

other than *¡Que viva México!*, *Limite* is the only Latin American silent film that radically critiques what Eisenstein called patriarchal exploitation, in this case through an oblique representation of three pillars of patriarchal liberalism: marriage, capitalism, and heteronormativity.

For example, the flashback that corresponds to Woman 1 deploys a scathing critique of marriage and capitalism. The sequence begins with her escape from a small rural prison that looks like a house, a fact that underscores the connection between marriage, domesticity, and imprisonment that had already been established in the opening sequence (in Spanish, coincidentally, the word for "handcuffs," *esposas,* is also the word for "wives"). After leaving prison, Woman 1 meanders through the countryside and eventually migrates by train to the city, where she finds a job as a seamstress. Machines are therefore initially associated with mobility, because the train facilitates her escape from the countryside where she had been jailed, but the machine's role quickly shifts to being associated with a different kind of limiting situation: not social, as marriage, nor legal, as during her imprisonment, but rather economic, because her work as a factory seamstress is poorly paid and alienates her from other human beings and from the fruit of her labor.

FIGURE 2.11 Mário Peixoto and Man 1 (Raul Schnoor) have a homoerotic encounter in *Limite*

Woman 2's flashback further develops this critique of traditional marriage as a form of imprisonment. And in the third and final flashback, the film broadens the critique of traditional gender relations to include heteronormativity, in a puzzling encounter between Man 1 and a character played by Peixoto in a country cemetery. The encounter is charged with homoerotism: there is Peixoto's play with a wedding ring, the emotion with which Peixoto grabs Man 1 by the tail of his jacket, the phallic connotations of a cigarette that turns out to be a piece of wood, and the intensity with which the characters look at each other (fig. 2.11). The encounter is followed by a long sequence where Man 1 frantically searches for Peixoto, and where the homoerotic double entendres of the encounter crystallize into an image of Man 1 as imprisoned by his acceptance of society's heteronormativity.[22]

Limite's radical critique of heteronormativity, marriage, and capitalism is supported by an equally radical treatment of space and time based on time-images. According to Gilles Deleuze, time-images are "pure optical and sound situations in which the character does not know how to respond, abandoned spaces in which he ceases to experience and to act so that he enters into flight, goes on a trip, comes and goes, vaguely indifferent to what happens to him, undecided as to what must be done. But he has gained in an ability to see what he has lost in action or reaction: he SEES so that the viewer's problem becomes 'What is there to see in the image?' (and not 'What are we going to see in the next image?')."[23]

One of the formal characteristics of the Deleuzian time-image is the elaboration of the kind of camerawork that separates the perspective of the camera from the perspective of the characters and their narratives, so that the representation of time is no longer tied to what the characters see, do, or feel. For Deleuze, it is a camerawork of "bizarre visions [produced by the] alternation of different lenses, zoom, extraordinary angles, abnormal movements, [and] halts,"[24] precisely the kind of camerawork that Edgar Brasil developed for *Limite*. In fact, *Limite* abounds, not with precursors to time-images (which according to Deleuze only appeared after World War II), but with highly elaborated examples of time-images of wind and water as metaphors of the ever-changing nature of time, space, identity, and social relations. The most bizarre of these time-images occurs around a fountain during Woman 2's flashback. The camera, placed in front of the fountain and looking up at the spout, suddenly moves toward the spout. The shot, unusual as it is, becomes all the more so because it is repeated three times, and then again five times. It is as if this image is so important that it deserves to be repeated, each time with more insistence, to the point that it forces the spectator into thinking of the camera's movement as a metaphor for time that can, like water, flow not only forward but also backward (as the camera's move toward the spout suggests), or in multiple directions, as when, at the end of the sequence, the camera, hanging from a rope, records the village rooftops freed from the impositions of conventional perspectives or narrative trajectories.

In effect, by suggesting that time can flow in multiple directions and in a rhythm based on repetition and variation, *Limite* represents an alternative temporality of modernity that is radically different from the teleological temporalities of conventional discourses of modernity. Concretely, the rhythmic flow of the camera and of the water in *Limite* generates a time that is measured by the lapses between time-images (shots of stagnant versus flowing water, of immobile plants versus plants that sway in the wind, of combed versus disheveled hair) instead of being measured by the lapses between action-images, as if what happened to the characters took place within the folds created by the time-images, and not the other way around.

Mário Peixoto himself may be the person who has best theorized the film's rhythmic and syncopated montage, in an article he wrote, quite tellingly, under the alias of "Sergei Eisenstein":

> [*Limite*] is a meticulously constructed film, with major shots surrounded by minor shots, like planetary systems intermediated by the intrinsic temporality of the regime. The totality remains standing and generates the desired atmosphere through an emancipated visual language that links and complements shots with one another, with the lucid precision of a meticulous poet or an expert watchmaker who makes all the parts work together. . . . The whole film is a luminous pain that unfolds rhythmically in images of rare precision and ingenuity. . . . And then one discovers in the object a beauty and a force that does not reside only at the level of human beings. [One discovers . . .] that things can have—or can come to have—their own or real existence, outside of human thought. In *Limite*, it is in an enlarged image, imposed suddenly, where this very particular process begins.[25]

As I interpret this passage, what Peixoto calls "major shots" are the equivalent of Deleuzian time-images around which revolve the "minor shots," or the equivalent of Deleuzian movement-images. Yet the only way for viewers to really *see* these major shots is to be shaken out of culturally ingrained expectations that shots tied to a particular narrative are somehow more meaningful than shots not tied to a narrative.

This shaking-out of the viewer is first hinted at during Woman 1's flashback: as she meanders through the countryside, the camera separates from her perspective and begins to observe things from a perspective that is clearly not hers. This decoupling of narrative and nonnarrative images is reiterated in the unexpected close-up of a dandelion seed head in Woman 2's flashback (fig. 2.12). This close-up of the dandelion may very well be the "enlarged image" that Peixoto says will help us discover an existence outside of human thought. It is, after all, an image imposed suddenly, by the camera's unexpected liberation from following Woman 2's point of view. The selection of a dandelion to represent this decoupling between narrative and nonnarrative images is also significant because from this point onward, the camera begins to move more and more like the seeds of the dandelion when liberated by the wind: increasingly in tune with the syncopated rhythms of the wind and the water, and less tied to the repetitive and fossilized rhythms of the character's mental and physical routines.

Limite's rhythmic time and fragmented space link it to the Latin American neobaroque, which arranges spatial and temporal fragments into new configurations marked by tension.[26] *Limite* constructs this

FIGURE 2.12 Dandelion seed head in Woman 2's flashback, *Limite*

neobaroque time-space through the tensile contrast between the free and rhythmic flow of a camera that is not conditioned by social and cultural prejudices or motivations, versus the limited lives of the three characters, trapped in a boat that functions as a metaphor for the stagnation they suffer because they have subjected themselves to the bourgeois norms of thought and behavior as manifested in traditional marriage, heteronormativity, and salaried work. Put another way, meaning in *Limite* emerges out of the tension between the rhythmic and pulsating liberty of the camera, the wind, and the water on the one hand, and the monotonous, repetitive, and routine existence of the characters on the other. In this reading, the free and rhythmic flow of the camera and the water represents the liberty that the characters could have, but do not enjoy, because they fear the transition from the liberal stability of "being" to the neobaroque instability of "becoming." Herein lies the radical message of the film: that the stability of epistemological binarisms, of linear time, and of continuous space (all of which underpin the bourgeois project of a liberal modernity) also condition ways of thinking and acting that limit the full development of our most human qualities, and that a more productive alternative would be to live in harmony with a nature—human and nonhuman—whose space is rhizomatic, whose time is rhythmic, and whose epistemology is relational.[27]

AN AVANT-GARDE MOMENT

While *Limite, Ganga Bruta, ¡Que viva México!,* and *São Paulo, A Sinfonia da Metrópole* do not constitute a movement, they do constitute what Marjorie Perloff calls an avant-garde moment:

> My sense is that neither the Italian or the Russian Futurist movements could, in the way they developed, be on par with the Futurist *moment.* Born in what were relatively young nation-states in the periphery of European culture, the Italian and Russian avant-gardes cultivated the new with more intensity than the avant-gardes at the centers of European culture. Futurism, notes Pontus Hultén, could never take root in the more established bourgeois cultures of the center. In nations like Italy and Russia, however, the contrast between the old and the new was sufficiently large so as to generate an aesthetics of excess, violence, and revolution.[28]

This understanding of the peripheral avant-garde moments as more radical than the avant-garde movements at the centers of production makes it possible to rescue the films of Latin American cinema's first avant-garde from the fringes of world film history, and in particular, *Limite* and *¡Que viva México!* as local expressions of a global avant-garde that eschews conventional boundaries between center and periphery. Furthermore, by asking what is or what should be the social role of machines, these four films contributed to a global debate that explored the relationship between human beings and technology in a context of rapid industrialization and intense struggles on every continent over the rights of workers. Many contemporaneous films represented this relationship as a contest where machines have the upper hand, for example *Metropolis* (Fritz Lang, Germany, 1927), *Frankenstein* (James Whale, United States, 1931), and *Modern Times* (Charlie Chaplin, United States, 1936). In Latin America, perhaps because industrialization was only beginning and most people still lived in the countryside, cinema does not represent machines as a threat to humanity. What we do see, however, is a Positivist representation of machines as harbingers of a liberal modernity in *São Paulo* and *Ganga Bruta,* and a more nuanced representation of machines in *¡Que viva México!* and *Limite* whereby the social function of machines depends on who uses them and to what end.

PART TWO

Studio Cinema

3

Transition to Sound

The Wall Street crash of 1929 precipitated the collapse of Latin America's period of export-led growth under oligarchic liberalism, and inaugurated a new era of mixed economies dominated by populist corporatist states. Slowly at first, then with increasing self-assurance in the 1940s and 1950s, these corporatist states implemented policies of import-substitution industrialization that rapidly accelerated Latin America's urbanization. In this context, Latin American cinema transitioned not only from silence to sound, but also from artisanal to industrial modes of production centered in studios and aimed at a rapidly growing urban population.

LATIN AMERICAN STUDIOS

From an economic perspective, Latin American studios functioned like Hollywood minors or B-film factories, dependent on Hollywood's majors for the distribution of a product that focused on lower-income audiences who could only afford the lower prices charged for most national productions. There was of course considerable overlap between the different sectors that made up Latin American audiences, yet its differentiation was such that, by focusing on the poorer sectors, filmmaking in Latin America became a sustainable enterprise for the first time in its history. Four studios—Lumitón, Argentina Sono Films, CLASA, and Churubusco—constituted the top tier of a tripartite pyramid of Latin

TABLE 3.1   Selected film Studios in Latin America

STUDIO	YEARS IN EXISTENCE	NUMBER OF FEATURES PRODUCED
Argentina		
Lumitón	1932–52	180
Argentina Sono Films	1933–77	240
Estudios San Miguel Inn	1937–57	35
Artistas Argentinos Asociados	1941–58	29
Aires Cinematográfica Argentina	1958–89	90
Brazil		
Cinédia	1930–70	50
Brasil Vita Filmes	1933–58	17
Atlântida	1943–62	62
Vera Cruz	1950–54	18
Maristela	1950–58	14
Chile		
Chile Films	1944–49	10
Mexico *(figures are unreliable because of frequent consolidations of studios)*		
Nacional Productora	1932–36	—
México Films	1933–47	—
CLASA (Cinematográfica Latinoamericana, S.A.)	1934–57	—
Estudios Azteca	1937–58	—
Churubusco	1945–today	—
Estudios San Ángel Inn	1949–68	—
Peru		
Amauta Films	1937–40	14
Venezuela		
Bolívar Films	1949–53	8

American studios. A middle tier included those studios that lasted for relatively short periods and/or whose production was relatively lower than that of the top four. The bottom tier of intermittent producers did not sustain production beyond a handful of films. Table 3.1 lists the top- and middle-tier film studios by country and chronologically, and the approximate number of feature films each one produced.[1] Figure 3.1 plots feature film production in Mexico, Argentina, and Brazil, the three major producing countries, between 1930 and 1962.[2]

Broadly speaking, studio cinema in Latin America developed in four phases:

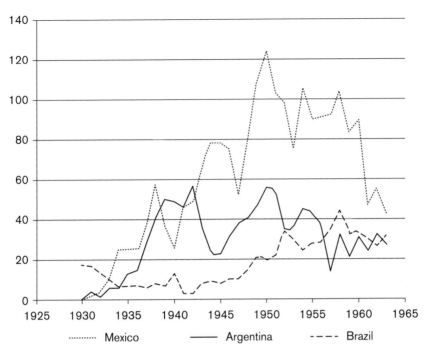

FIGURE 3.1   Feature film production in Mexico, Argentina, and Brazil, 1930–62.

1. *Transition to sound, early 1930s.* Studio cinema and corporatism
   are both embryonic, and because the new sound technologies
   require large amounts of capital investment for production
   precisely at a time when the effects of the Wall Street crash have
   sent Latin American economies into a deep depression, modes of
   production are artisanal and the number of films is correspondingly small.

2. *Early studio cinema, 1936–42.* Modes of production become
   increasingly industrial, state intervention in the film industry
   grows, and films begin to represent the values of corporatism as
   moral obligations limited to individual choices. Stories include
   interclass love, rich villains turned noble by still nobler peasants
   or workers, and a populist understanding of popular culture as
   synonymous with national culture. During these formative years
   of indigenous industrialization, Argentinean studios enjoyed a
   sustained increase in the quantity, quality, and diversity of

production, while in Mexico, a *ranchera* bubble generated by the 1936 hit *Out on the Big Ranch* burst in 1938. Argentina's lead seemed secure until the United States, as part of a broad Pan-American strategy to prod Latin American countries into joining the Allied war effort, punished Argentina's neutrality by banning U.S. exports of raw film to that country, and simultaneously rewarded Mexico's alliance with generous technical and financial support.

3. *Heyday of Studio Cinema, 1943–50.* As a result of the U.S. intervention, there was a marked turn in the fortunes of the two leading national industries, with Mexican studios the clear winners and Argentina's film industry enjoying a partial recovery only in the second half of the 1940s as a direct result of strong protectionist measures. Throughout this phase, industrial production expands and the corporatist state enters the screen via characters that represent its institutions as a mediating force between social actors with conflicting interests.

4. *Crisis of Studio Cinema, 1950s.* Studios suffer a decade-long road toward obsolescence as the United States vigorously reasserts the hegemony that it had partially ceded to Mexico because of the war, and as local audiences grow tired of the formulaic products coming out of an industry that is visibly in decline. Ideologically, films bear witness to the unraveling of corporatism's pact between state, capital, and labor.

This chapter focuses on the first phase. The next chapter ("Birth and Growth of an Industry") looks at phases two and three, and chapter 5 ("Crisis and Decline of Studio Cinema") covers the last phase.

LATIN AMERICAN STUDIO CINEMA AS A VERNACULAR OF HOLLYWOOD'S INTERNATIONAL STYLE

Since at least 1915, Hollywood studios had been developing a highly polished style that by the 1920s was the "classical" standard by which studio cinema worldwide was judged. At the level of the shot, this classical style is characterized by the use of cinematographic devices such as three-point lighting and centered framing to help create the illusion of continuous space. At the level of sequences and sets of sequences, the style is defined by the use of continuity editing to create the illusion of continuous time, and also the illusion of causal connections between narrative events. Finally, continuity of time and space are always at the service of narratives with clearly articulated Aristotelian arcs driven by psychologically motivated characters.[3] Because of its global reach, Santos Zunzunegui has called this style a global cinematic lingua franca whose position was analogous to that of architecture's international style, insofar as both provided practitioners the world over with "a basic model, a fixed format over which were stamped a multitude of particulars."[4] Miriam Hansen makes a similar argument when she calls Hollywood a "vernacular modernism," and Shanghai cinema of the 1920s and 1930s "a distinct brand of vernacular modernism . . . that evolved in a complex relation to American . . . models while drawing on and transforming [local] traditions in theater, literature, [and] graphic and print culture, both modernist and popular."[5] Building on Hansen and Zunzunegui, one could therefore define much of the cinema then being produced in cities such as Shanghai, Tokyo, Cairo, Mumbai, Paris, Rome, Berlin, Mexico City, and Buenos Aires as Hollywood vernaculars: hybrid versions of Hollywood's international style adapted to local tastes.

Latin American studios in particular adapted Hollywood's international style by incorporating archetypes and narrative forms already present in its popular theater (*género chico*), popular music, and popular literature. In the case of popular theater, for example, Latin American studio cinema borrowed directly from musical variety shows (*revistas de variedades*) and comedy skits (*sainetes*). Popular music entered cinema by way of radio, providing sound cinema with many of its early stars in films that were oftentimes little more than filmed songs. This practice quickly evolved into narrative films punctuated by songs that were nevertheless still the main attraction. In fact, by the end of the 1930s, cinema and radio had converged into a single entertainment industry, as evidenced by a specialized press that addressed both media: *Sintonía* (Buenos Aires, 1933–56), *Vea* (Mexico City, 1934–46), *Cine Radio Actualidad* (Montevideo, 1936–68), *Cine-Radio Jornal* (Rio de Janeiro, 1938–43), *Lente* (Havana, 1938), *Radiolandia* (Mexico City, 1938–58), and *Radiomanía* (Santiago de Chile, 1943–70).[6] Finally, from popular literature, and in particular serialized sentimental novels, studio cinema borrowed formulas such as an episodic structure full of improbable twists and turns, characters who are psychologically shallow, wailful yet ethical solutions to tense situations that are devoid of moral subtlety, and the salacious exploration of sexual problems faced by defenseless women in a rapidly modernizing and treacherous society. *Puerta cerrada* (*Closed Door*; Luis Saslavsky, Argentina, 1939), for example, adapted *Stella Dallas* (King Vidor, United States, 1937) by incorporating all three local influences—radio, popular theater, and serialized novels—into a product whose high production values were designed to attract higher-income audiences habituated to Hollywood modes of representation. As we will see in the next chapter, Saslavsky's adaptation of Hollywood melodrama to local tastes proved so successful that suspenseful, tearjerker melodramas focusing on women's problems in a treacherous society came to define Latin American cinema of the 1940s and 1950s.

From the perspective of production, Latin American studio cinema is also a Hollywood vernacular. As Silvia Oroz notes, Latin American studios "merely followed the same model adopted by the U.S. economy: standardized production. Therefore, the 'system of genres' and the star system are a logical economic consequence of the studio system. Genres were adopted to differentiate products and to rationalize the process of production as a function of [labor] specialization."[7] Such a system of production was clearly designed to decrease costs, but ultimately, box-office receipts drove profits. This meant that Latin American studios had to align the values represented in their standardized products with the values of their two intended audiences: corporatist states (and their censors) and the urban masses, which had their own forms of social censorship. Indeed, censorship, whether outright or self-imposed, is at the heart of why Latin American studio cinema is populated by patriarchal archetypes that respond to deeply entrenched corporatist values.

"HISPANIC" FILMS AND THE CONSOLIDATION OF HOLLYWOOD'S INTERNATIONAL STYLE

In the search for ways to emulate Hollywood's international style, "Hispanic" films came to play a pivotal role.[8] These were features made in Spanish by Hollywood studios for Spanish-speaking audiences in Latin America and Spain. More than one hundred such films were made between 1930 and 1939, by studios large and small, out of a misplaced fear that Spanish-speaking audiences did not want to see Spanish-subtitled, Hollywood-made, English-language features. The most famous of these studios was the one that Paramount built in Joinville, France, to make films not only in Spanish, but also in French, German, and other European languages. Carlos Gardel's first feature-length film was made here, and, like other popular musical films at the time, it made the most of an existing music industry built by radio and record sales.

The Day You Love Me (1935)

Carlos Gardel's films were exceptional "Hispanic" films because they were popular throughout Latin America (thus helping to crystallize a nascent pan–Latin American popular identity) and because they were by and large Argentinean. *El día que me quieras* (*The Day You Love Me*; John Reinhardt, United States, 1935), for example, was produced by Paramount and filmed in New York with a crew, cast, and storyline that were by and large Argentinean. The story, by the famed tango lyricist Alfredo Le Pera, is also unmistakably corporatist. Gardel plays Julio Argüelles, an aspiring tango singer and son of a wealthy financier who wants to marry him off to the daughter of an important business partner in order to gain control of the country's wheat sector. Julio, however, is in love with Marga (Rosita Moreno), a musical performer from the working class, and in order to marry her, he has to break ties with his father (fig. 3.2).

Fast forward a few years: Julio and Marga have a daughter, Margarita; Marga is gravely ill; and because Julio is chronically unemployed (a muted reference to the Great Depression), Marga sneaks out to look for work, which only worsens her health. Seeing that his father will not answer his phone calls, Julio breaks into his father's house, steals money for Marga's medical treatment, and returns home to find that Marga is already dead. Bereaved, Julio leaves the country with Margarita, becomes a famous tango singer with a grown Margarita as his sidekick, and one day receives a telegram with news that his father has died and left him his fortune. On the ship back to Buenos Aires, Margarita and her boyfriend announce their engagement to the chagrin of the groom's father, who considers Margarita below his class. However, as soon as he learns that Julio has inherited a fortune, he suddenly becomes friendly and gives his blessing to the young couple. Here are, in primitive form, the narrative formulas that will be repeated many times over the next two decades: egotistical capitalists reformed by the generosity of workers, women as symbolic objects of exchange between men of different classes, and narrative outcomes that celebrate unity and reconciliation for the benefit of the common good. The very premise of the film, a wealthy heir who becomes a working-class tango singer, underscores the centrality of popular culture in this process of class reconciliation and

FIGURE 3.2   Marga (Rosita Moreno) and Julio (Carlos Gardel) in the "Hispanic" musical melodrama *The Day You Love Me* (John Reinhardt, United States, 1935)

national unity. The fact that a culturally Argentinean film could break attendance records throughout Latin America and Spain proved that that there was an audience hungry for Spanish-language features with stars they already knew from radio and the recording industry, and that spoke to the specificity of national cultures and values rather than to a generic Hispanic culture artificially concocted by "Hispanic" films through a forced syncretism of accents, locations, and cultural practices. In any event, Hollywood soon found that subtitling its own productions in Spanish was more profitable and more palatable to Latin American audiences than making Spanish-language films or dubbing them into Spanish or Portuguese, and by 1933 most Hollywood studios had ceased or drastically decreased production of Hispanic films. As a result, many of the Latin American actors, directors, and technicians who had worked in Hispanic films returned to their respective countries, where they began adapting the methods they had learned to local productions. In the process, they helped to strip Hollywood's methods of their aura of inaccessibility and to legitimize Hollywood's international style as a viable alternative.[9]

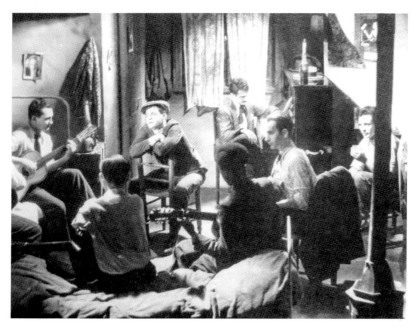

FIGURE 3.3   Eusebio (Luis Sandrini) daydreams of becoming a tango composer in the comedy *The Three Amateurs* (Enrique T. Susini, Argentina, 1933)

ALTERNATIVES TO HOLLYWOOD'S INTERNATIONAL STYLE

While for the most part Latin American studios sought to adapt Hollywood's international style to local tastes, the cinematic landscape in the early 1930s was still fluid and heterogeneous, and a number of films in fact pursued a strategy of differentiation from Hollywood productions.

The Three Amateurs (1933)

Los tres berretines (*The Three Amateurs*; Enrique T. Susini, Argentina, 1933), for example, takes a stab at Hollywood's consumerist values by making fun of a shopper who insists on buying a model of heater advertised in a film magazine. The style of the film is appropriately far from Hollywood's international style, its low production values a carryover from the kind of regular radio programming that its director had pioneered in 1920. The film tells the story of three brothers—an unemployed architect, an aspiring tango composer (fig. 3.3), and a talented football player—whose fortunes turn for the better thanks to the success of the

FIGURE 3.4 Antonio (Domingo Soler) and Rosario (Andrea Palma) before they find out they are brother and sister in the melodrama *The Woman of the Port* (Arcady Boytler, Mexico, 1934)

football player, the one son whose career choice seemed the least respectable to the father. It became Lumitón's first commercial success and launched the movie career of Luis Sandrini, a deft comedian who would become Argentina's biggest international star, along with Libertad Lamarque.

The Woman of the Port (1934)

In Mexico, *La mujer del puerto* (*The Woman of the Port*; Arcady Boytler, Mexico, 1934) also places formal heterogeneity at the service of a family drama, but with a tragic ending (fig. 3.4). The first part of the film focuses on how Rosario (Andrea Palma), a provincial young woman, gives herself to her boyfriend only to find out he is having a liaison with another woman. Distraught by her boyfriend's infidelity and by her father's death, she flees to Veracruz. In the film's most famous sequence, a physically transformed and Marlene Dietrich–like Rosario leans against a pole smoking a cigarette as Lina Boytler sings about "selling pleasure to men who come by sea." One of these men, an Argentinean sailor named Antonio Venegas (Domingo Soler), saves Rosario from a brawling sailor. They seem to fall in love and spend the night together, but after she finds out they are long-lost siblings, she throws herself into the sea.

Arcady Boytler was a Russian filmmaker who had worked with Konstantin Stanislavsky and Vsevolod Meyerhold in the theater, and with Sergei Eisenstein on *¡Que viva México!* (Mexico–United States, 1931). *The Woman of the Port* showcases this cosmopolitan background through visual references to *Zemlya* (*Earth*; Alexander Dovzhenko, USSR, 1930) in an early sequence of Rosario and her boyfriend framed against windswept fields of wheat; to the epilogue of *¡Que viva México!* in the documentary-like funeral precession of Rosario's father, when a group of revelers take off their Day of the Dead masks; to *Der blaue Engel* (*The Blue Angel*; Joseph von Sternberg, Germany, 1930) in the "selling pleasure to men" sequence where Rosario is framed and lit like Dietrich; and to *Das Cabinet des Dr. Caligari* (*The Cabinet of Dr. Caligari*; Robert Wiene, Germany, 1919) in the brothel sequence where Antonio follows Rosario to her room. However, these visual quotations do not function as intertexts to the political projects associated with German Expressionism, Soviet socialist realism, or Eisenstein's intellectual montage. Instead, they respond to a strategy of aesthetic differentiation vis-à-vis North American cinema, while supporting a pervasive melodramatic formula of fallen women in a treacherous world. Similarly, in *Dos monjes* (*Two Monks*; Juan Bustillo Oro, Mexico, 1934), the use of experimental forms (in this case expressionism) is at the service not of experimental politics but rather of a misogynist worldview that blames a woman's sexuality for disrupting the monks' idyllic friendship. In both *The Woman of the Port* and *Two Monks,* that is, experimentation is limited to visual forms, and the celebration of traditional patriarchal values in both films is in many respects a continuation of what Mexican filmmakers had been producing since *Tepeyac* (José Manuel Ramos, Carlos E. González, and Fernando Sáyago, 1917) and the first *Santa* (Luis G. Peredo, 1918).

Redes (1935)

Redes (Fishermen's Nets; Paul Strand, Fred Zinnemann, and Emilio Gómez Muriel, Mexico, 1935), on the other hand, stands out for Paul Strand's cinematography (clearly inspired by Eisenstein's framing of social types in *¡Que viva México!*) and for a soundtrack by Silvestre

FIGURE 3.5 Social types in the socialist realist *Redes* (Fishermen's Nets; Paul Strand, Fred Zinnemann, and Emilio Gómez Muriel, Mexico, 1935)

Revueltas that Aaron Copland praised for its "sense of the abundance and vitality of life" (fig. 3.5).[10] However, because the film represents the struggles of poor fishermen using Manichaean formulas of socialist realism, showing idealized individuals who unite in collective revolt against an evil profiteer, it ends up constructing a very simplified and romanticized rural landscape. It is a simplification and romanticism that Gabriel Figueroa, Emilio "El Indio" Fernández, and others would later transform into a full-blown indigenist school—no longer socialist, to be sure, but rather corporatist.

Fernando de Fuentes's Trilogy of the Mexican Revolution

By far the most important instance of early sound cinema's heterogeneity is a trilogy by Fernando de Fuentes that demystifies three different factions within the Mexican Revolution: Huertismo in *El prisionero 13* (*Prisoner 13*; 1933), Carrancismo in *El compadre Mendoza* (*Godfather Mendoza*; 1933), and Villismo in *¡Vámonos con Pancho Villa!* (*Let's Go with Pancho Villa!*; 1935). De Fuentes had his first break in the film industry as assistant director in *Santa* (Antonio Moreno, Mexico, 1931), and starting with the musical *Out on the Big Ranch* (Fernando de Fuentes, Mexico, 1936), he would come to define, along with Emilio Fernández and Gabriel Figueroa, the formulas of musicals and melodramas of Mexico's studio cinema of the 1940s.

In his trilogy of the Revolution, however, there are few narrative or visual formulas. Instead, he develops a highly individualized style reminiscent of John Ford—measured pace, static medium and long shots, terse dialogue, location shooting—to tell stories that are critical of the Revolution's destructive factionalism at a time when such factionalism was being definitively replaced by centralization measures under various presidents during the 1930s. Lázaro Cárdenas (1934–40), in particular, set this centralization on a clear corporatist path by helping to create two major unions, one for peasants (the Confederación Nacional Campesina, or CNC), and one for industrial workers (the Confederación de Trabajadores de México, or CTC); by reorganizing his political party along corporatist lines through what were called "sectors" (peasants, workers, the military, and urban microenterprises); by ending hostilities with the Catholic Church, and therefore recognizing it as a legitimate social actor; and by nationalizing railways and petroleum under a 1936 law that allowed the state to expropriate land and other assets for the common good. This is the context of production of de Fuentes's trilogy, and what is clear from the trilogy is that de Fuentes, like Cárdenas, roundly rejected the factionalism that had ruined much of the country during the tumultuous decade of 1910, when the films in the trilogy are set, and instead envisioned a country unified under the tutelage of a benevolent state.

Prisoner 13 (1933)

Prisoner 13 tells the story of Julián Carrasco (Alfredo del Diestro), a cruel and alcoholic officer in the army of Victoriano Huerta, possibly Mexico's least-liked president (1913–14) (fig. 3.6). In the film, Carrasco accepts a bribe to spare the life of a conspirator, and instead orders the shooting of a random prisoner who turns out to be his grown-up son. The mother, who had left Carrasco when their son was a baby because he repeatedly beat her, succeeds in warning her estranged husband of the tragedy that is about to happen, but Carrasco arrives too late to stop the execution. In a tagged-on ending, Carrasco wakes up and realizes it was all a nightmare, but to contemporary audiences, the references to

FIGURE 3.6 A bottle and an artillery shell serve as symbols of Victoriano Huerta's alcoholism and militarism in the social melodrama *Prisoner 13* (Fernando de Fuentes, Mexico, 1933)

Huerta's presidency must have been all too real. As John Mraz has noted, "In the film's visual narrative, the ubiquitous presence of a bottle (Huerta was famously alcoholic) and an artillery shell on Carrasco's desk is a constant reference to alcohol and militarism as the defining structures of Huerta's presidency."[11]

Godfather Mendoza (1933)

The action in *Godfather Mendoza,* the second film in the trilogy, begins during the presidency of Victoriano Huerta and ends during the presidency of Venustiano Carranza (1917–20). The film focuses on the economic and political choices faced by Rosalío Mendoza (Alfredo del Diestro), an opportunistic landowner who switches political allegiances as swiftly as he can swap the portraits of revolutionary leaders hanging in his dining room. The main characters are Mendoza, his beautiful and much younger wife, Dolores (Carmen Guerrero), and Felipe Nieto (Antonio R. Frausto), a handsome Zapatista general whom Mendoza welcomes with open arms when the Zapatistas first arrive in town (fig. 3.7). Felipe Nieto will later return the favor by saving Mendoza from

FIGURE 3.7 The bourgeois Dolores (Carmen Guerrero) and the Zapatista Felipe Nieto (Antonio R. Frausto) fall in love in the social melodrama *Godfather Mendoza* (Fernando de Fuentes, Mexico, 1933)

being executed by fellow Zapatistas when they identify him as Huertista, on the very night of Mendoza's wedding to Dolores. Over time, Dolores and Felipe become close friends with strong feelings for one another, and when Dolores becomes pregnant, Nieto gladly accepts the invitation to be the child's godfather (hence the title's "compadre," or godfather). De Fuentes, however, was not interested in happy endings: "We believe that the Latin audience is sufficiently cultivated and prepared to withstand the full force of reality's cruelty and harshness. It would have been very easy to finish with a happy ending of the kind we've grown accustomed to seeing in films from the United States, but it is our opinion that Mexican cinema should be a faithful reflection of our grim and tragic way of being—if we want, that is, to have a cinema with its very own characteristics, and not a cinema that is a poor imitation of what comes to us from Hollywood."[12]

In effect, *Godfather Mendoza* ends tragically. Mendoza, tired of the political instability of the countryside, decides to move to Mexico City as soon as he sells the year's crop. But when the train that carries the crop to market is intercepted and burned, Mendoza accepts a lucrative offer from a representative of the Carranza government to kill Felipe.

FIGURE 3.8 Pancho Villa (Domingo Soler) hands out corn in the social tragedy *Let's Go with Pancho Villa!* (Fernando de Fuentes, Mexico, 1935)

The unmistakable reference here is to Carranza's real-life offer of a ransom to kill Zapata, and with him the only real remaining opposition against Carranza's attempts to reinstall liberalism as the country's ruling ideology. Zapata's death of course did not lead to a return of liberalism, but in the film Nieto's death visibly secures Mendoza's economic future. And because the film methodically positions viewers to identify with Nieto and other Zapatistas over both Huertistas and Carrancistas, it therefore highlights the similarities between the latter two as ideologically bankrupt factions that were more interested in grabbing power than in improving the lot of the majority of Mexicans, as the Zapatistas clearly were.

Let's Go with Pancho Villa! (1935)

With *Let's Go with Pancho Villa!*, the last film in the trilogy, de Fuentes turns his critical eye on Villa (played brilliantly by Domingo Soler) to portray him as yet another ideologically bankrupt caudillo of the Revolution. The story centers on the "Tigers of San Pablo," seven men who enlist in Villa's army after they see him arrive by train and distribute corn to the needy (fig. 3.8). Their allegiance, however, is to Villa, and not to a clearly defined social or political program. One by one the Tigers die, and each new death is more senseless than the last. The senselessness reaches a low point in a game of Russian roulette where one of the few surviving protagonists deliberately shoots and kills himself after the game has ended, simply to prove that he was not afraid of playing the game, as someone had implied. Soon after, Villa orders Tiburcio (Antonio Fausto), the leader of the Tigers, to shoot his tubercular friend Miguel Ángel (Ramón Vallarino). Tiburcio complies, but then leaves Villa's army for good, disenchanted with what he now sees as Villa's cowardice and selfishness.

The common theme throughout the trilogy is the tragic fate of conscientious yet powerless men (Carrasco's son in *Prisoner 13*, Felipe Nieto in *Godfather Mendoza,* and the San Pablo Tigers in *Let's Go with Pancho Villa!*) at the hands of egotistical and power-hungry caudillos. The solution to this problem, the trilogy seems to suggest, is a strong and benevolent state, with correspondingly strong and benevolent institutions, that can harness the energies unleashed by the Revolution and productively redirect them toward the peaceful coordination of the different social actors that make up the great Mexican family. From this perspective, de Fuentes's trilogy, together with his next film, *Out on the Big Ranch* (discussed in the next chapter), can be read as the work of an intellectual of the state. On the one hand, the trilogy demystifies the caudillos that stand in the way of the corporatist state, and on the other, *Out on the Big Ranch* offers a new national mythology with clear corporatist values, where opposing sides (landowner and peasant, capital and labor) overcome their differences for the common good.

4

Birth and Growth of an Industry

THE MUSICAL BIRTH OF AN INDUSTRY

The unprecedented box-office success of three musicals in 1936—*Allá en el Rancho Grande* (*Out on the Big Ranch*; Fernando de Fuentes, Mexico), *Ayúdame a vivir* (Help Me to Live; José Agustín Ferreyra, Argentina), and *Alô Alô Carnaval* (Hello Hello Carnival; Adhemar Gonzaga, Brazil)—convinced local investors that national cinemas were ripe for industrialization. Consequently, the number of studios grew in Brazil, Mexico, and Argentina, while the first industrial-style studios were established in mid-size countries such as Venezuela, Peru, Chile, and Cuba. These three musicals followed Paramount's successful strategy, in *The Day You Love Me* (John Reinhardt, United States, 1935), of incorporating an artist already popular on the radio and in musical variety shows (*revistas de variedades*). *Alô Alô Carnaval*, for example, is little more than the story of the planning and subsequent filming of one of these shows, and it is important because its commercial success gave new impetus to *chanchadas*, a uniquely Brazilian genre that almost single-handedly sustained Brazilian cinema into the 1950s. *Ayúdame a vivir* is likewise forgettable, yet it is important because it inaugurated the film career of Libertad Lamarque, Argentina's biggest female star. Lamarque's next film, *Besos brujos* (*Bewitching Kisses*; José Agustín Ferreyra, Argentina, 1937), is much more interesting, with its seamless integration of musical numbers and dialogue, and a healthy female sensuality seldom seen in movies of the period.[1] Like *The Day You Love Me*, the story centers on interclass love, this time between Marga (Lamarque), a tango singer, and Alberto (Floren Delbene), a wealthy businessman who must overcome his family's opposition to the wedding and rescue Marga from Sebastián (Carlos Perelli), a brute landowner who kidnaps her. In the end, Sebastián willingly hands Marga over to Alberto, and the successful exchange represents the corporatist ideal of conciliation between different classes and regions.

Out on the Big Ranch (1936)

Unlike *Ayúdame a vivir* and *Alô Alô Carnaval,* which dated quickly, *Out on the Big Ranch* has survived the test of time thanks to de Fuentes's skillful directing, perfectly suited casting, a tightly woven script, Gabriel Figueroa's polished cinematography, and a catchy title song that is, to this day, popular throughout Latin America (fig. 4.1). The film broke all attendance records, spawned more than thirty imitations in just one year, and continued to inspire imitations and remakes into the 1940s, including a Colombian version titled *Allá en el Trapiche* (*Over at the Trapiche*; Roberto Saa Silva, 1943).

Out on the Big Ranch tells the love story of José Francisco (Tito Guízar) and Cruz (Esther Fernández), two young peasants who live in Rancho Grande, an idealized hacienda whose benevolent owner Don Felipe (René Cardona) takes good care his devoted workers. Through hard work and sheer likability, José Francisco rises to become the hacienda's foreman. He only lacks enough money to marry his sweetheart. One night, when almost everyone from Rancho Grande is away at neighboring Rancho Chico (Little Ranch) to see if José Francisco wins a horse race that will restore Rancho Grande's status (lost in the previous year's race) and in the process earn him enough money to marry Cruz, Cruz's evil caretaker brings the naive young woman to Don Felipe to exercise his *droit du seigneur* in exchange for a few pesos. Cruz faints and mutters José Francisco's name, whereupon Don Felipe backs off, apologizes to Cruz, and takes her back home. The next day José Francisco returns triumphant from the horse race, and during the celebrations at the local bar and supply store, the film's most famous sequence takes place, a duel of couplets between José Francisco and a would-be foreman who informs José Francisco that Cruz and Don Felipe were seen together the night before. With tensions running high, Don Felipe suddenly arrives, blames everything on Cruz's evil caretaker, and asks for José Francisco's forgiveness. The movie ends with three weddings:

FIGURE 4.1 José Francisco (Tito Guízar) sings the title song in the *ranchera* musical *Out on the Big Ranch* (Fernando de Fuentes, Mexico, 1936)

José Francisco and Cruz, Don Felipe and his fiancée, and the evil care-taker with her live-in partner.

The film's narrative trajectory is clearly patriarchal and corporatist, with everyone knowing their proper place throughout. The hacienda here functions as a metaphor for the Mexican nation, with characters who are less individuals than representatives of a social class—land-owner, manager, peasant, shop owner—all bound to each other in clearly defined hierarchical relations. The organicist nature of these relations is stated from the very beginning of the film, when José Fran-cisco's dying mother asks the boy's godmother to take good care of him, and it is further emphasized through a blood transfusion that José Francisco receives from Don Felipe after José Francisco valiantly inter-cepts a bullet in order to save Don Felipe's life. Following the transfu-sion, Don Felipe says they are now "brothers," but it is clearly not a brotherhood between equals. Rather, they are brothers in their shared commitment to the common good of the hacienda, with each doing his distinct part for the hacienda's smooth functioning as a whole.

Critics have unanimously read *Out on the Big Ranch* as a reaction-ary film that is nostalgic for a pre-Revolutionary past, and the reading is amply supported by the film's lack of references to the Mexican Revolution, and by the fact that it is set in a hacienda where feudal social relations are sugarcoated. However, given the film's corporatist values, where capitalist production and social justice are not mutually exclusive, it is equally valid to read the film as supportive of a contemporary state policy of confiscating inefficient or socially unjust haciendas, but not efficient and socially just ones. In 1936, for example, Lázaro Cárdenas famously expropriated the very profitable haciendas in La Laguna, a fertile cotton-producing valley that straddles southern Coahuila and Durango, because their model of production, with absentee owners, was efficient but socially unjust. Yet Cárdenas was not interested in converting all private haciendas into *ejidos*, or parcels of land farmed communally under a system supported by the state. Rather, Cárdenas walked the corporatist middle path between capitalism and socialism, stating once that "peasants always opt for organizations of productive activity that increase production and reduce costs, not because they are imposed on them, but because they see their profit in it. This does not mean that we wish to exclude all forms of organization that are not collective; far from it, wherever individual ownership and management is economically efficient, we will implement it and stimulate it."[2]

Cárdenas's corporatist stance, which simultaneously supported *ejidos* and private haciendas so long as they were efficient and socially responsible, would thus justify keeping Rancho Grande private because Don Felipe looks after the welfare of his workers while clearly making a profit. The message here is that not all haciendas are created equal. There is the good, corporatist kind, represented by Rancho Grande, and there is the "capitalist" kind that "exploits the poor," as a minor character dismisses Rancho Grande. The film explicitly disproves this take on Rancho Grande by making the minor character who voices it a villain, and by representing Don Felipe as a beloved, paternalistic leader who, like Cárdenas at the national level, ensures that the relationship between capital and labor is harmonious and directed toward the common good. Unlike Cárdenas, however, the film omits any references to *ejidos,* and this omission facilitates a more nuanced reading of the film's reactionary politics as grounded on a version of corporatism that favors capital over labor and the preservation of class, race, and gender hierarchies. It is a version that would take root during subsequent administrations, and eventually find its full cinematic expression in a Mexican school of cinema discussed later in this chapter.

ARGENTINEAN CINEMA'S "GOLDEN AGE"

The commercial success of *Out on the Big Ranch* generated in Mexico a slew of musicals at the expense of other genres, and when the bubble burst in 1938, the doors were wide open for Argentina to supply the newly created demand for Spanish-language films. Indeed, even though *Out on the Big Ranch* was far and away the most popular Latin American film of the decade, early studio cinema's center of gravity was Buenos Aires, not Mexico City. The political and economic context in Argentina at the time was not favorable for the development of a cinematic industry, for it coincided with what historians call the Infamous Decade (1930–43). This was a period characterized by fraudulent elections designed to keep Hipólito Yrigoyen and his Radical Civic Union Party from regaining political power, by widespread corruption, and by an economic policy that sought to satisfy two constituencies. On the one hand, the policy met the demands of the landowning oligarchy—most famously through the Roca-Runciman Pact of 1933, which guaranteed Argentina limited access to the British meat and grain consumer market in exchange for favorable concessions to British transnational corporations in Argentina. On the other hand, and increasingly after 1938, economic policy sought to satisfy the needs of workers for jobs by encouraging industrial development through policies of import substitution that included the creation of a publicly owned factory (Fabricaciones Militares, 1941) and a steel mill (Altos Hornos Zapala, 1943). This seemingly contradictory strategy of catering to both capital and labor was in fact consistent with an evolving corporatist policy that sought to protect both as parts of a national organism whose competing interests were best mediated by a strong—and, in Argentina's case, militarized—state.

Argentina's studio cinema reflected this shift toward corporatism through a variety of genres that shared the representation of corporatist resolutions to narrative conflicts as new foundational fictions for a united nation ruled by justice and love.[3] In the melodramatic detective film *La fuga* (The Escape; Luis Saslavsky, 1937), for example, Daniel (Santiago Arrieta) teaches a group of country schoolchildren the following civic lesson drawn from the country's heroic past: "San Martín then resolved to migrate to Europe. The man who had given America its independence lived his retirement in France. Too honest, too pure to mix himself in the pettiness of politics, he preferred ostracism. His life set an example that we should never forget."

Contemporary viewers would of course understand the "pettiness of politics" as referring to contemporary struggles for power between radicals and conservatives, and therefore as a call to rise above these differences for the common good of the nation. The fact that Daniel is a fugitive thief from Buenos Aires pretending to be a rural teacher is not meant to ironize the lesson, for by the time he teaches this class, he has reformed himself to the point of choosing the love of the simple yet honest Rosita (Niní Gambier), the schoolmistress's daughter, over the love of the sophisticated yet double-crossing cabaret star Cora (Tita Merello). Robles (Francisco Petrone), the police detective who arraigns Daniel, participates in Daniel's transformation, for when Robles realizes that Cora has used him to protect Daniel, he controls his individual desire, which urges him to kill Daniel, and instead acts for the common good by helping Daniel save face with the schoolchildren and schoolmistress, pretending to be a school inspector who must take Daniel away to Buenos Aires on important business.

Here then is a model of conciliation and reform based on redemption and love, a veritable corporatist roadmap out of Argentina's violent and corrupt present. It is the model followed in comedies (all pre–Perón) such as *Los muchachos de antes no usaban gomina* (Yesterday's Boys Didn't Use Hair Fixers; Manuel Romero, 1937), *La rubia del camino* (The Blonde on the Road; Manuel Romero, 1938), *Chingolo* (Lucas Demare, 1940), and *Los martes, orquídeas* (*On Tuesdays, Orchids*; Francisco Múgica, 1941), as well as in family melodramas such as *Así es la vida* (*Such Is Life*; Francisco Múgica, 1939) and *Puerta cerrada* (*Closed Door*; Luis Saslavsky, 1939). Yet family melodramas and popular comedies were not the only kinds of films coming out of Argentinean studios at the time. The studios also produced alternative films as diverse as *La vuelta al nido* (*Return to the Nest*; Leopoldo Torre Ríos, 1938), which confounded audiences through its use of indirect free style to represent the protagonist's deformed perspective on reality; *La guerra gaucha* (The Gaucho War; Lucas Demare, 1942), an epic drama based on the novel of the same name by Leopoldo Lugones (and ideologically a liberal holdover from the silent period); and *Prisioneros de la tierra* (Prisoners of the Land; Mario Soffici, 1939), the most consequential of the three.

Prisioneros de la tierra (1939)

Prisioneros de la tierra won over many critics with a cinematography that captures the exuberance of the tropics; the un-stylized acting by

Ángel Magaña (as the righteous hero, Esteban Podeley) and Francisco Petrone (as the evil Koerner); and its moral condemnation of working conditions in the yerba mate plantations in Misiones, in northern Argentina and southern Paraguay. Jorge Luis Borges hit the right note of restrained praise in his review for the journal *Sur*:

> It is superior—faint praise!—to many that our resigned republic has given birth to (and applauded). It is also superior to most of the films that California and Paris sent us recently. One incredible and sure touch: there is not a single comic scene in the course of this exemplary film. . . . There is a character—the vicious Koerner . . . who is more lifelike than the hero. I do not recall, in such a bloody picture, a more powerful scene than the next-to-last in *Prisioneros de la tierra*, where the man [Koerner] is horsewhipped into a final river. . . . In similar scenes in other pictures, brutal people are tasked to perform brutal acts; in *Prisioneros de la tierra* it is the hero [Esteban Podeley] who must perform it, and he is almost intolerably efficient.[4]

Prisioneros de la tierra is a hybrid film. Stylistically, its use of documentarist aesthetics to portray the exploitation of workers is in direct dialogue with the social-problem genre popularized by Warner Bros. in the 1930s. Thematically, on the other hand, its insistence on humankind's inability to escape the telluric forces of the Misiones region links it to contemporary authors of regionalist works, most notably Horacio Quiroga (four of whose psychologically complex stories the film adapts), but also José Eustasio Rivera, whose 1924 novel *La vorágine* (*The Vortex*) denounces the exploitation of rubber workers in the tropical jungles of Colombia. Narratively, the film is most clearly a melodrama, with a plot centered on a love triangle between Koerner (the greedy slave driver), Esteban (the noble, working-class protagonist), and Chinita (Elisa Galvé, the innocent daughter of the camp's alcoholic medical doctor) (fig. 4.2). It even makes unapologetic use of several of the formulas of melodrama, from the sudden plot reversal to justify the accidental killing of Chinita to the required return to the status quo ante via Esteban's impassioned decision to let Koerner's thugs kill him.

Ideologically, however, the film is not hybrid but squarely corporatist, with Esteban playing the role of an exploited national resource that a strong state should be able to protect (along with Chinita) from the predatory practices of foreign capital represented by Koerner. This reading is supported by a detail in one of the opening sequences, where one of the workers is paid with an IOU instead of cash. This practice, widespread in 1915, when the film is set, was declared illegal in 1925, yet the practice continued into the 1940s, when the Perón gov-

FIGURE 4.2 Chinita (Elisa Galvé) looks after her alcoholic father (Raúl de Lange) in the social-problem drama *Prisioneros de la tierra* (Prisoners of the Land; Mario Soffici, Argentina, 1939)

ernment finally enforced the provisions of the 1925 law. The film's political message for contemporary viewers is therefore that Argentina needs a benevolent state willing and able to protect the rights of workers like Esteban against the excesses of ruthless foreign capitalists and their local representatives like Koerner. This kind of populist nationalism was an important part of the political landscape in Buenos Aires when the film was released in 1939, so much so that Juan Perón would ride it all the way to the presidential palace in a few years' time. For his part, Mario Soffici, who sympathized and frequently collaborated with other artists affiliated with the leftist nationalist group FORJA—Fuerza de Orientación Radical de la Joven Argentina, whose motto was "We are a colonial Argentina; we want to be a free Argentina"—would go on to make dozens more films, chief among them *Barrio gris* (Gray Neighborhood; 1952), a Peronist film in the Neorealist style, and *Rosaura a las 10* (Rosaura at 10 O'clock; 1958), a smart murder mystery whose narrative structure recalls Akira Kurosawa's *Rashomon* (Japan, 1950).

FIGURE 4.3   Aunt Rosario (Angelina Pagano), Nina Miranda (Libertad Lamarque), and Raúl (Agustín Irusta) in the Hollywood vernacular melodrama *Closed Door* (Luis Saslavsky, Argentina, 1939)

Closed Door (1939)

Return to the Nest, Prisioneros de la tierra, and *La guerra gaucha* are exceptional in that all are of above-average quality, and none are lachrymose melodramas or popular comedies. Nevertheless, none of them was popular enough at the box office to inaugurate new trends in an industry that depended on hits for growth and sheer survival. That honor belongs to *Closed Door*, an over-the-top melodrama whose synthesis of existing melodramatic formulas set the industry standard for "quality productions" for years to come (fig. 4.3). The differences between Luis Saslavsky's earlier *La fuga* and *Closed Door* could not be greater: whereas *La fuga* is all about national conciliation and consummated love, *Closed Door* is about class antagonisms aggravated by treacherous friends and family, a fatal misunderstanding, a wrongful twenty-year incarceration, and the protagonist's ultimate sacrifice for a cause that is not her own. Yet despite first appearances, the film's corporatist logic is impeccable.

Nina Miranda (Libertad Lamarque, by now "the sweetheart of the Americas") is a working-class singer who marries Raúl (Agustín Irusta), an upper-class painter whose male identity is visibly threatened when one of his two rich aunts, Aunt Rosario (Angelina Pagano), disinherits him for marrying below his class status. Even as the couple descends into poverty, Raúl insists that Nina cannot go back to work, and when Nina becomes pregnant, all he does is hope it is a boy so that his aunts will take him back. The baby is indeed a boy, but the aunts do not soften. Only later, when Raúl is summoned to their mansion to say goodbye to his terminally ill Aunt Josefa (Ilde Pirovano), does Aunt Josefa manage to goad Aunt Rosario to welcome Raúl and his wife into the family. Everything will be perfect, Raúl writes to Nina, but Nina's treacherous brother and ex-manager Antonio (Sebastián Chiola) intercepts Raúl's letters to her, steals the money in them, and tricks Nina into going back to singing. When Raúl finds out that Nina has gone back to work, he confronts Antonio and Nina, and Nina accidentally shoots and kills Raúl. She is subsequently sentenced to twenty years and forced to give up her child for adoption to Aunt Rosario, who decides to keep the mother's identity a secret. Twenty years later, Nina is out of prison, and Antonio duplicitously steals money from Aunt Rosario. When Nina finds out, she sneaks out to return the money. In front of Aunt Rosario's mansion a group of hoodlums surrounds her, and when the now grown-up son Daniel (Ángel Magaña) intervenes, Nina steps in to take a bullet meant for him and dies without ever revealing her true identity as his mother.

Closed Door pits the archetype of the fallen woman who is doomed from the start (Lamarque as tango songstress) against the archetype of the suffering mother (Lamarque as the devoted mother who will sacrifice everything for her child). In the end, Nina's will and talent are no contest against her fate as a woman and as a working-class subject. The film's ideology is corporatist because by keeping her identity a secret, Nina avoids bequeathing to her son his Aunt Rosario's contempt toward the poor and his Uncle Antonio's resentment toward the rich. By forestalling both possibilities, Nina's silence leaves Daniel metaphorically free of any greed or resentment that could hinder the conciliation between labor and capital that his parents could not attain.

Closed Door is representative of what was by now a genre-driven, studio-produced cinema populated by patriarchal archetypes such as the suffering mother, the fallen woman, and the benevolent patriarch. These were in turn complemented by corporatist stereotypes such as the greedy rich and the resentful poor, two opposing figures whose immoral sentiments imperil the corporatist values embodied by two additional stereotypes, the noble rich and decent poor (*pobre pero bueno*). As melodrama, *Closed Door* reduces a complex history of class struggle to a few easily recognizable and atemporal feelings: love versus hate, generosity versus greed, contempt versus resentment. As tragedy, it justifies Nina's double sacrifice as essential for the reestablishment of a patriarchal status quo that is interwoven with the corporatist principles of organic class and gender hierarchies. First she sacrifices her promising career because her professional success threatened her husband's narrowly defined masculinity, and in the end she sacrifices her identity and her very life for the sake of her son's future, because otherwise, as Aunt Rosario puts it, "he cannot become a man."

Melodramas like *Closed Door,* with Oedipal narrative trajectories where women willingly sacrifice for the sake of their husbands and sons, were a staple of Latin American cinema during the studio era. The systematic reduction of female characters to mere accessories of male narrative trajectories, however, was not unique to Latin America. As Teresa de Lauretis points out, in Hollywood classical cinema, the mainstream female character

> simply awaits [the hero's] return like Darling Clementine; as she indeed does in countless Westerns, war, and adventure movies, providing the "love interest." [Even] when the film narrative centers on a female protagonist, in melodrama, in the "woman's film," etc., the narrative is patterned on a journey, whether inward or outward, whose possible outcomes are those outlined by Freud's mythical story of femininity. In the best of cases, that is, in the "happy" ending, the protagonist will reach the place (the space) where a modern Oedipus will find her and fulfill the promise of his (off-screen) journey.[5]

By the end of the 1930s, this Freudian mythical story of femininity was firmly established in Latin American cinema. Indeed, it was consistent with the region's reigning corporatist ideology at the time, which saw men as heads of households and women as lesser organs of the body politic.

SOCIAL COMEDIES

Throughout the 1930s and 1940s, social comedies rooted in the *sainete* (or comic opera, and its rough equivalent in Brazil, the *farsa*) celebrated the chaos of the world and the petty imperfections that make us all human. Only comedies came close to melodrama in popularity, so

FIGURE 4.4 The rich and over-serious Cayetano Lastre (Joaquín Pardavé) confers with the poor and easygoing Cantinflas (Mario Moreno) in the hit comedy *Ahí está el detalle* (You're Missing the Point; Juan Bustillo Oro, Mexico, 1940)

much so that by the second half of the 1930s, people spoke of going to the movies to see either "films for crying" or "films for laughing." Of the many film comedians who emerged during the 1930s and 1940s, the most important is Cantinflas. *Ahí está el detalle* (You're Missing the Point; Juan Bustillo Oro, Mexico, 1940), his fifth and best film, features him as a *peladito*, a sort of urban trickster (fig. 4.4). In the culminating sequence, after being sentenced to death for a crime he did not commit, he defends his innocence through a barrage of *cantinflismos*, nonsensical verbal acrobatics that end up contaminating the pompous language of the defense attorney, the prosecutor, and even the judge, who in a fit of despair declares him innocent and ends the trial.

Other popular comedians of the 1930s and 1940s include Luis Sandrini, who reprised his naive character in *Los tres berretines* (The Three Amateurs; Enrique T. Susini, Argentina, 1933) in dozens of films throughout the region; Niní Marshall, whose most famous character, Catita, simultaneously parodies and celebrates immigrant working-class culture in Buenos Aires; and the duo of Grande Otelo and Oscarito, whose popularity led to the first and only case in Latin America of a film studio, Atlântida, achieving vertical integration of production, distribution, and exhibition. As John King explains it: "The duo [of Grande Otelo and Oscarito] appeared in a number of successful comedies throughout the forties. This success attracted Luiz Severiano Ribeiro, who ran the country's major distribution and exhibition circuits. He bought Atlântida in 1947, and for the first time Brazil could boast a vertically integrated industry, making money essentially from *chanchadas,* exploiting the comic—and in particular verbal—skills of Oscarito, Grande Otelo and a number of other stars. . . . He thus made films for his own theaters, keeping profits within the family."[6]

Crucially, the social contrasts in social comedies and *chanchadas* of the 1930s and 1940s never lead to violent conflict, and in the end, all parties live in harmonious coexistence or else part ways amicably. Thus, while they critique prevailing class and racial prejudices by unmasking bourgeois pretentiousness, they also reveal a conservative social agenda that is compatible with corporatism's hierarchical values via a carnivalesque return to the status quo ante where the socially marginalized comic reverts to his or her "proper" place after having temporarily questioned the social order and its prevailing values.

THE IMPACT OF THE GOOD NEIGHBOR POLICY
ON LATIN AMERICAN CINEMA

The conditions of film production in Latin America changed dramatically with the start of World War II in 1939. Latin American economies boomed thanks to their ability to export raw materials to both sides of the conflict, and many governments, including the United States, declared their neutrality. But as the United States began to prepare to join the conflict on the side of the Allies, it made use of the Good Neighbor Policy to try to get Latin American governments to join the Allied effort. The policy included a three-pronged strategy for the Western hemisphere's film industries. First, the United States castigated Argentina for what it saw as the country's stubborn neutrality and Fascist sympathies by severely restricting U.S. supplies of raw film. Since the United States then held a near-monopoly on this supply, the result was that Argentinean studios could not make enough copies for distribution outside the home market. Predictably, Argentina's film industry collapsed. Second, in reward for Mexico's declaration of war against the Axis powers in 1942, the United States propped up Mexico's film industry with "loans, equipment, technical advice, and a practically unlimited supply of raw film."[7] As a result, Mexico quickly and decisively overtook Argentina as the region's cinematic leader, and by the second half of the 1940s was even competing head to head with Hollywood for market share in the region.[8] Finally, the United States encouraged Hollywood productions that represented relations with Latin America as friendly and cooperative, in films such as *Down Argentine Way* (Irving Cummings, Twentieth Century Fox, 1940), *That Night in Rio* (Irving Cummings, Twentieth Century Fox, 1941), *The Three Caballeros* (Norman Ferguson, Walt Disney Productions, 1944), and *It's All True*, an unfinished project entrusted to Orson Welles as Goodwill Ambassador to South America in late 1941.[9]

As World War II proceeded, Latin American economies continued to boom thanks to increasing commodity prices for the agricultural and mining products upon which many of the region's economies still depended, and by giving local manufacturing industries a breather from European and North American competition in the local consumer products market. The resulting balance of payments surplus allowed corporatist states, suddenly awash with resources unimagined in the 1930s, to consolidate and expand their roles in all aspects of national life, including cinema. This was the time of the Estado Novo in Brazil (1937–45), of Juan Perón's power behind the scenes (1943–45) and subsequent presidency (1946–55), and of Miguel Alemán's reinvention of Mexico's ruling party as a corporatist institution.

In this new geopolitical context, Latin American producers naturally turned to the state for additional help. In Argentina, they found it in the form of a series of protectionist measures that included screen quotas, loans, and subsidies; by 1948 these measures had reversed the downward trend in the quantity of films produced nationally, though at the expense of their quality and diversity, since many were "quota quickies" made simply to fill state-mandated quotas.[10] Protectionist measures in Mexico were likewise limited to quotas, loans, and subsidies, but the technical and financial support provided by the United States gave the Mexican industry an important strategic advantage during the first half of the 1940s. The Mexican government consolidated this advantage by creating three state companies to distribute Mexican films: one for the Latin American market (Pelmex, 1945), one for the U.S. market (Azteca, 1945), and one for the domestic market (Películas Nacionales, 1947). Pelmex, the biggest of the three, even built its own network of modern theaters, for instance the Mexico Theater in Bogotá and the Azteca

Theater in Rio de Janeiro.[11] So successful was this state-led effort at vertical integration that Mexican cinema in the second half of the 1940s became the country's biggest export after oil, and far and away the most important of the Latin American national cinemas in terms of quantity of production, cultural influence, and legacy. Other countries in the region followed Mexico's lead by experimenting with different levels of state intervention, from the creation of public-private partnerships such as Chile Films, to state production of documentaries and newsreels, to outright censorship.

Qualitatively, Mexican cinema's heyday (1943–48) is characterized by the high technical quality of the average film; the consolidation of a star system; the appearance on screen of the corporatist state (typically a law enforcement officer, a medical doctor, or a teacher) as a benevolent character who mediates between the decent poor and the noble rich while helping to keep everyone else (and their immoral sentiments) in check; and the continued dominance of comedy and melodrama, in part through their hybridization with new genres such as thrillers and social-problem films. A fine example of a thriller of this period is *Distinto amanecer* (*Another Dawn*; Julio Bracho, 1943), which tackles political corruption and labor activism using the visual conventions of film noir. Social-problem films, for their part, tackled issues such as juvenile delinquency (*Camino al crimen* [The Road to Crime; Don Napy, 1951]), prostitution (*Las abandonadas* [*The Abandoned*; Emilio Fernández, 1944]), alcoholism (*Campeón sin corona* [Champion Without a Crown; Alejandro Galindo, 1945]), racism (*Angelitos negros* [Little Black Angels; Joselito Rodríguez, 1948]), and migration (*Espaldas mojadas* [*Wetbacks*; Alejandro Galindo, 1953]).

THE MEXICAN SCHOOL OF CINEMA

Visually, the most original films of this period were the product of a team that the film producer Agustín J. Fink put together in 1942: director Emilio Fernández, cinematographer Gabriel Figueroa, writer Mauricio Magdaleno, and editor Gloria Schoemann. The team is credited with creating the first national aesthetic in Latin American cinema, an *escuela mexicana* that synthesized Hollywood melodrama and Mexican muralism (by way of Sergei Eisenstein's *¡Que viva México!* [Mexico–United States, 1931]) into an indigenist national mythology. From Hollywood the team adopted the use of established stars as a primary marketing device; a clear narrative trajectory whose rhythm "alternates the slowness associated with peace with the speed and violence of the crime scenes,"[12] something that Fernández had learned from studying John Ford films; and a preference for chiaroscuro lighting and composition in depth, something that Figueroa had learned as a student of the cinematographer Gregg Toland, of *Citizen Kane* fame, and that in Figueroa's hands "dramatizes the religiosity of indigenous and rural culture [and] seeks to unite the protagonists, regardless of their differences in gender, ethnicity, and class."[13] From Eisenstein, whose rushes and stills from *¡Que viva México!* Fernández and Figueroa closely studied, the team adopted the framing of indigenous subjects as organic elements of the natural landscape, though not the film's dialectical montage within and between shots, or its Marxist historiography. In synthesizing these influences, the team made the decision to privilege Hollywood-inspired long takes where everyone occupies a socially prescribed place within a unified space and time over Eisenstein's dialectical montage, which highlights social confrontation by accentuating spatial and temporal discontinuities. It was a most appropriate choice given the corporatist ideology that underpins all of Fernández's indigenist films: *María Candelaria* (1943), *La perla* (*The Pearl*; 1945), *Enamorada* (Enamored; 1946), *Río Escondido* (1947), *Maclovia* (1948), and *Pueblerina* (1948).

María Candelaria (1943)

María Candelaria put Mexican film on the world cinematic map after it won prizes in Cannes and Locarno. The film is set in the gardens of Xochimilco in 1909, just before the Revolution. María Candelaria (Dolores del Río, recently returned to Mexico after a successful but waning career in Hollywood) and Lorenzo Rafael (Pedro Armendáriz) are poor but dignified indigenous peasants who face two obstacles to marriage: money for their wedding, and their community's rejection of María Candelaria because her mother had been a prostitute. The atavism of the indigenous community contrasts sharply with the modern outlook of the white criollo characters: the priest (Rafael Icardo), the painter (Alberto Galán), the medical doctor (Arturo Soto Rangel), and the state workers who distribute medicine to prevent malaria. In between these two "races" is Don Damián (Miguel Inclán), the mestizo storeowner whose lust for María Candelaria sets off the chain of events that will lead to her death.

The plot advances melodramatically through misunderstandings driven by easily recognizable sentiments: Don Damián's lust and greed,

Lupe's (Margarita Cortés) envy toward María Candelaria, the painter's generosity, the priest's benevolence, and the dignified love that María Candelaria and Lorenzo Rafael feel for each other. The story begins with María Candelaria and Lorenzo Rafael already in love and raising a piglet whose offspring they plan to sell to pay for their wedding. Don Damián tries to leverage a debt that María Candelaria owes him to try to force her into marrying him, and when she refuses, he kills the piglet. To make matters worse, María Candelaria falls ill with malaria from a mosquito bite she suffered while being serenaded by Lorenzo Rafael, and even though state health sanitation workers had earlier distributed quinine, a malaria antidote, Don Damián hoards it and refuses to give any to Lorenzo Rafael. Undeterred, Lorenzo Rafael breaks into Don Damián's shop to steal the medicine, and while at it, he also steals a dress for María Candelaria to wear at their wedding.

That same night, the medical doctor sent by the benevolent painter administers the quinine. María Candelaria quickly recovers, but on the day of her wedding, Don Damián has Lorenzo Rafael arrested for stealing the dress that María Candelaria is wearing, public proof of Lorenzo Rafael's culpability. Desperate, María Candelaria agrees to model for a portrait in exchange for money to release Lorenzo Rafael from prison (fig. 4.5). After the painter has finished her face, he asks her to take off her clothes so that he can also paint her body, but María Candelaria balks at the idea and runs away. Disheartened, the painter accepts an offer from an indigenous-looking model who offers to pose nude in María Candelaria's stead, and the finished painting symbolically unites the two women into a harmonious whole. When an indigenous woman tells Lupe about the finished nude portrait, Lupe organizes a mob to kill María Candelaria for having offended their collective dignity, and this they do as Lorenzo Rafael watches helplessly from his prison window.

Throughout the film, sentiments are racialized, so that the worst ones are projected on the undifferentiated indigenous mob and on Don Damián, whereas the best sentiments are reserved for the white characters and the two protagonists who, while nominally indigenous, embody Western ideals of love, individualism, and beauty. The film's racist discourse is thus aligned with Mexico's official discourse toward indigenous subjects at the time the film was made, an *indigenismo* with roots in nineteenth-century Romanticism, but whose most immediate precedent was *La raza cósmica* (*The Cosmic Race,* 1925), a book-length essay by then–secretary of education and presidential hopeful José Vasconcelos. "On the surface," writes Joanne Hershfield,

FIGURE 4.5 María Candelaria (Dolores del Río) visits her wrongfully incarcerated fiancé Lorenzo Rafael (Pedro Armendáriz) in the indigenist melodrama *María Candelaria* (Emilio Fernández, Mexico, 1943)

Vasconcelos appeared to hail the mestizo as the "quintessential Mexican." He wrote of the coming of a new age wherein a fusion of races and classes in Latin America would culminate in the creation of a mestizo race, or what Vasconcelos called the "cosmic race." However, while proclaiming to celebrate Mexicans' racial mixture, Vasconcelos's thesis promoted the notion that this new race would emerge as a result of a "cleansing" of indigenous blood through European intermarriage. Vasconcelos's ideology of "fusion" (shared by many of his contemporaries) was thus actually a thinly disguised conviction that Mexico's pre-Colombian roots should and would eventually be whitened into extinction. It was, in essence, a thesis of spiritual eugenics, [that] rationalizes . . . a single way out to the Indian: Mexican nationality.[14]

In effect, one of the singular contributions made by Fernández to the development of *indigenismo* was to weave it into a corporatist discourse whereby Mexico is a body that can function properly only when every organ acts according to its role in a preestablished hierarchy. Don Damián, for example, represents the rising mestizo class that has not yet become spiritually whitened (hence his irrational and impulsive behavior). María Candelaria and Lorenzo Rafael, on the other hand, represent the defenseless noble savages at the bottom of the social hierarchy who must be protected by benevolent father figures (the criollo painter and the Catholic priest), from capitalism's greed (represented by Don Damián) and from socialism's irrational collectivism (represented by the indigenous mob that kills María Candelaria).

But doesn't María Candelaria's death signal the impossibility of *indigenismo* as a project of spiritual eugenics? At first glance, this seems to be the case, and yet the painting remains: an ideal of national beauty that seals María Candelaria's transformation into a Europeanized version of the Virgin of Guadalupe. Fernández achieves this transformation in several steps. First, he establishes María Candelaria's identification with the Virgin of Guadalupe when Lupe breaks the latter's altar to Guadalupe with a stone. Second, Fernández shifts María Candelaria's identification from the brown-skinned Guadalupe to the light-skinned Our Lady of Sorrows in the interior church sequence by having María Candelaria's tears and facial expressions visually mirror those of the European Virgin. Finally, because the finished painting features the head of Dolores del Río (an actress whose phenotype in Mexico would be considered European) and the body of a dark-skinned indigenous woman, the film can be read as positing the desirability of a Vasconcelian "cosmic race" that synthesizes Mexico's European and indigenous cultures into a national body politic whose cultural values are European and its labor force indigenous. An *indigenismo,* in short, that is both corporatist and Eurocentric.

Río Escondido (1947)

The corporatist ideal of a harmonious body politic with a benevolent state that mediates between social actors finds its fullest cinematic expression in *Río Escondido* (Emilio Fernández, Mexico, 1947), a film rightly praised for Gabriel Figueroa's stunning cinematography. The film tells the story of Rosaura Salazar (María Félix), a newly licensed teacher who, despite having a delicate heart, accepts an assignment in Río Escondido, a desolate hamlet in northern Mexico, where she will clash with Don Regino Sandoval (Carlos López Moctezuma), the greedy landowner who rules by terrorizing the indigenous inhabitants, the local priest (Domingo Soler), and the teacher she has come to replace (Columba Domínguez).

On her first day in town, Rosaura finds an indigenous woman ill with smallpox and sends for Felipe Navarro (Fernando Fernández), a young

FIGURE 4.6 Rosaura Salazar (María Félix) teaches a civics lesson in liberalism to illiterate indigenous children in *Río Escondido* (Emilio Fernández, Mexico, 1947)

medical student who is doing his medical service in a nearby town. Felipe cannot save the woman, but when Don Regino falls ill with the disease, Felipe offers to save him on condition that Don Regino reopen and restore the school, and that he order everyone to line up for vaccination. Don Regino agrees, yet when his thugs try to line up the Indians, they use lethal force. Rosaura stops the killing by ordering the priest to sound the church bells, and the Indians suddenly begin to walk devoutly toward the church, where Felipe vaccinates them with Rosaura's help. With the population vaccinated and the school restored, Rosaura begins her transformation of the indigenous children from dirty and illiterate Indians into clean and literate Mexican citizens. She teaches them the alphabet, of course, but she also tells them about Benito Juárez, an "Indian like yourselves who became president of the republic" (fig. 4.6).

Smitten by Rosaura's unique combination of beauty and determination—a combination that had by now made María Félix "the most important star to have emerged in Latin America and the principal myth created by Mexican cinema"[15]—Don Regino offers to set Rosaura up in a comfortable house if she will be his lover. Insulted, Rosaura storms out. When Don Regino visits her at school the next day, she responds to his offer with a veritable corporatist manifesto:

> A municipal president is a man who represents the people, a man who should lead by example and sacrifice himself for the common good. Unfortunately, this man, who is the municipal president of Río Escondido, like so many other authorities in Mexico, is only concerned with satisfying the pettiest of his ambitions and his basest instincts. . . . This man, like all his barbarous comrades-in-arms in the republic, has made a mistake this time around. And if they had any sense of shame, they would understand that their time is over, because now we have at the head of the government of Mexico a president who has resolved that his people regenerate, a president who aspires to end the terror spread by people like this one [pointing to Don Regino], and who wants Mexicans to help him build a fatherland so big and salubrious that it will be everyone's pride and sacred joy.

Humiliated, Don Regino leaves the school. Shortly thereafter, the water stops flowing from the town's only public water source (a clear corporatist metaphor), and Don Regino shoots and kills an Indian boy for stealing water from his private well. Tensions run high during the night of the vigil, and Don Regino is humiliated once again by Rosaura, this time in front of everyone in town. Don Regino plans his revenge for the following night, but as he is about to rape Rosaura, she pulls out a gun and kills him. Alerted by Rosaura's screams, the entire indigenous population shows up with lit torches to help her, and, seeing that she has killed Don Regino, they proceed to do the same to Don Regino's thugs. Rosaura collapses and soon dies of heart complications, but not before she receives a letter from the president of Mexico that reads:

> Miss Professor Rosaura Salazar:
> By means of my person, the fatherland expresses its gratitude to you for your sleepless nights, and congratulates you on the success achieved in your difficult mission. I know how great and painful have been the obstacles you have had to confront, but I also know that only the selflessness and abnegation of Mexicans like yourself will make possible the regeneration of our people. Today more than ever you must be certain that Mexico and I are with you, and that your sacrifices will translate into immediate fruits for the region in which you work as my representative. You have responded to my trust many times over, and as I write I give the order to initiate immediately the rehabilitation of Río Escondido.

Rosaura's sacrifice, as the president acknowledges, explicitly opens the doors for the birth of a new corporatist nation, the genesis of which had already been foreshadowed in the preface to the film. In the preface, a group of specially selected teachers is invited to meet President Miguel

Alemán to receive from him the orders for their first teaching assignments. Rosaura arrives late because on the way to his office, several of the objects in the presidential palace speak to her with an authoritative off-camera voice, as if brought to life by her visibly devout patriotism: first the Campana de Dolores, Mexico's bell of independence, then Diego Rivera's mural *The History of Mexico*, and finally two paintings in the Ambassador's Room, one of Benito Juárez and the other of Miguel Hidalgo. In front of *Mexico Today and Tomorrow*, the third part of Rivera's tripartite mural, the omniscient voice interprets the mural's narrative of class struggle and state repression using corporatist tropes such as blood, germination, clean souls, and fatherland. Timidly, Rosaura enters the Ambassador's Room, where the off-camera voice continues, "Yes, this is [a portrait of] Juárez, that little Indian shepherd and later president who fought against the European invaders and who dedicated his life to the service of his people. And this [Mexico's national hymn begins to play] is Hidalgo, the elder priest who broke chains and sounded bells, and who gave to his people their first flag."

The lesson here is that the Mexican Revolution was a destructive affair, and that in order to rebuild Mexico, the way forward is to move away from the socialism and anticlericalism of the previous constitution, and return instead toward the economic liberalism that is the legacy of Benito Juárez, but by way of Miguel Hidalgo's religious nationalism, whose use of the Virgin of Guadalupe successfully united criollos and indigenous peasants against the European invaders. In fact, only one year before the release of the film, Article 3 of the constitution had been changed from saying that public education was to be "socialist, and exclude any religious doctrine," to saying that it "will tend to develop harmonically all of the faculties of the human being, and foster in him love for country, and the awareness of international solidarity."[16]

Because Rosaura represents the first generation of teachers under the revised constitution, *Río Escondido* can be productively read as an allegory of a corporatist nation that successfully harmonizes all of the factions of the national body politic via education, rather than via land reform or other state interventions into the economy. In this reading, Rosaura is the state's heartfelt emissary who can harness the spiritual power of the Church in order to teach the indigenous inhabitants of Río Escondido how to harmonize the religious nationalism of Miguel Hidalgo and the economic liberalism of the Juárez Reformation. With this lesson in mind, Rosaura and viewers are now ready to receive the president's developmentalist message: "Water, roads, streets, education, and official morality. These are the priorities of the enterprise I have set out for myself, counting on, as I know I do, the fervent support of good Mexicans. . . . I invite you to join me in this effort to save our people. . . . Only by committing ourselves to meet the sacrifice will we be able to redeem Mexico, with our hearts." These words by the fictitious president reveal Fernández's remarkable alignment with President Alemán's developmentalist vision of a salubrious country headed by a benevolent patriarch who rules from the kindness of his heart, and whose subjects, in return, sacrifice their own private agendas for the common good of the nation.

Fernández's films, in fact, closely parallel official discourse, as a cursory comparison between *María Candelaria* and *Río Escondido* demonstrates. *María Candelaria*, for example, represents Indians as an irrational mob that acts against the interests of the nation (embodied in María Candelaria), and this representation parallels the view that then-president Manuel Ávila Camacho held regarding the country's powerful workers' unions. In *Río Escondido*, on the other hand, the Indians no longer coalesce into a resentful mob that acts independently of the state, embodied in Rosaura. Instead, they line up obediently and silently behind Rosaura's lead, very much like workers' unions lined up obediently and silently behind Miguel Alemán when they were incorporated into the formidable apparatus of the newly created PRI (Partido Revolucionario Institucional), heir to Lázaro Cárdenas's PRM (Partido de la Revolución Mexicana).[17] In short, between *María Candelaria* and *Río Escondido*, Fernández's *indigenista* discourse moved, as the Mexican state moved, from a socialist brand of corporatism championed by Cárdenas toward a liberal brand of corporatism that was institutionalized by Alemán through his government's drastic reductions in land redistribution and neutralization of workers' unions.[18]

STUDIO CINEMA AND PERONISM

The remarkable ideological convergence between studio cinema and the corporatist state was not limited to the Fernández-Figueroa films. Throughout Latin America, studio films celebrated the role of the state as a modernizing force through morally sound representatives that ranged from educators and medical doctors (like Rosaura and Felipe in *Río Escondido*) to police investigators and even minor bureaucrats. For example, in *Mercado de abasto* (Food Market; Lucas Demare, Argentina, 1955), a tax collector must convince a market stall owner to pay taxes because, he says, "You are not giving your money away. The state returns that money to the taxpayers . . . in the form of public services. Hospitals, for example, [as well as] bridges and roads used by everyone." The stall owner is not convinced, until his own son has an accident and his life is saved in a public hospital with a blood transfusion from an anonymous donor. "What you have done for my son," the stall owner tells the doctor, "has no price, and what is more, cannot be paid because you don't charge for services here. But at least I'd like to thank the blood donor." We have already seen, in *Out on the Big Ranch,* the use of blood as a corporatist metaphor that organically unites disparate social actors. In *Mercado de abasto,* this same metaphor is presented through a parallelism that explicitly incorporates the state as the coordinator of a body politic made up of a diversity of organs, for just as the blood donor gives life to the ailing son, the money that the tax collector collects "irrigates and saves society."[19]

The corporatist vision of society as an organic whole is also evident in *Apenas un delincuente* (*Hardly a Delinquent;* Hugo Fregonese, Argentina, 1949) and in the aforementioned *Camino al crimen.* As Clara Kriger notes,

> In these detective films the forces of law and order do not limit themselves to solving the crime. . . . In addition, they show a society that is affected by unlawful behavior, and a state that tries to mediate, to repair, and to articulate possible forms of conflict resolution. That is to say, they contextualize the private conflicts of the characters within the public sphere, . . . where the institutions of the state seem to have a relevant role. Generally speaking, . . . these symbolic productions tend to reinforce and legitimize the power of the state by promoting an image of the modern state that protects the community and adequately punishes and educates those who break the law. [The result is] a harmonious society where conflicts are resolved thanks to the mediation of an institution that defends everyone, including offenders of the law.[20]

Finally, even though the representation of medical professionals as full of conscience and generosity continues from the previous decade, medical doctors during Juan Perón's first presidency (1946–52) are additionally represented as "instruments or agents for the fulfillment of the obligations that the state has in the area of public health."[21] Such positive representations of the corporatist state via educators, health workers, the police, and other employees of the state is a constant throughout the studio era, a reflection not only of the ideological convergence between the state and national film industries, but also of censorship laws that proscribed negative representations of the state and its representatives.

God Bless You (1948)

The most ambitious Argentinean film of this period, however, did not represent the state directly because it was consciously produced for an international market. *Dios se lo pague* (literally "May God Repay You [Your Kindness]," but distributed as *God Bless You*; Luis César Amadori, 1948) is, in effect, representative of a strategy by Latin American studios to compete with Hollywood productions by sharing stars, directors, and technical personnel across borders.[22] An adaptation of a Brazilian play of the same name by Joracy Camargo, *God Bless You* tells the story of Mario Álvarez (Arturo de Córdova), a factory worker who in his spare time designs a machine that can produce as much textile material as one hundred workers. His boss steals the plans for the machine, and when Mario tries to get them back, he is accused of attempted theft and jailed for eight years. Unable to find work after his release, he becomes a beggar by the name of Juca, and accumulates so much capital that he begins a double life: humble beggar by night and wealthy businessman by day. When we first meet Juca/Mario, we do not know any of this. All we see is an old-looking beggar who willingly teaches a fellow beggar by the name of Barata (Enrique Chaico) the tricks of the trade wrapped up in nuggets of social wisdom such as "the rich live off of the labor of others" and "those who give alms are not generous; they give money in the hopes of being repaid with good luck." Juca works in shifts: in the early evening in front of a church, and later at night across the street in front of a clandestine casino.

This spatial arrangement, with the casino across from the church, reinforces the film's representation of the conflict between good and evil as a contest between the generosity of the working poor, who piously attend church, and the profligacy of the idle rich, who throw away their money in the casino. Moreover, the film's lack of temporal referents suggests a reading of this contest as timeless, a reading in keeping with an unwritten Peronist prohibition against the cinematic representation of social conflict in the present. Filmmakers routinely dealt with this prohibition by transferring any social conflict to a pre-Peronist past (hence the insistent use of flashbacks as a structuring narrative device) and by filming inside studios, so that viewers would not misinterpret a conflict that is represented via flashback as possibly being of the present. In *God Bless You*, social conflict is twice removed from the present via a stylized mise-en-scène that could be any city, and via the representation of class struggle as a moral problem rather than an economic one.

The main character embodies this struggle (and eventual conciliation) in his double role as a beggar (Juca) who gives generously of his popular wisdom and considers begging "work," and a capitalist (Mario) who gives generously to social causes while planning his revenge against the factory boss who caused him so much misery. But we only learn of this double identity after a melodramatic subplot has grown and taken over the narrative. The subplot begins when Nancy (Zully Moreno), a glamorous but poor woman who frequents the clandestine casino in search of a rich man, finds herself next to Juca as she hides from the police who have come to bust the casino. The two strike up an improbable conversation, and Nancy confesses that what she wants is a man who can give her the life of luxury she desperately desires. Intrigued, Mario anonymously sends flowers and a ticket to the opera to her hotel room. That night they have a grand time together: good music, smart conversation, and dinner at a fancy nightclub where Mario makes an offer she can't refuse: all the luxuries she desires in exchange for not asking him any questions about his life.

Their new life, as before, is one of appearances: he pretends to be married, and she pretends to love him. She grows restless, however, and soon finds herself in the company of Pericles Richardson (Florindo Ferrario), a compulsive gambler whom she first met in the clandestine casino, and who happens to be none other than the disinherited son of the factory boss who had made Mario's life miserable. After one of their many outings, Pericles asks Nancy to run away with him just as Mario unexpectedly returns home. Nonchalantly, Nancy introduces Pericles as a relative and excuses herself, whereupon Pericles "confesses" to Mario that he is Nancy's poor brother and is desperately in need of one hundred thousand pesos. Surprisingly, Mario gives the money to Pericles, who on the way out gives it to Nancy as evidence that he has the means to give her the life of luxury she is accustomed to.

The next day, just as Nancy is about to run away with Pericles, Mario asks her to be his witness as he informs Pericles's father that he, Mario, is now the majority stakeholder in the company, yet is willing (in the best corporatist tradition of seeking conciliation over confrontation) to keep him on board under a reconfigured administrative structure. Nancy, who is not privy to Mario's past, misinterprets Mario's revenge as being against her for planning to escape with Pericles, and Mario, hurt by what he sees as her betrayal, leaves the house, but not before giving her a jeweled box inside of which is a flower that reveals his identity as the beggar who once saved her from the police. When

FIGURE 4.7 Mario/Juca (Arturo de Córdova) and an Evita-looking Nancy (Zully Moreno) in the moral comedy *God Bless You* (Luis César Amadori, Argentina, 1948)

Nancy opens the box, she runs after Mario and finds him in front of the church, not disguised as the bearded Juca, nor sharply dressed like the Mario she knew, but rather a combination of the two, a metaphorical conciliation of his two personas and what they represent. Nancy is also dressed differently, with a white shawl over her head, like a halo that explains the purity of her intentions as she drops the misbegotten pesos and jewels into Mario's beggar's hat. Finally, and as if what we have just seen were not enough to make the moral of the story crystal clear, the two walk together into the church and bless themselves with holy water (fig. 4.7). They then kneel down in front of the altar, and Mario empties the money and jewels into the church's collection basket, thus practicing the life lesson that Barata had just taught him: to give freely of what one has, and to ask humbly for what one desires. In the end, that is to say, Mario successfully conciliates labor and capital by using his capital for the common good instead of personal gain or revenge.

THE CORPORATISM OF LATIN AMERICAN STUDIO CINEMA

In *God Bless You,* the corporatist discourse of conciliation between labor and capital meshes with Perón's nationalist discourse of a corporatist third way between capitalism and socialism via, for example, the fact that Mario's money comes from renting (a steady and national source of capital) as opposed to international stocks (a speculative and therefore socially destabilizing source of capital), and via the striking similarities, narrative and physical, between the fictional Nancy and Eva Perón. However, the corporatist discourse one finds in *God Bless You* did not have to wait for Perón's rise to power to make its appearance in Argentinean cinema. We already saw how in *The Day You Love Me* (John Reinhardt, United States, 1935), a wealthy heir becomes a working-class tango singer and in the process reconciles capital and labor by way of popular culture. Similarly, in *Puerta cerrada* (*Closed Door*; Luis Saslavsky, Argentina, 1939), Nina's son Daniel embodies the conciliation between his paternal family's capital and his maternal family's labor power via a denouement where Nina's silence forestalls the possibility that her son would inherit either the greed of his rich aunt or the resentment of his poor uncle. Surely it is not a coincidence that at the end of *God Bless You*, Mario and Nancy are likewise freed from the greed and resentment that had been impediments to their final conciliation, for the central metaphor in corporatist films is that of a body politic where disparate social classes and/or ethnicities are organically and harmoniously united. That body may be a character who inherits elements from disparate social groups, like the son in *Closed Door;* a character who harmonizes capital and labor through his or her own initiative, as in the Gardel character in *The Day You Love Me* and Mario/Juca in *God Bless You*; or a character who embodies different ethnicities, as in the virginal protagonist of *María Candelaria*.

Regardless of how the conciliation takes shape, studio cinema's representation of the Latin American nation as a corporatist body politic is strikingly consistent from the mid-1930s to the end of the 1940s. To put it as bluntly as the most populist films of the period—from *Navidad de los pobres* (Christmas with the Poor; Manuel Romero, Argentina, 1947) to *Nosotros los pobres* (We the Poor; Ismael Rodríguez, Mexico, 1948), *Ustedes los ricos* (You the Rich; Ismael Rodríguez, Mexico, 1948), and *Alma de bohemio* (Bohemian Soul; Julio Saraceni, Argentina, 1949)—the nation is one big happy family that, despite having members who enjoy very different degrees of power and privilege, can nevertheless get along superbly well thanks to the generosity of those who have more, the humility of those who have less, and the benevolence of a state that mediates between the two for the common good.

5

Crisis and Decline of Studio Cinema

FROM GOOD NEIGHBORS TO COLD WAR CONTAINMENT

When World War II ended in 1945, and just as Mexican films began to compete with Hollywood products in the Latin American market, the U.S. government suddenly shifted from its Good Neighbor Policy to a Cold War policy of containment. U.S. film policy shifted concomitantly, from one of helping Mexico's film industry to one that prioritized Hollywood's recuperation of lost markets in Latin America through block booking of Hollywood films, special arrangements for U.S. distributors and exhibitors in Mexico, and trade agreements with Spain that cut into Mexico's ability to export its films to that important market.[1] At the same time, union rules in Mexico made it difficult to innovate by keeping new talent out of the system, while the Mexican state in 1949 made the strategic decision not to protect as strongly as it could have its film industry from the U.S. government's aggressive promotion of Hollywood's interests.[2] As a result of these internal and external factors, Mexican cinema lost the ability, briefly held in the 1940s, to compete head to head with Hollywood for the lion's share of Latin American audiences. As Seth Fein puts it, "Despite notable exceptions, the U.S. and Mexican film industries settled into an international division of production for Spanish-speaking audiences: Mexico produced B-pictures, while Hollywood reconquered first-run screens surrendered during World War II."[3] The notorious Santo franchise is perhaps the best-known example of this new development in the case of Mexico, along with Cantinflas vehicles (which had largely lost their punch). The situation in Argentina and Brazil was somewhat similar, if less dramatic, for neither ever came close to challenging Hollywood's hegemony as Mexico briefly did. Nevertheless, their studios in the 1950s and 1960s also focused on producing B films, such as *chanchadas* in Brazil and sexploitation films in Argentina, for a second-tier market.[4]

PARODY AS SYMPTOM OF THE CRISIS OF STUDIO CINEMA

An interesting result of this shift to the production of B films is the emergence of comedies that turned to an increasingly formulaic studio cinema for material that was ripe for parodying. In Brazil, as João Luiz Vieira explains it,

> The dynamics of the inversions proper to carnival are found in the *chanchada*, and consequently, in the parody of American films, indicating also the existence of critical aspects in the functioning of the social structure. . . . There are frequent criticisms and observations about political life and the administration of the Federal Capital of the period, Rio de Janeiro. They criticize the lack of electricity and water, the increase in the cost of food, politicians with their populist rhetoric making grandiose and unfulfilled promises, the moving of the capital to Brasília, class differences, the bureaucracy and its bureaucrats, and the situation of blacks in Brazilian society. The public understood and identified with this language.[5]

Nem Sansão Nem Dalila (Neither Samson nor Delilah; Carlos Manga, Brazil, 1954), for example, parodies Cecil B. DeMille's *Samson and Delilah* (United States, 1949) not as an end in itself, but to expose how Brazil's elites ally themselves with populist politicians in order to retain power.[6] Meanwhile, in Mexico, the comic Germán Valdés, a.k.a. "Tin Tan," built a successful career through parodies whose titles advertised their irreverence: *La marca del Zorrillo* (The Mark of the Skunk; 1950), *Simbad el mareado* (Simbad the Seasick; 1950), *El ceniciento* (Cinderello; 1951), *El bello durmiente* (The Sleeping Beau; 1952), *El vizconde de Montecristo* (The Viscount of Montecristo; 1954), *Tres mosqueteros y medio* (Three and a Half Musketeers; 1956), *Rebelde sin casa* (Rebel Without a House; 1957), and *El rey del barrio* (The King of the Barrio; 1949), that last a parody of Hollywood gangster films and Mexican *cabareteras* (fig. 5.1). Carlos Monsiváis wrote that *El rey del barrio* is Tin Tan's best movie, and justified his assessment with words as expressive as the actor's performances: "Tin Tan is the crooner and the bolero singer filled with the onomatopoeia of boogie-woogie, who sings

FIGURE 5.1 Tin Tan (Germán Valdés) and Tongolele (Yolanda Montes) in the *cabaretera* and gangster film parody *El rey del barrio* (The King of the Barrio; Gilberto Martínez Solares, Mexico, 1949)

with his whole mouth ('my mouth spreads all over the place'). If he cannot be solemn like Juan Arvizu or Emilio Tuero, or sensual like Frank Sinatra, Tin Tan does succeed in parodying those diverse styles, unifying them into his own ironically pretentious and openly reticent one, through the careful use of the vocal virtues that are ultimately never very important."[7]

Sometimes comedy films go beyond parody to satire. In *Carnaval Atlântida* (Carnival Atlantida; José Carlos Burle and Carlos Manga, Brazil, 1952), a would-be director named Cecílio B. de Milho—"Cecil B. de Corn," a clear spoof of Cecil B. DeMille—sets out to film the epic story of Helen of Troy (fig. 5.2). But in a move worthy of Oswald de Andrade's "Manifesto Antropófago," the Brazilian carnival form narratively ingests and regurgitates as a *chanchada* what should have been a Hollywood-style superproduction of an Greek epic. The film begins self-reflexively, with two *malandros* (rascals), played by Colé Santana and Grande Otelo, trying to pass off their *chanchada* screenplay as the screenplay Mr. de Milho (Renato Restier) is looking for. De Milho quickly dismisses their

FIGURE 5.2 Grande Otelo and Eliana Macedo sing a duet in the *chanchada Carnaval Atlântida* (Carnival Atlantida; José Carlos Burle and Carlos Manga, Brazil, 1952)

manuscript but offers them jobs as janitors in the studio. Shortly thereafter, de Milho runs into them on one of the studio's sets and explains his grandiloquent vision for the tragedy he wants to direct, to which Grande Otelo responds with a vision of his own, a carnival remake of the same scene but with Helen transformed into a samba dancer moving happily to that year's carnival hit song, "Dona Cegonha." Here we are still in the territory of parody, yet the film does not parody DeMille's style throughout. Instead, the rest plays like a *chanchada*, with musical numbers and comedy skits galore, so that it ends up being a satire that holds up to ridicule the idiocy of those like de Milho, who would make a European epic using Hollywood's high production values in a country like Brazil. Toward the end of the movie, when Lolita (María Antonia Pons) implores her uncle de Milho to give up the epic in favor of a musical, because "people want to sing, dance, have fun!," his response, "A musical, in my studio?!," is a jab at the Vera Cruz studios (see the next chapter). It is also a nod to viewers who would answer that yes, a musical comedy like the one we've been enjoying, and with which the film in effect ends, is a more appropriate form to pursue in Brazil.

Aventurera (1950)

As a satire, *Carnaval Atlântida* does not pack much of a sting because the narrative trajectory always points toward conciliation, and in the end, bourgeois morality is upheld. By contrast, *Aventurera* (The Adventuress; Alberto Gout, Mexico, 1950) is particularly biting, far less conciliatory, and in many ways a brilliant and exceptional commentary on the twin crises of state corporatism and studio cinema. Ninón Sevilla, the Cuban bombshell who complicated every role she took in Mexico, plays Elena, a young middle-class woman who, after being tricked into working as a dancer and a prostitute in a cabaret (hence the genre's name, *cabaretera*), exacts revenge on all of those who have hurt her, and, incredibly for its time, is not punished for it. The film parodies melodrama and *cabaretera* films to satirize the hypocrisy and classism of the bourgeoisie and to question women's subservient role in society. The parody of melodrama is achieved via acting that is excessively stylized even by contemporary standards—what Ana M. López calls "Sevilla's exaggeratedly sexual glance . . . excessive laughter, and menacing smoking"—while the parody of the *cabareteras* is evident in dance numbers that border on kitsch thanks to Sevilla's imperfect dancing, "overabundant figure, extraordinarily tight dresses [and] rolling hips."[8]

Narratively, the film adheres to the typology of characters already established for *cabareteras,* a genre whose numbers grew exponentially in the second half of the 1940s.[9] The two primary character types in *cabaretera* films are the virtuous woman who is tricked into prostitution but rises above it thanks to her dancing and singing skills, and the villain who tricks her into prostitution and keeps her in a position of subservience.[10] Secondary types are a reflection of the primary ones, and so they either help or obstruct the protagonist in her attempts to escape her predicament. In *Aventurera*, however, there is a twist, in that the main characters are split: Elena is both the virtuous girl and the avenging woman, while her nemesis Rosaura (Andrea Palma) is both the villainous madam who forces Elena into prostitution and the mother who sacrificed herself for her sons, one of whom, Mario (Rubén Rojo), falls in love with Elena and offers to marry her. Secondary characters are similarly doubled: Lucio (Tito Junco) is the pimp who at first sells Elena to Rosaura, then saves her from death, and in the end tries to kill her; while Rengo (Miguel Inclán) is Rosaura's thug who becomes Elena's protector (fig. 5.3).

The only character who escapes this doubling is Mario. Yet even though Mario offers Elena the respectability that she had lost, *Aventur-*

FIGURE 5.3 The thug Rengo (Miguel Inclán) temporarily holds back Elena (Ninón Sevilla) while Rosaura (Andrea Palma) explains the rules of the game in *Aventurera* (The Adventuress; Alberto Gout, Mexico, 1950)

era is not about Mario's search for love or about Elena's search for respectability. Rather, the film's main narrative trajectory is that of Elena's search for revenge, so much so that Elena is only interested in marriage with Mario as a vehicle to exact it. After she has gone back to cabaret dancing using Mario's last name and revealed Rosaura's second life to him, Elena is finally satisfied, and feels safe enough to tell Rengo, who by now is her bodyguard, that he need not keep watch on her that night. This is the first and most important conclusion to the film. The second conclusion is a tag-on that seals, as with a ribbon, Elena's hard-earned success: Lucio, having escaped from prison, shows up in her hotel room to kidnap her. Mario also shows up, to tell Elena he still loves her despite everything. Lucio, who had been hiding, interrupts the love scene. The two men fight it out. Lucio beats Mario unconscious, and then forces Elena to leave with him. Happily, Rengo has been keeping watch outside the hotel and kills Lucio in the nick of time as Elena, having now really fallen in love with Mario, walks away from a dying Lucio to her waiting husband. The film thus concludes with Elena and Mario together and ready to embark on a life happily ever after. And yet the sensation that remains after watching the film is that Elena's spiritedness has opened a Pandora's box of sexual and economic liberation for women on and off screen, for Elena, the film has made clear, will never be a traditional wife, and will instead go on to be a liberated woman in charge of her own sexuality and her own livelihood.[11]

From this perspective, *Aventurera* is more a comedy than a melodrama, and more specifically a comedy of errors whose resolution is the emancipation of the female character from the straitjacket of the whore-saint binary that Latin American cinema had imposed on female characters for the past fifty years. Indeed, inasmuch as Latin American cinema of the first half of the twentieth century is a projection of male desire, it transformed the patriarchal binary of love and desire into mutually exclusive roles for female characters: motherly saint or devilish prostitute. This not only denies women subjectivity, but also forces both male and female characters to make a choice between love and desire that is framed in terms of a false binarism. *Aventurera* is remarkable because it pushes this false binarism to its limits by presenting Mario with a choice between a wife and a mother who are both sexualized, rather than the more traditional choice between a hypersexual prostitute and an asexual mother figure. Just as important, neither Elena nor Rosaura has to sacrifice her life (as do the female protagonists in *Closed Door*, *María Candelaria*, and *Río Escondido*, all discussed in the previous chapter) or her liberty (like Nancy in *God Bless You*) in order for Mario to complete an Oedipal trajectory that is, in any case, secondary to Elena's narrative of revenge. Last but not least, *Aventurera* represents a country without a benevolent state, and a heroine whose father has committed suicide, two factors that, when placed in the context of two decades' worth of positive representations of patriarchy and the corporatist state, signal the end of the hegemony of corporatist discourse in Latin American studio cinema.

DOCUMENTARY AND NEWSREEL PRODUCTION
DURING THE STUDIO ERA

While only Mexico and Argentina (and to a lesser extent Brazil) developed studio-based industrial cinemas during the 1930s, 1940s, and 1950s, many more Latin American countries reached sustainable levels of production of newsreels during the same period. Paulo Antonio Paranaguá has identified more than forty newsreels during the studio era, chief among them *Cinédia Jornal* and *Atualidades Atlântida* in Brazil; *Noticiario Panamericano* and *Reflejos Argentinos* in Argentina;

Noticiario Clasa-Excelsior and *Noticiario EMA* (España México Argentina S.A.) in Mexico; *Noticiario Royal News* and *Cineperiódico* in Cuba; and *Noticiario Nacional* in Peru.[12] While Latin American newsreel companies were privately owned, their productions were oftentimes commissioned or financed directly by the state. The exception was *Cine Jornal Brasileiro*, which was directly produced by Brazil's Department of Print and Propaganda.

The production of documentaries was much more limited than the production of newsreels, with Brazil again providing the exception. In 1932, a law was passed that required the screening of a nationally produced short before the main feature. Not content with the quality of these shorts, the Brazilian Ministry of Education and Health created INCE (Instituto Nacional do Cinema Educativo) in 1936, the first initiative of its kind in Latin America.[13] An instrument of Getúlio Vargas's corporatist state, INCE did not, however, reproduce the kind of racist discourse produced by INCE's two models, Italy's Istituto Luce and Germany's Reichsstelle für den Unterrichtsfilm. Instead, under the forceful direction of the anthropologist Edgar Roquette-Pinto, INCE developed "a discourse that valued the multiracial dimension of the Brazilian people [and] the role of education and public hygiene in its development."[14] In its thirty years of existence (1936–66), INCE produced more than 350 documentaries, most of them directed by Humberto Mauro. Production developed in two distinct periods: 1936–47 and 1947–66. During the first period, which coincides with Roquette-Pinto's tenure as director, Mauro drew an image of Brazil that was consistent with Roquette-Pinto's vision of a progressive nation characterized by the harmonization of social and racial conflicts, and united by a common history peopled by larger-than-life heroes who established the founding myths of the nation.[15] Typical of this period are documentaries on Brazilian flora, fauna, industries, towns, and natural resources; reconstructions of historical episodes; biographies of famous Brazilian statesmen, musicians, novelists, and poets; stories about artisanal culture; and newsreels of civic and political events.[16] As a group, these productions speak to a strong belief that mass education can speed up the process of corporatist modernization. The legacy of this first period is remarkable, as evidenced by the fact that institutions with similar structures and pedagogical missions were founded elsewhere in Latin America, including Puerto Rico's DIVECO (División de la Comunidad de Puerto Rico, 1949), Bolivia's Instituto Boliviano Cinematográfico (1953), Uruguay's SODRE (Servicio Oficial de Difusión Radio Eléctrica, 1954), and Cuba's

FIGURE 5.4 Galdino (Mário Mascarenhas) courts Maria (Cláudia Montenegro) in the bucolic *O Canto da Saudade* (The Song of Yearning; Humberto Mauro, Brazil, 1952)

ICAIC (Instituto Cubano del Arte e Industria Cinematográficos, 1959), whose earliest productions were almost exclusively didactic documentaries in the INCE tradition.

During INCE's second period, no longer limited by Roquette-Pinto's grandiloquent vision of a modernizing Brazil, Mauro gave free rein to his lyrical-nostalgic vision of the rural Brazil of his youth. This line of work culminated in the *Brasilianas* series, seven short films made between 1945 and 1956 that celebrate the dying musical traditions in his native state of Minas Gerais. Fernão Pessoa Ramos explains the importance of the series: "The representation of popular culture (the songs that accompany work) wakes in Mauro a new degree of attention. The rigor of the mise-en-scène reaches here a high point that explains why Mauro is considered one of the most vigorous directors of style in Latin American cinema. Mauro does not strain to achieve genial images or framings in the style of Gabriel Figueroa, Ruy Santos, or Mário Peixoto. Instead, his shots seem to be composed naturally, demonstrating the maturity of a style whose forms emerge from the simplicity of the culture being recorded."[17]

6

Neorealism and Art Cinema

After the defeat of the Axis powers in World War II, Latin American corporatism shed many of its Fascist garments and adopted, under the guise of developmentalism, elements of economic liberalism and representative democracy. The most famous example of Latin American developmentalism is the presidency of Juscelino Kubitschek (1956–61), whose motto of "fifty years of progress in five" culminated in the construction of a new capital for Brazil, Brasília. Paradoxically, given the financial, political, and military power that the United States exerted over the region during the 1950s, Latin American cinema witnessed a profound recalibration in its triangulated practices away from Hollywood as the primary reference for the region's filmmakers. The leadership role of audiences in this recalibration cannot be overstated, for it first took place among audiences and critics who increasingly saw in European cinema models of production and representation that were more adequate to the new postwar realities and sensibilities in Latin America. During the studio era, people in Latin America commonly went to the cinema to see melodramas or comedies, and studios focused on feeding the continued demand of what was in many ways a standardized product. By the 1950s, however, films that addressed social and psychological themes more directly and through innovative cinematic forms found a receptive audience in rapidly growing urban centers throughout the region.

TABLE 6.1   Cinephilic Publications of the 1950s

FILM JOURNALS

Cine Club (Montevideo, Uruguay, 1948–53)
Filme (Rio de Janeiro, 1949)
Gente de cine (Buenos Aires, 1951–57)
Film (Montevideo, Uruguay, 1952–55)
Cine-Guía (Havana, 1953)
Revista de Cinema (Belo Horizonte, Brazil, 1954–57)
Revista de Cultura Cinematográfica (Belo Horizonte, Brazil, 1957–63)
Séptimo Arte (Mexico City, 1957–62)
Delirio (São Paulo, 1960)
Cine-Clube (Rio de Janeiro, 1960)
Revista de Cinema (Belo Horizonte, Brazil, 1961–64)
Nuevo Cine (Mexico City, 1961–62)

HISTORY, THEORY, AND CRITICISM

Alberto Cavalcanti, *Filme e Realidade* (Film and Reality, 1953)
Luis Buñuel, "El cine, instrumento de poesía" ("Cinema, Instrument of Poetry," 1958)
Domingo Di Núbila, *Historia del cine argentino* (History of Argentinean Cinema, 1959)
Alex Viany, *Uma introdução ao cinema brasileiro* (An Introduction to Brazilian Cinema, 1959)

EMERGENCE OF A CINEPHILE CULTURE

The new cinephile culture developed in several distinct venues. Commercial theaters regularly played Italian Neorealist films by directors such as Luchino Visconti, Roberto Rossellini, and Vittorio De Sica, as well as psychological dramas by the likes of Ingmar Bergman, Yasujirō Ozu, and Robert Bresson. Meanwhile, in newly formed cinematheques, university courses, and film clubs (variously sponsored by universities, the Catholic Church, and Communist groups), film enthusiasts could reconsider films of earlier eras and discuss contemporary developments in the medium. In other words, film was now accepted as a cultural fact, and the best evidence of this new status was the emergence of a critical print culture that included a wide variety of film journals, the first national film histories, and the first theoretical texts since Mário Peixoto's essay on *Limite* in 1931. Tables 6.1 and 6.2 give a sense of the scope of these developments.[1]

CONVERGENCE OF NEOREALISM AND ART CINEMA IN LATIN AMERICA

Two major cinematic modes emerged alongside the new film culture: neorealism and art cinema. The salient features of neorealism are well

TABLE 6.2 Cinephilic Institutions of the 1950s

FILM CLUBS

1940	Clube de Cinema de São Paulo (censored and reopened in 1946)
1942	Club Gente de Cine (Buenos Aires, precursor to Cine Club Núcleo, 1954)
1948	First Cuban film society established
1948	Cine Club del Uruguay
1949	Cine Club de Colombia
1950	First congress of film societies of Brazil
1951	Cine Club de Medellín, Colombia
1952	Cine Club de Lima
1955	Federación Mexicana de Cineclubes

FILM ARCHIVES

1948	Filmoteca, São Paulo Museu de Arte Moderna (Cinemateca Brasileira after 1956)
1951	Cinemateca de Cuba
1952	Cinemateca Uruguaya
1957	Cinemateca, Rio de Janeiro Museu de Arte Moderna
1957	Instituto Nacional de Cine, Buenos Aires
1960	Filmoteca de la UNAM (Universidad Nacional Autónoma de México)
1962	Cinemateca Universitaria, Universidad de Chile

UNIVERSITY PROGRAMS

1950	Instituto Cinematográfico de la Universidad de la República (Montevideo, Uruguay)
1955	Instituto Fílmico, Universidad Católica, Santiago de Chile
1956	Instituto de Cinematografía, Universidad del Litoral, Santa Fe, Argentina
1959	Departamento de Actividades Cinematográficas, UNAM
1960	Departamento de Cine Experimental, Universidad de Chile
1963	Centro Universitario de Estudios Cinematográficos, UNAM

known: on-location shooting with direct sound and ambient light, frequent use of nonprofessional actors, and linear storylines that paint a sympathetic picture of the daily life struggles of poor people. Art cinema, on the other hand, is a more amorphous category. Broadly speaking, it refers to films that value technical quality, reject classical cinema's generic conventions, and see the director as the author (auteur) of a unique, expressive, and poetic work of art marked by ambiguity.[2] The idea that some directors are the primary authors of a film was first proposed by the French critic Alexandre Astruc in a 1948 manifesto titled "The Birth of a New Avant-Garde: The Camera-Stylo," and later elaborated in the pages of the influential *Cahiers du Cinéma* in the 1950s, in articles such as François Truffaut's "A Certain Tendency in French

Cinema" (1954) and André Bazin's "On the Auteur Cinema" (1957).[3] The idea of the director as author is problematic, given the collective nature of filmmaking, but it is useful as long as we avoid viewing auteurs in the Romantic tradition of the lone artist. With this in mind, we can distinguish at least three kinds of Latin American auteurs:

1. hegemonic studio auteurs: directors such as Luis Saslavsky and Emilio Fernández, who developed their own personal styles within the constraints of studio productions, and in so doing helped crystallize the corporatist values and generic conventions of studio cinema,

2. counterhegemonic studio auteurs: directors such as Luis Buñuel and Leopoldo Torre Nilsson, who managed to impose their personal styles and world vision on studio productions while questioning the corporatist values and generic conventions of studio cinema, and

3. independent auteurs: directors such as Nelson Pereira dos Santos and Glauber Rocha, whose personal styles and world vision were developed outside the studio system, in their case in close dialogue with the French New Wave that emerged in the late 1950s and early 1960s.

Art cinema is most closely associated with the work of auteurs in the second category, and this chapter highlights the work of Luis Buñuel and Leopoldo Torre Nilsson as representative of a generation of art cinema directors that also includes Alberto Cavalcanti, Lima Barreto, Walter Hugo Khouri, Carlos Velo, Roberto Gavaldón, David José Kohon, and Lautaro Murúa. At the same time, the chapter also considers two early films by Nelson Pereira dos Santos that straddle neorealism and independent auteurism. Taken together, the work of these directors demonstrates that the relationship between neorealism and art cinema in Latin America was dialogic rather than dialectical, a point that deserves some elaboration.

While neorealism and art cinema are distinct—neorealism is didactic, moral, and utilitarian, and art cinema tends to be poetic, ambiguous in its morality, and therefore hard to instrumentalize—they nevertheless shared the assumption, widespread in Latin American film clubs at the time, that cinema could help improve society by raising viewers' awareness of seldom-seen aspects of reality. They also shared a common rejection of studio cinema's aesthetic and thematic conventions, as well as a commitment to social reform that remained surprisingly consistent until the triumph of the Cuban Revolution in 1959, and longer in some cases.

Paulo Antonio Paranaguá, who has undertaken the most thorough comparative analysis of Latin American Neorealism, argues that the enthusiasm with which Latin Americans embraced Italian Neorealism can be explained by the fact that it spoke to the two main ideological currents then in contention within film clubs. "Both sides," he writes, "agreed that film has a messianic mission to fulfill: Marxists could project their desire for transparency onto Neo-realism, while Catholics could see their own aspirations to immanence reflected there."[4] Paranaguá does not elaborate on this point, but a summary comparison between Cesare Zavattini and André Bazin neatly illustrates it. On the one hand, Zavattini, an active member of the Italian Communist Party, insisted on neorealism's capacity to elicit feelings of solidarity with the poor.[5] By contrast, Bazin, who was politically a Christian Democrat and philosophically a Personalist (a Christian philosophy that sees the world as mysterious and life's goal as the revolution of the human spirit), celebrated what he saw as Italian Neorealism's immanence, specifically its photographic ability to reveal the divine presence in everyday reality.[6] In other words, whereas Zavattini emphasizes neorealism's ability to increase viewers' awareness of social reality because its mode of representation is transparent and indexical, Bazin sees in neorealism's poetic "self-effacement before reality" an acknowledgment of the immanence of everyday life.[7] Italian Neorealism's multivalence—at once indexical and immanent—thus supports the thesis of convergence, in Latin American cinema of the 1950s, between socially progressive politics and poetic expression, between neorealism and art cinema. This chapter analyzes and evaluates, in chronological order, the richness of this convergence in films whose heterogeneity laid the foundation for the future convergence, in the New Latin American Cinema, between documentary modes of representation and revolutionary expressionism.

LUIS BUÑUEL

Luis Buñuel, a Spaniard who made a name for himself as a French Surrealist filmmaker with *Un chien andalou* (An Andalusian Dog; France, 1929) and *L'Age d'or* (*The Golden Age*; France, 1930), was by far the most celebrated filmmaker in Latin America in the 1950s. Between 1946 and 1965 he directed twenty films in Mexico: sixteen fully

Mexican productions, two coproductions with France, and two coproductions with the United States. Given Buñuel's Surrealist pedigree prior to his arrival in Mexico, it is striking that his Mexican films so often participate in the conventions of Mexico's studio cinema. The most obvious example of this practice is *Susana* (1950), a hybrid between melodrama and *comedia ranchera*, where the corporatist values traditionally associated with these two genres are put to the test by Susana (Rosita Quintana), a beautifully seductive convict teeming with sexual energy. After an improbable escape from prison, Susana arrives at a version of Fernando de Fuentes's Rancho Grande in the middle of a stormy night, and, like a storm, she begins to wreak havoc on the perfectly ordered hacienda. First she seduces the foreman, then the son of the patriarch, then the patriarch himself. And just when the house of cards based on appearances and upheld by hypocrisy is about to fall down, the police take Susana back to jail and everyone merrily resettles into the roles they played before her arrival.

This is studio melodrama pure and simple, complete with sudden reversals of fortune, the return to the status quo ante, formulaic acting, flawless continuity editing, and a bourgeois morality summed up by the maid at the end of the film: "That was a nightmare. This [the hacienda's return to patriarchal normalcy] is the pure truth of God." That said, one is left with a feeling that things really can't go back to the way they were, as Susana has revealed the masquerade that is Mexican society and its cinema by unleashing repressed desires. Buñuel's better Mexican films, notably *Los olvidados* (The Forgotten Ones; 1950), and *Él* (literally "He" but distributed as *This Strange Passion*; 1953), similarly use many of the stylistic conventions of studio cinema, but as vessels for a Surrealist critique of conventional values.

Los olvidados (1950)

Los olvidados was Buñuel's first personal film in Mexico, a kind of reward from the producer Óscar Dancigers for Buñuel's supple direction of a commercially successful but inconsequential musical comedy.[8] The film tells the story of Pedro (Alfonso Mejía), a prepubescent boy who yearns for his mother's love, and Jaibo (Roberto Cobo), a young man recently escaped from a youth correctional facility. The two belong to a neighborhood gang of petty thieves who pick on easy targets such as Don Carmelo (Miguel Inclán), a blind beggar, and Ojitos (Mario Ramírez), an Indian boy whom Don Carmelo recruits as his assistant. Pedro

FIGURE 6.1   Pedro's (Alfonso Mejía) Oedipal dream in *Los olvidados* (The Forgotten Ones; Luis Buñuel, Mexico, 1950), with Stella Inda in the role of Pedro's mother

at first sees Jaibo as an older-brother type who is willing to teach him how to survive the mean streets of Mexico City, but the relationship quickly sours when Pedro witnesses Jaibo's brutal murder of Julián (Javier Amezcua), an upright neighbor whom Jaibo blamed for his recent incarceration. Terrified, Pedro accepts part of the money that Jaibo steals from Julián, and in so doing becomes an accomplice to murder.

That night, Pedro's trauma is dramatized via a Freudian dream sequence whose slow motion and nondiegetic sound contrasts sharply with the film's otherwise realist aesthetics (fig. 6.1). The dream begins with a white hen falling from the ceiling. Pedro gets up to see where it landed and finds an agonized and bloodied Julián under his bed. Pedro's mother (Stella Inda) also gets up and begins to walk toward her son. As we hear the following acoustically off-kilter dialogue, her white and heavily starched nightgown and the way she walks over mattresses makes her look like the Virgin Mary floating on air:

> *Mother:* What are you doing, Pedro? Listen, my little boy. You are good. Why did you do this?
>
> *Pedro:* I didn't do anything. It was Jaibo. I only saw it. I just want to be with you, but you don't love me.

> *Mother:* It's just that I'm so tired. Look at my hands, destroyed from washing so much.
>
> *Pedro:* Why don't you ever give me a kiss? Mamá, I promise I'll behave. I'll get a job and you'll be able to rest.
>
> *Mother:* Yes, my little boy.

The mother gives Pedro a tender hug, lays him down to sleep, and begins to walk away when Pedro jumps up and calls: "Mamá, mamá, why didn't you give me meat the other night?" The mother turns around and, with an enormous piece of raw meat in her hands and a smile on her face, begins to approach Pedro as we hear the sounds and lights of a thunderstorm. Finally, just as Pedro grabs the piece of meat, Jaibo appears from under Pedro's bed and snatches it while the mother turns back and walks away. Startled, Pedro wakes up, looks around, and goes back to sleep.

The next day, Pedro makes good on his dream promise by securing a job as a blacksmith's apprentice. Things are starting to go well for him until one day, when he is alone in the shop, Jaibo shows up, steals a knife without Pedro noticing, and then goes to Pedro's house to seduce Pedro's mother with a saccharine story about his orphanhood.

When a policeman subsequently visits Pedro's house to investigate the case of the missing knife, Pedro scrams, thinking the visit has to do with Julián's murder. The mother, when asked about the knife, is sure that it was Pedro who stole it and even asks the policeman to punish the boy in order to teach him a lesson. A few days later, when Pedro returns home and tells his mother that the reason she's upset with him is "because of Jaibo," she mistakenly thinks that he is referring to her affair with Jaibo instead of his own friendship with a hoodlum, and proceeds to give him a beating. Then, just as Pedro is about to fight back, he stops himself and tells her that he will do whatever she asks of him.

The mother, still certain that Pedro stole the knife, takes him to the authorities. A male judicial caseworker tells her that without evidence of the theft, Pedro cannot be jailed, and offers instead to send him to a reformatory school. She quickly agrees and the caseworker scolds her for not giving the boy the maternal love he needs. "Why should I love him," she responds, "if I did not even know his father. I was a weakling and could not defend myself." In the waiting cell, however, after Pedro finally convinces her that he did not steal the knife, she is moved and gives him a tender, motherly kiss.

FIGURE 6.2   Jaibo's (Roberto Cobo) death dream in *Los olvidados*

At the reformatory school Pedro gets into trouble, but the director, rather than castigating him, sends him on an errand to prove that the school is not a jail and to give Pedro a chance to prove himself a responsible man. Jaibo, however, intercepts him just outside the school's gate, steals the money with which Pedro has been entrusted, and runs away. When Pedro catches up to Jaibo in front of the other members of the gang, he is no longer afraid. He demands the money back, and after Jaibo beats him up, Pedro picks up the stolen knife that has fallen from Jaibo's pocket and defies him: "Now run! I won't let you kill me behind my back like you killed Julián!" The scene is now set for the denouement. Jaibo runs away, but soon finds and kills Pedro inside a stable. The police, who have been informed of Jaibo's hiding place, shoot him, and as he lays dying, he imagines a mangy dog running toward him and a tender conversation with his absent mother (fig. 6.2):

> *Jaibo, to himself:* Now they've got you, Jaibo. They gave you a bullet right between the eyes.
>
> *Mother:* Watch out, Jaibo. The mangy dog is coming.
>
> *Jaibo:* No, no. I'm falling into the black hole. I'm alone. Alone.
>
> *Mother:* Like always, my son . . . like always. Go to sleep and don't think. Go to sleep, my child . . . Sleep . . .

The last shot of the film shows the owner of the stable where Pedro was killed and his daughter, dumping Pedro's body into a ravine shortly after having crossed paths with Pedro's mother, who senses something is wrong but does not stop to inquire.

With this tragic ending, *Los olvidados* highlights the limits of reformism, narratively represented in the film by the inability of the reformatory school to stop delinquency outside its walls. But the film says something much more profound by asking how one can represent the reality of juvenile delinquency among poor children and adolescents without repeating cinematic clichés about poverty that do not contribute to a more complex understanding of the problem, and, potentially, to its solution. Buñuel's answer is twofold: on the one hand, to systematically reveal the superficiality of established forms of representing poverty (social documentary, socialist realism, social realism, neorealism, and studio cinema), and on the other, to dig deeper into that reality through a combination of Hispanic realism and Surrealism in dialogue with one another.

Consider for example the film's relationship to Mexican studio cinema and to the political and economic context of Mexico in 1950, a time when President Miguel Alemán's policies of corporatist developmentalism were transforming Mexico City into the chaotic megalopolis it is today. *Los olvidados* is an *arrabalera*, a genre whose exploration of life in the *arrabales*—seedier parts of rapidly modernizing Mexican cities—became hugely popular between 1948 and 1952. The genre, which includes social dramas such as Alejandro Galindo's *Campeón sin corona* (Champion Without a Crown; Mexico, 1945) and *cabareteras* such as Alberto Gout's *Aventurera* (The Adventuress; Mexico, 1950), speaks to the profound crisis of a nationalist and edifying cinema that depended on and reflected the values of state corporatism. In the specific case of *Los olvidados,* the film critiques Alemán's economic policies by focusing on a social class that, far from enjoying the fruits of developmentalism, becomes ever more entrenched as an underclass.

In the film, the gap between the official discourse of developmentalism and the social reality of widespread poverty has its aesthetic counterpart in the sequences at the waiting cell and in the reformatory school. The fact that these two sequences are filmed in the style of the Fernández-Figueroa Mexican school of cinema, and not with the gritty realism prevalent throughout the rest of the film, signals to viewers that the values associated with the Fernández-Figueroa Mexican school style are as hollowed and clichéd as the words uttered by the representatives of the state who occupy those spaces, whether it is the caseworker telling Pedro's mother that "we should lock up the parents instead" or the school director who, after a long silence, tells his assistant, "I was just thinking we should be locking up misery instead of these kids." By filming these two sequences in the style of the Mexican school of cinema, *Los olvidados* suggests that the gap between the Mexico depicted through this style and the Mexico in the streets is as wide as the gap between the official state discourse of economic growth through developmentalism, and the rising inequality that is its underside.

The film's critique of the limits of the social documentary is equally pointed, and made at the very beginning by way of several disclaimers. The first proclaims that "this film is based entirely on real-life incidents, and all its characters are authentic." The second gives thanks to three specific government officials for "their valuable help in making this film." The third and longest disclaimer shows touristy shots of New York, Paris, London, and Mexico City with the following voice-over:

> The great modern cities—New York, Paris, London—hide behind their magnificent buildings villages of misery that house malnourished children, without hygiene or schooling—seedbeds of future delinquency. Society has tried to fix this problem, but the fruit of its efforts is very limited. Only in a proximate future will the rights of children and adolescents be attained so that their lives can be productive and beneficial to society. Mexico City, the great modern city, is no exception to this universal rule. That is why this film, based on real-life events, is not optimistic, and leaves the solution to the problem to the progressive forces of society.

In the disclaimers, the authoritative voice of the omniscient narrator in direct verbal address, the use of images to illustrate the narrated text, and the use of nonsynchronous sound are all features of what Julianne Burton-Carvajal calls the expository mode of social documentary, a mode that emphasizes objectivity, generalization, economy of analysis, and the filmmaker's privileged knowledge.[9] It is possible to read these disclaimers as ironic because we have come to expect irony from Buñuel, but it is not necessary to do so in order to extract their meaning and their two functions. On the one hand, they help neutralize expected attacks against the film's unsavory representation of the nation by defining Mexico City as a modern city with problems similar to those experienced in New York, Paris, and London. And on the other hand, because they insist on the film's basis on reality, they predispose viewers to ask a central question that the film explores in depth: what is reality, and how can cinema best represent it?

Following these expository-mode disclaimers, the film shifts modes to neorealism (on-location shooting, mostly nonprofessional actors) in a sequence that sympathetically portrays a group of street children playing and then welcoming Jaibo back to the neighborhood. The sudden shift of registers implies that the expository mode of social documentary—with its sets of statistics, "objective" facts, and omniscient point of view—is too limited a format to investigate the daily life of poor children, something Italian Neorealism had famously explored. Buñuel, however, was no fan of neorealism, and in a 1958 conference titled "Cinema, an Instrument of Poetry," he justified Pedro's dream and Jaibo's hallucination as the film's most important contributions to the language of cinema:

> The cinema seems to have been invented to express the subconscious life, whose roots penetrate so deeply into poetry; but it is almost never used for that end. Among modern tendencies of cinema, the best known is what is called "neo-realism." Its films present to the eyes of the spectator slices of real life, with people taken from the street, and with real buildings and exteriors. With a few exceptions, among which I would especially instance *Bicycle Thieves*, neo-realism has done nothing to produce in its films what is proper to the cinema, that is to say, the mysterious and fantastic.[10]

Los olvidados specifically targets neorealism by discrediting the essentialist construction of characters in *Sciuscià* (*Shoeshine*; Vittorio De Sica, Italy, 1946), a neorealist film that also deals with young delinquents. That is to say, whereas *Shoeshine* depicts the likable Pasquale (Franco Interlenghi) and Giuseppe (Rinaldo Smordoni) as inherently purehearted, and their antagonists Attilio (Guido Gentili) and Panza (Gino Saltamerenda) as inherently criminal, in *Los olvidados*, the likable Pedro is as violent as any other kid in the gang (and as willing to kill as Jaibo), while his antagonist Jaibo is, as Buñuel put it, "not entirely bad, no. In my films, nobody is fatally bad or entirely good."[11]

Two other key intertexts of *Los olvidados* are *Putevka v zhinzn'* (*Road to Life*; Nikolai Ekk, USSR, 1931), a classic of early socialist realism about a reformatory school for orphans where children unlearn their impulse to steal through the joys of collective work; and *Boys Town* (Norman Taurog, United States, 1938), a thesis film in the style of social realism, where a priest runs a progressive orphanage with the goal of proving that there is no such thing as a bad boy. As in *Road to Life*, Pedro goes to a reformatory school where collective work is used to help students unlearn antisocial behavior; and as in *Boys Town*, the director of the reformatory school believes there is no such thing as a bad boy. Buñuel, however, "did not want at all to make a thesis film,"[12] but "to denounce the sad condition of the poor without beautifying it, because I hate the sweetening of the character of the poor."[13] Thus, just as Buñuel references the expository mode of social documentaries and neorealism to point out their aesthetic limitations in capturing the full complexity of reality, he references *Road to Life* and *Boys Town* to highlight the narrative limitations of socialist realism and social realism as vehicles to explore reality and its contradictions. Unlike the characters in *Road to Life* and *Boys Town,* that is, Pedro and Jaibo are psychologically complex characters whose violence cannot be explained (away) by simply referring to their physically brutal environment, as in *Road to Life,* or by referring to a simple lack of love, as in *Boys Town*. Instead, *Los olvidados* calls attention to the interaction between the social and the psychological roots of juvenile delinquency by using Hispanic realism (including the picaresque) to represent the economic poverty that is the sociological explanation of juvenile delinquency, and Surrealism to represent its psychological roots, a poverty of love that is narrated as Pedro's (and to a lesser extent Jaibo's) frustrated Oedipal trajectory.

Octavio Paz, who was Mexico's cultural attaché in France at the time and salvaged the film's initial rejection by doggedly promoting it at the Cannes Film Festival, recognized the convergence of these two traditions. Regarding the film's Hispanic realism, he wrote:

> Misery and abandonment can take place in any part of the world, but the bitter passion with which the film describes it belongs to the great Spanish artistic tradition. Those women, those drunkards, those cretins, those murderers, those innocents, we have seen them in Quevedo and in Galdós, caught a glimpse of them in Cervantes, seen them painted by Velázquez and Murillo. . . . And the children, the forgotten ones, their mythology, their passive rebelliousness, their suicidal loyalty, their thundering sweetness, their tenderness full of exquisite ferocities, their ripping affirmation of their selves in and through death, their search without end for communion—even through criminal behavior—cannot be but Mexican. Thus, in the film's key scene—the oneiric scene—the theme of the mother is resolved in the shared dinner, that is, in the sacred feast.[14]

Paz then goes on to interpret Pedro's dream sequence and Jaibo's final hallucination as the Surrealist unmasking of "the archetypal images of the Mexican people: Coatlicue [the Earth goddess of the Mexicas], and sacrifice." "The theme of the mother," Paz concludes,

> is [not only] one of Mexico's obsessions, it is also inexorably linked to the theme of friendship till death. Together, they make up the secret backdrop of

this film. The world of *Los olvidados* is inhabited by orphans, by solitaires who seek communion and who do not back down in the face of blood. The search for the "other," of our likeness, is the other side of the search for the mother. . . . Pedro, Jaibo, and their friends thus reveal to us the ultimate nature of mankind, which might be a permanent and constant state of orphanhood.[15]

Paz's incisive review provides the basis of a reading of *Los olvidados* as the most Mexican of Buñuel's Mexican films. For Paz, that is to say, the film participates in a national debate on the nature of Mexican identity that began with the publication in 1934 of Samuel Ramos's *El perfil del hombre y la cultura en México* (Profile of Man and Culture in Mexico) and culminated with the 1950 publication of his own *El laberinto de la soledad* (The Labyrinth of Solitude). This influential essay by Paz, who was a friend of Buñuel and a fellow Surrealist, was published the same year as the release of *Los olvidados*. Not coincidentally, Buñuel's film and the essay by Paz share an understanding of Mexican identity as the product of the interaction between the social reality of a modern nation where human relations (like human relations in modern nations everywhere) are impersonal and competitive, and a foundational fiction (Hernán Cortés, La Malinche, and their illegitimate children) that the film rereads as an unresolved Oedipal narrative trajectory between a negative father figure (Jaibo), a humiliated mother (Pedro's mother), and a traumatized son (Pedro).

This Strange Passion (1953)

Los olvidados's exploration of the interaction between an individual's Oedipal trajectory and a specific social reality continues in *This Strange Passion* (1953), only this time the specific social reality is the closed world of Mexico's traditional landed bourgeoisie. Moreover, whereas the cultural archetype that informs Pedro's Oedipal trajectory in *Los olvidados* is the story of La Malinche and her illegitimate sons (some recognized by her, some forgotten), in *This Strange Passion* the cultural archetype that informs the protagonist's Oedipal trajectory is the Holy Trinity: Father, Son, and Holy Spirit. The film tells the story of Francisco Galván de Montemayor (Arturo de Córdova), a forty-year-old virgin and scion of an aristocratic family with roots in the conservative stronghold of Guanajuato, and Gloria (Delia Garcés), a beautiful and much younger woman recently arrived from Argentina. The two meet in a baroque church in Mexico City, where they both live. It is Maundy

Thursday. During the Washing of the Feet ceremony, he is visibly aroused by Father Velasco's (Carlos Martínez Baena) washing and kissing of the bare feet of young boys. Francisco quickly averts his gaze, and projects his awakened desire onto Gloria's bare legs in the front row of parishioners. After Mass he tries to approach her, but is frustrated first by Gloria's mother (Aurora Walker), who takes her daughter away just when the two are about to share holy water, and then by Father Velasco, who stops Francisco for small talk.

Back home, Francisco's frustration grows when his lawyer informs him that the lawsuit to regain the family's expropriated properties in Guanajuato is going nowhere. Francisco fires the lawyer and is forced to escort him out of the house personally because the butler (Pablo, played by Manuel Dondé) is nowhere in sight. As Francisco ascends the stairs calling for Pablo, a maid runs down, disturbed, buttoning her shirt. "What is going on?," Francisco demands. "Ask don Pablo," she replies and runs away. Upstairs, in Francisco's bedroom, he chastises Pablo for disrespecting the "honor of the house." Pablo asks for forgiveness, adding, "Nobody respects and loves you as much as I do," whereupon Francisco orders Pablo to fire the maid so that "this shameful situation will not happen again."

In these first ten minutes of the film, Buñuel skillfully establishes the central conflict as one between Francisco's private homosexual desire and his patriarchal duty to marry and produce heirs. The conflict develops as a reversed Oedipal trajectory. Francisco begins as a full-blown patriarchal figure. He subdues Gloria through the power of his objectifying gaze, takes her away from her fiancé, his engineer friend Raúl Conde (Luis Beristáin), and quickly marries her. The story of their terrible marriage is told from Gloria's point of view. "I got my first surprise the very day we were married," she tells Raúl in the first of a series of confessions structured as one long flashback. On their wedding night, when Francisco is confronted with his own lack of heterosexual desire, his jealousy attacks begin, outward symptoms of a paranoiac fear that his own unacknowledged homosexuality will be discovered. As his paranoia grows, so do his attempts to control and humiliate Gloria. During their honeymoon in Guanajuato, the city of his childhood, he controls how she is to take pictures of him (from below), while in the hotel he unjustly accuses her of causing a fight with a guest.

Back in Mexico City, the situation only gets worse. He won't let anyone, including Gloria's mother, see her. One night he asks her to entertain his new lawyer and then accuses her, in front of Pablo, of flirting

FIGURE 6.3   Francisco (Arturo de Córdova) tries to strangle his wife, Gloria (Delia Garcés), in *This Strange Passion* (Luis Buñuel, Mexico, 1953)

with him. After the guests have left, we hear her screaming as he apparently rapes her offscreen. The next morning she asks her mother to come see her right away, and she does, but not before Francisco has explained what happened from his point of view. "You should be more understanding," the mother tells Gloria, "more loving with him. . . . Listen to your mother, who loves you more than anything in this world." Unlike Pablo, who declares his love for Francisco over any*one*, Gloria's mother participates in her daughter's objectification by saying she loves her more than any*thing*. In desperation, Gloria goes to see Father Velasco, "the only person who had influence over him," only to learn that Francisco has already confessed that Gloria was "the first woman he had been with." Back home, Francisco shoots her with blanks, and Gloria has a nervous breakdown. When she recovers, he invites her on an outing to a bell tower, and after describing the people below as worms, he tries to throw her over the ledge (fig. 6.3). Gloria escapes and the flashbacks end.

We are back in Raúl's car. He drops her off a block away from her house, but Francisco sees them nevertheless. Distraught, Francisco seeks solace from Pablo:

Francisco: My wife is cheating on me. I know it. I'm certain. You know how much I love her. She is the first and last woman in my life. That's why I come to you.

Pablo: But I . . . how can I help you?

Francisco: By advising me what to do. What would you do if you were married and your wife cheated on you?

Pablo: Well, I'd leave her, I'd divorce her.

Francisco: What?

Pablo: I'd divorce her, sir.

Francisco: You wouldn't kill her?

Pablo: And spend the rest of my life in prison? No way, sir. Forgive me for being sincere, sir, but since you married you have not been cheerful. If you are sure of what you are saying, kick her out and be done with it. You will never lack for someone to love you and take care of you.

Upon hearing Pablo's awkward profession of love, Francisco leaves Pablo's room and stops halfway up the stairs that lead to his and Gloria's bedrooms, sits down, rips out one of the rods that holds the carpet in place, and begins to clank it against the railings in an ever-increasing rhythm, as if masturbating.[16]

The next day Francisco locks himself up in his studio to write a letter to the president of Mexico, asking for help with his land claims. He can't manage to finish it, and asks Gloria to help him. She obliges, and even consoles him like a mother would a helpless child, but Francisco bursts out with another jealousy attack over Raúl. That night, in his bedroom, Francisco wraps a shaving blade, a large threaded needle, and a pair of scissors into a roll of cloth, puts it and some rope in his pockets, and heads to Gloria's bedroom, where she is asleep. Francisco begins to carefully tie one of Gloria's arms, but she wakes up and starts to scream. Francisco, hearing the servants coming, locks himself in his bedroom and throws himself on the floor, crying and throwing a fit like a boy punished for bad behavior. The next morning Pablo informs Francisco in a revealingly intimate tone that "the madam has just escaped." With his gun loaded, Francisco runs out looking for Gloria, first at her mother's house, then at Raúl's office, and finally in church, where he thinks he sees Gloria and Raúl enter together. Inside, he realizes that it is not Gloria and Raúl, but an unknown couple, and begins to imagine that everyone, including Father Velasco, is making fun of him. He finally snaps, starts to strangle Father Velasco, and is taken away.

The closing sequences take place at a monastery in Colombia, where Francisco has been living for many years after his release from a mental hospital. Gloria and Raúl, accompanied by a boy of about ten, have come to see how he is doing. "If you like, I can ask him to come," says the head monk, but both Gloria and Raúl agree it is not a good idea. When the monk learns that the boy's name is Francisco, he asks Raúl and Gloria if the child is theirs, and instead of answering, they bid their farewells. Later, when Francisco asks the head monk if the child was theirs, the head monk says yes. "You see, Father," Francisco tells the head monk, "how I was not as perturbed, as they said. . . . Time has proven me right," to which the monk replies, "Continue with your pious reading (*lectura piadosa*)," a response with at least two possible meanings: one literal (i.e., continue reading the Bible as you were doing), the other ironic (i.e., continue believing that lie if it gives you peace of mind). The double meaning is underscored in a final shot of Francisco zigzagging toward a dark, womblike arch at the end of a path in the monastery's garden.

Like a zigzag, the film provides viewers with two equally valid explanations for Francisco's regression from his full participation in the symbolic order of patriarchy before he marries, to a mirror-stage boyhood when he grapples with contradictory images of Gloria as fetishized object and mother figure, to fetal unity with the mother, represented by his last steps in the direction of the womblike opening at the end of the garden path. The first interpretation of Francisco's regression is an Oedipal trajectory in reverse, where Raúl is the father, Gloria the mother, and Francisco their child. This is the reading suggested by the visit to the monastery, with Gloria and Raúl the proud parents of a boy aptly named Francisco. Francisco's repressed homosexuality is an obstacle to sleeping with his symbolic mother, and his inability to recuperate his family's ancestral lands is an obstacle to killing his symbolic father because Raúl represents the professional bourgeoisie that has displaced the landed elite from the traditional center of power in post-Revolutionary Mexico.

The second interpretation of Francisco's regression is an allegorical reading of the Catholic Holy Trinity where Father Velasco embodies the Father, Francisco the Son, and Pablo the Holy Spirit. If one recalls that the film begins with a shot of a triangular candelabra framing first a couple of altar boys, then three priests, and finally a group of laymen who will help with the ceremony of the Washing of the Feet, it is easy to imagine that Francisco, who is part of that group of laymen, was once one of the boys whose feet Father Velasco washed and tenderly kissed. The homosocial ceremony takes place in a baroque church that echoes Francisco's mansion because both are excessively decorated and both arrange space hierarchically through stairs and a theatrical space (the altar in the church and the landing/foyer in Francisco's mansion) that underscore vertical social relations. However, the baroque of the mansion is not one of complementary opposites between male and female, Francisco and Gloria, but rather one of masculine exclusion of the feminine, with Father Velasco an invisible presence, Francisco the Son who moves effortlessly between the first and second floors of the mansion, and Pablo a kind of Holy Spirit that is everywhere and always about. Psychoanalytically speaking, it makes sense that Francisco would want to kill Father Velasco in his moment of greatest madness, for it is in madness that Francisco intuited that Velasco is a father figure he must symbolically kill in order for him to exit the patriarchal symbolic order and live out his homosexuality.

Both *Los olvidados* and *This Strange Passion* use Oedipal narrative trajectories and patriarchal binary oppositions—above/below, male/female, heterosexuality/homosexuality—to reveal their contingent nature and to explore the cultural specificity of desire. In *This Strange Passion*, Francisco's frustrated homosexual desire is specifically linked to the dogmas of the Catholic Church. In *Los olvidados*, Pedro's desire for maternal love is inseparable from the story of La Malinche as a foundational fiction that the film rereads as a frustrated Oedipal narrative trajectory. In both cases, Buñuel situates his main character in an unresolved Oedipal situation in order to observe, like a scientist, the workings and outcomes of frustrated desire. In *Los olvidados*, the outcome of frustrated desire is death; in *This Strange Passion*, insanity. Common to both outcomes is a crisis of masculine identity, a similarity that indicates that ultimately, what Buñuel may be exploring is a broader crisis of masculinity and its institutions in contemporary Mexico, a crisis so profound that it cuts across socioeconomic lines and cinematic genres.[17]

VERA CRUZ STUDIO AND ITS AFTERMATH

At the same time that Buñuel was regaining his international stature through very personal films, a group of wealthy industrialists in São Paulo set out to transform Brazilian cinema from a backwater dependent on *chanchadas* to a world-class industry à la Hollywood. They founded Vera

Cruz Studio in 1949, and hired Alberto Cavalcanti as its first director. Cavalcanti, a Brazilian national who had made a name for himself in France with the avant-garde film *Rien que les heures* (Nothing but the Hours; 1926) and in Britain's General Post Office Film Unit, imported the latest equipment and many technicians from Europe, especially Italy, but was soon forced out, in part because his vision collided with the vision of the financial backers of Vera Cruz, and in part because of his homosexuality. In any case, the studio did not last much longer. In 1954, after having produced eighteen features and some documentaries, Vera Cruz declared bankruptcy. Its failure was both commercial, because its business model focused on production and ignored distribution and exhibition, and artistic, because it chose to emulate Hollywood's international style at a time when studio cinema was in crisis. However, the experience of Vera Cruz is important in the history of Brazilian cinema because its use of Hollywood's international style generated a response so intense and profound that it helped set the stage for Cinema Novo, the first of several national new cinemas that would coalesce into the New Latin American Cinema.

The harshest criticisms were reserved for *O Cangaceiro* (The Backlands Bandit; Victor Lima Barreto, 1953), winner of two awards at Cannes and the studio's most widely distributed film. The film tells the story of a band of *cangaceiros*, armed peasants from the arid and desolate *sertão* in northeastern Brazil, who between the 1880s and the 1930s constituted a movement (the *cangaço*) to battle the big landowners and their government allies. The importance of the *cangaço* to the creation of a modern Brazilian identity is suggested by the *literatura de cordel*— a kind of pulp fiction that was very popular in northeastern Brazil in the 1920s and 1930s, about *cangaceiros* such as the famous Lampião—and by the book *Os Sertões* (*Rebellion in the Backlands*; 1902) by Euclides da Cunha, widely considered a classic of Brazilian and world literature. Though very different in style, the representations of the *cangaço* found in the *literatura de cordel* and in *Rebellion in the Backlands* share a view of the *cangaceiros* as brutally courageous bandits whose struggles against social injustice were informed by a highly developed mysticism.

Because *O Cangaceiro* followed Vera Cruz's institutional adoption of Hollywood's international style as its mode of representation, the film ended up transforming the historical reality of the *cangaço* into a myth in the tradition of the Western, and the psychological complexity of the *cangaceiros* into a historically inaccurate Manichaeism. Specifically, the film uncharacteristically divided the *cangaceiros* into good bandits and bad bandits, and then privileged the love story between the "good" ban-

FIGURE 6.4 Milton Ribeiro as the "bad bandit" Galdino in *O Cangaceiro* (The Backlands Bandit; Victor Lima Barreto, Brazil, 1953)

dit Teodoro (Alberto Ruschel) and the teacher Olívia (Marisa Prado) over the social struggle centered on the "bad" bandit Galdino (Milton Ribeiro) (fig. 6.4). The fact that the film was shot in the verdant high plains of São Paulo instead of the rugged *sertão* only added to what many Brazilians considered its overall inauthenticity.[18] The charges against O *Cangaceiro* were summed up by a young Glauber Rocha, who blasted Lima Barreto for having created "a conventional and psychologically basic adventure drama illustrated by mystical figures with leather hats, silver stars, and comic cruelties. The *cangaço*, as a phenomenon of mystic, anarchic revolt born from the northeastern *latifundio* system and worsened by droughts, was not represented."[19]

Rocha was equally dismissive of another film set in the northeast: *O Canto do Mar* (*Song of the Sea*; Alberto Cavalcanti, 1954), one of three films Cavalcanti directed between 1951, when he was forced to resign as director of Vera Cruz, and 1954, when he returned to Europe to resume his high-profile career. *Song of the Sea* stands out among his Brazilian films for putting into practice his own call for a national cinema freed from the constraints of Hollywood's international style:

FIGURE 6.5 The funeral procession for a drowned child in *Song of the Sea* (Alberto Cavalcanti, Brazil, 1954). Courtesy Maristela Films

We've made great progress when it comes to technique. But it's not technique that counts. On the contrary, it can turn dangerous in the hands of irresponsible people, and serve as an excuse to launch the worst of films under the guise of profitability.

It is the true sense of cinema that needs to be encouraged, and the knowledge of its international value that we must cultivate. Above all, it is the awareness of its role, the responsibility toward its audience that we must inculcate to neophytes, so that their youthfulness, their character, and their strength can triumph over the powerful enemies at the very center of national cinema.[20]

In effect, *Song of the Sea* mixes studio melodrama with several nonstudio modes of representation, from the British documentary film movement in the opening sequences, to the Surrealism of Buñuel's *Los olvidados* in the young protagonist's nightmare sequence, to neorealism's humanism and interest in the daily lives of the poor, to avant-garde cinematography in the film's funeral procession for a drowned child (fig. 6.5). Rocha was not impressed:

Cavalcanti . . . was enchanted with the exotic, and the struggle of his character—the young man who hears the sea and yearns to see other horizons—is romantic, abstract, and is filled with . . . antinationalist feeling. In directing his actors—some professionals, some not—he imposed on the young

Ruy Saraiva a ridiculous affectation that clashed with the rest of the human landscape of Recife. . . . From a historical perspective for the development of Brazilian cinema, it is one of those artifices that must be studied so as not to be repeated.[21]

To his credit, Rocha called the opening sequences of *Song of the Sea* "suggestive," and quoted them in his own *Deus e o Diabo na Terra do Sol* (literally, "God and the Devil in the Land of the Sun," but distributed as *Black God, White Devil*; Brazil, 1963). And if nothing else, Rocha's combativeness confirms the important role that *O Cangaceiro* and *Song of the Sea* played as inspiration for Rocha, Nelson Pereira dos Santos, and Ruy Guerra to rectify what they saw as inauthentic and exotic images of the northeast, in films that turned out to be Cinema Novo's founding trilogy: *Vidas Secas* (*Barren Lives*; Nelson Pereira dos Santos, 1963), *Os Fuzis* (*The Guns*; Ruy Guerra, 1964), and the aforementioned *Black God, White Devil*.

Rio, 40 Graus (1955) and *Rio, Zona Norte* (1957)

For many progressive filmmakers and critics, the failure of Vera Cruz—and of similar "quality" studios such as Kino Films, which produced Cavalcanti's *Song of the Sea*—confirmed the need for Brazilian cinema to go in an altogether different direction from both *chanchadas* and Hollywood's international style. If only by elimination, that direction seemed to be neorealism, and the young Nelson Pereira dos Santos, an admirer of Cesare Zavattini, set out to prove that this was indeed the case. *Rio, 40 Graus* (Rio, 100 Degrees F; Brazil, 1955), as Heliodoro San Miguel notes,

> follows the happenings of five black *manisero* [peanut vendor] kids from Cabaçu [a working-class favela] that sell their peanuts all over the city, from the stadium of Maracanã to the Pão de Açucar. One of the most original features of this film, and one of its main achievements, was to point the camera towards the poorest urban classes of a major city, ignored for the most part by the previous Brazilian cinema. *Rio, 40 Graus* portrays their marginal and oppressed condition, and exposes the people of Rio in all their diversity and multiracial complexity, exploring the subtle interactions between skin color and social status. The black population is shown without stereotypes, without a hint of the typical patronizing attitude all too frequent in earlier films. It is not a coincidence that one of the sambas they sing at the end of the movie refers to the end of slavery.[22]

The critical success of *Rio, 40 Graus* opened the door for dos Santos to make *Rio, Zona Norte* (Rio, North Zone; Brazil, 1957), a much more complex film set in the city's poor north side that pushes neorealism in a new direction. The film stars Grande Otelo, already famous from his many years working as a comic sidekick in *chanchadas,* in a dramatic performance as Espírito da Luz Cardoso, a poor composer of sambas who dreams of making a living from the music he writes. The film is structured as a series of flashbacks from Espírito's point of view, as he lays dying after an accident. The result of the use of subjective flashbacks is a marked shift of perspective away from the privileging of surface reality so evident in dos Santos's previous neorealist film, and toward the privileging of an interior reality that is framed but not fully contained by the social context of the favelas. Moreover, because the story centers on Espírito's failed attempts to make a living from selling his carnival songs to exploitative hawks in the recording industry, the film takes on a political and self-reflexive position regarding the commoditization of popular culture, something absent from conventional neorealist films.

The film begins with the camera recording the passenger-level view from a train that is leaving Rio's central station toward Zona Norte. The shot seems objective enough, but when it is repeated toward the end of the film, we realize we were sharing Espírito's point of view shortly before he accidentally fell down. As he lays semiconscious on the ground, Espírito recalls his recent life: how he was tricked into selling a song for a pittance; how a sympathetic violinist by the name of Moacyr (Paulo Goulart) never followed through on his promise to help him professionally; how the girl from the samba school who moved in with him left him after it became clear he would not be famous (fig. 6.6); and how, after all these setbacks, he vowed never to be tricked again, and started to improvise a new samba for the next carnival:

> It's my samba, and Brazil's too
> They want to make you into
> A despised João Nobody
> But the favelas don't forget you
> For the slums, the samba doesn't die.

Here the flashbacks end. When he wakes up, he is at the hospital, post-surgery. He sees his good friend Lourival (Haroldo de Oliveira) standing next to Moacyr, and dies. On their way to the train station, Moacyr asks Lourival if he knows Espírito's sambas, and Lourival responds that everyone in the neighborhood does. The film thus leaves open the possibility for Moacyr, a white middle-class intellectual like

FIGURE 6.6 Samba composer Espírito (Grande Otelo) falls in love with Angela Maria (as herself) in *Rio, Zona Norte* (Rio, North Zone; Nelson Pereira dos Santos, Brazil, 1957)

dos Santos, to break with his class prejudices in order to help rescue an authentically national popular culture without manipulating it for the benefit of a more dominant class.[23]

There is no denying dos Santos's social commitment and positive representation of Afro-Brazilians in *Rio, Zona Norte* and *Rio, 40 Graus*. Robert Stam acknowledges as much in a defense worthy of Zavattini: "*Rio, 40 Graus* represents a giant step forward for Brazilian cinema in general and for the representation of blacks in particular. Unlike the *chanchadas*, the film takes the existential dilemmas of its black characters seriously, according them the unpretentious sympathy and solidarity which was to become the hallmark of dos Santos' work."[24] However, even dos Santos himself acknowledged the films' aesthetic shortcomings, and blamed them on the structural lack of continuity in Brazilian filmmaking:

> We wanted to confront Brazilian reality with our own eyes, with our own way of seeing the world, as if it were original. . . . Every filmmaker in the world wants that and one other thing: originality in the way of seeing the world. . . . [But] in Brazil, a director makes a film and has to wait years until another

opportunity arises. This is detrimental for our cinema. The best time to begin a film is immediately after making one [and to thereby correct] the most evident or even the most subtle defects. But that does not happen in Brazil.[25]

In fact, there was only one place in the late 1950s where a Latin American director could still enjoy a modicum of continuity in their work: a studio system whose very crisis favored the expansion of themes and forms well beyond the expansion of themes and forms offered by neorealism. The most undervalued example of this expansion is the work of the Argentinean director Leopoldo Torre Nilsson, whose trilogy of female sexual awakening closes the transitory 1950s on a highly dissonant note.

LEOPOLDO TORRE NILSSON'S GOTHIC TRILOGY (1957–61)

In Leopoldo Torre Nilsson, the son of director Leopoldo Torres Ríos, we find a consummate professional who uses the full arsenal of cinematic techniques available to him neither instinctually, as does José Agustín Ferreyra, nor as showy adornment, as in Luis Saslavsky's *Closed Door,* but in a very calculated way to visually underscore the psychological imbalance of his characters and their social milieu.[26] Out of the eighteen features he directed between 1956 and 1976, his most important work is a Gothic trilogy made in collaboration with his wife, the award-winning novelist Beatriz Guido. The trilogy works like a fugue, with each film repeating variations of the same theme (the sexual awakening of a female victim-hero, always played by Elsa Daniel) in the oppressively patriarchal world of Argentina's decadent oligarchic milieu.

La casa del ángel (1957)

In *La casa del ángel* (The House of the Angel; 1957), Ana Castro (Elsa Daniel) is the youngest of three daughters growing up in an opulent Buenos Aires mansion in the 1920s. Her mother is exceedingly prudish, to the point of forcing her daughters to bathe while clothed; and her father is old-school criollo, heir to the military traditions of nineteenth-century independence heroes. Into this rarified world walks Pablo Aguirre (Lautaro Murúa), a handsome parliamentarian who has made a name for himself by proposing a liberal law to protect the freedom of the press. When a member of the governing party accuses him of hypocrisy because Pablo's father had blocked a similar law in order to cover up a corrupt deal that made the family rich, Pablo forgets his liberal principles, and in

FIGURE 6.7 Ana (Elsa Daniel) with the (literally) shadowy Pablo (Lautaro Murúa) in *La casa del ángel* (The House of the Angel; Leopoldo Torre Nilsson, Argentina, 1957)

a burst of traditionalist bravura challenges the accuser to a duel. Ana's father, who sees his own values reflected in Pablo, offers to host the duel in his house, and even invites him to sleep there the night before. During dinner, Ana and Pablo exchange intense, desiring glances. The dinner sequence is shot with unconventional angles and with spotlighting that together help create an ominous atmosphere. This almost expressionist cinematography is repeated later that night, this time to underscore Ana's shock at being raped by Pablo. Ana never speaks of the experience to anyone, and after Pablo goes on to win the duel, he becomes an inseparable friend of Ana's father, and a specter who haunts Ana for years to come (fig. 6.7). "He was always waiting for me," Ana's voice informs us in the second-to-last sequence, framed in tilted low-angle shots to underscore her alienation. "I did not know if we were two ghosts or something else."

The Fall (1959)

In *La caída* (*The Fall*; 1959), Albertina Barden (Elsa Daniel) is a self-assured university student of French literature in 1950s Buenos Aires.

Tired of living with her overbearing aunts and having to commute to school, she decides to rent a room in a spacious house where four unruly children live with their bedridden, asthmatic mother. Even though the house is spacious, the crowded mise-en-scène, dark lighting, and extensive use of medium shots and close-ups successfully creates a claustrophobic atmosphere that mirrors Albertina's social condition as an intelligent, desiring woman trapped by patriarchy. Outside, the situation is not much different. At the local bookstore, which is crowded to the ceiling with books, Albertina meets José María Indarregui (Duilio Marzio), a male chauvinist and nationalist who tells her that she should not read Proust but rather a revisionist account of the nineteenth-century dictatorship of Juan Manuel Rosas. They begin an unlikely relationship, which Albertina eventually ends because José María does not appreciate her studies (he wants her to marry and raise his children, something she calls *la caída*, "the fall"), but also because she begins to vicariously fall in love with Lucas Foster (Lautaro Murúa), the children's absent uncle. The children adore their uncle, who visits them on occasion from his trips abroad, and when Albertina sees the many books and exotic artifacts in his bedroom, it is as if she has seen what Gonzalo Aguilar describes as "the ghost of her own father, a lover of books and the bohemian lifestyle."[27]

One day, while Albertina is at school, the mother has an asthma attack and the children, tired of hearing her scream (or so they say), lock her in her bedroom, where she dies. Albertina is traumatized because she feels complicit in what she considers a matricide. When she explains this to Lucas, who has just arrived, he responds by making romantic overtures to her, first in a nearby bar, and then in her bedroom, until the youngest boy interrupts them. Lucas lays the boy down next to Albertina and goes to sleep alone in his bedroom. Albertina, however, does not fall asleep. Instead, she packs her bags and leaves the house, aware that otherwise she will end up falling, as the title suggests, into the trap of domesticity that Lucas has set out for her so that he can continue his adventurous life uninterrupted. When the children realize that Albertina has left, they wake Lucas, who runs off after her, leaving the children, in the words of the eldest, "alone, once again."

The Hand in the Trap (1961)

In *La mano en la trampa* (*The Hand in the Trap*; 1961), the third and best film of the trilogy, Elsa Daniel plays Laura Lavigne, a high school student who is intent on solving the mystery of the freak illegitimate son

FIGURE 6.8 Laura (Elsa Daniel) confronts Inés (María Rosa Gallo) in *The Hand in the Trap* (Leopoldo Torre Nilsson, Argentina, 1961)

who lives locked up on the third floor of her opulent but decaying home in a small town on the outskirts of Buenos Aires. Laura's hope is that by solving the mystery she will be able to live in a present (late 1950s) freed from the ghosts of the family's past. To this end, she enlists the help of her working-class boyfriend, Miguel (Leonardo Fabio). In the house, there is a dumbwaiter that her mother uses to send food to the third floor. Laura gets in it, Miguel pulls the lever, and what Laura sees is not a deformed man but an elegant woman sleeping under a canopied bed. Once down, Laura's demeanor unsettles Miguel, as does her insistence that he sleep with her in payment for his help. "I don't like ghost stories," he tells her, and her own response conflates the mystery of her family's past with the mystery that sex is for her: "Ghosts must be eliminated, and tonight you've missed the opportunity to kill one." Clearly, Laura has an amorphous sensation that if she solves the mystery of the woman's identity, she will avoid repeating her fate. As Laura gets closer to uncovering the sleeping woman's identity as that of Aunt Inés (María Rosa Gallo), she also gets closer to unveiling the history of gender violence in the family's past (fig. 6.8). Despite Laura's best attempts, however, that history is repeated when in one of the final sequences Laura is raped and driven mad by Cristóbal Achával (Francisco Rabal), the very man who drove Inés mad by dumping her in favor of a virgin shortly before they were to be married.

The style in which Torre Nilsson chose to film Laura's search for clues to the family's past is realism. This is important because realism anchors the expressionist sequences inside Laura's house to a broader reality. During her search, for example, we learn that the wealth of the town's two most prominent families is tainted with Indian blood. On a bright and sunny day in the town square, the Achával family is filmed across from the Lavigne family in the most conventionally realist style, with an establishing shot followed by alternating 180-degree shots of each family. As they stand facing each other, the mayor reads the following: "Today we celebrate the one-hundred-year anniversary of the founding of this town, and it was precisely here that the noble founders had the audacity to establish the first barbed-wire fence that signified civilization in the struggle—ahem, ahem—the struggle against the Indian. Two illustrious families, the inheritors of those first leaders, maintain an honorable and noble patrimony. We are lucky to have among us their dignified descendants, the Achával family and the Lavignes, who carry on the unshakable values of tradition and lineage."

Susan Martin-Márquez has perceptively read the mayor's declaration as Torre Nilsson's way of establishing a parallel "between the enclosure of women . . . and the 'walling off' of both the working class (in the numerous scenes in which Miguel is pointedly situated outside of metal gates and chain link fences) and Argentina's native population."[28] The parallel between women and indigenous communities, in particular, is further emphasized by a confession that Cristóbal makes to Laura, which clearly links the subjugation of indigenous peoples to the systematic rape of their women: "Our old patrician families also have their eccentricities: liaisons with Indian squaws, fevers. I hope that our descendants don't pay the price for our faults." Despite Cristóbal's protestations, it is the women descendants such as Aunt Inés and Laura (not to mention the Indians) who end up paying a price that, in Laura's case, is tinged with incestuous overtones because the film hints that she may be Inés's daughter from Cristóbal, and not her niece.

Visually and aurally, the mechanisms of attraction and repulsion at play throughout the trilogy are those of the gothic horror genre: indoor spaces whose claustrophobic atmospheres simultaneously protect and asphyxiate their female dwellers; statues that seem to be half-dead and half-alive (the faun in *La casa del ángel*, the statue that covers the illicit tomb in *The Hand in the Trap*); unsettling animals (burned birds in *The Fall*, rats and cockroaches in *The Hand in the Trap*); and ghostlike characters (Pablo Aguirre in *La casa del ángel*, the absent Lucas Foster in *The Fall*, and Aunt Inés in *The Hand in the Trap*). All these elements are filmed in an expressionistic manner achieved via extreme angle shots, chiaroscuro, and the judicious use of unbalanced mise-en-scène. Narratively, however, the trilogy does not conform to the gothic horror genre's convention of following the monster's trajectory until it kills or is killed. Instead, each film follows the narrative trajectory of an intelligent and daring woman who is simultaneously repulsed by and attracted to the monster of patriarchy, and in each case, the outcome is open-ended and ambiguous. The result is that viewers are forced to think not in terms of absolute attraction or rejection vis-à-vis the monsters of patriarchy—Pablo Aguirre in *La casa del ángel*, José María Indarregui and Lucas Foster in *The Fall*, Cristóbal Achával in *The Hand in the Trap*—but to what degree the female protagonists are complicit with these monsters.

Complicity is such a central concern in the trilogy that the protagonists in *The Fall* and in *The Hand in the Trap* mention it by name. In *The Fall*, Albertina Barden tells Lucas Foster that she is complicit in the death of the children's mother, and in *The Hand in the Trap*, Laura Lavigne tells Cristóbal that she is complicit in the death of her Aunt Inés. Even in *La casa del ángel*, where complicity is not mentioned by name, there is no doubt that Ana Castro feels complicit in the dueling death of Pablo Aguirre's political enemy. In short, the female protagonists' complicity is not framed as a question of either/or (either they actively participated or they passively accepted), but rather as a question of degree. Ana Castro did not kill Pablo Aguirre's enemy, but she did give Pablo a good-luck charm. Albertina Barden did not kill the children's mother, but she did indulge the children's whims and did not heed their mother's warnings not to trust them. And Laura Lavigne did not kill Inés, but she did lead Cristóbal into Inés's bedroom, and the sight of him killed her.

By positioning viewers to more readily identify with the narrative trajectory of strong, desiring women who are partially complicit with patriarchy, the trilogy indirectly explores the degree to which we as viewers are also complicit with patriarchy's values. How emotionally invested are we, for example, in Ana's offer of help to Pablo in advance of the duel in *La casa del ángel*, even though the duel represents the values of oligarchic liberalism and the violence that sustains it? Or with Lucas's offer of matrimony to Albertina in *The Fall,* even though it would signal the end of Albertina's studies and independence? Or with Laura's decision to leave her working-class boyfriend Miguel to go after the rich Cristóbal, even though we know that Cristóbal could be her father and sees Laura only as a sex object? These open-ended outcomes invite viewers to think back on the films and ask correspondingly open-ended questions, such as how and to what degree we are patriarchy's accomplices, rather than close-ended questions, such as whether or not we are complicit with patriarchy's class and gender hierarchies.

"I hope," Torre Nilsson said in an interview while filming *The Hand in the Trap,* that in this film, "the subjective world of *La casa del ángel* and *The Fall* connects with a realist world [and that] the presence of an unconscious world is felt [as much as] the documentation of reality."[29] In effect, even though the preceding discussion has privileged the trilogy's "universal" message by highlighting the protagonists' complicity with patriarchy, the films are anchored to the concrete reality of Argentina in the 1950s, and this specific reality is as important as the psychological dynamics of the characters to an understanding of the critique that the trilogy makes of Argentina's particular brand of patriarchy. To put it bluntly, *The Hand in the Trap* crystallizes the trilogy's indictment against the social value attached to getting ahead at the expense of others, a value known as "putting the hand in the trap," or, more popularly, *viveza criolla.*

The sociological phenomenon of *viveza criolla* was so entrenched during Torre Nilsson's lifetime that several book-length studies, the best known of which is Julio Mafud's *Psicología de la viveza criolla* (Psychology of Criollo Liveliness, 1965), saw it as an essential component of Argentinean cultural identity. Edmund Stephen Urbanski summarizes Mafud's thesis as follows:

> During the immigration waves of the early twentieth century to Buenos Aires, a rift developed between the old and the new inhabitants of the metropolis. . . . It was then that the *viveza criolla* emerged as a reaction by the established criollos against the most enterprising European immigrants. The *viveza* consists of a "vivo" who uses all the faculties of his intelligence to take advantage of a foreigner by means of deception and tricks. This "vivo" . . . is an egotistical and unscrupulous man whose thwarted ambitions, economic anxiety, and concealed desires lead him time and again to all sorts of violations, yet always under the cover of well-disguised intentions. The *viveza criolla* is a degradation of human values that, thanks to its moral per-

version, is now considered, ironically, as synonymous with manhood, virility, and machismo. And like a chain reaction, the immigrants adopted the *viveza* as a way to become criollos themselves. It thus turned into a collective vice.[30]

Insofar as the women in the trilogy are intelligent and daring, and think and act for themselves, they are like the foreign upstarts who caused so much anxiety among established criollos by threatening their privileges in the early part of the twentieth century. From this perspective, Torre Nilsson's trilogy can be read as a feminist critique of a local variety of patriarchy—*viveza criolla*—that must be condoned because it justifies rape in all its forms, from the rape of individual women like Ana in *La casa del ángel* and Laura in *The Hand in the Trap*, to the economic rape represented by the stealing of indigenous lands by families like the Lavignes and the Achávals in *The Hand in the Trap*, to the systematic rape of indigenous women to which *The Hand in the Trap* obliquely refers to by way of Cristóbal's comments on miscegenation. Given the practice, then and now, of rape as a widespread strategy of gender dominance in Argentina and throughout the world, the trilogy is utterly contemporary, and those who dismiss the films as elitist or backward-looking are missing this central point.[31]

THE LEGACY OF NEOREALISM AND ART CINEMA

Because Italian Neorealism was embraced with such militancy in the Latin American film culture of the 1950s, and because some of its key practitioners who studied at Rome's Centro Sperimentale would go on to play leading roles in the New Latin American Cinema, critics over the years have privileged it over other European influences in the development of Latin American cinema in the 1950s. This is a mistake, for while it is true that many young Latin American filmmakers studied at the Centro Sperimentale in Rome, including Fernando Birri, Julio García Espinosa, Tomás Gutiérrez Alea, Néstor Almendros, and Gustavo Dahl, many more studied at the Institut des hautes études cinématographiques (IDHEC) in Paris, for example Margot Benacerraf, Ruy Guerra, Eduardo Coutinho, and Paul Leduc, and still others in London and Moscow.[32] Therefore, the full extent of Latin American cinema's recalibration away from Hollywood in the 1950s can only be fully appreciated if we consider Italian Neorealism as one among several European referents. Paulo Antonio Paranaguá compares the depth of this recalibration to the impact of Hispanic films in the early years of sound cinema:

We can compare these one hundred and fifty Latin Americans who passed through a European experience [in the late 1940s and early 1950s] with the large group of Latin Americans ... who in the late 1920s and early 1930s worked in Spanish-language production in the United States. In both cases, what we have is not [only a] cultural or ideological influence, but [also] direct, practical, sustained professional contact. . . . The post-war period also means a new [shift] towards European influence in film culture, an alternative model both for production and expression crystallized around the example of Italian Neo-realism, but in fact much broader, with strong links to French criticism, certainly, but also to British documentary and East-European film-making.[33]

That said, however, Latin American cinema of the 1950s is neither an echo of European developments (a Eurocentric bias) nor a mere prelude to the revolutionary praxis of the New Latin American cinema (a hindsight bias). As I see it, the best Latin American cinema of the 1950s reveals something much more interesting, namely, a very productive struggle to adapt a multiplicity of European ideas and practices to a studio system in crisis.

It is certainly true that thanks to new lightweight and inexpensive cameras, many filmmakers were suddenly in a position to work outside the studios, and many of these efforts drew inspiration from Italian Neorealism: *La escalinata* (The Staircase; César Enríquez, Venezuela, 1950), *Agulha no Palheiro* (Needle in a Haystack; Alex Viany, Brazil, 1953), *Rua Sem Sol* (Street Without Sun; Alex Viany, Brazil, 1954), *Rio, 40 Graus* (Rio, 100 Degrees F; Nelson Pereira dos Santos, Brazil, 1955), *O Grande Momento* (*The Grand Moment*; Roberto Santos, Brazil, 1958), *El mégano* (The Charcoal Worker; Julio García Espinosa and Tomás Gutiérrez Alea, Cuba, 1955), *Tire dié* (Throw Me a Dime; Fernando Birri, Argentina, 1958/1960), *Un vintén p'al Judas* (A Dime for Judas; Ugo Ulive, Uruguay, 1959), *Crónica cubana* (Cuban Chronicle; Ugo Ulive, Cuba, 1963), and *Raíces de piedra* (Roots of Stone; José María Arzuaga, Colombia, 1962), among others. It is also true that neorealism's modes of production have continued to be an option for Latin American filmmakers to this day, in films that are far more sophisticated than their counterparts of the 1950s: *Rodrigo D: no futuro* (*Rodrigo D: No Future*; Víctor Gaviria, Colombia, 1990), *Vendedora de rosas* (*The Rose Seller*; Víctor Gaviria, Colombia, 1999), *Mundo grúa* (*Crane World*; Pablo Trapero, Argentina, 1999), *Bolivia* (Adrián Caetano, Argentina–the Netherlands, 2001), and *Temporada de patos* (*Duck Season*; Fernando Eimbcke, Mexico, 2004). However, the more critical filmmakers of the 1950s openly acknowledged the shortcomings of their own neorealist films, from dos Santos, who called the distance between his idea for *Rio, Zona Norte* and the actual film "considerable"; to Tomás Gutiérrez Alea, who thought his tripartite film *Historias de la Revolución* (Stories of the Revolution; Cuba, 1960) was "full of good intentions but with a total lack of experience"; to Torre Nilsson, who acknowledged that his neorealist approach to documenting reality in *El secuestrador* (*The Kidnapper*; Argentina, 1958) was a partial failure.[34]

Because of these shortcomings, individual neorealist films are less important than neorealism as a set of practices that made it possible for young filmmakers who would have otherwise been unable to make films to enter the profession. In turn, neorealism as a set of practices is less important in the development of Latin American cinema in the 1950s than the dialogic cross-fertilization between neorealism and the expressiveness associated with art cinema. Ultimately, it is this dialogism, and not neorealism by itself, that inaugurated a new era in Latin American cinema defined by heterogeneous modes of production and representation. Films that exemplify this dialogic cross-fertilization include *Raíces* (*Roots*; Benito Alazraki, Mexico, 1953), *La langosta azul* (The Blue Lobster; Álvaro Cepeda Samudio and Gabriel García Márquez, Colombia, 1954), *¡Torero!* (*Bullfighter!*; Carlos Velo, Mexico, 1956), and *Macario* (Roberto Gavaldón, Mexico, 1960). But it was Buñuel and Torre Nilsson—particularly in *Los olvidados* and *The Hand in the Trap*—who made the most of the expressive and critical potential of this dialogic cross-fertilization before filmmakers of the New Latin American Cinema took the idea and ran with it in a completely new direction.

PART FOUR

New Latin American Cinema

7

New Latin American Cinema's Militant Phase

DOCUMENTARY FOUNDATIONS

The stirrings of what became the New Latin American Cinema (NLAC) can be detected in the 1950s, in the social concerns of neorealism and in the poetics of art cinema. In the early 1960s these two tendencies combined under the sign not of reform but of revolution—specifically, the 1959 Cuban Revolution. Revolution had been in the air throughout the 1950s, from Guatemala, where Jacobo Arbenz initiated a series of liberal reforms cut short by a U.S.-backed coup in 1954, to Bolivia, where a government led by the multiclass MNR party (Movimiento Revolucionario Nacionalista) changed the future direction of the country by declaring universal suffrage, nationalizing key industries, and drastically reducing the military. It was this government that created the Instituto Boliviano Cinematográfico in 1953, not to sing the praises of the nation's elite, but to produce expository social documentaries focused on the needs of the country's marginalized groups.

Tire dié (1958/1960)

Meanwhile, in Argentina, where a 1955 coup against Juan Perón further radicalized the country's political and cultural landscape, Fernando Birri, with students from the Film Institute of the Universidad del Litoral in Santa Fe, set out to film not an expository social documentary in the tradition of INCE or the Instituto Boliviano Cinematográfico, but

FIGURE 7.1 A poor boy begs for money in *Tire dié* (Throw Me a Dime; Fernando Birri, Argentina, 1958/1960)

"the first filmed social investigation of underdevelopment in Latin America."[1] Stylistically, *Tire dié* (Throw Me a Dime; 1958/1960) begins in the expository mode and very quickly shifts to neorealist representational strategies such as on-location shooting, the use of direct sound and nonprofessional actors, and a sympathetic treatment of the plight of the poor. However, the film's historical importance derives not from its chosen modes of representation, but from the now-iconic images of children as they run along the parapet of a metal bridge, begging for alms from well-to-do passengers in a moving train (fig. 7.1). Such powerfully denunciatory images of social inequality were unprecedented in Latin American cinema, and it is this new use of the medium to condemn social inequality that makes *Tire dié* an important precursor of the NLAC.[2]

Araya (1959)

A lesser-known precursor of the NLAC is *¡Que viva México!* (Sergei Eisenstein, Mexico–United States, 1931). The influence is not direct but rhizomatic, in the sense that Eisenstein's film established themes and forms that were effectively suppressed by the commercial exigencies of

FIGURE 7.2   A salt worker in *Araya* (Margot Benacerraf, Venezuela, 1959)

studio cinema until the 1960s, when conditions were once again ripe for the emergence of a second avant-garde. These conditions included the political impact of recent revolutions; a vibrant alternative cinematic culture diffused through film clubs, magazines, and universities; and the search for an autochthonous culture through experimental themes and forms.

The first film of the NLAC to draw on Eisenstein's legacy was Margot Benacerraf's *Araya* (Venezuela, 1959), which is linked to *¡Que viva México!* in at least two ways: stylistically, in its use of social types set against highly stylized landscapes, and narratively, in its use of a prologue, a central narrative, and an epilogue, each representing a distinct mode of production filmed in different styles. The prologue tells, in an expository mode of representation, of the origins of Araya as a salt harvesting port founded by the Spanish in 1630, and the importance of salt for the expanding Spanish empire. The central narrative documents in great detail the artisanal harvesting and processing of salt and the domestic life that revolves around it (fig. 7.2). Hauntingly poetic shots of salt pyramids, the seashore, and a sun-bleached cemetery punctuate a routine that has seen little change in more than three hundred years. Then suddenly, a jump cut—so abrupt that it can be read as the formal equivalent of the ideological breaks that revolutions embody—takes us to an epilogue shot in the rudimentary style of newsreels, showing the arrival in Araya of new salt-processing industrial machines that announce the end of artisanal harvesting as a way of life. Remarkably, the film is free of any nostalgia for the way of life that is ending, and free also of any celebration of new technology as a panacea. Instead, *Araya* leaves viewers with a single question: how will Arayans respond to a new reality that is so radically different from anything they have known before? It is a question contemporary Venezuelan audiences could very well have asked themselves, given the end of that country's military dictatorship in 1958, but also Latin American audiences everywhere, if we consider the enormous impact that the Cuban Revolution had on the region's political economy.

Araya left a deep mark on a young Glauber Rocha when he saw it as a journalist in Cannes in 1959. As Julianne Burton-Carvajal explains:

> [Rocha] interviewed [Benacerraf] and kept in subsequent touch with her until his death in the early 1980s because he was so profoundly impacted, personally and aesthetically, by the example of what she had accomplished in such independent and artisanal fashion. . . . Like *Araya*, Rocha's opera prima [*Barravento* (The Turning Wind; Brazil, 1962)] emphasizes the natural setting through a similar virtuosity of camera angles, movements, and montage. In *Barravento*'s intricate parable, it is not the machine but the ambiguous promise of the remote city that rends the cohesive fabric of tradition in this Edenic, predominantly Afro-Brazilian fishing community. Rocha's film brings to the foreground narratively and visually what Benacerraf's relegated to one level of her multi-leveled soundtrack: music, dance, religious ritual, patterns of belief and practices of cultural expression.[3]

A year after *Barravento,* Rocha applied to *Black God, White Devil* (Brazil, 1963) another lesson learned in *Araya*: how to represent historical discontinuity through an abrupt shift in focus and tone. In *Araya*, this happens once, via the jump cut and shift of registers that sets the epilogue apart from the film's main narrative, while in *Black God, White Devil* it happens three times—as it also does in *The Hour of the Furnaces* (Fernando Solanas and Octavio Getino, Argentina, 1968) and in *Lucía* (Humberto Solás, Cuba, 1968), two other films I discuss in this chapter—all of which suggests a thread of continuity between the first and second avant-gardes in Latin American cinema, characterized by the use of dialectical metanarratives that Sergei Eisenstein first developed and put into practice in *¡Que viva México!*

Santiago Álvarez

The New Latin American Cinema's initial militancy and creative innovation developed within a global context framed primarily as a Manichaean struggle between socialism, led by the Soviet Union, and capitalism, led by the United States. In this context, the Cuban Revolution represented for many Latin Americans a model for the region to liberate itself from the physical and cultural poverty engendered by North American imperialism. The feeling, moreover, was that this liberation was at hand, for if a small country like Cuba, dependent as it had been on U.S. capital, could liberate itself through a popular revolution and go on to eliminate illiteracy and drastically reduce poverty in five years, then what could larger and far richer countries such as Argentina and Brazil not accomplish? The sudden and by all accounts impressive transformation of Cuban society during the 1960s had a profound impact on how Latin American filmmakers saw their profession. Most rethought their roles, for if society was in effect in the throes or on the cusp of radical transformation, as in Cuba, then their function should be to document this transformation in film and/or to use film to help bring about the transformation. Not surprisingly, as Zuzana Pick points out, Latin American filmmakers suddenly saw the documentary with new eyes, not just as a witness to reality, but as a tool to analyze and in principle transform that reality.[4]

Santiago Álvarez, for example, developed a unique montage technique for the Cuban Film Institute's weekly newsreels, whereby he rediscovered the principles of montage that had been originally developed by the likes of Sergei Eisenstein, Lev Kuleshov, and Dziga Vertov in the 1920s (fig. 7.3). The result, which could have easily been formulaic given the genre (newsreels) and the form (agitprop) with which Álvarez chose to work, is instead a corpus of films that together constitute one of Latin America's most important contributions to the history of documentary cinema. John Mraz explains how Álvarez's appropriation and recontextualization of still photos and music, timidly used in *Muerte al invasor* (*Death to the Invader*; 1961) and *Ciclón* (Hurricane; 1963), achieve full expressiveness and force in *Now!* (1965), *Cerro Pelado* (Barren Hill; 1966), *Hanoi, martes 13* (Hanoi, Tuesday the 13th; 1967), *Hasta la victoria siempre* (Ever Onward to Victory; 1967), and *79 primaveras* (*79 Springs*; 1969): "By using U.S. photos in his dramatic montages, [Álvarez] consciously 'reappropriated' images produced under imperialism, transforming their meaning and 'restoring

FIGURE 7.3   Superimposed images in *Now!* (Santiago Álvarez, Cuba, 1965)

their truth' by inserting them into a revolutionary cinematic context. Álvarez performed a similar operation with music, using a variety of strategies—from the mocking association of the U.S. television themes with counterrevolutionaries to the appropriation of rock and roll to express the energy and international solidarity unleashed by the struggle against imperialism both inside and beyond U.S. borders."[5]

EPIC PROJECTIONS

The formal and thematic innovations initiated by Álvarez made their way into *The Hour of the Furnaces* (Fernando Solanas and Octavio Getino, Argentina, 1968), an agitprop documentary of epic proportions that has been rightly considered "the paradigm of activist revolutionary cinema."[6] This film, along with two others of equally epic proportions whose protagonists are no longer individual but collective, are exemplary of the militant phase of the New Latin American Cinema. The first is the aforementioned *Black God, White Devil*, a film that announced, more than any other, that a new cinema was afoot in Latin America and indeed the world. The other is *La batalla de Chile* (*The Battle of Chile*; Patricio Guzmán, Chile-Cuba, 1975–79), a film that in many ways marks the end of the NLAC's militant phase.

FIGURE 7.4   Rosa (Yoná Magalhães) isolated from her husband Manuel (Geraldo Del Rey) by the *beato* Sebastião (Lidio Silva) in *Black God, White Devil* (Glauber Rocha, Brazil, 1963)

Black God, White Devil (1963)

Deus e o Diabo na Terra do Sol (*Black God, White Devil*; Glauber Rocha, Brazil, 1963) is an extraordinary film in many ways, from the richly layered symbolism of its guiding metaphor of the *sertão* as complementary opposite to the sea, to the Brechtian and highly expressive acting by Othon Bastos as Corisco, to its creative appropriation and transformation of elements of spaghetti Westerns and samurai films, to its construction of a dialectical temporality and discontinuous space. Broadly speaking, the film interprets the history of the *sertão* through the lives of Manuel (Geraldo Del Rey) and his wife, Rosa (Yoná Magalhães), as they go from being (a) poor peasants and hired hands, to (b) followers of the messianic leader Sebastião (Lidio Silva), to (c) followers of the revolutionary bandit Corisco, and finally to (d) an uncertain future where it is not even clear whether Manuel and Rosa will continue to be together after the mercenary Antonio das Mortes (Maurício do Valle) has killed Corisco (figs. 7.4, 7.5).

In this journey across the *sertão*, they also journey across different periods in Brazilian history. As Ivana Bentes has noted, the narrative covers "three important cycles of the Northeast: the *coronelismo* (a system

FIGURE 7.5 Antonio das Mortes (Maurício do Valle) kills a willing Corisco (Othon Bastos) in front of Corisco's pleading wife Dadá (Sonia Dos Humildes) in *Black God, White Devil*

in which large extensions of land are concentrated in the hands of a few powerful owners, the *coronéis*); the *beatismo* (the belief in saints, pious men—beatos—who led messianic movements); and the cycle of the *cangaço* (social banditry that flourished in the *sertão* from 1870 to 1940)."[7]

In the film, these cycles are narratively connected not by seamless transitions, as in classical cinema, but rather by violent transitions in the tradition of Marxist historiography. Indeed, like Eisenstein's *¡Que viva México!*, *Black God, White Devil* explores Brazilian history through a series of discrete narratives made intelligible by their dialectical relationship to one another (fig. 7.6). In this dialectical metanarrative, *coronelismo* serves as an original thesis, the episodes with Sebastião and Corisco as a prolonged antithesis, and the suggested utopia at the end as a potential synthesis. These narratives are, in turn, connected by transition sequences defined by their violence. In the first transition, between *coronelismo* and *beatismo*, Manuel brutally murders the *coronel* with his machete. In the second transition, between *beatismo* and the *cangaço*, Rosa murders Sebastião with a knife, and this is followed by the mass shooting by Antonio das Mortes of the *beato*'s followers. In the third transition, between the *cangaço* and the final sequence, Antonio das Mortes repeatedly shoots Corisco.

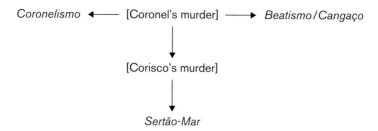

FIGURE 7.6 Dialectical structure of *Black God, White Devil*

Violence has one of two functions in the film: either it is a disruptive force that leads from one form of exploitation to another, as in the first two transitions, or it has the potential to be not merely disruptive but also liberatory, as in the transition to the film's closing sequence, a series of dynamic shots that track Rosa and Manuel as they frantically run away from Antonio das Mortes, followed, after an abrupt jump cut, by a set of aerial shots of the sea, which functions as a metaphor for the limitless possibilities that have suddenly opened up for Manuel to chart his own course. The end of the film is therefore not a closed synthesis, as in socialist realism, but rather an open call for spectators to chart their own path to liberation free of the traps of religious and political populism represented by the figures of Sebastião and Corisco, respectively. Moreover, because at one point in the closing sequence Rosa and Manuel are separated, the film suggests that this new path to liberation must also include liberation from institutions such as marriage and the traditional gender roles it mandates.

In his 1965 manifesto "Aesthetics of Hunger," Rocha theorized the differences between exploitative and liberatory violence by distinguishing between reactionary and revolutionary violence, and calling the latter "the most noble cultural manifestation of hunger." Cinema Novo, he writes,

> shows that the normal behavior of the starving is violence; and the violence of the starving is not primitive. . . . From Cinema Novo it should be learned that an esthetic of violence, before being primitive, is revolutionary. It is the initial moment when the colonizer becomes aware of the colonized. Only when confronted with violence does the colonizer understand, through horror, the strength of the culture he exploits. As long as they do not take up arms, the colonized remain slaves; a first policeman had to die for the French to become aware of the Algerians.[8]

For Rocha, then, horror marks the difference between reactionary violence and revolutionary violence: reactionary violence causes the colonizer

FIGURE 7.7   Rosa kills a horrified Sebastião in *Black God, White Devil*

to feel joy and a sense of self-affirmation, while revolutionary violence causes that same colonizer to feel horror. For example, when Manuel turns against his exploitative coronel boss, the look in the coronel's face is that of horror: not just the horror of facing death, but more important, the incredulous horror of a man who suddenly realizes the strength of those he has been exploiting with impunity. The same may be said of Sebastião's horror when Rosa approaches him, dagger in hand, with the obvious intent of killing him (fig. 7.7). The horror in his face marks him as a colonizer and exploiter in the same vein as the coronel. In the case of the mass murder of Sebastião's followers, by contrast, there is no horror in Antonio das Mortes's face, a fact that underscores the victims' position as colonized and marks das Mortes's violence as reactionary.

Another way the film distinguishes between revolutionary and reactionary violence is through an editing that slows down time and encloses spaces during periods of reactionary violence, while accelerating time and exploding spaces during moments of potentially revolutionary violence. An example of reactionary violence linked to enclosed space and slow-moving time comes early in the film, when Manuel and Rosa are grating tapioca to prepare flour. Throughout the sequence, Rocha lets the camera stand still and record in *cinéma vérité* style the repetitiveness of this chore, forcing the viewer to take in the enclosed space and the temporal stagnation associated with the feudal system of *coronelismo*. Later, when Manuel is under the spell of Sebastião, the slowness of time and the compression of space are taken even further in a purposely monotonous sequence where Manuel performs a Sisyphean kind of *via crucis* with a huge stone over his head, under the watchful eye of Sebastião. Finally, under Corisco, time comes to a standstill when Manuel, Rosa, Corisco, and Corisco's wife Dadá (Sonia Dos Humildes) pause their journey across the *sertão* and begin a series of dialogues, monologues, and silent exchanges within an inexplicably limited space framed by Corisco's immobile followers on the left and the right, and a barely visible horizon on the upper edge of the frame. In all these examples, the slow movement of time and the closing off of space is linked to reactionary violence and to history at a standstill that slows the progress of revolutionary liberation or brings it to a halt.

By contrast, when violence is potentially revolutionary, time rushes forward and space seems to explode. For example, when Manuel kills his coronel boss, the camera is suddenly freed from the confines of classical camera positioning (i.e., establishing and over-the-shoulder shots) and instead takes flight with Manuel, sometimes alongside him, sometimes behind him, sometimes ahead of him, but always in feverish motion. Likewise, after Rosa kills Sebastião, the editing favors jump cuts while the music's tempo becomes much more accelerated than during the sequences that precede it. Finally, after Antonio das Mortes kills Corisco, the camera becomes so free from the confines of any previous use in the film that it literally takes off from the ground and follows Manuel and Rosa as they escape Antonio das Mortes, and then only Manuel after Rosa trips and falls to the ground, all the while the soundtrack playing a chorus singing that "the *sertão* will become the sea."

The music's celebratory tone in this last sequence, just before the final jump cut to the sea, seals a reading of this last act of violence as full of liberatory potential, a reading that stands in sharp contrast to Sebastião's populist claims that someday "the *sertão* will become the sea and the sea will become the *sertão*," which he used to justify pillage and murder. By positioning viewers in the same space as that occupied by Manuel, a place of having overcome feudal bondage, messianism, and social banditry, and confronted with a sea devoid of any physical or mental chains that might take their place, Rocha in effect turns the open sea into a metaphor for the boundless possibilities of a national popular culture freed from religious and political populism.[9] In short, a veritable clarion call for viewers to liberate themselves from present-day false prophets and their facile promises.

The Hour of the Furnaces (1968)

By contrast, *La hora de los hornos* (*The Hour of the Furnaces*; Fernando Solanas and Octavio Getino, Argentina, 1968) is far from open in its reading of the contemporary situation in Argentina, and in fact assumes that a Cuban-style socialist revolution is inevitable. In keeping with this assumption, the film—parts of which were regularly used between 1969 and 1973 as agitprop at clandestine meetings of radicalized workers' unions and their sympathizers—organizes its materialist interpretation of Argentina's history into three parts that are conceived as privileged moments within a dialectical metanarrative spanning several centuries and glued together by violence.

The title of the film comes from the epigraph Che Guevara used to open what became one of his last political statements, the "Message to the Tricontinental," in 1967.[10] The author of the epigraph is José Martí, Cuba's nineteenth-century national hero.[11] This double reference, to a revolutionary who died fighting Spanish colonialism and a revolutionary who had just died fighting neocolonialism, cues the spectator to think of the parallels between contemporary liberation struggles and Latin American wars of independence in the nineteenth century. To get around the differences between these earlier liberation movements and those of the 1960s (the political and economic discourses of Simón Bolívar and José Martí were in the main liberal, whereas the film constructs a discourse that identifies Peronism with socialism), the film successfully highlights their shared anti-imperialism and a voluntarist virility that masks the film's blind spots regarding gender and sexuality. These limitations, however, should not blind us to the film's greatest strength: the clear articulation of a revolutionary discourse through an equally revolutionary means of representation.

For example, the film presents and defines, through intertitles, omniscient narrators and documentary material, terms, and concepts such as "imperialism," "the system," "neocolonialism," "patriotism," "nationalism," "class struggle," "oligarchy," "the bourgeoisie," "proletariat," "liberation," "domination," "power," "ideology," "revolution," "dehumanization," "dependency," "racism," "mass media," "intellectuals," "artists," "the people," "the Third World," "internationalism," "tricon-

FIGURE 7.8 Didactic intertitle in *The Hour of the Furnaces* (Fernando Solanas and Octavio Getino, Argentina, 1968)

tinental brotherhood," "solidarity," "commitment," "revolution," "reformism," "coexistence," "resistance," "the New Man," "film-act," "national populism," "clandestinity," "syndicalism," "developmentalism," "neocolonial" versus "anticolonial" armed forces, "*toma de conciencia*," "impunity," and, above all, "violence" in various forms: political, systemic, neocolonial, cultural, and revolutionary (fig. 7.8).

Robert Stam has perceptively noted that

> much of *La hora*'s persuasive power derives from its ability to render ideas visual. Abstract concepts are given clear and accessible form. The sociological abstraction "oligarchy" is characterized by shots of the "fifty families" that monopolize much of Argentina's wealth. "Here they are . . . " says the text; the "oligarchy" comes into focus as the actual faces of real people, recognizable and accountable. "Class society" becomes the image ("quoted" from Birri's *Tire dié*) of desperate child beggars running alongside trains in hopes of a few pennies from blasé passengers. "Systemic violence" is rendered by images of the state's apparatus of repression—prisons, armored trucks, bombers.[12]

Another good example of this strategy is when a photomontage is effectively used to visually ground the following off-camera narration of neocolonialism:

> The independence of the Latin American peoples was betrayed in its origins. The betrayal was carried out by the exporting elites of the port-cities. . . . England, since then, would substitute for Spain in the dominion of almost all the continent. Its lenders secured what its armies did not achieve. In exchange for wool, we received fabrics; in exchange for meat and leather, grand pianos. The agro-exporting bourgeoisie became the agrarian appendix of European industry. For the first time in the history of Latin America there began to be applied a new form of dominion: the exportation of colonial business through the native bourgeoisie. Thus was born neocolonialism.

Text in the form of intertitles or quotations from the likes of Franz Fanon, Jean-Paul Sartre, Ernesto "Che" Guevara, and José de San Martín also guide viewers' readings of the film's visuals, while intertitles make explicit the conceptualization of part 1 of the film as twelve didactic lessons: (1) history, (2) the country, (3) systemic violence, (4) the port-city, (5) the oligarchy, (6) the system, (7) political violence, (8) dependency, (9) cultural violence, (10) the models, (11) ideological war, and (12) the option.

The Hour of the Furnaces is structured in three parts that are dialectically related to one another. Part 1 of the film ("Neocolonialism and Violence") corresponds to a thesis equated with the current status quo; part 2 ("Act of Liberation") to a prolonged antithesis of Peronist struggle; and part 3 ("Violence and Liberation") to a soon-to-be-achieved synthesis. The film, moreover, rearticulates popular violence not as something negative, to be actively suppressed by the state, but rather as a symptom of the changes in modes of production, and also as a tool to be actively wielded against the oppressively violent "system" of institutionalized fear and terror. The film achieves the positive rearticulation of popular violence in three steps, each one corresponding to a part in the film. Part 1 defines different kinds of violence under the current system, and introduces the possibility of a counterviolence that will liberate the masses of their oppressors; part 2 elaborates a historical and theoretical justification for that counterviolence; and part 3 uses techniques from Augusto Boal's theater of the oppressed to encourage viewers to actively transform not just their worldview but their reality as well.

Part 1: Neocolonialism and Violence

Part 1 describes neocolonial violence as having several manifestations: daily violence (violence that is "constant, meticulous, systemic"); neocolonial violence (violence that does not have to be acted out because by being potential it is already effective); political violence (the farce that is a system where out of the last twenty governments, seventeen have come to power as a result of fraudulent elections or coups); cultural violence (the widespread illiteracy that effectively substitutes for colonial policing); sublimated violence (disorienting forms that bear the load that should correspond to the dominant classes, for example God, fatality, destiny, and immortality); and ideological violence (through a mass media that alienates and thus depoliticizes potential enemies of the system). Finally, we are told in an intertitle that under neocolonialism,

VIOLENCE
CRIME
DESTRUCTION
BECOME
PEACE
ORDER
NORMALITY

At this point a rapid-fire visual montage of neocolonial violence not only in Argentina but also in Africa, Vietnam, and even the United States is superimposed with the frivolous laughter of a woman. The contrast between the monstrosity of the images and the frivolity of the audio track is then driven home by the intertitle MONSTROSITY DRESSES ITSELF UP AS BEAUTY, which effectively links physical violence to the neocolonial system's Orwellian doublespeak. The climax of part 1, a call for inventing a new vocabulary, a new theory, and a new aesthetic, becomes in this context a call for revolution, even if it leads to certain death. The closing sequence, with a still of the murdered Che lying in state and the following voice-over narration of Che's own words, is set up as an example of how to become that invention, the New Man theorized by Che himself: "What is the only option left open for the American native? To choose with his rebellion his own life and his own death. When he inserts himself in the struggle for liberation, death ceases to be the final state. It becomes a liberating act. A conquest. The man who chooses his death is choosing also a life. He is already life and liberation itself."

The film cuts to an extreme close-up of Che's face in death, and the narrator adds, "In his rebellion, the Latin American recuperates his existence" (fig. 7.9). The shot is held for three minutes (longer in some versions), to the accompaniment of the same Afro-Cuban music that opened the film, a viscerally effective move that elicits the viewer's tacit approval of violence as the only viable act of liberation. It will be up to part 2 to develop the necessary historical and theoretical justification

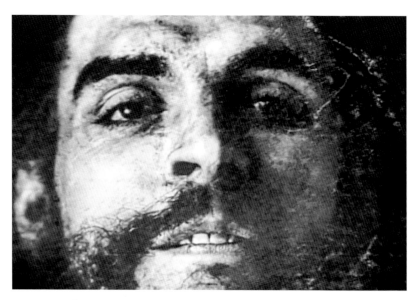

FIGURE 7.9   Freeze-frame of a dead Che Guevara in *The Hour of the Furnaces*

for this conclusion, and up to part 3 to give more examples (besides Che's) on how to proceed.

Part 2: Act of Liberation

Part 2 begins very much like part 1, with an agitprop montage of intertitles, shots, stills, and narration over the pulsating rhythm of an Afro-Cuban song. Two of the opening intertitles explicitly establish the main ideas of this part: that liberation is achieved through revolutionary violence, and that revolutionary violence at the national level cannot succeed unless it is linked to revolution at the international level:

REVOLUTIONARY VIOLENCE WILL PUT AN END TO THE CRIMES OF IMPERIALISM

IMPERIALISM IS AN INTERNATIONAL SYSTEM AND IT MUST BE DEFEATED IN AN INTERNATIONAL BATTLE

THE THIRD WORLD

AFRICA
LATIN AMERICA
ASIA

Despite this internationalism, part 2 concentrates on the specific case of Argentina, the idea being that the road to liberation goes through the nation, and that the nation, defined in the case of Argentina as incarnated in the Peronists, is the most effective conduit for confronting neocolonialism.

Part 2 is divided into two subparts. The first, "Chronicle of Peronism (1945–1955)," focuses on Peronism between 1945, when Juan Perón first gave official voice to the Argentinean proletariat, and 1955, when he was ousted by a reactionary coup. This period is presented as a partial antithesis to neocolonialism because Perón failed to secure and consolidate his achievements against the constant attempts by the opposition to undermine and overthrow him. The second subpart, "Chronicle of Resistance (1955–1966)," documents the strategies that the now-in-opposition Peronists assumed after the coup. One by one the strategies adopted by the different groups that had supported Perón are reviewed: the spontaneous and clandestine modus operandi of the labor unions, the self-critique of sympathetic middle-class intellectuals, the ideological realignment of the armed forces, the radicalization of the student movement, the workers' occupation of factories throughout the 1960s. After this survey, the filmmakers conclude with shots of workers being ejected from occupied factories and the following voice-over: "Spontaneous resistance reaches today a critical moment. If until yesterday labor unions were the axis of resistance, they have today lost political effectiveness. As instruments of revolutionary struggle, they have reached the limit of their possibilities. If the initiative of the masses is not channeled in a revolutionary manner, everything stays at the level of response: resistance, self-defense. The initiative is only in the hands of the enemy."

The narration continues with an overview of the increase in U.S. military interventions in Latin America since the Cuban Revolution, and concludes: "Power rests only with he who has weapons, or with he who is set on taking hold of them. The language of arms is today the most effective political language. Shouldn't the people prepare itself for its use? Will this not mean a long and painful war? Are there other alternatives for liberation?" These were not rhetorical questions asked to an undifferentiated audience, but rather questions regarding strategy aimed at Peronists who had tried different means of nonviolent resistance without success, under the full weight of the state's repressive apparatus.

Part 3: Violence and Liberation

The answer to these questions comes in the third and final part of the film, with the call for violent insurrection defined as legitimate (because it is in self-defense), and even sanctioned by Christianity, as when the filmmakers quote from the liberation theology of Father Juan Carlos Saparodi:

> The issue of violence is but an issue of truth and sincerity. The value of armed violence consists in its efficacy in unmasking the truth. Only hypocrites oppose the violence of the oppressed. One cannot exploit man without hating man. Against this devastating force of hatred there is no other force capable of counteracting it but the violence of love. The violent love of combatants is in essence a sublime form of love for truth. The love of Jesus Christ led him to the cross. He was killed because he made the people rebel.

To this unequivocal nature of the film's conclusions regarding violence and liberation, Paulo Antonio Paranaguá has countered that its open structure "relativizes the contentiousness of its discourse."[13] The following excerpt from the concluding narration supports this reading of the film: "*Compañeros*, this is an unfinished film and it is so for different reasons. One of them, because many testimonials, experiences, or letters we thought of including in this film-act could not be incorporated for reasons too long to enumerate. Another reason, the fundamental one, is that the topic that we have developed, violence and liberation, is historically an open topic. A topic that cannot have an ending. Its development depends on none other than you."

In the end, however, the film's overall Manichaeism betrays the filmmakers' concluding remarks, and the best one can do to account for this contradiction is to note, as Robert Stam does, that "*La hora* is brilliant in its critique. And history has not shown its authors to be totally failed prophets. . . . The film's indictment of neocolonialism remains shatteringly relevant. . . . The film also accurately points up the ruling class potentiality for violent repression. . . . It respects the people by offering quality, proposing a cinema which is simultaneously a tool for consciousness-raising, an instrument for analysis, and a catalyst for action."[14]

Whether or not one agrees with the kind of violent action the film proposes, there is no denying the validity of the questions and issues it raises, even today.

The Battle of Chile (1975–79)

The last great film of the NLAC's militant period is *La batalla de Chile* (*The Battle of Chile*; Patricio Guzmán, Chile-Cuba, 1975–79), a documentary that analyzes the six months leading up to the 1973 coup against Salvador Allende. It does so from three distinct perspectives: that of the bourgeoisie, of Allende's Unidad Popular (UP), and of the workers who supported Allende but were not necessarily wedded to any one of the political parties that made up Unidad Popular. Each of the film's three parts focuses on one of these perspectives, as their titles suggest: "La insurrección de la burguesía" (The Insurrection of the Bourgeoisie, 1975), "El golpe de estado" (The Coup d'État, 1976), and "Poder popular" (Popular Power, 1979). This organization was not preplanned; it emerged over several years of exhaustive editing work in Cuba in the 1970s. Following the coup, Guzmán and the filmed material made it safely to Paris, where he met and accepted an offer from Alfredo Guevara, the head of Cuba's Film Institute, to edit the film in Havana. Julio García Espinosa, who helped in the editing, remembers the experience "as being part of an extraordinary creative fever. Locked up in that editing room, Patricio [Guzmán], Pedro Chaskel, and I were confronted with a material that defied us to give it coherence."[15] The coherence they found, both structurally and ideologically, was rooted in the particular experience of exile in Cuba:[16] structurally, because the film's organization in three parts remits the viewer to *Lucía*, which García Espinosa cowrote, and to *The Hour of the Furnaces*, which was widely screened and discussed in Cuba;[17] and ideologically, because being in Cuba gave Guzmán the uniquely combative perspective of having lost a political and economic battle,[18] but not the ideological war for Chileans' hearts and minds.[19]

"The Insurrection of the Bourgeoisie" famously begins with a disorienting soundtrack of jets, and no visuals. The subsequent images of the bombing of the presidential palace suddenly place us in the position occupied by Allende supporters after the coup: in the dark, and on the receiving end of rightist violence. This positioning of the spectator is maintained in parts 1 and 2, both of which Guzmán succinctly summarized in an interview with Julianne Burton-Carvajal:

> Part 1, "The Insurrection of the Bourgeoisie," tries to shed light on a fundamental aspect of the problem in Chile: the mass uprising of the middle and upper sectors of the population, in collaboration with foreign interests, and the actions taken by the government and by the left as a whole to curb this right-wing insurrectionary escalation.
>
> The primary contradiction in the first film is thus between fascism/imperialism/bourgeoisie on the one hand and the working masses on the other. The masses are only present in part 1 as a point of reference, since the major focus of this segment is to demonstrate how the right, through its use of the

mass media, and financed by imperialist interests, succeeded in mobilizing the middle class "masses," thus preparing the way for the coup d'etat. This is, of course, the most unique aspect of the Chilean coup: the right succeeded in arousing massive resistance among all sectors of the bourgeoisie and in the armed forces, as well as among one sector of the proletariat, the copper miners of El Teniente mine.

Part 2, "The Coup d'État" . . . continues to show the mass agitation of the bourgeoisie in opposition to the democratic popular forces, but it adds a third dimension: the diverse and competing strategies that existed within the various groups on the left. This is why the second part is much more difficult than the first. Our decision to maintain the same dialectical style of narration (the voice-over narrator provides only the most essential background information; the bulk of the analysis is given directly by those who participated in the events the film records) means that the viewers have to grasp this triple contradiction for themselves.[20]

In part 3, "Popular Power," the perspective shifts to position viewers not on the receiving end of the opposition's violence, but in the safe space occupied by workers as they created popular cooperatives free from state guidance or right-wing violence. Again, Guzmán provides a good summary of this "simplest of the three" parts:

Part 3, "Popular Power" . . . is a very affectionate evocation of the mass organizations during the Popular Unity government, and in particular during 1973. These were very practical organizations that answered concrete needs like how to get food and supplies to the population, how to get a greater yield from a plot of land, how to organize a people's supply store [almacén popular], how to set up a production committee in the factory.

There were many times during the struggle in Chile that the popular forces would distance themselves temporarily from the action to discuss the nature of the socialist state that was then in the early stages of construction. This was a very calm and measured progress, very touching at times. This theoretical development of the workers and peasants—always based on their practical experience—was extremely impressive. The footage we have of these occasions is the most convincing proof of the enormous level of awareness among the Chilean people. Yet if we had inserted these sequences along with the rest of the footage, such discussions would have appeared unreal in the midst of pre–civil war conditions. So, as we edited the first and second parts of the film, we set aside all these sequences that depicted the incipient stages of people's power in Chile for a third segment, which would complement but be different from the first two.[21]

While not as dramatic as part 1 or part 2, this third part narratively completes the film as the potential future synthesis of an ongoing dialectical historical process. By this I mean that even though part 3 represents something that happened before the coup, the fact that Guzmán and Chaskel placed it separately at the end of the film effectively re-imagines the coup as a temporary setback in a historical dialectic where the synthesis is not some theoretical utopia, but a very concrete stateless socialism practiced by the workers' self-governing *cordones industriales*. This strategic move transforms what would have been a simpler historical record, albeit an excellent one, into a call for future generations to pick up where the *cordones* left off. Clearly, then, the film is not only a testimony. It is also an aesthetic object whose impact is, as Ana M. López notes, "determined by the fictive strategies that are invoked to represent what we necessarily recognize as important documentary footage of crucial historical events." "The most important of these strategies," she argues, is

> Guzmán's extensive use of sequence shots. Rather than depend on montage (like *The Hour of the Furnaces* and, in fact, most political documentaries) to organize and construct an a posteriori reading of the social and political events of this particular moment in Chilean history, the filmmakers set out to film in long takes whenever possible. . . . This explicit aesthetic decision required the complex orchestration of the filming process. Guzmán often served as the peripheral eyes of the cameraman Jorge Müller, surveying the action, anticipating what was about to happen, and instructing him [here quoting Guzmán] "to make certain movements [pans, tilts, manual cranes] that are much more readily identified with fictional than with documentary filmmaking."[22]

There are several instances of this strategy at work. In part 1, for example, Guzmán asks a working-class woman enjoying a picnic with her family in a public park, "What do you think that will happen in the future?" Her answer is filmed in close-up: "We'll have to keep fighting a lot more than we have, *compañero*. . . . What can I tell you about Frei [the last president]? Under him I had a hut that was falling apart. There was water everywhere, and my four children were sick with pneumonia. I asked for help here and there, and nobody listened to my pleas. In contrast, I now get help wherever I go, and thanks to my president [Allende], I have a nice home. I don't have any luxuries, but I have not gone hungry."

Jorge Müller pulls back from the woman slowly enough and long enough for viewers to be able to clearly see the pin of a hammer and sickle that she wears on her shirt (fig. 7.10). Thus, as Jorge Ruffinelli notes, "her position as a militant in the Communist Party reveals the ideological inclination of her answer and, without taking away from its veracity, places it in perspective."[23] It is a perspective, one might add, with which the viewer

FIGURE 7.10 A working-class woman wearing a hammer-and-sickle pin in *The Battle of Chile* (Patricio Guzmán, Chile-Cuba, 1975–79)

easily identifies because of the woman's easygoing manner, the sincerity of her voice, and the contagious optimism of her story.

When Müller repeats a similar pullback of the camera later in the film, in the well-appointed apartment of a middle-class family that opposes Allende, the results are very different. The film crew was able to enter the apartment posing as reporters for one of the opposition's television channels. Inside, a woman responds enthusiastically yet superficially to Guzmán's question regarding that day's municipal elections (fig. 7.11). The camera leaves her in order to record the objects in the apartment: a cigarette holder that the woman's adolescent son picks up, a wall unit filled with curios, and a panoramic view of the city from the living room window. Instead of helping us feel closer to the interviewee, as happened in the previous example, the camera's slow and lengthy take in this case hinders the development of any real sympathy by establishing a metonymic connection between the apartment's superfluous objects and the equally superfluous political position of their owners.

At other times, images gain significance not so much through cinematography as through the raw intensity and directness of what they reveal, as when a Fascist woman practically jumps in front of the camera and screams at the top of her lungs: "This is a corrupt and degenerate government, sir! Degenerate and corrupt! Unclean! Dirty Communists, they all have to leave Chile! On May 21 we will have, thanks be

FIGURE 7.11 A middle-class woman interviewed inside her apartment in *The Battle of Chile*

to God, the cleanest and most beautiful government that we have ever known, winning with democracy and kicking out these communists, rotten Marxists. . . . Let them all be damned!"

This kind of unmediated documentation reaches eerie proportions in part 2 during the funeral of Allende's aide-de-camp, Arturo Araya. Jacqueline Mouesca describes the sequence as "difficult to forget": "The camera pans to show those present, [including] the faces of those in the military whose eyes show the sign of treason. The director was not aware that he was gathering at that moment, and in those images, testimonial proof of the coup that was already under way, [or that] he had recorded the military officials [including Pinochet] with their faces uncovered, without their masks on."[24]

From a standpoint of dramatic effectiveness, *The Battle of Chile* could have ended here, just as it could have ended with the sequence that closes part 1, where the Argentinean cinematographer Leonardo Henrichsen films his own death at the hands of the military. The film reaches full significance, however, with part 3, where Guzmán points not only to the tensions within the Left, but also to the promise of the workers' ability to overcome these tensions by valuing lived experience over abstract political theory or political directives from above, as evidenced in this dialogue between a worker and his interviewer:

> *Interviewer:* You don't support the Popular Front. Who do you support?
> *Worker:* I support the workers.

Interviewer: And who do the workers in this factory support?

Worker: The Popular Front.

Interviewer: Did you [plural] work during the strike?

Worker: Of course.

Interviewer: Why?

Worker: Because we are conscious of being workers.

Interviewer: And did you [singular] show up to work during the strike?

Worker: Yes.

Interviewer: Does this mean that you support the Popular Front?

Worker: It means I support the workers.

This exchange, which on the surface sounds like a Cantinflas routine, in fact reveals how much the struggle for power in Chile had shifted to popular organizations such as *cordones industriales,* which took power in their own hands and were not beholden to the interests of political parties or workers' unions. "Suddenly," writes Jorge Ruffinelli, "the simple existence of popular power [as practiced in the *cordones industriales*] gave conclusive meaning to the great fresco that is *The Battle of Chile.*"[25] It is not strictly a historical conclusion (Ruffinelli acknowledges that the military coup had usurped this conclusion), but rather a conclusion that legitimizes the phenomenon of the *cordones industriales* as the most innovative and revolutionary practice to have been developed in Chile at the time, and as a model to adopt and adapt in ongoing battles for social justice throughout Latin America.

TRANSITION TO A NEOBAROQUE PRAXIS

The filming and editing of *The Battle of Chile* coincides with a transition in Latin American cinema toward a neobaroque praxis whose center of gravity was none other than Cuba during the Revolution's period of greatest cultural and political tension, the late 1960s and early 1970s. Three Cuban films—*Memories of Underdevelopment, Lucía,* and *One Way or Another*—represent especially well the many contradictions and the enormous creativity of this transition.

Memories of Underdevelopment (1968)

In *Memorias del subdesarrollo* (*Memories of Underdevelopment*; Tomás Gutiérrez Alea, Cuba, 1968), a film that critics consistently rank as the best Latin American film of all time, Tomás Gutiérrez Alea successfully synthesizes the comic with the tragic, and incorporates the formal lessons of Jean-Luc Godard, the narrative expressiveness of Sergei Eisenstein, the intellectualism of Bertolt Brecht, and the political commitment of Cinema Novo to create a tour de force that is not derivative but highly original and contentious. The film, loosely adapted from the novel of the same name by Edmundo Desnoes, takes place in Havana between two defining moments in post-Revolutionary Cuban history: the Bay of Pigs invasion in 1961 and the Cuban Missile Crisis in 1962. Sergio (Sergio Corrieri) is an aspiring intellectual from the commercial bourgeoisie. When his wife and parents leave for the United States, he sees their departure as an opportunity to become the writer he always wanted to be. Instead of committing himself to this task, however, he spends his days reflecting upon his past life and looking for love. In the end, his failure to communicate with the women he courts parallels his failure to integrate into the rapidly transforming society around him.

This synopsis, while accurate, misses the point that the main protagonist of the film is not Sergio, but the viewer, who must make sense of the film's disparate and oftentimes contradictory representations of Sergio and those around him. For example, the film demystifies bourgeois individualism through a lucid character who embodies much of what can be positive about bourgeois life (high levels of education, cosmopolitanism, lots of free time, disposable income, and a capacity for critical thought), but also much of what can be negative about it (objectification of women, compulsory heterosexuality, racism, classism, and a lack of solidarity with one's fellow humans). Critics who read the film as either revolutionary or counterrevolutionary therefore ignore the structuring contradictions that make this film an enduring classic of Cuban (and world) cinema.

Memories of Underdevelopment is a composite of film material broadly divided into fiction and documentary, and each of these modes is in turn an amalgam of audiovisual styles. The most important antecedents of the film's documentary mode can be found in ICAIC's (Instituto Cubano del Arte e Industria Cinematográficos) own newsreel production, and more specifically in the documentaries of Santiago Álvarez, with their signature montages of clashing images and sounds. Virtually all kinds of "documents" are used in *Memories of Underdevelopment*: hidden-camera footage, photo essays, newsreels, TV reports, radio broadcasts, newspaper clippings, and even a sociological treatise. For the fictional segments, on the other hand, the film draws from European sources, the more obvious ones being contemporary Italian cinema and the French New Wave.

Gutiérrez Alea's masterful appropriation of European auteur practices, however, should not be read as evidence of Eurocentrism on his part. Rather, it was a means to hook a specific audience, that of Latin American intellectuals, and not an end in itself. Thus, from the French New Wave, *Memories of Underdevelopment* appropriates Alain Resnais's continuous shifting between objective and subjective modes of narration, as well as Godard's formal experimentation with montage and the handheld camera. From Italian contemporary cinema, Michelangelo Antonioni and Federico Fellini come to mind: Antonioni for having popularized the theme of the brooding intellectual, and Fellini for his sympathetic portrayals of middle-aged men looking for love in all the wrong places. Indeed, Sergio bears a striking resemblance in terms of taste, outlook, luck, and even looks to Marcello Mastroianni in *La dolce vita* (Federico Fellini, Italy, 1960) and *8 ½* (Federico Fellini, Italy, 1963): a good-looking, intelligent, and cultivated man with money, time, and wit to spare. This characterization may not have been accidental, as *La dolce vita* was at the center of a 1963 debate between Alfredo Guevara, ICAIC's founding director, and Blas Roca, an orthodox Marxist politician, who, in trying to impose socialist realism on Cuban artists, had criticized *La dolce vita* as an example of decadent art. In this light, *Memories of Underdevelopment* can be read as part of Alea's career-long criticism of the bureaucratization of art and the revolutionary process, examples of which include his earlier *La muerte de un burócrata* (*Death of a Bureaucrat*; Cuba, 1966), and his last two films, codirected with Juan Carlos Tabío: *Strawberry and Chocolate* (Cuba-Spain, 1993) and *Guantanamera* (Cuba-Spain, 1995).[26]

The documentary and fictional elements in *Memories of Underdevelopment* are edited using what Sergei Eisenstein called intellectual montage, whereby the juxtaposition of shots or sequences that are dialectically opposed to one another creates a new, abstract idea, for example "alienation" or "solidarity." The abundance of such juxtapositions also makes the film a collage, which is precisely the word Alea uses to describe it during his cameo appearance as a film director in the offices of ICAIC (fig. 7.12).

The main drawback of theorizing the film as a collage, however, is that collages are taken in all at once, whereas films must be seen in time. Indeed, it is impossible to step back from a film as one would step back from a collage. Take for example the way in which Noemí (Eslinda

FIGURE 7.12 Tomás Gutiérrez Alea (center, as himself) and colleagues at the Cuban Film Institute discuss censorship in *Memories of Underdevelopment* (Tomás Gutiérrez Alea, Cuba, 1968); Sergio (Sergio Corrieri, second from the right) listens and Elena (Daisy Granados) grooms herself

Núñez) is incorporated into the narrative. Like Elena (Daisy Granados), Noemí gets her own subtitle, but unlike Elena's narrative, which is Aristotelian and therefore easy to follow, Noemí's narrative is presented out of sequence and glued together only by Sergio's own fragmented imagination. Thus, the viewer's ability to incorporate Noemí's dispersed and disconnected appearances into the film's overall narrative is limited by his or her ability to make the necessary connections not only between relevant and easily identifiable fragments that are close in time (easily done), but also between relevant fragments that are not so easily identifiable or are far apart in time (not so easily done). For example, the opening sequence is shot from Sergio's point of view, but we only find this out when the scene is revisited more than an hour later, at which point the viewer is unlikely to make the connection with the opening sequence (fig. 7.13). Making such connections between separate sequences is all the more challenging because nearly all of the fictional sequences, including some of Sergio's most subjective ruminations, incorporate material typically associated with documentaries, for instance the use of photographs as historical evidence, radio and television broadcasts, and hidden cameras.

By centering its narrative on a politically underdeveloped and far-from-exemplary character, and by mixing fiction and documentary in ways that erase the boundaries between them, *Memories of Underdevelopment* in

FIGURE 7.13 The "double repetition" of Sergio's date with Noemí (Eslinda Núñez) in *Memories of Underdevelopment*

effect stakes an important heterodox position with respect to the Revolution's political and artistic orthodoxy, which claimed that a documentary mode of representation is intrinsically more authentic and revolutionary than a fictional mode of representation, and which called on artists to follow the precepts of socialist realism, chief among them the representation of exemplary heroes and the use of inspirational endings. Alea theorized his brand of heterodoxy in *La dialéctica del espectador* (*The Viewer's Dialectic*), a collection of six essays on cinema published in 1982. The book is part film history, part film theory, and part manifesto. It includes a brief, materialist history of cinema, a discussion of what kinds of viewers have emerged from that history, a plan on how to change things, and a case study of *Memories of Underdevelopment,* where Alea examines how the film promotes the development of viewers' ability to think critically by revisiting four key moments from different points of view: (1) Sergio's date with Noemí (in sequences 1 and 22); (2) Sergio's farewell to his family at the airport (in sequence 2); (3) Sergio's tape-recorded argument with his wife (in sequences 3 and 11); and (4) regular people in the streets of Havana before and after the Cuban Missile Crisis (in sequences 4 and 30).

In each of these double repetitions, as Alea called them, Sergio's point of view of an event is contrasted with a point of view of that same event from a perspective that is not Sergio's. At the airport, for example, the roving, handheld camera randomly follows various people who will board planes to the United States. Some are clearly suffering, some look stoic, and some children play, unaware of what is going on. The sequence looks and feels like a documentary up to this point. Then we see Sergio hugging his parents goodbye. Sergio is clearly unmoved, and when he turns to his wife, Laura (Beatriz Ponchera), as if saying, "Well, this is it," Laura turns around and leaves. In the next shot, the camera's perspective is that of someone standing next to Sergio, who is himself standing behind and apart from a group of people who are waving to the plane as it rolls down the runway. When the camera begins to move, it tracks around him until we see him in close-up, whistling, with an air of contentment. The shot, therefore, begins the viewer looking *with* Sergio, and ends up with the viewer looking *at* Sergio. This shifting of perspectives is then underscored in the next few shots, which repeat Sergio's farewell to his family from another perspective, so that now we can see that Sergio's mother was crying and that his wife was upset. In other words, both the 180-degree tracking shot of Sergio and the double repetition of Sergio's farewell to his family show essentially the same thing from incompatible perspectives. The result is that, as viewers, we suspect that Sergio's reality is not to be found in either his perspective of himself or in the perspective others have of him, but rather in the confrontation between the two.

The film similarly juxtaposes documentary and fictional modes to generate a critical viewing practice by setting up a dialectic between the fictional mode's predominantly individual perspectives and the documentary mode's predominantly collective perspective. By constantly and insistently alternating between these two perspectives on the Cuban Revolution, the film proposes that the truth of the Revolution is not to be found in either of these perspectives by themselves, but rather in their confrontation, and in what this confrontation suggests in a context of continuing struggles to develop a socialism that productively incorporates the needs of the individual and the needs of the collectivity.

The strategy of confronting perspectives is also used to structure Sergio's narrative trajectories with Laura and Elena, each of whom represents a social class in somewhat problematic ways. The first time we see Laura is at the airport, from Sergio's perspective. Here she represents the petit-bourgeoisie that flees, leaving behind what she sees as the filth, the sweat, and what she pejoratively calls the *chusma* of Cuba. But does she really? Judging from what we learn in a later sequence, in a flashback to a bedroom quarrel with Sergio, Laura seems to have fled Sergio's machinations as much as the Revolution. Elena, on the other hand, represents the popular masses in whose interest the Revolution was ostensibly fought. And yet she lives by the rules and appearances of the pre-Revolutionary petit bourgeoisie, as when she accuses Sergio of raping her so that he will marry her. And then there is Noemí, who represents the hopes and aspirations of the Revolution, the woman who may yet save Sergio from himself. Unlike Laura and Elena, Sergio is attracted to Noemí as much by her beauty as by her innocence, an innocence signified by her baptism and in no small degree associated with the early years of the Revolution. Like Cuba after 1959, the newly baptized Noemí is the embodiment of hope and the possibility of a new beginning for Sergio.

But Sergio's inability to make the most of this opportunity is underscored via a double repetition of their first and only date. The first part of this double repetition takes place during the opening sequence. The scene is shot with a handheld camera moving and jostling through a crowd of dancing, sweating bodies. The camera loses focus at times, and the dancers, seemingly unaware of its presence, obstruct its view. In the midst of this *cinéma vérité* shooting, one of the dancers, an Afro-Cuban woman, looks directly into the camera. The camera moves on. Several gunshots sound above the rhythmic music, an Afro-Cuban *mozambique* by Pello el Afrokán. Confusion ensues as people gather around the victim on the ground. The camera moves rapidly through the crowd, calling more attention to its subjective use and reminding the viewer of its operator (or is it Sergio, the protagonist, whom we haven't seen yet?). It then comes to rest on the face of the same Afro-Cuban woman, who addresses the camera (Sergio?) with her bold gaze. The frame freezes on the woman, music fades out, then the image cuts to the next sequence. The second part of the double repetition takes place more than an hour later, with the difference that this time the music is no longer that of Pello el Afrokán, but a very dissonant arrangement by Leo Brouwer. The effect is that we see the same tumultuous scene through Sergio's eyes, and with a better appreciation of how much his inner world has distanced itself from outer reality. We also come to realize that the black woman's gaze at the beginning of the film was directed at Sergio. What was the nature of that gaze? Do we recall? Are we now in the same position she was in, looking at Sergio as one looks at a strange animal? Or are we still the object of her gaze, thrown off and even threatened by the new society which in so many ways she represents?

Like a satyr in a classic Greek tragedy, Sergio is torn between two opposing and seemingly irreconcilable forces. Before the Revolution, his desire to be a bohemian writer and live with his German-born girlfriend Hanna (Felicia Hirsch) in New York clashed with his family's demands for him to settle down into a life of work and responsibility as a furniture store owner. Sergio grudgingly chooses the latter and settles for Laura, whom he tries to mold into the Hanna of his dreams. But Laura is not Hanna, which is like saying Cuba is not Europe. After his family's departure for Miami, Sergio gets an unexpected chance to redeem himself. He tries to find a new Hanna and to live the life of a bohemian writer, but fails on both counts. Sergio's ideal of feminine beauty and sophistication is not to be found in Cuba, and even if he did find it, it is doubtful that he would meet his end of the bargain by treating her as an equal subject rather than an object of desire. The second possibility of redemption, becoming a bohemian writer, also falls short of expectations. Before his family's departure, Sergio was half-integrated into his social class. He loathed its shallowness and consumerism, yet grudgingly participated in them by not articulating and acting out a productive alternative. After his family leaves Cuba, Sergio follows the same pattern of behavior: he loathes the Revolution's populism and the physical deterioration that accompanies its economic policies, yet he grudgingly participates in them by not articulating and acting out a productive alternative.

Sergio's inability to articulate and act out productive alternatives to a society he loathes generates alienation, a feeling visually captured in the shot of him looking down on Havana through a telescope. The original script, in fact, called for Sergio's death, the logical outcome given his role as a tragic hero who cannot overcome his alienation. Many scenes throughout the film prepare the viewer for this eventuality, from the scene where he says to himself: "You are nothing. Nothing. You are dead," to the shot of a man walking in front of a wall with MUERTE written in huge letters. Against all expectations, however, Sergio does not die, and his survival leaves open two possible outcomes: either he will continue down the road of ambiguity, which will exacerbate his alienation and precipitate his eventual death, or he will confront the cause of his alienation by using his ability to think critically, his only redeeming quality, in order to transform himself through what was then theorized as a *desgarramiento*. Literally, the word means to tear or rip, as one would a piece of cloth. Figuratively, it means to shatter, to crush. Both definitions underscore the destruction of something, in this case a pre-Revolutionary consciousness that includes racial prejudice, class privilege, compulsory heterosexuality, and the reification of metropolitan values at the expense of local culture, all of which, as the film's title suggests, are forms of underdevelopment that stand in the way of socialism. But the road from underdevelopment to socialism is not limited to the *desgarramiento* of the intellectual class. It also includes overcoming the bureaucratization of everyday life that the housing censors embody, and the kind of spiteful retribution sought by people like Elena's father and brother. In effect, by asking how far someone like Sergio has gone down the road from underdevelopment to socialism, *Memories of Underdevelopment* is also asking the timely question of how the Revolution itself has fared, eight years into the project. In trying to answer this question, the film steers clear of simplistic representations of the new order while avoiding a categorical dismissal of the old. Instead, it sets up a dialectic between individual and collective perspectives that validates, in Alea's own words, both individual fulfillment and collective achievement.[27]

Lucía (1968)

In *Lucía* (Humberto Solás, Cuba, 1968), as in *Memories of Underdevelopment,* the dialectic between the individual and the collectivity and between form and content is also explored through a corresponding confrontation of narratives and styles. *Lucía* is a composite film made up of three parts: "Lucía 1895," a melodrama; "Lucía 1932," a noir film; and "Lucía 196..," a social comedy. The result is a dialectical metanarrative of the kind Sergei Eisenstein developed for *¡Que viva México!,* where several relatively independent episodes are combined into a coherent whole by placing them in successive and dialectical relationships to one another, and in such a way that each semi-independent episode may be read allegorically as a stage in the dialectical development of national history. *Lucía*'s Marxist historiography is graphically suggested by the film's silkscreen poster by Raúl Martínez, with the first Lucía—the aristocratic Lucía of 1895—at the upper left, occupying the position of thesis, the second Lucía—the bourgeois Lucía of 1932—at the upper right, occupying the position of antithesis, and the third Lucía—the peasant Lucía of the 1960s—below and centered, occupying the position reserved for the synthesis.

By filming the three episodes in three very different styles and genres, however, the film simultaneously undermines the Marxist orthodox position that one art form is intrinsically more revolutionary than another, simply based on that form's class origins. Needless to say, the film does something else, and in fact comes very close to Che Guevara's understanding of art as creative expression based on free inquiry:

[W]hy try to find the only valid prescription in the frozen forms of socialist realism? We cannot counterpose "freedom" to socialist realism, because the former does not yet exist and will not exist until the complete development of the new society. We must not, from the pontifical throne of realism-at-all-costs, condemn all art forms since the first half of the nineteenth century, for we would then fall into the Proudhonian mistake of going back to the past, of putting a straitjacket on the artistic expression of the people who are being born and are in the process of making themselves.[28]

For Che Guevara, then, a radical shift in consciousness is the sine qua non for revolutionary change and not, as Marxist economic orthodoxy stipulates, the other way around. This is, briefly stated, the so-called Guevarian heresy. In *Lucía,* as in *Memories of Underdevelopment,* the corresponding heresy is the articulation of narratives that privilege psychological conflict over moral certitudes, and not, as socialist realism requires, the other way around.[29]

"Lucía 1895"

In *The Melodramatic Imagination,* Peter Brooks argues that melodrama first emerged after the French Revolution as "a response to the loss of the tragic vision. It comes into being in a world where the traditional imperatives of truth and ethics have been violently thrown into question, yet where the promulgation of truth and ethics, their installation as a way of life, is of immediate daily, political concern."[30]

When *Lucía* was first released, the reception of the first episode was less positive than the reception for the second and especially the third, chiefly because many thought that melodrama was an inappropriate genre in a country where traditional imperatives of truth and ethics had already been superseded by revolutionary ones.[31] More recently, Eduardo López Morales has taken a more productive approach by asking how melodrama suits the specific narrative needs of "Lucía 1895." His answer? That Solás consciously assumes the form of melodrama and its attendant kitsch "as a demystifying expression of our cultural personality, as a de-alienating vehicle for Cubans to recognize themselves without false prudishness,"[32] and more importantly, that melodrama highlights the fact that "the political, sentimental and existential treason against Lucía . . . reflects an obliterating colonial society that is based on swindling and on treason."[33] In other words, the use of melodrama in "Lucía 1895" serves as a conduit to explore the crisis in Cuba's colonial relationship with Spain precisely because melodrama underscores the crisis of the protagonist's class and its truth imperatives. One of the ways the episode underscores this crisis is by contrasting the protagonist's social class in decline with an ascendant Cuban collectivity represented by the young, black, naked *mambises* who defeat the older, clothed Spaniards in the episode's climactic battle sequence.

Similarly, when Lucía's crisis reaches a turning point, it is a procession of Afro-Cubans, rather than individuals of her own class, who give her the strength to redeem herself. The procession is part of the episode's denouement, which begins when Lucía (Raquel Revuelta) realizes that her lover, Rafael (Eduardo Moure), is in fact a Spanish spy who has used her to find and destroy the rebels' hideout in her family's coffee plantation. Taken together, the expressive acting, the shift in the soundtrack to a subjective point of hearing (i.e., we start to hear her own breathing and steps over other sounds in the environment), and the overexposure of the film stock all signal to the viewer that Lucía has become hyperconscious of her condition as an object within the hegemonic colonial and patriarchal order, and more precisely, as an object exploited by Rafael for the protection of that order. Lucía's exact moment of lucidity comes as she is frantically banging her hands against a wall and pacing back and forth within her mansion-cage. Suddenly, in a flash-forward so short it is almost imperceptible, she sees herself walking toward the plaza where she will meet and kill Rafael. She then slowly leaves the darkness of the home's interior and enters the light-drenched patio, where she sits down and looks straight into the camera, as if asking for the viewer's complicity in the plan she is about to carry out (fig. 7.14).

The final sequence of "Lucía 1895" begins in a side street with an old, frail woman, dressed as a *santera*, telling a disoriented Lucía where to find Rafael. The next shot opens with the brief flash-forward mentioned above, and zooms out to reveal an Afro-Cuban procession in front of the cathedral where the two lovers first met. In a handheld medium shot, we now see Lucía stride toward the plaza as one of her friends appears out of nowhere to try to stop her. She easily breaks free. The camera turns to follow her as she continues on her way, so that we are no longer looking at Lucía but rather with her, and over her shoulder at the Afro-Cuban procession behind her. Finally, Lucía immerses herself in the procession's collective dance, and with the strength of that collectivity now backing her, she lunges forward to finish off her plan, transformed now from an act of personal revenge to an act of collective retribution. The closing shot, an overexposed close-up of a visibly alienated Lucía, with Fernandina's (Idalia Anreus) hand gently supporting and consoling the

FIGURE 7.14 Lucía's (Raquel Revuelta) newfound political awareness is underscored by the overexposed film and her intense gaze into the camera in the "Lucía 1895" episode of *Lucía* (Humberto Solás, Cuba, 1968)

bereaved lover, illustrates the two women's common fate and underscores how colonialism relegates visionary lucidity to the realm of madness.

Notwithstanding the centrality of transformation in these sequences, "Lucía 1895" closes with the assault's quick suppression, and is therefore in keeping with the melodramatic convention that social structures revert to the status quo ante. However, this ensuing return, with Spaniards still in charge and women still in positions of submission, is not a nostalgic yearning for a lost order, as in a typical melodrama, but rather the condemnation of a colonial order that held back the historical development of both individual women and the colonized nation as a whole. If anything, the assault's quick suppression underscores the insufficiency of the nationalist aristocracy's actions for the successful liberation of the island nation. From this perspective, Lucía's personal heroism is a necessary but insufficient element for her own liberation and the liberation of Cuba. The missing element, in this episode as in the next, is the development, at a strategic level, of a political alliance between the nationalist elite and the popular masses.

"Lucía 1932"

In the second episode, Solás employs the narrative and stylistic conventions of film noir for several reasons. For one, the use of noir conventions such as dimly lit interiors, rainy backdrops, and long takes in enclosed spaces heightens the sense of hopelessness, disillusionment, and lost time that permeated Cuban politics when, between the over-throw of Gerardo Machado in 1933 and the reactionary crushing of the general strike of 1935, opportunistic forces conspired against the pro-gressive government of Ramón Grau San Martín to return Cuba back to the kind of neocolonialism that led to the overthrow of Machado in the first place. In terms of narrative, film noir's emphasis on self-doubt, questionable morality, and the uncertain future also made this genre an appropriate vehicle through which Solás could explore the kind of inse-curity and anxiety that gripped Cuba, and especially Cuban men, after the world crash of 1929. For example, because the crash forced many women to look for work outside the house, male dominance was directly questioned, thus fueling the kind of male anxiety toward women that is one of the hallmarks of film noir.[34] And while the kind of extreme male anxiety that one finds in "black widow" type film noirs is missing in "Lucía 1932," Aldo (Ramón Brito) sees Lucía (Eslinda Núñez) as primarily a domestic subject who will return to her "proper" domestic role of housewife and mother once the political struggle is over. In effect, what Lucía's marginalization and domestication allegorizes is the nationalist bourgeoisie's marginalization of its radical wing, under-scored in the episode's final sequence of a pregnant but isolated Lucía contemplating suicide in a noir urbanscape, with nowhere to go but down and under the river in front of her (fig. 7.15).

The use of noir conventions in "Lucía 1932" highlights the ideologi-cal limits of a bourgeoisie that identifies with what Paul Schrader calls the "overriding noir theme: a passion for the past and present, but also a fear of the future. Noir heroes dread to look ahead, but instead try to survive by the day, and if unsuccessful at that, they retreat to the past. Thus film noir's techniques emphasize loss, nostalgia, lack of clear pri-orities, and insecurity."[35]

Indeed, Aldo and Lucía, the noir heroes in "Lucía 1932," are doomed precisely because they cannot see far into the future. Critically, they fail to realize that their struggle against tyranny and neocolonialism cannot be won through the kinds of romantic and isolated attacks Aldo helps to organize and carry out against soft targets of the dictatorial regime, or even through the kind of collective mobilization Lucía engages in during a tobacco workers' protest against Machado, but rather through the strategic alliance between the progressive urban bourgeoisie and the island's majority population in the countryside. This is in effect the pri-mary political lesson of "Lucía 1932," that even though the progressive

FIGURE 7.15 A pregnant Lucía (Eslinda Núñez), weighed down by an oppressive urbanscape, contemplates suicide in "Lucía 1932"

bourgeoisie had the right intentions, it lacked the necessary ideological grounding and strategic foresight to realize that it needed the support of the island's rural proletariat and an understanding of their needs and interests if it was to be successful not only in its attempts to seize power, but in using that power to lift the masses out of poverty and break Cuba's neocolonial relationship with the United States.

"Lucía 196.."

The last part is not, as one might expect given the film's overall dialectical structure, a historical synthesis where the working class has already achieved its paradise on earth. Rather, the episode uses social comedy to present machismo as the main impediment to the full development of the revolutionary process, and more specifically, as a problem that is symptomatic of customs and manners requiring reform at that level, rather than as a problem whose solution requires structural changes in the economy. Crucially, then, the machismo in "Lucía 196.." is shown to belong to a resilient tradition of patriarchal customs that have been little affected by changes in economic structures across time. The title of the last episode gives us an important clue as to how to interpret the film's take on this problem. Just as 1895 and 1932 are three years before the historical breaks of 1898 and 1935, respectively, perhaps the third part takes place two or three years before another historical break. The fact that the ellipsis is incomplete—"Lucía 196.." only has two dots—suggests that this break is just about to take place, and that we as spectators have a role to play in finishing that narrative.

In this reading, the 1959 Revolution is but a prelude to a more thorough revolution that goes beyond economic changes to a radical transformation of patriarchal customs and manners. And ideologically as well, beyond crude Marxism (which posits that changes in modes of production mechanically transform social relations) to a critical Marxism that is more open and nuanced. This critical Marxism is visually and narratively encapsulated in the closing shot of the laughing girl. The girl is several things at once. Narratively, she is a convention of socialist realism, and therefore represents the next generation that will overcome the outdated customs and attitudes of both Tomás (Adolfo Llauradó) and Lucía (Adela Legrá) to fulfill the promise of Communism. In the context of contemporary debates over the direction of the Revolution, however, her laughter is directed at the orthodox Marxists who argued that because patriarchy arose alongside capitalism, patriarchal relations will automatically give way to egalitarian relations between the sexes now that Cuba has advanced to socialism. The girl's irreverent laughter may also be directed at those whose only solution would be for Lucía to abandon Tomás. The fact that Solás did not choose this plausible end signals the film's project of imagining an inclusive community identified with the interests and needs of an agricultural cooperative whose social relations are egalitarian and even matriarchal, a project rendered visually in the salt flats sequence when Tomás is brought down from his position of power by the collective force of Lucía's female coworkers (fig. 7.16).

In light of this project, Lucía's attempt to transform Tomás is of paramount importance, and what she tells Tomás in the last sequence is directed as much to her recalcitrant husband as to viewers of both sexes:

> *Lucía:* I have returned because I cannot live without you. But, but . . . I cannot go on the way you were treating me. I have to work. Understand me, Tomás. I have to be productive at something. Otherwise, what is the reason for living?
>
> *Tomás:* *Coño,* if that's what you wanted to tell me you should not have come! To tell me all that trash you might as well go to hell! You hear me? Go to hell!
>
> *Lucía:* No, I am going to stay with you! I will work at the farm! I will stay with you and I won't leave you! I will stay because that's why I married you!

FIGURE 7.16 Female workers take down the *machista* Tomás (Adolfo Llauradó) in "Lucía 196.." The book's cover image shows Lucía (Adela Legrá) defiantly looking at Tomás (and the viewer) just before this incident

This final exchange cements the film's overall thesis that the abolition of all forms of exploitation is an ongoing struggle. Throughout the film, this struggle centers most obviously on the transformation of patriarchal social relations, capitalist and otherwise, but it is also a struggle, at the artistic level, to transform the melodramatic impulse that underlines all three episodes in the film, regardless of their genre, into a politically viable alternative.

A testament to Solás's creativity is the fact that none of the episodes in *Lucía* is an uncritical appropriation of the genre in question. On the contrary, each illustrates the director's thorough assimilation and subsequent transmutation of generic conventions into appropriate vessels for the film's overall metanarrative of national liberation. In "Lucía 1895," for example, Solás inserts into the overarching melodrama several highly stylized, documentary-like sequences that serve at least three functions: to anchor the episode's sentimental narrative to a very concrete and brutal historical context, to contrast the worlds of the exploited versus those who benefit from their exploitation, and to highlight the intensity with which characters, especially Fernandina and Lucía, experience transformative events such as rape, treason, or sexual awakening. Likewise, "Lucía 1932" plays with the conventions of film noir by incorporating into the narrative historical events such as the overthrow of Machado, and by having a female instead of a male as the protagonist. Finally, the third episode mixes social comedy, whose sympathetic critique of customs and manners is ideologically reformist, with socialist realism, a Soviet genre that calls for working-class heroes and a narrative closure identified with revolutionary praxis.

The film's hyper-heterogeneity—that is, the fact that there is heterogeneity between and within episodes—has as its corollary a corresponding heterodoxy in meaning. In this sense, *Lucía* is much more than a Marxist-feminist rereading of Cuban history; it is also a film manifesto that exemplifies the kind of unorthodox praxis that Alfredo Guevara, the founding director of Cuba's film company (ICAIC), approvingly called heretical: "Heresy is not easy. However, to practice it is a source of profound and encouraging satisfaction, the better when the rupture with, or ignorance of, the generally accepted dogmas is authentic. . . . No adult life is possible without systematic heresy, without the commitment to continually take risks. And while this adventurous attitude toward life implies the possibility of failure, it is nevertheless the only real way to approach truth: from its many edges."[36]

Written in 1963 in the context of a bitter polemic between Alfredo Guevara and the orthodox Marxist politician Blas Roca, Guevara's position prevailed for the rest of the decade and became identified with ICAIC for a much longer period. The polemic was part of a broader debate on the limits of artistic expression, which incidentally included Fidel Castro's 1961 speech "Words to the Intellectuals," and its celebrated yet ambiguous refrain, "Within the Revolution, everything, outside the Revolution, nothing." Recently, Rufo Caballero and Joel del Río picked up on Alfredo Guevara's thesis and concluded that Cuban cinema "has been a cinema of a ferocious heresy that reflects, like a luminous mirror, a self-image as subverted as it is transparent, as devout as it is uncomfortable."[37] While overly generous, their description of Cuban cinema as both subversive and devout, a good definition of heresy as well as of heterodoxy, applies especially well to *Lucía*: it is devout because the film's materialist teleology points toward Communism, and it is subversive because it embodies that evolving teleology in three lucid protagonists whose motivations and actions cannot be reduced to their class positions. Rather, each Lucía is caught between equally valid collective aspirations and individual desires at odds with one another. At the same time, the film's guiding visual metaphor, where light equals conflict equals lucidity, helps to interweave the three episodes into an aesthetically and narratively cohesive whole that may also explain the decision to privilege light-skinned women in the casting. This is not to say that the film is systematically racist, for, as we have seen, it identifies Cuba's liberation with black *mambises* in the first episode, while in the third episode, the model revolutionary couple is played by the black actors Teté Vergara and Flavio Calderín. In the final analysis, however, the film does reproduce conventional categories of race (and sexuality) even as it develops a thoroughly unconventional narrative of national, gender, and class liberation.

Glauber Rocha once told Julio García Espinosa that "we are not interested in the problems of neurosis; we are interested in the problems of lucidity."[38] Rocha may have well been speaking of *Lucía*, whose multiple protagonist embodies, as her name suggests, the lucidity to see beyond a conflictive present to a future utopia where, as Che Guevara put it, "The material possibilities for the integrated development of absolutely all members of society make the task [of transforming society] much more fruitful. The present is a time of struggle; the future is ours."[39] By locating the drama of history precisely at the intersection between a present time of struggle and a future that is ours for the making, *Lucía* participates in the creation of a new national history based not on the linear organization of extraordinary events and people (as in liberal historiography), or the preordained outcome of a materialist teleology (as in orthodox Marxism), but on the ongoing confrontation of contested socioeconomic structures and cultural values.

One Way or Another (1974)

Sara Gómez took the idea of history as an ongoing dialectical unfolding to its logical conclusion in *De cierta manera* (*One Way or Another*; Cuba, 1974), a film that borrows themes and forms from both *Lucía* and *Memories of Underdevelopment,* but gives them a uniquely Afro-Cuban and female perspective. The conflict, as in *Memories of Underdevelopment* and the third part of *Lucía,* centers on the struggles of a male protagonist who cannot fully incorporate himself into the Revolution because of his sexism. Mario (Mario Balmaseda), a dark-skinned Afro-Cuban man who grew up poor and has a past history of delinquency, falls in love with Yolanda (Yolanda Cuéllar), a light-skinned Afro-Cuban woman of the middle class who works as an elementary school teacher in a poor neighborhood where the housing is new, thanks to the Revolution, but where the attitudes are still racist, classist, and sexist. Gómez directs their acting with great skill in a variety of settings, ranging from private and semiprivate scenes, framed mostly in close-ups

FIGURE 7.17 Mario (Mario Balmaseda) and Yolanda (Yolanda Cuéllar) do not see eye to eye in *One Way or Another* (Sara Gómez, Cuba, 1974)

linked to fictional modes of representation, to public scenes of confrontation and negotiation captured in medium or long shots and indebted to documentarist modes of representation (fig. 7.17).

It is in this conflictive space between public persona and private self that Mario's narrative trajectory develops. On the one hand, he is in love with Yolanda and wants to develop their relationship further. On the other, his social web lies elsewhere, with a buddy system whose machismo is personified in Humberto (Mario Limonta), a close friend and coworker at a bike factory, and institutionalized in the Afro-Cuban secret society Abakuá. The film opens *in media res*, at the point of highest tension between Mario and Humberto. Humberto is defending himself from accusations of absenteeism in front of his coworkers, claiming that he had to leave to care for his ailing mother. In truth, he had been absent to be with his lover, and Mario had agreed to cover for him out of a sense of male solidarity. When Mario hears Humberto tell the story of his supposedly sick mother, however, he can no longer contain himself and calls Humberto's bluff.

The rest of the film is the backstory to this climax, but instead of ending where it began, with Mario confronting Humberto, the film closes with a memorable sequence where Mario bumps into Yolanda and tries to convince her that he has changed for the better. The sequence, which does not include the audio of their dialogue, begins with a frontal full shot of the two walking down a sidewalk, cuts to a close-up from behind, quickly zooms out to a wide-angle shot that reveals them walking into Miraflores (the neighborhood of new apartment buildings that was built to house the people who once lived in the slum of Las Yaguas), and closes with a leitmotif that has by now become the central metaphor of the film: a documentary shot of a wrecking ball demolishing a concrete building. Here and elsewhere, this leitmotif represents an ongoing process of demolishing any lingering sexism, racism, and classism that stands in the way of a truly relational praxis between the protagonists, and of a truly egalitarian society in general. By choosing to film the protagonists' visibly difficult conversation in a variety of shots, Gómez underscores the need to take into account a wide variety of angles and perspectives in this ongoing demolition, including the social, historical, cultural, and affective factors that still sustain the structures of sexism, racism, and classism despite fifteen years of revolutionary change.

8

New Latin American Cinema's Neobaroque Phase

THE COLONIAL ROOTS OF THE LATIN AMERICAN NEOBAROQUE

In the late 1960s and early 1970s, filmmakers of the New Latin American Cinema looked for new and more sophisticated modes of expression to address the more complex reality of the times, but also to avoid censorship, exile, or even outright death at the hands of newly installed or newly turned authoritarian states. Many found what they were looking for in Latin America's own popular baroque traditions. A first, popular Latin American baroque flourished in the eighteenth century, when confraternities freely adapted the European baroque to their own ends. Confraternities were societies of mutual assistance regularly founded on the basis of sharing a common patron saint, a common profession, or a common social, legal, or ethnic standing. They had existed in Europe during the Middle Ages, and the institution was imported to major cities and towns in the Americas from the beginning of the colonial period. In the eighteenth century, however, they became widespread and influential beyond urban centers, often without official approval, to the point where "it could be said that there was no church or altar without its own confraternity."[1] In the specific case of the Andes, the popularity of confraternities was tied to the practice of reinventing *ayllus* (indigenous units of land farmed communally by several extended families) as confraternities. A case in point is the community of Santa Lucía de Pacaraos, where each of its four *ayllus* formed a confraternity:

Ayllu Roca = Cofradía Rorca o del Señor de los Auxilios

Ayllu Ninucushma = Cofradía ninucushma o de la Virgen Purísima

Ayllu Mariac = Cofradía Mariac o de San Antonio de Padua

Ayllu Jayec = Cofradía Jayec o de la Virgen Candelaria[2]

As the wealth of these confraternities/*ayllus* grew, so did their political activity, with many going so far as giving moral and material support to Túpac Amaru's Great Rebellion in the late eighteenth century in an attempt to protect their newfound status.[3]

The Bourbons of course succeeded in suppressing the Great Rebellion, and proceeded to institutionalize their victory by outlawing most confraternities, confiscating their property, and imposing neoclassicism as the official style of the Church and the state. However, before confraternities were outlawed and their property confiscated, their patronage was instrumental in the flowering of a colonial baroque art that expressed a local worldview of mixed cultures. Two examples stand out: the indigenous confraternities devoted to San Miguel Arcángel in the Andes, one of which commissioned the famous facade attributed to José Kondori at the Church of San Lorenzo de Potosí;[4] and the confraternities of free slaves and mulattos in Minas Gerais, several of which commissioned works by Aleijadinho.[5]

The popular baroque works of Kondori and Aleijadinho stand in sharp contrast to the official baroque art of the Counter-Reformation. Instead of reaffirming existing structures of power and social relations, as the official baroque does, Kondori and Aleijadinho created works that invited viewers to identify with those whom society marginalizes.[6] Kondori and Aleijadinho are for this reason the two central figures in an ongoing reinterpretation of the Latin American Baroque as different from, and not merely derivative of, the European Baroque. The Argentinean Ángel Guido, the Dominican Pedro Henríquez Ureña, and the Venezuelan Mariano Picón Salas were the first to explore, during the first half of the twentieth century, the idea of a Latin American colonial Baroque that was qualitatively different from the European one.[7] The Cuban José Lezama Lima took this idea one step further by defining Latin America's colonial baroque as rebellious (he called it "the art of the Counter-Conquest");[8] and Severo Sarduy, also Cuban, added that much of twentieth-century literature is, in its eccentricity and artificiality, aesthetically neobaroque and politically revolutionary.[9] Curiously, Sarduy never explored the differences between the (neo)baroque in the metropolis versus the periphery, opting instead to speak of them separately. But their differences are fundamental for an accurate evaluation of the baroque and the neobaroque in general, and of neobaroque cinema in particular.

Generally speaking, works of the baroque and the neobaroque in the global economic metropolis tend to situate those in power at the center of clearly demarcated social hierarchies, whereas baroque and neobaroque works in the global economic periphery tend to situate marginalized subjects at the heart of narrative and/or visual compositions in such a way that existing social and cultural distinctions, rather than being reinforced, are inverted or else altogether lost in an excess of signifiers. In terms of reception, this means that baroque and neobaroque works in the metropolis tend to position viewers to more readily identify with existing structures of power and social relations, whereas baroque and neobaroque works in the periphery tend to position viewers to more readily identify with those whom society marginalizes.[10]

Frida Still Life (1983)

Consider for example how Hollywood and Latin American cinema have variously represented Frida Kahlo. Stylistically, both Paul Leduc's *Frida, naturaleza viva* (*Frida Still Life*; Mexico, 1983) and Julie Taymor's *Frida* (United States, 2002) are neobaroque films: both feature rich color palettes, object-filled sets, and the use of mirrors and paintings to call attention to the nature of representation. Yet while Taymor's *Frida* depoliticizes Kahlo by portraying her as a primarily ethnic subject with little or no commitment to class-based struggles, Leduc's *Frida* does the opposite, highlighting Kahlo's heterodox Marxism precisely at a time when her public memory had been thoroughly depoliticized so as to better serve the interests of the international art market and a Mexican government that had, under Miguel de la Madrid, begun the transition to neoliberalism in earnest. This is not to say that Taymor's *Frida* is apolitical; rather, its portrayal of Kahlo as primarily an ethnic and gendered subject plays down the class dimensions of Kahlo's life and work in favor of a very U.S.-specific identity politics rooted in liberal individualism.

In Leduc's *Frida,* by contrast, Leduc makes the personal openly political by counterpointing sequences that focus on Kahlo's intimate life with sequences that focus on her political beliefs. Interspersed between these intimate and political sequences are sequences where both the personal and the political combine, as in the sequence where Kahlo passionately orders David Alfaro Siqueiros to stop speaking negatively of Leon Trotsky, whom she loves as a man and admires as a political thinker. Trotsky reciprocates Kahlo's love and admiration in a sequence where he walks alone and meditates in the forest. Here, Leduc highlights Kahlo's heterodox Marxism by incorporating the thesis of André Breton and Trotsky's "Manifesto for an Independent Revolutionary Art"—the idea that "independent revolutionary art must proclaim aloud its right to exist . . . against the usurpers of the revolution"[11]—into Trotsky's fictional love letter to Kahlo: "My dear Frida, I want to share with you some thoughts about the connection between genuine art and revolution. Proletarian art and the pedagogical use of art are not the only forms of revolutionary culture. The workers of the world are in need of what you can offer them: the idea of mankind's psychological complexity, the expression of the force of an instant of passion."

The love letter functions as Trotsky's validation of the kind of heterodox art that Kahlo's intimate paintings represent in a context dominated by epic muralism, and of the kind of heterodox politics that cost Trotsky his life. At the same time, the letter validates Leduc's use of neobaroque forms to narrate Kahlo's life, for three reasons: first, because the film constructs a discontinuous space and fragmented time that undermines the kind of spatial and temporal continuity required by monologic discourses such as liberalism, state socialism, and state corporatism. Second, because the film explores a subject whose contradictions, far from making her seem less than exemplary, confirm her humanity; for example, Leduc's Kahlo is a politically progressive woman who nevertheless feels incomplete because she cannot have a child, and a sexually liberated woman who practices free love yet feels jealous when Diego Rivera does the same. Finally, Leduc's Kahlo reveals, in her most intimate moments—whether with a carpenter, a domestic worker, Rivera, or Trotsky—her commitment to living the present not as an instrumentalized moment that points toward some future utopia, but rather as a privileged instant where social relations are inclusive and horizontal.

The differences between the Hollywood and Latin American versions of the neobaroque are also evident in the relationship these two Fridas establish with viewers. Taymor's *Frida* follows Hollywood's standard practice of absorbing the viewer in a closed and linear narrative that facilitates spectatorial identification with a protagonist whose privileged position within society is highlighted through costume design and through the narrative emphasis on psychological motivations over social and political ones. By contrast, Leduc's version of Kahlo's life develops a critical viewing practice by highlighting her marginality as a woman and an artist, and by shattering conventional cinematic constructions of time and space. Leduc's use of mirrors is especially revealing in this regard. In the film's third sequence, which takes place inside Kahlo's studio, two mirrors and a sketch underscore the malleable and positional nature of representation and identity. The composition references Diego Velázquez's *Las Meninas* (1656), a key painting of the European Baroque whose only mirror, strategically positioned at the center of the painting, reflects the king and queen of Spain. Because the mirror would reflect us viewers were it real, the painting in effect makes it easier for the viewer to identify with those at the very center of power, and to regard the structures of power as stable. In the film, on the other hand, the reflection in the small, beveled mirror is that of a marginalized subject, and is only one among several reflections in mirrors, thereby radically questioning the kind of subject stability anchored by the single mirror in *Las Meninas*. The deconstruction of the stable subject is further developed by two metaphors of identity as a malleable construct: first, the unfinished self-portrait to the left of the frame, which suggests that identity is a work in progress, and second, the shot of Kahlo carefully testing a color on her skin, as if she were literally painting her self into existence (fig. 8.1).

This visual deconstruction of the stable subject is not a mere formal exercise in neobaroque aesthetics. In fact, it supports the narrative deconstruction of dominant values via the centering of a protagonist who is marginalized from the center of power four times over: first, as a non-heteronormative female in an androcentric and homophobic society; second, as a committed Marxist who supported Trotsky at a time (1930s) when Marxist orthodoxy was Stalinist; third, as an artist who painted small-scale autobiographical canvases at a time when public, epic murals had become the hegemonic art form in Mexico; and finally, as a woman with physical disabilities. This alternative narrative of Kahlo's life as a marginal subject, combined with a polycentric and fragmented mise-en-scène, together produce a neobaroque time-image where the artist serves as a metaphor of a marginalized civil society struggling to come to terms with the painful traumas inflicted by the authoritarian regimes of the previous two decades (the 1960s and 1970s). Furthermore, by having Kahlo overcome her traumas only after the public exhibition of her paintings, the film suggests that without an

FIGURE 8.1 Frida (Ofelia Medina) paints multiple, complementary selves into existence in *Frida Still Life* (Paul Leduc, Mexico, 1983)

equally public examination of collective traumas, there is little chance for any reconciliation, let alone the kind of reconciliation that many Latin American governments at the time pretended could be achieved without facing the past and bringing to justice those responsible for state-sponsored terror. The film's narrative of psychological healing, culminating in the solo exhibit at Mexico City's gallery of contemporary art, functions to drive home the point that the only way for contemporary civil society to begin the process of national reconciliation is to make public the sufferings of those who, like Kahlo, fought for social justice at home and throughout Latin America.

Frida Still Life is an exemplary film of the neobaroque NLAC because its fractured narrative, theatrical mise-en-scène, and complex protagonist reject the unity of time, space, and subject identity favored by monologistic discourses such as liberalism and corporativism. Just as important, *Frida* uses neobaroque aesthetics to revisit the socialist assumptions of the NLAC's militant phase in light of politically altered landscapes: authoritarian regimes in the 1970s and vulnerable democracies in the 1980s. Similar concerns inform *La última cena* (*The Last Supper*; Tomás Gutiérrez Alea, Cuba, 1976) and *La nación clandestina* (The Clandestine Nation; Jorge Sanjinés, Bolivia, 1989), two films that explore alternative modernities of African and indigenous cultures in the Americas in the context of colonialism and neocolonialism.

The Last Supper (1976)

The Last Supper was part of a hemispheric debate in the 1970s and 1980s on the origins, forms, and consequences of African slavery in the Americas. The debate was especially pronounced in countries such as Cuba and Brazil, where the percentage of people of African descent is the highest. In Brazil, several films in the 1970s and 1980s sought to demystify Gilberto Freyre's *Casa-grande e Senzala* (*The Masters and the Slaves*; 1933), a foundational text that inaugurated the myth of Brazilian racial democracy. Two of these films stand out: Carlos Diegues's beautiful and poignant *Xica da Silva* (Brazil, 1976), which mythologizes the real-life story of a slave woman in the middle of the eighteenth century who attained freedom, wealth, and power by becoming the lover of Brazil's richest diamond contractor; and *Quilombo* (Brazil, 1984), also by Carlos Diegues, which dramatizes the creation, growth, and subsequent demise of Quilombo do Palmares, the largest maroon community in the history of the Americas, which lasted almost a century until it finally succumbed to Portuguese attacks in the 1690s. In Cuba, where Fernando Ortiz's *Cuban Counterpoint: Tobacco and Sugar* (1940) played a role similar to Freyre's Brazilian text by theorizing Cuban culture as the synthesis between Euro-Cuban and Afro-Cuban cultures, films in the 1970s and 1980s revisited this idea by highlighting African resistance to European colonialism and slavery. The best examples of this phenomenon are *El otro Francisco* (*The Other Francisco*; Sergio Giral, 1975), a highly original deconstruction of nineteenth-century abolitionist discourse in Cuba, and *The Last Supper*, a historical drama based on a real-life incident that took place in 1727 and is recorded in a footnote to Manuel Moreno Fraginals's *The Sugarmill*, a classic of postrevolutionary historiography:

> His Excellency the Count of the House of Bayona, in an act of profound Christian fervor, decided to humble himself in front of his slaves. And following the example of Christ, on a Maundy Thursday he washed the feet of twelve blacks, sat them at his table, and served them his food. As things turned out, the slaves, whose theological knowledge was not very profound, did not behave like the Apostles. Instead, and encouraged by the prestige they had acquired in the eyes of the other slaves, they rebelled and burned

the sugar mill. The Count's overseers finished off this most Christian act by hunting down the runaway slaves, and then displaying on top of twelve spears the decapitated heads of the slaves for whom the Most Excellent Count of the House of Bayona had humbled himself.[12]

The film dramatizes these events, but instead of reproducing the interpretation above that the slaves rebel because the count encouraged them to do so, it places historical agency squarely on the slaves, and in particular on the rebel slave Sebastián (Idelfonso Tamayo). The film also moves the action to the 1790s, after the Haitian Revolution, in part to make a connection between that Revolution and the Cuban one, and in part to underscore the count's conflict between Christian piety and the economic opportunity to expand sugar production in order to take advantage of the rise in world sugar prices after the Haitian Revolution.

The film is structured like a triptych. The first part sets the stage, and includes episodes such as the overseer Don Manuel's (Luis Alberto García) brutal treatment of slaves, the count's (Nelson Villagra) highly anticipated arrival, and the preparations for the supper. The second and central part of the triptych is the supper sequence, a fifty-five-minute-long tour de force where the count's attempts to evangelize the slaves are met with reactions ranging from piety to incredulity to outright rejection. Finally, the third part of the triptych plays out the consequences of what happened during the dinner: the slaves rebel, and when the count wakes and realizes what has happened, he gives the orders to round up and decapitate the twelve slaves and display their heads on the location where he intends to build a church in honor of the killed overseer. Only Sebastián manages to escape capture, by using shamanistic powers to transform himself into animals in order to continue the fight against repression at some other place and time, much like Mackandal and Ti Noel in Alejo Carpentier's novel *The Kingdom of This World* (1949).

Aesthetically, the film is realist, with great attention paid to the historical accuracy of costumes, speech, and mise-en-scène. However, whereas the realism in the first and third parts of the film is conventional, with extensive use of a handheld camera and natural lighting, the realism in the supper sequence spills over to the neobaroque, with a theatrical mise-en-scène that is structured as a tableau vivant of Leonardo da Vinci's *The Last Supper,* a cinematography saturated by sumptuous colors and chiaroscuro, the extensive use of parables as a narrative device, and the structuring use of counterpoints in dialogues that pit the count's monologistic Christianity against the pluralism of the slaves'

FIGURE 8.2 *Tableau vivant* of Leonardo da Vinci's *The Last Supper* (1495–98) and Luis Buñuel's *Viridiana* (1961) as intertextual signifiers in *The Last Supper* (Tomás Gutiérrez Alea, Cuba, 1976)

worldviews, as well as between the disparate perspectives of the slaves themselves (fig. 8.2). The aesthetic contrast between the central and side panels of this cinematic triptych underscores the neobaroque theatricality of the supper sequence, inviting viewers to read its mise-en-scène as allegorizing a colonial power structure where the count sits at the center of a slave economy, and on another, complementary level, as a critique of the count's instrumentalization of Christianity because the mise-en-scène, modeled as it is after da Vinci's *The Last Supper,* identifies the abusive count with Christ and the exploited slaves with the apostles.[13]

The count's instrumentalization of Christianity is historically accurate. When he admonishes Sebastián for trying to escape, for example, his words are a close transliteration of a sermon published in 1797, where the author recommends that priests in *ingenios* never side with the blacks, but should rather say to them, in pidgin Spanish, "You yourselves are to blame because not all of you fulfill your obligations; you are many; overseer only one; today one is missing, tomorrow another one, today one does a naughty thing, tomorrow someone else does it: every day overseer must put up with this: every day the same story, but he doesn't like it; of course, he gets mad."[14]

Sebastián's response is to spit in the count's face, a dramatic climax that Dennis West has read in light of Georg Wilhelm Friedrich Hegel's master-slave dialectic: "In *The Phenomenology of Mind,* Hegel's notion of recognition means that the master depends on his bondmen for acknowledgment of his power, indeed, for assurance of his very self-hood. As the count reiterates his order that Sebastián recognize him, the camera emphatically dollies on their juxtaposed faces, and a tense silence reigns. The slave's eventual answer is to spit in the master's face—a brutal refusal to recognize the other's lordship and the graphic expression of the birth of the bondman's true self-consciousness: in spite of his actual bondage, the slave's mind is his own."[15]

Unlike Sebastián, other slaves engage the count with questions about Christ and his followers, and even add comments and interpretations of their own. Bangoché (Tito Junco), for example, accepts slavery as natural, but unlike the count, interprets equality from a positional perspective. When the count asks Bangoché whether he prefers Africa or the *ingenio*, Bangoché, who claims to have been a king in Africa, answers adroitly: "Bangoché is a slave." For Bangoché, roles may change, but the notion of slavery is not questioned. The same may be said of Antonio (Samuel Claxon), a domestic slave who has internalized his Uncle Tom–ism to the point of not considering the possibility of being something other than a slave. Sebastián's defiant silence, of course, is a more powerful indictment than all the questions and comments made by the other slaves, and when he finally speaks, after the count falls asleep because he has had too much wine, his words carry a performative dimension lacking in the preceding dialogues:

> Oloffi made the World, he made all of it; he made day, he made night; he made good thing, he made bad thing; he also made pretty thing and ugly thing too. Oloffi made good everything in the world: he made Truth, and he made False too. Truth came out pretty. False came out not good: she was ugly and skinny like a stick, like a sick person. Oloffi felt pity of her and gave her a sharp machete to defend herself. Time passed and everyone always wanted to be with Truth. Nobody, I mean nobody, wanted to be with False. . . . One day Truth and False met in the woods, and since they are enemies, they fight each other. Truth is more strong than False, but False had the sharp machete that Oloffi gave her. When Truth look the other way, False—chaz!—and cuts off the head of Truth. Truth now don't have no eyes and she starts to touch everything to find her head. [Sebastián imitates Truth by closing his eyes and feeling the table.] She looks and she looks with her hands until she finds the head of False and—wham!—she rips the head off False and puts it on where her head was before. And from that day she goes around and around, fooling everybody with the body of Truth and the head of False.[16]

Rather than discarding the discourse of Christianity *in toto* because it has been instrumentalized, the parable recovers those fragments of

FIGURE 8.3 Sebastián's (Idelfonso Tamayo) performative truth-telling in *The Last Supper*

Christianity that are emancipatory (i.e., the body of Truth), and discards those that are not (i.e., the count's instrumentalization of that Truth). The way Alea frames Sebastián as he tells the parable, in a single close-up shot, is important, for it helps identify Sebastián with the body of Truth and the count with the head of False. To be precise, just as Sebastián says that the headless Truth rips out the head of False, he grabs the head of the pig in front of the count and places it in front of his own face (fig. 8.3). This signals to viewers that Sebastián is to Truth what the count is to False.

Moreover, when Sebastián moves the pig head away from his face, what remains in the frame is no longer his previous self, but a self that has, through the performative language of African oral tradition, incorporated what is valuable from a European emancipatory discourse into his own shamanic tradition. This means that in his final escape from the slave hunters, when Sebastián transforms himself into a succession of animals, he is not simply seeking individual freedom. That would be a very narrow reading of his escape, in line with liberalism's emphasis on individual freedom. Rather, he is also transforming himself for a future return as a messiah in line with an African tradition of shamanism à la Mackandal in Carpentier's *The Kingdom of This World*—who transforms himself into animals so that he can return at a more propitious time to continue the struggle for justice and freedom for his people—and also in line with a European tradition of messianism à la Christ, who died and returned to this world to continue the struggle for the equivalent of Truth in Sebastián's parable.

Some critics have rejected Sebastián's final transformation because it is not historically accurate. Nevertheless, the symbolic reading of Sebastián as messiah makes clear that his final escape should not to be read according to the documentarist codes of the first and last parts of the film-as-triptych, but in light of Carpentier's notion of a marvelous reality (*lo real maravilloso*):

> [D]uring my stay in Haiti . . . I found myself in daily contact with something we could call the marvelous real. I was treading earth where thousands of men, eager for liberty, believed in Mackandal's lycanthropic powers, to the point that their collective faith produced a miracle on the day of his execution. . . .
>
> There is a moment in the sixth *Song of Maldoror* when the hero, chased by all the police in the world, escapes from "an army of agents and spies" by taking on the shape of diverse animals and making use of his ability to transport himself instantly to Peking, Madrid, or Saint Petersburg. This is "marvelous literature" at its peak. But in the Americas, where nothing like that has been written, there did exist a Mackandal who possessed the same powers because of the faith of his contemporaries, and who used that magic to encourage one of the most dramatic and strange uprisings in History.[17]

From this perspective, *The Last Supper* conceives of Cuban culture as the tensile combination of two "faiths" that are equally real and marvelous: African shamanism and European Christianity. Insofar as Sebastián embodies, as we have seen, the emancipatory potential of both, *The Last Supper* interprets European and African cultures as having equal status. Unlike mainstream theories of *mestizaje,* racial democracy, and transculturation, this neobaroque understanding of the tensile interplay between European and African cultures as opposites that do not cancel each other out does not downplay the brutality Europeans have brought upon Africans, or suggest that African culture will be absorbed into a Cuban national culture that is European in the main. Instead, it suggests the possibility that Cuba will someday free itself from the legacy of European colonialism (racism, Eurocentrism, gross inequalities) without having to renounce what is liberatory about its European and African heritages.

The reconstruction of history implies a comment on contemporary events, and just as the film explicitly critiques the Count's monologistic Christianity, it implicitly critiques contemporary Cuba's monologistic Marxism. Consider the following two citations. The first, taken from Manuel Moreno Fraginals's *The Sugarmill,* refers to the first sugar boom in Cuba's history in 1792, the timeframe of the film. The second comes from Carmelo Mesa-Lago's *Cuba in the 1970s,* and refers to the ten-million-ton harvest of 1970. Their dates could be switched and still they would remain valid.

> [The sugar harvest] was characterized by the abandonment, to incredible limits, of all activities that did not affect, directly or indirectly, sugar production.[18]

> [The sugar harvest was] achieved by depleting resources from other sectors of the economy, which in turn suffered output declines offsetting the increase in sugar output.[19]

In the first few years of the Revolution, economic policy prioritized reducing Cuba's historic dependence on sugar through industrialization and agricultural diversification. By 1964, however, these efforts were abandoned because output in all sectors had declined to unacceptable levels, and sugar once again became the primary target of agricultural planning.[20] Two factors spoke in favor of this reversal: the rise in 1963 of the commodity's price, and the realization that sugar offered "an obvious and relatively cost-effective method of reversing the mounting balance of trade deficits by mobilizing efforts around a sector in which Cuba possessed adequate personnel and sufficient experience."[21] In March 1968, Fidel Castro proclaimed that "the question of a sugar harvest of 10 million tons [for the 1970 harvest] has become something more than an economic goal; it is something that has been converted into a point of honor for this Revolution, it has become a yardstick by which to judge the capability of the Revolution . . . and if a yardstick is put up to the Revolution, there is no doubt about the Revolution meeting the mark."[22]

The sugar harvest was to be the basis for Cuba's great leap forward into the developed world. As in China, this economic leap was to be achieved with a parallel shift in subjective consciousness, a veritable cultural revolution. The blueprint for this new "moral economy" is spelled out in Che Guevara's essay "The New Man":

> The resulting [economic] theory will unfailingly give preeminence to the two pillars of the construction [of a moral economy]: the formation of the new man, and the development of technical knowledge. Much remains to be done on both counts, but the backwardness in science is less excusable, because in this respect it is not a matter of walking blindly, but of following for a good stretch of the way the path opened by the most advanced nations of the world. [Our youth] is the malleable clay with which we must build the new man. . . . We will make a new man for the twenty-first century. We will forge ourselves in daily action, and create a new man with a new science.[23]

The essay's messianic tone—not to mention its author's own heroic example—set the tone for Sino-Guevarism, a fusion of Maoist ideological purity with Guevara's charismatic zeal and humanistic ideals. Like Christianity in the 1790s, Sino-Guevarism was a powerful emancipatory discourse in the 1960s. The main features of the New Man were discipline, selfless motivation, and a strong work ethic, the combination of which would purge persisting bourgeois sins and help usher in stateless Communism. Two events in 1968, however, did not bode well for the development of this vision. One was the nationalization of all the small businesses, and the other was Castro's approval of the Soviet invasion of Czechoslovakia. Then, beginning in 1970, the Cuban state gained increasing control over more aspects of Cuban life, a state of affairs achieved at the expense of the openness, freshness, and promise that characterized the 1960s. Finally, even though the target of harvesting ten million tons of sugar was achieved, disappointment set in and cynicism grew, and instead of shaking off the monoculture economy, Cuba became even more defined by it.

The sugar economy of the late eighteenth and early nineteenth centuries differed in many important ways from the Cuban "moral economy" of 1966–70. One cannot help but note, however, how these two widely divergent economic models, which differed so much in professed ends and actual practice, shared many outward features. Both concentrated economic decisions in the hands of a few. Both treated workers paternalistically, tying them to their masters through "free" services. Both minimized material stimuli in their compensation of workers. And both responded to the attendant decrease in production by militarizing the workplace. All of this was facilitated, and some would say made possible, by the instrumentalization of two otherwise liberatory discourses: Christianity in the 1790s, and Marxism in the 1970s. These parallelisms cannot have escaped Alea, and *The Last Supper* may have been his attempt to recover the emancipatory potential of both Christianity and Marxism through a neobaroque praxis that is contrapuntal, pluralist, and, in this particular case, as didactic as the Christian triptychs that perhaps inspired its structure.

La nación clandestina (1989)

La nación clandestina (The Clandestine Nation; Jorge Sanjinés, Bolivia, 1989) offers what may be the most sophisticated treatment of indigenous subjectivity in all of Latin American narrative cinema.[24] It tells the story of Sebastián Mamani (Reynaldo Yujra), an Aymara man who revisits his life, after death, through a series of flashbacks and flashbacks within flashbacks. Sebastián's first flashback is to an ancient dance to the death that he witnessed as a child, the *jacha tata danzante,* whose objective was to help ease/forgive the community's collective faults so that its harmony with nature could be restored, and with it, the rains that had not arrived for several years. New flashbacks follow, each activated, à la Proust, by a chance sensation. His own family hands him over as domestic help to a criollo family from La Paz, because the mother believes that this will give Sebastián better opportunities in life. As an adult, Sebastián lives in one of the many poor, working-class neighborhoods that ring La Paz, where he earns his living as a builder of wooden coffins. To earn more money, he enlists in the national army, and then in the Bolivian secret service. Alienated from his own roots, he becomes an alcoholic and at one point, just before participating in a secret service raid on the home of criollo political dissidents, he changes his last name from the indigenous Mamani to the European-sounding Maisman. This is Sebastián's nadir, the point in the narrative when he has fully internalized the racist values of the criollo family that had adopted/bought him, of the army, and of the secret service. After the raid Sebastián feels worse than ever, and when his brother Vicente (Orlando Huanca) finds him drunk in a cantina, he takes Sebastián with him to Willkani, the *ayllu* where they grew up.

In Willkani, Sebastián is welcomed like a prodigal son, and he falls for the young Basilia (Delfina Mamani). But instead of treating her with respect, one day he finds her alone and begins to throw pebbles at her until she is trapped between him and a precipice. The sequence is shot in extreme wide angles intended to help viewers maintain a critical distance from what could easily have been a melodramatic subplot, and ends abruptly without showing us what happened next: a likely rape. Notwithstanding this violence, Sebastián is elected to speak with state officials in La Paz regarding an offer of food aid. The offer of aid divides the *ayllu.* Some are in favor of accepting it because of the prolonged drought, while others warn that this type of aid has always brought with it more dependency and poverty. Without a mandate, Sebastián leaves for La Paz as Willkani's representative, and once there, unilaterally accepts the aid as part of a corrupt deal to sell part of it and keep the proceeds. In his violence toward Basilia and in his betrayal of the community's trust in order to enrich himself, this first Sebastián embodies the androcentric and racist attitude of the official criollo nation toward the clandestine, indigenous nation, as if it were completely natural for criollos (and those who internalize their values) to rape indigenous women and to sell what belongs to everyone for personal profit.

When the elders of the *ayllu* find out about Sebastián's corruption, they call a meeting and resolve to exile him from Willkani. Ironically, it is here that Sebastián's decolonization begins. Back in La Paz, and after a superbly acted drunken spree, Sebastián commissions an Aymara artist to make a mask for the *jacha tata danzante*, and with the mask strapped to a backpack, begins his trek back to Willkani by foot. During his journey there are additional flashbacks, and a key sequence where a criollo university student is being persecuted by state armed forces. When it becomes evident that a group of indigenous women cannot help him because they do not speak Spanish, the student hurls racist insults at them and leaves. All in all, it is a critical commentary on the hypocrisy of a sector of the intellectual left that claims to fight on behalf of the Indians, yet never takes the time to learn their language, culture, or history.

After a tense encounter with the same armed forces that are following (and in fact kill) the university student, Sebastián finally arrives at the outskirts of Willkani. The children welcome him, curious about the outfit he is now wearing (fig. 8.4). Soon the community's shaman (Roque Salgado) arrives. Sebastián respectfully explains his intentions, and the shaman lets him proceed after having consulted with the *ayllu*'s elders. At this point, survivors of a massacre at the nearby mines also arrive. The first wide-angle shot of the returning survivors is very similar to the opening sequence in Jorge Sanjinés's militant feature *El coraje del pueblo* (The Courage of the People; Bolivia, 1971), where a group of indigenous miners march together toward the mines to claim better wages and working conditions. In *La nación clandestina*, however, the confrontation is no longer between workers and employers, which are Marxist categories, but between different groups within the indigenous community, and within Sebastián himself. In this sense, *La nación clandestina* is what Freya Schiwy has called an Indianized film, a film focused on "decolonizing the soul [by] strengthening indigenous cultures and their perceived value [and by] integrating independent filmmakers and consultants into a cultural politics designed by indigenous social movements. . . . The process is aimed at broadening the procedure of analyzing and generating proposals within communities, rather than at raising consciousness from without."[25]

FIGURE 8.4 Sebastián (Reynaldo Yujra), prepared for the performative ritual dance, in *La nación clandestina* (The Clandestine Nation; Jorge Sanjinés, Bolivia, 1989). Courtesy Cinemateca Boliviana

In effect, *La nación clandestina* breaks with the Marxist interpretation that *El coraje del pueblo* makes of the historical Massacre of San Juan in 1961 at the Siglo XX Mine in Bolivia, to instead explore the cultural dynamics of inclusion and exclusion within an indigenous community torn between two options: one militant, with survivors solemnly carrying martyred heroes on their backs, and the other neobaroque, with a shaman pleading on behalf of an outcast to take the community in an altogether different direction. The sequence, filmed in what Sanjinés called an "integral sequence shot" (see explanation below), culminates with the shaman prevailing over the indignant miners. This opens the way for the film's denouement, which is Sebastián's ritual dance to the death and the subsequent funeral procession, with Sebastián now carried solemnly on the backs of the Indians who only recently rejected him. Finally, in the last shot of the film, Sebastián emerges from behind the camera, observing with us his own funeral/reincorporation into the *ayllu*.

The ending of *La nación clandestina* facilitates a neobaroque reading of the reborn Sebastián as a collective individual who combines the indigenous values of reciprocity and solidarity with the Enlightenment values of democracy and individual freedom (see "neobaroque" in the appendix to this book). This new Sebastián redeems himself not by sacrificing his own individuality to an undifferentiated collectivity, but by harmonizing his own individual aspirations with the needs of the collectivity, and his own personal memory with the memory of the collectivity in a way that is analogous to the popular nineteenth-century belief (now discredited) that ontogeny recapitulates phylogeny.[26] By this I mean that just as Sebastián at first loses his communion with nature and with his own people because he is sold off as labor power, then survives a long period of disharmony when he becomes more and more assimilated into Western culture until he even changes last names, and finally returns to a renewed harmonization with nature after a dance to the death that symbolizes the beginning of a new, different Sebastián, the indigenous (Aymara) nation was likewise bought and sold as labor power when the Spaniards arrived, then survived a long period of disharmony lasting more than four centuries (first under colonialism and then under republican neocolonialism), and now stands at the cusp of a rebirth when the clandestine nation shall give way to an indigenous nation free to choose its own path and openly celebrate its own culture, as equals in their humanity to the criollos and every other group in Bolivia. It is a modern nation whose modernity is no longer liberal but rather neobaroque, like Sebastián himself—a highly complex subject who, having overcome the traumas of the colonial and neocolonial experience, is ultimately able to productively combine elements from what Aníbal Quijano calls an original Andean rationality, namely reciprocity and solidarity, with elements from what Quijano calls the original Enlightenment reason, with its emphasis on individual freedom and democracy.[27]

In a 1989 article titled "The Integral Sequence Shot," Sanjinés explained why a sequence filmed with very few or no cuts is the most appropriate form to represent these values:

> In Andean culture, the preeminence of group interests—the collectivist tradition, the practices of solidarity, the view of the whole, of integration and participation—together constitute, in their ideological signifiers and in their daily practice, a befitting way to face reality, to solve the problems of life and of society as well as the problems of selfhood, subordinated to the collective needs. . . . It seemed fundamental to us to propose a narrative technique fitting the Andean worldview. . . . Little by little, it became clear to us that the camera should move without interruption and motivated by the internal dynamic of the scene. Only then could we achieve its imperceptibility and the integration of the space. By not splitting the sequence into diverse shots

we could transmit a new ordering, an ordering that is befitting to the peoples who conceive of everything as a continuation of themselves.[28]

The unifying impulse behind this theorization of the integral sequence shot is reflective of a neobaroque praxis far removed from the militancy of Sanjinés's earlier films, whose dialectical montage underscored the impossibility of a negotiated resolution to the narrated social conflicts. In *La nación clandestina,* to be more exact, opposite sides (Sebastián Mamani and the returning miners) do not cancel each other out, as they would have in Sanjinés's earlier films. Instead, Sebastián and the returning miners enter into a contrapuntal and highly productive dialogue within a single integral sequence shot. This neobaroque counterpoint between opposites that do not cancel each other out is then sealed in the two closing sequences, both of which are also filmed as integral sequence shots: first, the *jacha tata danzante,* a highly stylized and masked ritual that is both individual and collective, and then the closing funeral sequence, where the two Sebastiáns are clearly different (one is dead, the other alive) and yet the same, because the relationship between life and death, body and spirit, individual and collectivity, even mestizo and Aymara, is no longer oppositional but rather relational and dialogical.

THEORY OF THE NEW LATIN AMERICAN CINEMA

Any discussion of the New Latin American Cinema that does not consider filmmakers' own theorizations would be incomplete. José Carlos Avellar considers it a continuation of the directors' filmmaking by other means, "a way of imagining forms that do not yet exist, a way to rethink experiences that have already been lived, a way of generating images and suggesting narrative and cinematographic models in the same ways that an unfilmed script suggests."[29] Indeed, the transition from militancy to the neobaroque also takes place in the filmmakers' theorizations of their own work, in an arc that goes from Glauber Rocha's militant "Eztetyka do Fame" (a.k.a. "Aesthetics of Hunger" and "Aesthetics of Violence"; 1965) to his irrationalist "Eztetyka do Sonho" ("Aesthetics of Dream"; 1971); from Fernando Birri's analytical "For a National, Realist, and Popular Cinema" (1962) to his poetic "For a Cosmic, Delirious, and Lumpen Cinema (Manifesto for Cosmunism, or Cosmic Communism)" (1978); and from Jorge Sanjinés's Marxist "Problems of Form and Content in Revolutionary Cinema" (1978) to his neo-indigenist "The Integral Sequence Shot" (1989).

For most people, militancy is the first thing that comes to mind when hearing "New Latin American Cinema." Three anthologies have helped to popularize this view: *Twenty-Five Years of New Latin American Cinema* (1983), edited by Michael Chanan for a London retrospective of the movement; *Hojas de Cine*, a major three-volume undertaking by several cultural and educational institutions in Mexico (1988); and the two-volume *New Latin American Cinema*, edited by Michael T. Martin in 1997.[30] In all three anthologies one can read the militant manifestos from the 1960s cited above, but none of the neobaroque ones from the 1970s and 1980s. Yet the neobaroque manifestos (among which Raúl Ruiz's 1995 *Poetics of Cinema* must be included) are as important as the earlier ones in understanding the evolution of the NLAC's project of cultural nationalism.[31]

Take Rocha, for example. In "Aesthetics of Hunger," discussed in the previous chapter in relation to *Black God, White Devil*, Rocha uses the famous sequence where Manuel kills the landholding coronel as an example of justified violence because it crystallizes Manuel's dilemma as a clear-cut choice between continued oppression or liberation. In *Terra em Transe* (Land in Anguish; Brazil, 1967), however, Rocha explores Manuel's dilemma in more subtle ways, via the figure of a male intellectual who is, like Manuel, torn between charismatic leaders, and whose conscience is, like Rosa in *Black God, White Devil*, a woman far more intelligent than he is. The experience, coupled with the new political reality post-coup, led him to write "Aesthetics of Dream," a manifesto whose title is a clear reference to the baroque reality-dream dyad, and whose main argument is that revolutionary art should be as concerned with aesthetics and philosophical speculation as it is with politics:

> A work of revolutionary art should not only act in an immediate political way, but also promote philosophical speculation and create an aesthetic of humankind's eternal movement toward cosmic integration. The discontinuous existence of such revolutionary art in the Third World is due fundamentally to the repressions caused by [instrumental] reason. . . . Today's filmmakers, those from the Right as much as those from the Left, are imprisoned by conservative reasoning. . . . The Right thinks according to the logic of order and progress . . . while the responses from the Left, in the case of Brazil, have been paternalistic in relation to the central topic of political conflicts: the impoverished masses.[32]

An aesthetics of dream should therefore supersede an aesthetics of reality, where reality is the kind of raw violence and hunger Rocha highlighted in "Aesthetics of Violence," and dream is the kind of philosophical art he proposes in "Aesthetics of Dream." Rocha put this call into practice in *Der Leone Have Sept Cabeças* (The Lion Has Seven Heads; Brazil, 1971), but it is in *A Idade da Terra* (*The Age of the Earth*; Brazil, 1980) where the development of a neobaroque language filled with symbols and theatricality to critique instrumental rationality points the way toward what he calls the cosmic integration of humanity. The narrative of *The Age of the Earth* is difficult to summarize. Conceptually, however, Rocha's own synopsis captures the epic sweep and allegorical complexity of his most experimental film:

> The film shows a Fisherman-Christ, the Christ performed by Jece Valadão; a Black Christ, performed by Antônio Pitanga; [it] shows the Christ who is a Portuguese Conqueror, Dom Sebastião, performed by Tarcísio Meira; and [it] shows the Warrior-Christ Ogum de Lampião, performed by Geraldo Del Rey. That means, the Four Horsemen of the Apocalypse which reanimate Christ in the Third World, retelling the myth through the Four Evangelists: Matthew, Mark, Luke and John, whose identity is revealed in the movie almost as if it would be a Third Testament. And the film assumes a prophetic tone, really biblical and religious.[33]

In a key sequence, the Black Christ begins a sermon by yelling "All this sea of mud!," a clear reference to *Black God, White Devil*'s motif-ideal of the *sertão* that turns into the sea, only this time the two are thoroughly mixed. And as the Black Christ continues with his sermon about the rights of men, Rocha's own voice-over sermon takes over the soundtrack: "All this ideology of love would concentrate in a Christianity born of the African, Asian, European, Latin American peoples, from the 'total peoples.' A Christianity that is not embodied solely in the Catholic Church, but in all religions that find the figure of Christ in their most subterranean, recondite, eternal, and lost symbols. A Christ that is not dead, but alive and outpouring love and creativity. The search for eternity and for victory over death."

For Rocha, one could say, the crucified Christ is to instrumental rationality what the living Christs are to substantive reason, so that *The Age of the Earth*, with all its Christs, both living and dead, represents Brazil as a microcosm of a global community where substantive reason is on the verge of declaring victory over instrumental reason, an idea embodied in the film by the plurality of living Christs who are about to displace the crucified Christ.

Birri's transition from militancy to the neobaroque parallels that of Rocha. Birri's early militancy is evidenced in "Cinema and Underdevel-

FIGURE 8.5   Baroque fragmentation in *Org* (Fernando Birri, Italy, 1979)

opment" (1962), where he writes, "Our purpose is to create a new person, a new society, a new history and therefore a new art and a new cinema. Urgently. . . . *Conclusion*: to confront reality with a camera and to document it, filming realistically, filming critically, filming underdevelopment with the optic of the people."[34] Here is as good a list of the tropes of the militant phase as any other: a new man, a new cinema, a new history, urgency, realism, from the perspective of the people, critical, underdevelopment. All were put into practice in *Tire dié* (Argentina, 1958/1960), yet fifteen years later Birri's praxis had changed dramatically. After an intense effort that lasted fully ten years, he finished and screened *Org* (Italy, 1979) (fig. 8.5). Hermann Herlinghaus notes that in contrast to a typical feature film,

> which has between 600 and 800 shots, the number of splices in *Org* reaches 26,625, the result of 8,340 hours of work by three women. The soundtrack (one year's worth of work), with its 616 premixed and 429 mixed tracks, synthesizes 102 hours of conversation, sounds, and music, including 500 repertoire sound effects. The color scheme, with its 6,524 lighting changes, is the equivalent to that in 10 films (compared to the average of 700 in a typical film). There are 257,368 stills, and a total of 419,922 meters of filmed material shot on 33 different types of film stock. . . . A kaleidoscopic multitude of

more than 300 hypothetical characters appear, from Salvador Allende [to] Johann Sebastian Bach, Roland Barthes [and] Ernesto "Che" Guevara . . . in addition to beggars, skeletons, alchemists. The aesthetic procedure that makes it possible to present such a plurality is the principle of the montage-collage, whose roots can be found in the Dadaist photomontage. . . . The spectator feels implicated in . . . an indigestible baroque audiovisual chaos whereby the video clip method is taken to its limits.[35]

This excess of signifiers situates the film squarely in the neobaroque phase of the NLAC.[36] *Org*, says Birri, "is an invented name whose etymological root is the word *orgasm*. I dedicate it to Che Guevara, to Méliès, author of *A Trip to the Moon,* and to Wilhelm Reich, author of the sexual revolution, because I believe them to be three emblematic figures who remain from the 1960s, a decade when a man lands on the moon, when Che is assassinated, and when the political situation explodes in France. . . . It is also a film that shares the tensions in Glauber [Rocha]'s *A Idade da Terra,* its filmic sibling."[37]

The anarchist celebration of excess of signifiers in *Org*, made explicit by the film's opening quote by the English poet William Blake ("The road of excess leads to the palace of wisdom"), points also to the symbolic character of the film's protagonists, as described in the official synopsis:

Several years after the explosion of the atomic mushroom, the Black Grr helps his friend, the White Zohom, to successfully conquer the love of Shuick. Later, out of jealousy, Zohom interrogates an old electronic sibyl about his love . . ., confirms his suspicions, and in desperation, cuts off his head. Grr . . ., upon finding him, also kills himself. Shuick tries to throw herself off a cliff, but the electronic sibyl stops her and offers to resuscitate her two friends. [When they come back to life], their heads have been exchanged (accidentally?), whereupon a dispute emerges between the two bodies to decide who will stay with Shuick.[38]

By creating a fiction filled with a plethora of signifiers that are emptied of their referentiality (for example the nonsensical names of the protagonists, or the insertion of documentary clips with no direct relationship to the fictional narrative), *Org* offers a fresh perspective on the extra-filmic world, no longer tied to rationalizations of the Right or the Left, but rather as an upside-down world (a baroque motif) where war is normal, peace is impossible, sex is a tool of power, and the horizon of possibilities does not extend beyond surface reality. The intra-filmic world, on the other hand, puts into practice Rocha's call, in "Aesthetics of Dream," for a cosmic cinema, in the sense of going beyond what is directly material and rational. Little wonder Birri titled the manifesto that accompanies *Org* "For a Cosmic, Delirious, and Lumpen Cinema (Manifesto of Cosmunism or Cosmic Communism)." The text, written in an appropriately neobaroque style, is nothing short of a clarion call to revolutionize the NLAC:

> We will not have a lasting revolution without a revolution in language sensual hedonist erotic communism thinking entrails: cosmunism fabrication of a poem or a novella clash craft versus industry cosmic and magical communism for a cosmic delirious and lumpen cinema (between cinema and noncinema or beyond-cinema: filmunculus). . . . (Pythagoric montage techniques, oracular and alchemical) . . . for a cosmic delirious and lumpen cinema sensual communism hedonist erotica thinking entrails: cosmunism (a Rorschach film test) therefore ideologize everything but also sensorialize everything tabula rasa: cinema from zero to experiment ORG ("only for lunatics") fabrication of a poem or of a . . .[39]

The manifesto justifies the plethora of contrasting images in the film with a language that is also plethoric in opposites that do not cancel each other out (for example "between cinema and non-cinema," "thinking entrails"). More to the point, Birri theorizes *Org* as a "tabula rasa: cinema from zero," a trope analogous to the "founding space" that Severo Sarduy theorized in his book *Barroco*: "In the symbolic space of the baroque . . . we find the textual citation or the metaphor of the foundational space, as posited by contemporary Astronomy; in contemporary [artistic] production, the expansion of the stability of the universe that today's Cosmology supposes is indistinguishable from Astronomy: we can no longer observe without having the facts that we collect remit us, thanks to their magnitude, to the 'origin' of the universe."[40]

Org is like that symbolic space of the baroque where the excess of contrasting images remits us not to a future utopia, but to the construction of a utopia in the present. It is therefore a symbolic space that includes all of our creative possibilities without some of these possibilities having to, by necessity, precede other possibilities, as in orthodox Marxism's stagist historiography. Not in vain does Sarduy title the first chapter in *Barroco* "o: Echo Chamber," with a number zero instead of a number one. And not in vain is the central image of this first chapter a chamber where "sometimes the echo precedes the voice."[41] Applied to *Org*, this idea of an effect that can precede a cause suggests that Birri's project is nothing short of the creation of a present utopia where love, embodied by the sexually liberated Shuick (Lidija Juracik), and solidarity, embodied in the brotherhood between the white Zohom (Terence Hill) and the black Grr (Isaac Tweg Obn), are starting points and not endpoints of a radically revolutionary praxis based on quotidian love and solidarity.

A third case of a director whose theory makes the transition from militancy to the neobaroque is Jorge Sanjinés. As late as 1977, Sanjinés saw militant, documentarist cinema as the most appropriate kind of cinema for the anti-imperialist struggle: "Today's militant cinema has its clearest origin in the first important documentaries that are done in Bolivia through the official organism [the Bolivian Cinematographic Institute] created by the revolutionary government in 1952. . . . Out of this production a revolutionary cinema developed, oriented toward the anti-imperialist struggle."[42]

This political function of cinema, mediated through documentarist modes of representation, is clearly seen in *Yawar Mallku* (*Blood of the Condor*; Bolivia, 1969), and especially in the aforementioned *El coraje del pueblo* (Bolivia, 1971). With *El enemigo principal* (The Principal Enemy; Bolivia, 1974), Sanjinés begins to shift away from his early documentarism by not specifying when and where the re-created events take place. His best-known manifesto, "Problems of Form and Content in Revolutionary Cinema" (1978), points to the change that his thinking is undergoing, as when he writes that "communication in revolutionary art should seek the development of reflexivity."[43] This transition from militancy to reflexivity culminates, as we have already seen, in *La nación clandestina* and in the article titled "The Integral Sequence Shot," discussed earlier, where he explains why this particular cinematic form best serves the core values of the film.

Rocha, Birri, and Sanjinés are exceptional theoreticians of the NLAC because they wrote about both their militant and their neobaroque practices. Other filmmakers theorized primarily militancy (Julio García Espinosa) or primarily the neobaroque (Raúl Ruiz), and still others opted to incorporate their theorization into the films themselves. In *Macunaíma* (Joaquim Pedro de Andrade, Brazil, 1969), for example, the main character suffers realistically impossible transformations that impede a unity of perspective. Born as a black adult (Grande Otelo) to an old white woman (Paulo José), and then turning white (also played by Paulo José) halfway through the film, Macunaíma's life trajectory demystifies the legend of Brazil's harmony between three races by exaggerating baroque formulae such as reversals of fortune, allegorical signification, and anachronism. Such exaggeration highlights the precedence of role

FIGURE 8.6 The climactic cannibalistic orgy in *Macunaíma* (Joaquim Pedro de Andrade, Brazil, 1969)

over character in Brazilian society at the time, and becomes, in the context of a brutal military dictatorship, a subversive appropriation of the *chanchada*. At the same time, there is also in *Macunaíma* an appropriation and revaluation of Brazilian Modernismo, not only because the film adapts Mario de Andrade's eponymous 1928 novel, but also because it references, in the climactic anthropophagous orgy (fig. 8.6) and in the white Macunaíma's subsequent fall into senseless consumption, the kind of low cannibalism that Oswald de Andrade criticized in his 1928 "Manifesto Antropófago": "Cannibalism. Absorption of the sacred enemy. . . . Carnal at first, [the cannibal] instinct becomes elective, and creates friendship. When it is affective, it creates love. When it is speculative, it creates science. It takes detours and moves around. At times it is degraded. Low cannibalism, agglomerated with the sins of catechism—envy, usury, calumny, murder. We are acting against this plague of a supposedly cultured and Christianized peoples. Cannibals."[44]

This kind of recuperation and reinsertion of the historical avant-garde (in this case Brazilian Modernismo) into broad-based popular culture is a hallmark of the NLAC's neobaroque phase. We saw it already in Paul Leduc's incorporation of the 1938 "Manifesto for an Independent Revolutionary Art" into the narrative of *Frida Still Life,* and it can also be seen in Fernando Solanas's *Sur* (The South; Argentina-France, 1988) in the many parallels between the film's Proyecto Sur (a clandestine operation led by one of the characters to recalibrate Argentina's cultural and economic compass away from the metropolitan North), and Joaquín Torres García's 1935 manifesto "The School of the South":

> *Our north is the South.* There should be no north for us, except in opposition to our South. That is why we now turn the map upside down, and now we know what our true position is, and it is not the way the rest of the world would like to have it. From now on, the elongated tip of South America will point insistently at the South, our North. Our compass as well; it will incline irremediably and forever towards the South, towards our pole. When ships sail from here traveling north, they will *be traveling down, not up* as before. Because the North is now below. And as we face our South, the East is to our left. This is a necessary rectification; so that now we know where we are.[45]

This intertextual reference functions as part of a neobaroque strategy of inversion that repositions the marginal as central, and in so doing negates Eurocentric teleologies, in particular that of the Euro-liberal nation as the privileged and desired social and cultural narrative of progress. Thus, Solanas often shows the protagonist and his friends reflected in mirrors and shrouded in a bluish fog, as if signaling to the viewer that the discourse of progress used by the military dictatorship of the previous decade is an exercise in smoke and mirrors that can conceal neither the memory of the disappeared nor the omnipresence (and therefore centrality) of the socially and politically marginalized (fig. 8.7).

It should be clear from these examples that when artists such as Rocha, Birri, Sanjinés, Pedro de Andrade, Leduc, and Solanas point out, in their films and in their theoretical writings, the limits of the orthodox Left, they do so not as rightist reactionaries would. Rather, they do it as committed artists who are keenly aware that the crisis of the Left in the 1970s and 1980s should be a transit toward more inclusivity, and they do so also as artists who saw in the neobaroque a praxis befitting the new ideal of cosmic integration and this ideal's core values of reciprocity, solidarity, and democracy.

FIGURE 8.7 Smoke and mirrors as neobaroque tropes in *Sur* (The South; Fernando Solanas, Argentina-France, 1988)

ARC OF THE NEW LATIN AMERICAN CINEMA

The New Latin American Cinema begins with films that are overwhelmingly militant and documentarist. It then enters a short period of transition in the late 1960s and early 1970s when many filmmakers mix documentary modes of representation with neobaroque strategies of representation. Finally, it enters a long period in the 1970s and into the 1980s when an explicitly neobaroque praxis is widespread. What links the militant and the neobaroque phases is neither a unified aesthetics nor a comparable political landscape, but rather the continuity in the filmmakers' unwavering commitment to a revolutionary political project, and to the creation of a cinematic language appropriate for that task. Thus, whether the NLAC served a populist and militant political project of national liberation that seemed achievable and oftentimes even inevitable (as in the 1960s), or a project of denouncing and undermining authoritarianism and in some cases totalitarianism (as in the

1970s and 1980s), the uniting factor of these two phases of the NLAC was the systematic critique of unequal power structures and social relations through inventive and experimental forms. Throughout the movement, that is, the filmmakers' search for an aesthetic language they could call their own was as important as, and in fact inseparable from, the search for other forms of emancipation. The price that filmmakers of the NLAC paid for this search was, generally speaking, the loss of broad audience appeal, yet it was a loss many willingly paid, because they saw the continued use of conventional genres and identification techniques as reproducing traditional values, and therefore unacceptable.

The trajectory of some of the best-known filmmakers of the NLAC—Fernando Birri, Glauber Rocha, Tomás Gutiérrez Alea, Julio García Espinosa, Fernando Solanas, Jorge Sanjinés, Carlos Diegues, Humberto Solás, Nelson Pereira dos Santos, and Paul Leduc—suggests that the NLAC was a generational movement. Four of these directors began their careers as neorealists, with films such as *Rio, 40 Graus* (Rio, 100 Degrees F; Nelson Pereira Dos Santos, Brazil, 1955), *El mégano* (The Charcoal Worker; Julio García Espinosa, Cuba, 1955), *Tire dié*, and *Historias de la Revolución* (Stories of the Revolution; Tomás Gutiérrez Alea, Cuba, 1960). In the early 1960s they pushed neorealism to its aesthetic and political limits in films such as *Barravento* (The Turning Wind; Glauber Rocha, Brazil, 1962), *Vidas Secas* (*Barren Lives*; Nelson Pereira dos Santos, Brazil, 1963), and *Ganga Zumba* (Great Lord; Carlos Diegues, Brazil, 1964).

Almost immediately, they adopted the kind of openly Marxist and documentarist filmmaking most people associate with the NLAC: *Black God, White Devil* (Glauber Rocha, Brazil, 1963), *Os Fuzis* (*The Guns*; Ruy Guerra, Brazil, 1964), the short *Manuela* (Humberto Solás, Cuba, 1966), *The Hour of the Furnaces* (Fernando Solanas and Octavio Getino, Argentina, 1968), *Blood of the Condor* (Jorge Sanjinés, Bolivia, 1969), and *El coraje del pueblo* (The Courage of the People; Jorge Sanjinés, Bolivia, 1971). During the transition between militancy and the neobaroque, in the late 1960s and early 1970s, films such as *Terra em Transe* (Land in Anguish; Glauber Rocha, Brazil, 1967), *Lucía* (Humberto Solás, Cuba, 1968), *Memories of Underdevelopment* (Tomás Gutiérrez Alea, Cuba, 1968), and *Reed, México insurgente* (*Reed: Insurgent Mexico*; Paul Leduc, Mexico, 1972) combined documentarist modes of representation with fragmentary, self-reflexive, highly stylized, and/or poetic elements. Finally, from the middle of the 1970s and into the 1980s, these directors largely abandoned documentarist modes of representation in favor of a neobaroque praxis in films such as *The Last Supper* (Tomás Gutiérrez Alea, Cuba, 1976), *Xica da Silva* (Carlos Diegues, Brazil, 1976), *Org* (Fernando Birri, Italy, 1979), *Como era Gostoso o Meu Francês* (*How Tasty Was My Little Frenchman*; Nelson Pereira dos Santos, Brazil, 1971), *Frida Still Life* (Paul Leduc, Mexico, 1983), *Cecilia* (Humberto Solás, Cuba-Spain, 1981), *The Age of the Earth* (Glauber Rocha, Brazil, 1980), *Sur* (Fernando Solanas, Argentina-France, 1988), *La nación clandestina* (Jorge Sanjinés, Bolivia, 1989), and the appropriately titled *Barroco* (Paul Leduc, Mexico-Spain, 1989).

Many other equally important directors contributed to the development of the NLAC without participating in all of its phases. Among those who helped define the movement's early militancy are Margot Benacerraf, via her visually stunning *Araya* (Venezuela, 1959); the husband-and-wife team of Marta Rodríguez and Jorge Silva, whose *Chircales* (*Brickmakers*; Colombia, 1971) effectively invented an ethical audiovisual anthropology; Santiago Álvarez, whose newsreels revolutionized the genre by editing found footage using what might be called syncopated hypermontage; Miguel Littín, whose *El Chacal de Nahueltoro* (*The Jackal of Nahueltoro*; Chile, 1969) advocates social revolution by pointing to the limits and ironies of reformism; Luis Valdez, whose *I Am Joaquin* (United States, 1972) adapts Rodolfo Gonzales's homonymous epic poem of militant resistance based on Chicano pride; and Felipe Cazals, whose *Canoa* (Mexico, 1975) combines the language of television reportage and social realism to reconstruct a lynching episode as a microcosm of Mexico's social, political, and religious ills.

In the 1970s, Sara Gómez's *One Way or Another* (Cuba, 1974) and Sergio Giral's *The Other Francisco* (Cuba, 1975) mark high points in the transition between militancy and the neobaroque thanks to their inventive synthesis of documentarist militancy and neobaroque self-reflexivity. And finally, in the late 1970s and throughout the 1980s, the neobaroque flourishes in the work of directors such as Alejandro Jodorowsky, whose psychedelic and symbolically rich *La montaña sagrada* (*The Holy Mountain*; United States–Mexico, 1973) has become a cult classic; Arturo Ripstein, whose parody of the clichés of Mexican classical cinema and TV melodramas in *El lugar sin límites* (*The Place Without Limits*; Mexico, 1978), *El imperio de la fortuna* (*The Realm of Fortune*; Mexico, 1986), and *Principio y fin* (*The Beginning and the End*; Mexico, 1993) invent what Daniel Sauvaget calls a social baroque;[46] Diego Rísquez, whose neobaroque trilogy *Bolívar, Sinfonía*

FIGURE 8.8 *Tableau vivant* of Caravaggio's *St. Jerome* (1605–6) and Georges de la Tour's *The Repentant Magdalene* (1635) as intertextual signifiers in *I, the Worst of All* (María Luisa Bemberg, Argentina, 1990)

Tropikal (Venezuela, 1979), *Orinoko* (Venezuela, 1984), and *Amerika, Terra Incognita* (Venezuela, 1988) allegorizes Latin American history through a highly symbolic language and a rich color palette;[47] María Luisa Bemberg, who uses neobaroque aesthetics in *Yo, la peor de todas* (*I, the Worst of All*; Argentina, 1990) to draw analogies between a repressive seventeenth-century state baroque and the Fascism of Argentina's recent military dictatorship (fig. 8.8);[48] Luis Valdez, whose *Zoot Suit* (United States, 1982) links the baroque excess of the protagonists' colorful suits and stylized acting to their rebellious inconformity to dominant discourses of cultural assimilation and bourgeois economic efficiency; and Raúl Ruiz, whose early films in Chile and then in exile in France have almost always been neobaroque.[49] These examples illustrate the many unfoldings of the New Latin American Cinema and the varieties of its contours. Just as important, they disprove the popular view of the New Latin American Cinema as reducible to what Fernando Solanas and Octavio Getino called Third Cinema.[50]

It is generally accepted that the films I have discussed in these last two chapters fall under the category "New Latin American Cinema," and those who have attempted to account for the radical aesthetic and thematic differences between the earlier and later examples have done so by speaking of two, and sometimes three, phases of the NLAC. The case of Brazil is instructive. Critics agree that Cinema Novo entered a second phase after the 1964 military coup. Then, when the military government turned more openly authoritarian in 1968, what one sees is a parallel development of two filmmaking modes: first, *udigrudi* (underground) cinema, a clandestine continuation of militant Cinema Novo that culminated with Eduardo Coutinho's extraordinary documentary *Cabra Marcado para Morrer* (literally "Man Marked to Die," but distributed as *Twenty Years Later*; Brazil, 1984); and, second, the better known Tropicalismo, whose themes and aesthetics are visibly neobaroque. Yet rather than understanding Tropicalismo narrowly as a third phase of Cinema Novo, it is more productive to understand it more broadly, as the Brazilian version of a neobaroque NLAC, much like the term "Cinema Novo" is used to speak of Brazil's version of New Latin American Cinema. Neobaroque NLAC has, then, different manifestations depending on national and subnational circumstances. Regardless of the country, however, the neobaroque NLAC's critique of teleological narratives (in particular that of the liberal nation) justifies its study as a continental movement whose aesthetics may be distinct from those of the militant NLAC, but whose radical critique of existing power structures unfolds out of, and indeed elaborates on, militant NLAC. By drawing on genres that the militant NLAC had shunned because it considered them intrinsically conservative, neobaroque NLAC effectively expanded the militant NLAC's narrow political/aesthetic horizon, in such a way that even when opting for conventional genres, their formulas are brought into play to denounce the artifice of unequal social relations, not to represent them as natural or desirable.

In Argentina, for example, the commercial success of the social melodrama *La historia oficial* (*The Official Story*; Luis Puenzo, 1985) and of the science fiction *Hombre mirando al sudeste* (*Man Facing Southeast*; Eliseo Subiela, Argentina, 1986) may rest on their adoption of generic conventions, which already points to the cinema of the 1990s and 2000s, but their inclusion as part of the New Latin American Cinema rests on their neobaroque transformation of those genres. In *The Official Story,* the protagonist's name, Alicia (Norma Aleandro), and the musical motif of María Elena Walsh's children's song "En el país de no me acuerdo" (In the Country of I Don't Remember) together invite the viewer to read the film's Argentina as a baroque nightmare in the tradition of Lewis Carroll's *Alice's Adventures in Wonderland*. Likewise, in

Man Facing Southeast, the claim by Rantes (Hugo Soto) to be a holographic image from outer space functions as an intertextual reference to Adolfo Bioy Casares's *The Invention of Morel* (1940), a novella from which the psychiatrist (Lorenzo Quinteros) reads out loud a passage describing a hologram capable of reproducing "the sounds, the resistance to touch, the taste, smells, and temperature, all perfectly synchronized."

In both cases, the use of the baroque trope of parallel worlds suggests alternative forms of being and socializing. Even in Cuba, where the state played an important role in the institutionalization of a militant version of the NLAC, one sees a similar shift in the 1970s and 1980s away from a militant and nationalist position mediated by agitprop aesthetics that favor documentary modes of representation (as exemplified by Santiago Álvarez's documentaries of the 1960s) toward neobaroque films such as *The Last Supper, Son o no son* ([the title is a play on the two meanings of the word *son*: the third-person plural of the verb "to be" and the popular musical form], Julio García Espinosa, 1977), *Maluala* (Sergio Giral, 1979), *Cecilia* (Humberto Solás, Cuba-Spain, 1981), *Papeles secundarios* (Supporting Roles; Orlando Rojas, 1989), and *Alicia en el pueblo de Maravillas* (*Alice in Wondertown*; Daniel Díaz Torres, 1991). Unlike many of the films of the 1960s, these later films are characterized by rich color palettes, claustrophobic mise-en-scènes, and characters who play roles in narrowly defined vertical social relations, all of which function together to denounce or parody patriarchal patterns of thought and behavior that stand in the way of reclaiming the Revolution as a project defined by horizontal social relations.

Irrespective of the nation, then, the reason for the NLAC's shift from militancy to a neobaroque praxis in the 1970s and 1980s is clear: in a context of contemporary or very recent control by authoritarian regimes over the representation of self-serving truths, and of truths that were represented as if they were stable, universal, and eternal, an effective way of questioning the reification of these supposed truths is through the neobaroque strategy—a strategy capable, perhaps more than any other, of highlighting the constructed and in principle malleable nature of socioeconomic structures and cultural values.

PART FIVE

Contemporary Cinema

9

Collapse and Rebirth of an Industry

NEOLIBERAL RESTRUCTURING

In 1985, Fernando Birri accepted Cuba's first Félix Valera Order for intellectual merits. "Twenty five years ago," he told his audience of peer directors from throughout the region, "the New Latin American Cinema was a utopia." He then challenged them with a question, "What is the new utopia?"[1] The NLAC, which had come to be defined over the previous twenty-five years by a shared Marxism and a marked preference for experimental modes of representation, was being shaken to the core by the crisis in Cuba's socialism—highlighted later by the implosion of the Soviet Union and the ensuing Special Period, but already well established in 1985—and by a different kind of crisis in the rest of Latin America, where the imposition of neoliberal economic measures by the IMF and the World Bank sparked a period of economic contraction and widening income disparities that came to be known as the lost decade. As part of these neoliberal measures, many Latin American governments systematically cut back on social and cultural programs, including direct investment and incentives for the film sector. Things came to a head in 1990, when the governments of the three largest film producers in the region—Mexico, Argentina, and Brazil—announced draconian cuts to (and in the case of Brazil, the dismantling of), their respective film companies: IMCINE (Instituto Mexicano de Cinematografía), INCAA (Instituto Nacional de Cine y Artes Audiovisuales), and Embrafilme (Empresa Brasileira de Filmes).

Given the key role these state-funded enterprises had played in film production during the previous decades, it is not surprising that production practically collapsed as a result. In Brazil, it declined from seventy-four features made in 1989 to less than ten features per year during the first half of the 1990s. In Mexico, production declined from ninety-eight features made in 1989 to an average of twenty-eight features per year during the 1990s. And in Argentina, production went from an average of twenty-three features per year during Raúl Alfonsín's presidency (1983–89), to an average of eleven films per year during the first half of the 1990s.[2] Just as dramatically, Cuban production dropped from an average of six films per year during the 1980s to an average of three during the 1990s, a 50 percent decline explained by the sudden end of state funding to its national film company, ICAIC (Instituto Cubano de Arte e Industria Cinematográficos), after the new Russian Federation announced it would not continue subsidizing the Cuban state. This is the context in which Néstor García Canclini famously asked, in an article published in 1993, "Will There Be a Latin American Cinema in 2000?"[3] Yet Canclini's essay was not only about numbers. It also captured the sense, generalized at the time, that in the new post-Soviet, neoliberal order, where cultural products were increasingly seen as regular items of consumption, and where Latin American films were increasingly transatlantic coproductions, New Latin American Cinema's radical politics and its sustained search for cultural autonomy and national identity might have become a relic of the past.

Looking back, it seems that the unprecedented commercial success of a conventional melodrama—*Como agua para chocolate* (*Like Water for Chocolate*; Alfonso Arau, Mexico, 1992)—marked a turning point, at least in terms of numbers (fig. 9.1). Slowly at first, but steadily since the mid-1990s, capital from both the public and the private sectors, attracted by the possibility of similar commercial successes, began to flow once again toward film production. The growth can be attributed to the confluence of several factors: the emergence of low-cost digital technologies since the end of the 1990s; the reactivation of some state incentives, such as Brazil's 1993 Audiovisual Law (a tax break) and Argentina's Law #24,377 of 1995 (which provided outright funds); and the revitalization of the international film circuit, which includes initiatives such as the Sundance Institute's Feature Film Program (1981), France's Canal Plus (1984), the Rotterdam Film Festival's Hubert Bals Fund (1988), Ibermedia (1997), and the Films in Progress Initiative between the San Sebastián Film Festival and the Latin American Film Festival in Toulouse, France (2002).[4]

FIGURE 9.1 Magical tears cause an outbreak of nostalgic longing for a liberal past, visually rendered here via ocher light and a faded photograph of a dead husband in military uniform in *Like Water for Chocolate* (Alfonso Arau, Mexico, 1992)

This is a very different cinematic landscape from the 1960s, the 1970s, and even the 1980s in terms of production and distribution, not to mention the fact that filmmakers of the New Latin American Cinema always saw their work as part of a larger project of cultural nationalism and autonomy. And while cultural nationalism is still evident in many specific films of the 1990s, the tendency was for filmmakers to create transnational products through casting, setting, narrative, and aesthetic choices that facilitate the films' marketing to international audiences and help satisfy the differing economic and political interests of the coproducing parties. In this sense alone, Latin American cinema of the 1990s was radically different from what Birri had in mind when calling for the renewal of the New Latin American Cinema in 1985.

Very likely because of this radical difference, critics in Latin America and elsewhere began citing the success of films starting in the second half of the 1990s as evidence of a New Brazilian, New Mexican, and New Argentinean Cinema, respectively.[5] But the use of the adjective *new* to describe the cinema of the past two decades is problematic, because it suggests a continuity with the New Latin American Cinema when evidence points to the contrary, and because, in suggesting this continuity, it perpetuates a kind of historical amnesia that may advance the marketing of contemporary films, but not our understanding of the complex history that led to their specific modes of production and representation.

A more productive way to frame the discussion of the differences between the New Latin American Cinema and the cinema of the past two decades may be to ask what is the "old" against which each of these two cinemas affirm their newness. In the case of the New Latin American Cinema, the consensus is that it reacted to the old studio cinema of formulaic genres and corporatist values by affirming instead a praxis that effectively married avant-garde politics with avant-garde aesthetics in order to create something broadly defined as epic, spectacular, and revolutionary. The cinema of the last two decades, by contrast, reacts not so much against the early militant films of the NLAC, but to the more recent neobaroque cinema, which, because it often failed at the box office, was increasingly dismissed as a poor investment of cultural and financial capital. This context of declining audience and investor interest in a neobaroque cinema was the backdrop of Birri's legendary call for a "New, New, New Latin American Cinema" in 1985, and served also as context for a seminal debate that took place two years later. Patricia Aufderheide describes the debate as follows:

> The 1987 seminar at the Havana festival, celebrating the twentieth anniversary of the 1967 film festival held in Viña del Mar, Chile, provided a moment of often anguishing reflection on the direction of Latin [American] cinema. The 1967 festival had marked the self-awareness of an international film movement then generating some of the most remarkable film work anywhere, by such internationally renowned figures as Fernando Birri, Glauber Rocha, Nelson Pereira dos Santos, Tomás Gutiérrez Alea, and Humberto Solás. . . . The 1987 debate openly raised the question of this movement's historicity and its legacy. Had New Latin American Cinema achieved its objectives? Was it still alive?[6]

Many of the filmmakers present answered these questions with a resounding "yes," followed immediately by a call to revitalize the movement. But an unnamed Colombian student of the School of the Three Worlds (just inaugurated in the outskirts of Havana) articulated the emerging rift between the old guard, who dominated the debate, and the younger generation that was about to take over and redefine the direction of Latin American cinema, by saying, "I don't even understand this talk of the legacy of New Latin American Cinema. I haven't seen most of these films; they're not my model. My job is to figure out how to make something that will reach people today."[7]

At the conference, Paul Leduc also called for new ways of making films. In a talk he titled, with provocative irony, "New Latin American Cinema and Industrial Reconversion (A Reactionary Thesis)," he first outlined the lack of financing available from traditional state, studio, and independent sources. On funding by the state, he noted how "between the external debt as an implacable reality and the external debt as an excuse to eliminate 'non-priority' help to national film industries, our governments have simply dissociated themselves from the task, following instead the policies of the International Monetary Fund and the Motion Picture Association [of America]." Addressing funding by private studios, he lamented that Churubusco Studios had been rented out for two years to shoot *Dune* (David Lynch, United States, 1984) and had just been rented out by Walt Disney for another two, effectively making that studio's Union of Film Industry Workers "an organization maintained by U.S. dollars . . . to *maquilar* films for Hollywood at lower costs." And finally, he pointed out that funding by independent producers was nonexistent, because "by simply depositing money in the bank, converting it to dollars or taking it to the U.S., [independent producers] secure solid earnings that cinema will never be able to guarantee."[8] This dire situation led Leduc to conclude:

> Cinema, the cinema we always knew, is a dinosaur becoming extinct; but the lizards and salamanders that survived the catastrophe are beginning to appear. We need to see how they did it. . . . We need solidarity and collective action. . . . We must rescue from Viña del Mar the principle of organization, and of course we have to use, as are already being used, the VHS, JVC, NTSC and TBC, the satellites, the computers and cable. . . .
> Dinosaur cinema is extinct.
> Long live the cinema of the lizards!
> Long live the salamander cinema![9]

One way this proclamation has been read is as a scoff against Leduc's embattled colleagues, the earnest founding figures of the New Latin American Cinema that many considered to be a generation of giants on the road to extinction. But a closer reading of Leduc's text suggests something else. If dinosaur cinema was, as Leduc defines it, the cinema with high production values that was hardly being produced because there was less and less money for it, the cinema of the lizards and of the salamanders would then be a qualitatively different kind of cinema produced with low-cost technologies that make it possible for filmmakers to adjust quickly and strategically to ever-changing circumstances. Perhaps the most important example of this low-cost cinema is the indigenous video movement that has been flourishing since the 1980s throughout Latin America.[10] And yet, as important as this movement is, feature narrative cinema with high production values has turned out to be a dinosaur that refuses to die.

A MELOREALIST CINEMA

In fact, since the implosion of the Soviet Union, and in a context defined by the rapid acceleration of capitalist globalization, a new generation of filmmakers has succeeded in reinserting Latin American cinema into the global cinematic marketplace through the reactivation of some of the very conventions that the New Latin American Cinema rejected out of principle—for example the use of traditional genres such as melodrama or road movies, and the unabashed use of formulaic identification techniques—and by redirecting the NLAC's emphasis on societies or extraordinary individuals in upheaval to focus instead on the micropolitics of everyday life. Jorge Ruffinelli was the first to document this shift, in an essay published in 2001 in the Cuban journal *Nuevo cine latinoamericano*: "One of the most important transformations in the cinema of the 1990s vis-à-vis the New Latin American Cinema of the 1960s is the rediscovery of the individual character and the individual dimension of experience. . . . The reinsertion of the individual in his/her history is closely linked to the dissolution of those grandiose collective utopias [of the 1960s] and the reencounter of meaning in small things, in quotidian life, in microhistory."[11]

No longer epic, spectacular, or revolutionary, but rather intimist, realist, and ultimately reformist, the most innovative cinema in Latin America of the last twenty years strategically incorporates a multiplicity of cinematic practices in order to highlight what Ruffinelli calls microhistory and what Damián Fernández calls, in another context, affective realism: "the politics of emotions and their reasons" found in the "informal relations of everyday life."[12] Aesthetically, moreover, we are dealing with a cinema that recycles earlier cinematic styles into multiple configurations that are distinct from these styles' historical unfoldings, yet linked to them by their shared antecedent: a tradition, going back to silent cinema but really flourishing under the aegis of corporatist states during the 1940s, of films as marketable culture.

For these reasons, much of the cinema of the past two decades is what could be called *melorealist,* a neologism that captures the marked preference for narratives that center on affect and emotion, yet without the excess emotion associated with much of classical melodrama. Melorealism as a category also points to the prevalence of a realist visual style constructed through the use of natural acting, continuity editing, on-location shooting, and the restrained use of nondiegetic sound. Thus, melorealist cinema does not explicitly call attention to its own cinematic construction, as the NLAC often does, but rather self-consciously crafts seamless narratives in homogeneous styles in order to exploit audiences' willingness and desire to be swept up in emotionally charged narratives in realistic settings. Finally, whereas situations and aesthetic forms in the NLAC are typically larger than life, underscoring the NLAC's preference for analytical perspectives on the *grand récit* of history, the choice of characters, situations, and aesthetic forms in melorealist cinema is decidedly limited, and in tune with the recent and profound shift in historiography and other forms of narration toward critical *petit histoires*.[13] Melorealist cinema appears to have developed in two phases: a phase characterized by nostalgia in the 1990s, and a phase beginning around 2000 that is characterized by immediacy, in the sense of projecting an intuitive awareness or apprehension of a complex and nuanced present. The rest of this chapter focuses on this first nostalgic phase; the next and final chapter takes up the second, suspenseful phase.

THE MARKETING OF NOSTALGIA

The unprecedented commercial success of films such as *Like Water for Chocolate* (Alfonso Arau, Mexico, 1992) and *Central Station* (Walter Salles, Brazil-France, 1998) showed that a commercially viable cinema based on international formulas was possible. The key novelty of these films is the way they combine the local (through the use of realism in the tradition of customs and manners to represent social landscapes) and the global (through the use of commercial genres such as the road movie, melodrama, and comedy), into *glocal* commodities (themselves the result of glocal modes of coproduction, marketing, and distribution). In terms of content, these glocal commodities oscillate between representing Latin America critically, for local audiences familiar with references the films frequently make to local histories, and touristically, for global audiences who need not understand these references in order to enjoy stories that are often marketed as universal.[14] Just as important, these films were commercially successful because they tapped into a pervasive nostalgic yearning that swept the globe in the years that followed the collapse of the Soviet Union and reached its peak with the global phenomenon that was Wim Wenders's *Buena Vista Social Club* (Germany-United States-England-France-Cuba, 1999) (fig. 9.2).

In using nostalgia as a category, I am thinking not only of Fredric Jameson's use of the term to describe films whose "glossy image" transforms the present "into a simulacrum by the process of wrapping, or quotation," an effect often achieved with the help of ocher lighting that

FIGURE 9.2 Ry Cooder (in the driver's seat) and Joachim Cooder ride the global wave of nostalgia for a socialist past in *Buena Vista Social Club* (Wim Wenders, Germany-United States-England-France-Cuba, 1999)

evokes a simpler past of more primitive (photographic) technologies;[15] but also of films whose glossy ideology transforms present reality into a simulacrum of a socialist, corporatist, or liberal past when human relations were supposed to have been more stable than in the neoliberal present of the 1990s. For example, films such as *Confesión a Laura* (*Confession to Laura*; Jaime Osorio Gómez, Colombia-Cuba-Spain, 1990), *Strawberry and Chocolate* (Tomás Gutiérrez Alea and Juan Carlos Tabío, Cuba-Spain, 1993), and *La estrategia del caracol* (The Strategy of the Snail; Sergio Cabrera, Colombia-Italy, 1993) use nostalgia to reprise a socialist discourse of modernity. Films that use nostalgia to reprise a Euro-liberal discourse of modernity include *Like Water for Chocolate* and *Amores perros* (Love's a Bitch; Alejandro González Iñárritu, Mexico, 2000). And among those that use nostalgia to reprise a corporatist discourse of modernity one can cite *Danzón* (María Novaro, Mexico-Spain, 1991) and *Central Station* (Walter Salles, Brazil-France, 1998). The following discussions of *Strawberry and Chocolate*, *Amores perros*, and *Central Station* will serve to illustrate this point.

Strawberry and Chocolate (1993)

Fresa y chocolate (*Strawberry and Chocolate*; Tomás Gutiérrez Alea and Juan Carlos Tabío, Cuba-Spain, 1993) tells the story of David

FIGURE 9.4 A *tableau vivant* of the pietà, bathed in nostalgic ocher light, as a corporatist plea for a more compassionate state (of affairs) in *Central Station* (Walter Salles, Brazil-France, 1998)

run away), she becomes increasingly disoriented and enters a "house of miracles" where believers post ex-votos and pray for loved ones. At the end of a brilliantly shot sequence that visually underscores Dora's spiritual transformation, she faints. The next shot has Josué holding Dora outside, in a pose that recalls the pietà and the Christian message of corporatist redemption that is at the heart of the film (fig. 9.4).

The religious references suddenly begin to multiply. When Josué and Dora finally reach the house where Josué's brothers live, we learn that Isaías (Matheus Nachtergaele) unconditionally loves their father, whereas Moisés (Caio Junqueira) resents him. The film skillfully synthesizes these positions in Josué through an emotionally stirring sequence where Dora leaves unannounced and Josué finds out just a minute too late to catch up and say goodbye. The sequence begins with Josué asleep between his two brothers, thereby symbolizing his (and the film's) corporatist "third way" between Isaías's blind faith and Moisés's resentment, and allegorically, between liberalism's resentment toward the state and socialism's blind faith in it. The film ends with a convention of socialist realism: Josué, having realized he won't catch up with Dora, yet reassured of their bond thanks to a picture souvenir of the two of them together, is shot from below and framed against a clear blue sky, thereby embodying the bright future that awaits the nation if it keeps to a centrist, corporatist path.[19]

Ideologically, then, the film is much closer to the social conventionalism one normally associates with melodramas than to the potential for social transformation normally associated with socialist realism, for in the end it reaffirms Josué's traditional blood relations over horizontal ones born out of solidarity and mutual respect. Indeed, while it is conceivable that we ask ourselves whether it would have been better for Josué to return to Rio with Dora and consolidate the relationship they had constructed, the film privileges Josué's nostalgic search for a patriarchal and corporatist family structure, visually represented in the hand-tinted photographic portrait of Josué's parents below which Dora leaves her parting gifts. Dora's final decision to return alone to Rio, based as it is on the logic of blood family relations, thereby deflects attention away from Brazil's own less-than-savory present, and toward an idealized corporatist past when social relations were supposed to have been stable, organic, and patriarchal all at once.

Amores perros (2000)

A first draft of the script for *Amores perros* (Love's a Bitch; Alejandro González Iñárritu, Mexico, 2000) neatly summarizes the film's innovative audiovisual language: "The film will be structured around three loosely connected stories linked by a car accident; it will use documentary-style camerawork, with the film stock processed with silver retention to create stronger contrast and texture in color; the dog fights will not be explicit and the dogs will be handled with extreme care; the cast will largely consist of unknowns; and there will be a strong soundtrack."[20]

The relevance of *Amores perros* for our discussion, however, does not reside in its masterful interweaving of loosely connected narrative threads (which already point to the suspenseful dramas of the next decade), or in its aesthetics of violence (which have less to do with Glauber Rocha's call for unmasking the systemic violence of capitalism than with the capitalist commoditization of violence). Instead, its relevance as an example of a film that uses nostalgia to reprise a liberal discourse of modernity resides in the stories themselves. The three stories are all melodramatic, with that genre's attendant emphasis on emotion through narrative trajectories that punish those who threaten conventional social relations and reward those who reaffirm the status quo ante after having temporarily strayed from it. A first story centers on Octavio (Gael García Bernal), a lower-middle-class lad who proposes to run away with his battered sister-in-law Susana (Vanessa Bauche). On the day of the planned escape, however, she steals his money and escapes with her abusive husband. A second story centers on business executive

FIGURE 9.5 El Chivo (Emilio Echevarría) uses a snapshot to symbolically reinsert himself into the liberal family/nation in *Amores perros* (Love's a Bitch; Alejandro González Iñárritu, Mexico, 2000)

Daniel (Álvaro Guerrero) and his supermodel lover Valeria (Goya Toledo), both of whom are at the top of their game. Shortly after they move into a smartly decorated modern apartment, however, Valeria loses her leg, her dog, and her career. At this low point in her life, when Valeria needs him the most, Daniel decides to return to his wife and their traditional home/marriage, iconically defined by the oversize crucifix that hangs over their matrimonial bed. The first and second stories thus reassert the sanctity of marriage, even when that marriage is plagued by violence, as in Susana's case, or is loveless, as in Daniel's.

Finally, a third story centers on El Chivo (Emilio Echevarría), a middle-class intellectual who gave up his university teaching job to join the Mexican urban guerillas in the 1970s. In his story, as in all three stories, the film proposes a nostalgic return to liberal individualism and to conventional family structures, in his case through a sequence where El Chivo unlawfully enters his daughter's apartment. As he spies a collection of glossy family pictures, he nostalgically yearns to become the father he never was because of his revolutionary activities (fig. 9.5). Framed as a story of individual redemption, El Chivo's narrative trajectory thereby equates the revolutionary activity of the 1970s (and the more contemporary activities of someone such as Subcomandante Marcos) to irresponsible parenting and mercenary crimes. It is a move that—very much in the tradition of *El automóvil gris* (The Gray Automobile; Enrique Rosas, Joaquín Coss, and Juan Canals de Homs, Mexico, 1919)—allays criollo fears and anxieties of losing their racial and class privileges by reducing very complex social ills to individual narrative trajectories of crime and redemption featuring middle-class and upper-class white characters.

10

Latin American Cinema in the Twenty-First Century

SUSPENSEFUL NARRATIVES FOR PRECARIOUS TIMES

Argentina's currency collapse of 2001 (the infamous *corralito*) and the subsequent collapse of the Washington Consensus in Latin America invalidated the nostalgic impulse of the 1990s and heightened instead a sense of social and economic precariousness throughout most of the region. Perhaps for this reason, many of the most innovative Latin American films in the twenty-first century have been privileging suspense, a narrative and audiovisual strategy that is especially well suited to the critical examination of the precarious present. Ironically, this examination has been taking place within a context of relatively strong economic growth and political stability since the mid-2000s, when an ongoing geopolitical and economic realignment toward China facilitated the region-wide rejection of the neoliberal orthodoxy of the 1990s, and the adoption, in its place, of moderately interventionist audiovisual policies. Examples of such policies included the doubling of IMCINE's budget in 2004; the creation in 2006 of Villa del Cine, a large state-owned TV and film studio in Venezuela; and regional initiatives to integrate distribution and exhibition, such as the Mercosur Film Market (2005) and the Ibero-American Film Market (2006).

At the same time, private conglomerates and institutional investors have entered the market. Brazil's Grupo Globo, the largest media group in Latin America, inaugurated Globo Films in 1997, while more recently, private equity fund firms such as the New York and Berlin–based

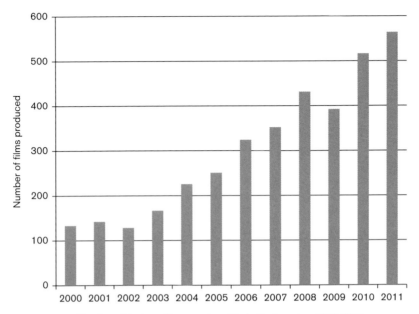

FIGURE 10.1   Number of feature films produced in Latin America, 2000–2011

D Street Media Group, the Buenos Aires–based Costa Films, and Colombia's Dynamo Capital have become important players in the Latin American media landscape, with capitalization ranging between $10 and $50 million each, and with the objective, as D Street chief executive Dexter Davis puts it, "to make commercially viable stories in Latin America for the world, not just the U.S. market."[1] Bigger still are transnational conglomerates such as Sony, Twentieth Century Fox, and Warner Bros., all of which regularly coproduce what they call local-language productions in Latin American countries.[2] The combined effect of these new state policies, fresh sources of capital, and low-cost digital technologies has been an explosion in the number of narrative films to levels far beyond those reached during studio cinema's "golden age" in the 1940s (fig. 10.1).[3]

¡Y tu mamá también! (2001)

In terms of modes of representation, the cinema of the twenty-first century continues to be mostly melorealist (see the previous chapter for an explanation of this term). In terms of content, on the other hand, the shift away from the nostalgia of the 1990s toward a more critical perspective on the immediate present is brilliantly registered in ¡Y tu mamá también! (And Your Mother Too!; Alfonso Cuarón, Mexico-Spain, 2001), a coming-of-age road movie whose narrative focuses on Tenoch Iturbide (Diego Luna) and Julio Zapata (Gael García Bernal) the summer before they begin university studies. Bored and looking for an adventure, they invite Luisa Cortés (Maribel Verdú), the estranged Spanish wife of Tenoch's cousin, on a road trip to a pristine beach on the Oaxacan coast. The trip is as much physical as psychological, for the closer they get to their destination, the more the class differences and homosexual attraction between the two young men rise to the surface. The attraction culminates in a ménage à trois where they kiss and wake up naked, lying next to each other, while the class differences, as we will see, jump to the surface in a final sequence where the onetime friends run into each other and decide to chat "because it [is] easier to sit down for coffee than to come up with excuses to avoid it."

The film self-consciously uses themes and audiovisual codes of international youth culture—chief among them music video aesthetics and the exploration of sex and drugs as part of consumer culture—to market itself globally. But it does not reproduce the neoliberal ideology typically associated with globalized middle-class youth culture at the beginning of the twenty-first century. Instead, it skillfully denounces the rise of neoliberal politics and economics in Mexico through a voice-over that fills us in about the local histories and class conflicts that always lurk just beneath the surface, as when it tells the audience how Tenoch's father (Emilio Echevarría) struck it rich through a corruption scheme facilitated by Mexico's entry into NAFTA, or that Tenoch's indigenous *nana* grew up in a poor hamlet they drive by. In the end, and unlike what happens in *Central Station* (Walter Salles, Brazil-France, 1998), class conflict does enter the filmic space, most visibly in a final sequence where the lower-middle-class Julio ends up paying the bill for upper-middle-class Tenoch. This final sequence also opens up the film to a richly suggestive allegorical reading, where the homosocial and homosexual attraction between Julio and Tenoch represents the neoliberal alignment of the PRI (Partido Revolucionario Institucional) with the PAN (Partido Acción Nacional) throughout the 1990s, while their final parting of ways, in which Tenoch is in a far better political and economic position, represents the PAN's consolidation of power in the 2000 elections as the logical consequence of this alignment.

FIGURE 10.2 The dialectical composition in depth calls attention to Mexico's social inequalities in ¡*Y tu mamá también!* (And Your Mother Too!; Alfonso Cuarón, Mexico-Spain, 2001)

The irony of the allegory is not lost on viewers familiar with Mexican history, for Zapata (a reference to the revolutionary Emiliano Zapata) is an ironic last name for a depoliticized middle-class kid like Julio, who wishes to become part of the country's elite, while Tenoch (a reference to the Aztec ruler who brought the Mexicas to Mexico's central valley) is an ironic name for someone who belongs to the country's Eurocentric elite (the off-camera narrator wryly explains that Tenoch's father chose this name for his son in a fit of nationalist fervor, meaning he wanted to ascend in the government hierarchy). The irony extends to the female lead, Luisa Cortés, for Cortés, the name of the Spanish conqueror of Mexico, is an ironic choice for a character who is female and who can communicate with locals from all walks of life from a position that is free of prejudices of class, gender, sexuality, race, or national origin.

Indeed, the ironic allegorization extends to practically all the characters, whose names read like a who's who of official Mexican history: Morelos, Huerta, Madero, Montes de Oca, Carranza. This discrepancy between signifiers and signifieds is visually complemented by a composition in depth where the foreground, occupied by the main fictional characters, contrasts with a background oftentimes populated with working-class people displaced by Mexico's neoliberal turn and ignored by both the PRI and the PAN (fig. 10.2). The dialectical composition in depth thus facilitates a powerful and sophisticated critique of the distance between an official discourse that celebrates Mexico's entry into neoliberal modernity, and the brutal reality of neoliberal Mexico's class-based, gendered, and racialized social relations.

THE RISE OF THE WOMAN DIRECTOR

A key development in the new century has been the rise to prominence of female directors. Before the 1980s, noteworthy Latin American women directors were few and far between. During the silent period, for example, we know of Mimí Derba (codirector with Enrique Rosas of *La tigresa* [The Tigress; Mexico, 1917]); during the studio era, Carmen Santos (*Inconfidência Mineira* [Minas Gerais Conspiracy; Brazil, 1948]) and Matilde Landeta (*La negra Angustias* [The Black Angustias; Mexico, 1950]); during the transitional 1950s, Margot Benacerraf; and during the militant phase of the NLAC, Marta Rodríguez and Sara Gómez. Then, quite suddenly, the 1980s witnessed what Paulo Antonio Paranaguá calls a "feminization of the profession" linked to profound changes in the social status of women broadly speaking, and in the specific case of cinema, to a proliferation of film schools that began in earnest in the 1960s: CUEC (Centro Universitario de Estudios Cinematográficos at Mexico's Autonomous University, 1963), CERC (Centro de Experimentación y Realización Cinematográfica in Argentina's Instituto Nacional de Cinematografía, 1965), ECA (Escola de Comunicações e Artes at the University of São Paulo, 1968), the Department of Cinema at the University of the Andes in Mérida, Venezuela (1969), the International School of Cinema and Television in San Antonio de los Baños in Cuba (1986), and FUC (Fundación Universidad del Cine in Argentina, 1991).[4]

Two distinct generations of professional female directors have emerged since then. The first is loosely linked to the New Latin American Cinema. It includes the Chilean Valeria Sarmiento (*El hombre cuando es hombre* [A Man, When He Is a Man; Costa Rica, 1982]); the Brazilians Vera de Figueiredo (*Femenino Plural* [Plural Feminine; Brazil, 1976]), Ana Carolina (*Mar de Rosas* [Sea of Roses; Brazil, 1977]), Suzana Amaral (*A Hora da Estrela* [The Hour of the Star; Brazil, 1985]), Tizuka Yamazaki (*Gaijin, Os Caminhos da Liberdade* [Gaijin, Roads to Freedom; Brazil, 1980]), and Helena Solberg (*Carmen Miranda: Bananas Is My Business*; United States, 1994); the Mexicans Marcela

Fernández Violante (*De todos modos Juan te llamas* [*The General's Daughter*; Mexico, 1974]), Busi Cortés (*El secreto de Romelia* [Romelia's Secret; Mexico, 1988]), María Novaro (*Danzón*; Mexico-Spain, 1991), and Dana Rotberg (*Ángel de fuego* [Angel of Fire; Mexico, 1991]); the Venezuelan Fina Torres (*Oriana*; Venezuela, 1985); and most famously, the Argentinean María Luisa Bemberg (*Camila* [Argentina, 1984] and *Yo, la peor de todas* [*I, the Worst of All* [Argentina, 1991]). Despite its increasing prevalence, the work of this first generation remained marginal within the New Latin American Cinema, and continuity of production remained an elusive goal for all but Bemberg.

Today, on the other hand, women directors are at the center of a cinematic revival that includes the work of Tata Amaral (*Um Céu de Estrelas* [*A Starry Sky*; Brazil, 1997]); Marisa Sistach (*Perfume de violetas* [*Violet Perfume: No One Is Listening*; Mexico, 2001]); Claudia Llosa (*La teta asustada* [*The Milk of Sorrow*; Peru-Spain, 2009]); Paz Encina (*Hamaca paraguaya* [*Paraguayan Hammock*; Paraguay-Germany-Denmark-Argentina-France-Spain, 2008]); Mariana Rondón (*Pelo malo* [*Bad Hair*; Venezuela-Peru-Argentina-Germany, 2013]); Verónica Chen (*Agua* [*Water*; Argentina, 2006]), Lucía Puenzo (*XXY* [Argentina, 2007]), Albertina Carri (*La rabia* [Anger; Argentina, 2008]), and, most notably, Lucrecia Martel.

Lucrecia Martel's Salta Trilogy (2001–8)

Martel's filmic trilogy about life in the province of Salta, Argentina, explores the country's incomplete transition to democracy from the perspective of strong, intelligent, and socially privileged female protagonists who do not conform to dominant patriarchal values: first during childhood in *La Ciénaga* (*The Swamp*; 2001); then during sexual awakening in *La niña santa* (*The Holy Girl*; 2004); and finally in adulthood, in *La mujer sin cabeza* (*The Headless Woman*; 2008).[5] What makes Lucrecia Martel stand out among her female cohorts is not so much her critique of patriarchy's traditional gender roles and normative sexuality (something all of them do), but the way she delivers that critique through a multilayered and innovative cinematic language that privileges nonlinearity over causality, sound over sight, and suspense over closure.

The Swamp is a snapshot of the lives of two cousins and their corresponding families (fig. 10.3). Martel's synopsis captures the film's emphasis on tone and atmosphere over character motivation and action:

FIGURE 10.3 Suspense fills the air when Momi (Sofía Bertolotto) does not reemerge from the pool in *The Swamp* (Lucrecia Martel, Argentina, 2001)

February in the Argentine northwest. Scorching sun and tropical rain. In the jungle some areas flood into swamps that trap heavy-footed animals but shelter swarms of happy vermin. This is not a story about swamps, but about the town of La Ciénaga [The Swamp] and its environs.

Located 90 kilometers away is the town of Rey Muerto [Dead King] and close by the estate called La Mandrágora [Mandrake]. Mandrágora is a plant that was used as a sedative before ether and morphine replaced it, when it was necessary to bear painful experiences such as amputation. In this story it is the name of an estate where red peppers are grown and dried, and where Mecha, a fifty-something woman with four grown-up children and a husband who dyes his hair, spends her summer. All of this is worth forgetting with a couple of drinks and yet, as Tali says, alcohol enters through one door but does not leave through another.

Tali is Mecha's cousin. She also has four children and a husband who loves his house, his children, and hunting. She lives in La Ciénaga, in a house without a pool. Two accidents will unite these two families out in the country, where they'll try to survive a summer from hell.[6]

In this living hell, Mecha (Graciela Borges) and her daughter Momi (Sofía Bertolotto) move as if having just woken from a long sleep. Both seem to be headed in the direction of Mecha's mother, who one day decided not to leave her bed, and died there many years later. Mecha's oldest son, José (Juan Cruz Bordeu), is a Freudian Oedipus: he sleeps with his father's ex-lover, naps and showers with his twenty-something sister Verónica (Leonora Balcare), and sleeps in his mother's bed, from which his father has been banished. On the side of Tali (Mercedes Morán), none of these rarified relationships exist, and yet it is her son Luciano (Sebastián Montaga), the most innocent of all the characters, who dies in the end.

By cutting off the strongest affective link viewers have to the film, Luciano's death invites us to take a much more critical look at the rest of the characters. In this critical reappraisal, only Momi is worth rescuing because she is the only one who perceives what goes on beneath the thin veneer of what the camera's eye records. Momi, for example, warns her mother that she will end up bedridden like the grandmother, a fate that *The Headless Woman* explores in more detail. It is also Momi who first notices that the maid Isabel (Andrea López) is pregnant. And in the closing sequence, Momi tells her sister Verónica that she went to see the image of the apparition of the Virgin Mary that was reported on television, but did not see anything. Momi's awareness, based on her own senses rather than what others say, thus points to a way out of an otherwise oppressive and suffocating environment.

The Holy Girl, the next film in the trilogy, takes place almost entirely in a hotel-spa that has seen better days, during a medical congress that promises participants a mix of work and pleasure. The narrative centers on the love triangle between Dr. Jano (Carlos Belloso), one of the congress participants, Helena (Mercedes Morán), who played Tali in *The Swamp* and in *The Holy Girl* plays the owner of the hotel where the congress takes place, and Amalia (María Alche), Helena's adolescent daughter. Dr. Jano, like the name suggests, is two-faced. Publicly, he is a respectable physician who specializes in hearing disorders. Secretly, he is a sexual molester. Both Helena and Amalia fall for Dr. Jano: Helena for his public facade and the power that he represents in a patriarchal society, and Amalia, unexpectedly, for his sexual advances. Amalia also sees it as her holy mission to bring him back into the fold of society by forgiving him, in a tender sequence where she insists to him that he is a "good man."

The Headless Woman concludes the trilogy. Unlike *The Swamp* and *The Holy Girl,* which have fully developed narrative threads for three or more characters, *The Headless Woman* focuses almost exclusively on Vero (María Onetto), a forty-something dentist who bears several striking resemblances to Verónica in *The Swamp,* chief among them their names (Vero is short for Verónica), their introspective demeanors, the fact that both sustain uncomfortably close relations with physically strong men in the family, and the fact that their mothers at one point decided to spend the rest of their lives in bed.

In Spanish, *sin cabeza* ("headless") refers to a mental state of having lost one's bearings, typically when falling in love. In this case, however, the title refers to Vero's having lost her bearings after she accidentally hits something (an animal, a young working-class mestizo man, or both?) with her car. Throughout this key sequence we see and feel what happens from Vero's perspective. We experience with her an unexpected thump, our perspective is limited to what she can see in the rear- and side-view mirrors, and we hear a 1970s pop song playing on her car radio. Rather than stop and confirm what she has hit, Vero stays in the car, and the camera with her, so that we can study and reflect on her actions. After a long pause she drives off, and only when she is safely out of range from the site of the accident does she stop to inspect the car and drive herself to the hospital. The rest of the film is about how her husband, brother, and male cousin join forces to cover up all the evidence of her hit-and-run—from the X-ray records at the hospital, to the dent in her car, to the record of her stay that night at a hotel—and more importantly, about how people convince themselves of a reality that suits their interests. And herein lies the film's (and the trilogy's) political dimension, for if we can create one reality to suit one set of interests, surely we can create another reality in support of another set of interests. As Martel herself explains:

> In *The Headless Woman*, the mere suspicion—never confirmed—of having perhaps killed a person or a dog leads the protagonist to make a series of decisions that will mark the rest of her life. That happens a lot with oral language. I can say something—regardless of whether or not it is true—but your reaction and the emotion it generates will be real. It happens a lot in amorous relationships: when one has an argument, one says things that one may not feel, but once they're said, the other party reacts as if they were true. The person who listens to these words is the one who gives them their power, so that the consequences of words become materially real. My cinema has this political dimension. It demonstrates that one can transform the world through the combination of one's will with the will of others. Reality is something we author, not something that exists. It is something we have constructed, and if we have constructed it one way, we could also construct it some other way.[7]

Entangled Sounds, Entangled Narratives

Martel's films can certainly be read individually, but their full richness comes through when read as narratives whose protagonists are entangled in ways that are nonlinear yet measurable, like points on a string whose defining feature is female desire in patriarchy. In quantum mechanics, entanglement refers to the phenomenon whereby particles that are not physically connected can still affect one other. String theory, the best explanation so far for this phenomenon, argues that this can happen because particles are parts of the same wave, or string. It is in this sense that Martel's female protagonists are entangled: the string is the protagonists' condition as privileged, intelligent, and desiring women in patriarchy, and the particles are events and situations connected non-causally across films in the trilogy. One instance of a non-causally connected event comes early in *The Swamp*, when two girls sing a children's song that foreshadows the plot in *The Holy Girl* and even the name of one of its protagonists, Dr. Jano:

> Doctor Jano, surgeon
> today we have to operate
> in the emergency room
> a girl your age
> She is twenty-one
> You are one year older
> Doctor Jano, surgeon
> Don't go falling in love

Another example of entanglement is the song that plays during the closing credits of *The Swamp*, because the song, a cumbia titled "Amor divino" (Divine Love), references both *The Swamp*, whose young protagonist sublimates the love she feels toward the housemaid, and *The Holy Girl*, whose adolescent protagonist sublimates the love she feels toward Dr. Jano.

As if to test how an alternative to the prevailing patriarchal reality could be constructed, each of the films is set up as a dialectic between a desiring female subject and the hegemonic patriarchal reality. Martel underscores this dialectic through a contrast between images of flow that are linked to female desire, and images of stagnation that are linked to patriarchy. Thus, spaces where air, sound, and water flow freely are linked to the unprejudiced expression of intersubjective desire, whereas stagnant air, sound, and water are linked to the suppression or the instrumentalization of desire. For example, in *The Swamp,* there is a memorable sequence where Verónica asks a young mestizo man to take her and Momi to the town's dam. The sequence, which contains the moment of greatest narrative pleasure in the whole of the trilogy, comes when the dam doors open and the overflowing water metaphorically washes away and visually erases class, gender, and ethnic differences. By contrast, the closing sequence of each film shows its protagonist in a tellingly stagnant setting. In *The Swamp*, Momi's suppressed desire is visually represented by her sitting idly next to the dirty pool. In *The Holy Girl*, Amalia's sublimated desire is underscored by her floating in the still waters of the hotel pool. And in *The Headless Woman*, Vero's loss of her ethical self and her subsequent dependency on men is visually represented when she, after having confirmed that the last bit of the incriminating evidence has been destroyed, is flanked and protected by her brother and male cousin, yet trapped behind the tinted glass doors of the hotel's activity room as if inside a dirty pool.

These suspended narrative endings make it clear that Martel is not interested in representing a resolution to the dialectic between female desire and patriarchy. Instead, she heeds Teresa de Lauretis's call for a feminist cinema that explores the contradictions that are inherent in the Oedipal narrative trajectory:

> I am not advocating for the replacement or the appropriation or, even less, the emasculation of Oedipus. What I have been arguing for, instead, is an interruption of the triple track by which narrative, meaning, and pleasure are constructed from his point of view. The most exciting work in cinema and in feminism today is not anti-narrative or anti-Oedipal; quite the opposite. It is narrative and Oedipal with a vengeance, for it seeks to stress the duplicity of that scenario and the specific contradiction of the female subject in it, the contradiction by which historical women must work with and against Oedipus.[8]

Martel's films are, in effect, both narrative and Oedipal with a vengeance. Specifically, they explore Freud's Oedipal complex, the archetypal narrative of patriarchy, through stories that highlight the contrast between two kinds of female desire: that which is subjected to the narrative trajectory of the male hero and his gaze, and that which is not. This contrast is most fully developed in *The Holy Girl*, through a dialectic of sight and sound embodied in Helena, who willingly subjects herself to Jano's desiring gaze, and Amalia, who does not. For instance, Gonzalo Aguilar notes that Helena's hearing problems "speak of a deficiency that is compensated with visual exuberance: her image is trapped in the mirror where Jano finds her or when she dances in her bedroom. . . . Helena finds pleasure in the visual field dominated by the male gaze. Amalia, by contrast, ensconces herself in the acoustic labyrinth and uses sounds, touch, and even the sense of smell to trap Jano, the man she wants to save."[9]

The shots of Helena's image trapped in the mirror, or behind glass in the hearing-test booth, invite a reading of her character as being caught in a Lacanian mirror stage, whereby her self-perception depends on external validation by male characters, whether Jano or the little boy who dances with her in the bedroom. Narratively, she is what de Lauretis calls a mainstream female character whose narrative function is to help the male protagonist fulfill his Oedipal journey and achieve narrative closure.[10]

Amalia, by contrast, is not contained by Jano's Oedipal narrative or his gaze. Her desire clearly exceeds the patriarchal bounds of appropriate female behavior, but Martel neither rewards nor punishes her for it, preferring instead to suspend the kind of closure required by the Oedipal narrative trajectory. Here then is a film that simultaneously develops (via Helena) and counters (via Amalia) the Oedipal narrative trajectory that characterizes mainstream cinema, and skillfully uses suspense to transfer that unresolved dialectic to the viewer.

Unlike horror films, which generate fear by making dangers explicit, suspense films generate anxiety by hiding dangers, whether literally behind objects or, more effectively, by making what is dangerous inseparable from what is not.[11] Martel uses sound to generate the anxiety that is central to suspense films by hiding and containing possible sources of looming danger. Her strategy is to create what Michel Chion calls a "phantom audio-vision," that "other side of the image" where sounds sometimes go, "disengaged from the present."[12] More specifically, Martel privileges a subset of phantom audio-visions that Chion calls null extension, or the shrinking of the sonic universe to the sounds heard by a single character.[13]

In the Salta trilogy, the most powerful use of null extension to create a phantom audio-vision occurs early in *The Headless Woman*, in the accident sequence. It begins with Vero driving on a gravel road along a concrete ditch where two mestizo boys and their dog had been playing earlier in the film. The radio is playing "Soley Soley," a pop song from the 1970s. Vero's cell phone rings, and just as she bends to reach for it, a sudden thump throws her (and viewers) off balance. The radio keeps playing and drowns out any sound that may come from the outside, so that the effect is that we look more actively at the image in front of us: Vero looking through the car's side mirror, her hesitancy to get out of the car, her putting on the fallen sunglasses (as if this could somehow protect her), her driving off, the accident site as seen through the car's rear window, her turning off the radio, and, most eerily, the marks on her side window as silent witnesses of what just happened (more on this later). Yet what we see, dense as it is with meaning, cannot explain the evocative power of the sequence. Only sound can—or more specifically, the use of null extension to create a phantom audio-vision. Thus, after the thump, the pop song is suddenly transformed into an insidious sound that transports viewers to another side of the image, a ghostly world that is in this case Argentina's dictatorial past, not only because the song on the radio was typical of the escapist fare favored by the dictatorial regime, but more importantly because the silenced echoes of the disembodied thump mysteriously and inexplicably reverberate in our memory in much the same way that the silenced memory of the dictatorship's victims reverberates in Argentina to this day.

Additional examples of phantom audio-visions can be found throughout the trilogy, and are especially evident whenever an ominous atmosphere crystallizes: in *The Swamp*, the dragging of chairs in the opening sequence, or the unidentified sound that comes from the second floor in Tali's house; in *The Holy Girl*, Amalia's pounding on the pool's railings to catch Jano's attention, or the announcements over the speakers calling for Jano as Helena waits for him to assume his double role on stage; and in *The Headless Woman*, the aforementioned accident sequence, and the muffled sound through the tinted doors in the final sequence. In each of these examples, the effective use of null extension creates a phantom audio-vision whose strength depends on sound's ability to evoke a mysterious other side of the image, rather than on sound's capacity to anchor the image to a specific referent.

In an interview, Martel was very explicit about why sound, so central to suspense, is for her more important than the visual:

> Sound requires an elastic medium for transmission; it propagates and touches, and passes through everything that might be blocking its path. That's what we are in the movie theater, where we are touched by sound. When we watch a horror film or any other kind of film that impresses us, we can close our eyes to avoid watching a stabbing, or a shooting, or a car crash, or anything else like that. But we don't have eyelids for the ears. . . . I say this to underscore the fact that sound is the inevitable in cinema. Of course now we can lower the volume if we're watching a DVD, but that would completely transform the film. In a movie theater, however, we cannot avoid sound. . . . Sound in cinema has always been disqualified, perhaps because our society has been organized much more around visual perception.[14]

For Martel, then, visual representation is more limited than aural representation, because whereas light waves travel in direct paths and cannot traverse or go around solid objects, sound waves can. In the accident sequence, for example, we hear two thumps, yet only see one body on the road. Perhaps Vero killed not only the dog we see lying there as she drives off, but also the dog's owner. The film never answers this question. It does, however, point to an important consequence of the distinction between sight and sound in cinema, for whereas conventional narrative films, centered as they are on vision, reproduce an understanding of reality as something that is static and best represented via the one-point perspective typically associated with the realist tradition, Martel's films routinely place the camera behind or near objects that obstruct the one-point perspective, thereby creating a counter-understanding of reality as something malleable that is best represented from multiple perspectives, and, more precisely, via the multiple marginal perspectives afforded by the diverse nooks and crannies where sound can reach but light cannot.

Martel's appreciation for sound's ability to reach beyond the surface of visible reality grows out an oral storytelling tradition that is alive and well in provincial settings like Salta. In a revealing interview, Martel recounts the childhood experience of listening to her grandmother use different sounds, tones, and carefully selected pauses to tell scary stories designed to keep children immobilized while the adults took their afternoon siesta:

> My grandmother loved to tell stories, and she was very good at it because she completely captured our attention. The stories she would tell us were versions of well-known stories—by the Brothers Grimm, and above all by Horacio Quiroga, an Uruguayan-Argentinean writer whose feverish and wild literature takes place in Misiones, in the Argentinean northeast, and in which there are crimes, deaths, and fantastic animals. My grandmother never told us that her stories were by a writer. I always thought that they were things that had taken place in our house. . . . The story by Quiroga that she always told us is titled "The Feather Pillow," about a woman [named Amalia] who is sick and nobody knows why. She grows increasingly weak, and when she finally dies, her husband sees on her pillow a small spot of blood, and inside a parasite that had been sucking all her blood. And then the husband kills it with an ax. I always thought that had happened to a friend of my grandmother's.[15]

This story by Quiroga bears striking similarities to the story of Little Red Riding Hood: a convalescent woman in bed, a male hero who kills the menacing creature, the striking symbolism of the color red. And while in Quiroga's version there is no ax (only that the husband ripped open the woman's pillow after her death), the insertion of the ax in

Martel's retelling of the story, and her decision to name the protagonist in *The Holy Girl* Amalia, in clear intertextual reference to the protagonist of Quiroga's story, reveals Martel's ambitious project of rewriting Little Red Riding Hood so that the protagonist no longer accepts the subordinate role that patriarchy requires of her, and instead claims agency over her body, her gaze, and, ultimately, her life's narrative.

Why Little Red Riding Hood? In his book *The Irresistible Fairy Tale*, Jack Zipes writes that "it is well known that Little Red Riding Hood in the two classical versions by Perrault and the Brothers Grimm is not a heroine. She is more of a wimp. Either she stupidly agrees to an assignation with the hungry wolf and thus is complicit in her own rape/violation and death (Perrault), or she needs the help of a hunter to free her from the wolf's belly (Grimm)."[16] In this book Zipes studies works by a number of female visual artists, including Kiki Smith and Sharon Singer, who in the past few decades have created alternative versions of Little Red Riding Hood. In Kiki Smith's *Born* (2002), Zipes argues, the artist may be asking whether women "were born with blood-red hoods and capes from wolves . . . [since] the wolf's hair appears to stream into the hairy capes and hoods of mother and daughter like blood or red flames."[17] Likewise, Sharon Singer's *Little Dread Riding Hood* (2004) "gives the story [of Little Red Riding Hood] a radically different slant," with a "feisty young woman with deadlocks seemingly riding on a wolf, tamed and muzzled."[18] Martel participates in this ongoing revisionism through the representation of girls and adolescents who are not wimps, victims, or, worse, deserving of punishment, and who never give up loving their mothers or other women, as required by the Oedipal trajectory, even as they partake in the privileges that patriarchy and capitalism offer them.

In *The Holy Girl,* in particular, Martel troubles the conflicted relationship between female desire and patriarchy by insistently returning to the equivalent of Red Riding Hood's encounter with the wolf in the forest. In three separate but very similar sequences, a group of people gathers outside to watch a musician play a theremin, an early electronic instrument that underscores Martel's interest in the density of the invisible because it is played without direct physical contact. The first time, Dr. Jano approaches the group of spectators, stands behind Amalia, and nonchalantly rubs his crotch against her derriere as the theremin plays an adagio. Rather than react with consternation, as one would expect, Amalia turns with curiosity to see who her molester is, and Dr. Jano, startled by her unexpected response, sheepishly walks away.

The second such encounter begins with the theremin playing music reminiscent of science-fiction B films of the 1950s, as if cuing the spectator to a looming danger. The music quickly shifts to the melody of "Cielito Lindo," a popular Mexican folk song about unrequited love, as Dr. Jano gets out of a cab and heads to the crowd where Amalia is already listening to the music with her friend Josefina (Julieta Zylberberg) close by. The way the next shot is framed leaves room for interpretation, but it seems as if Amalia turns to observe Dr. Jano molesting someone before the sequence abruptly ends. Finally, the third encounter begins with the theremin playing "La Habanera" from Georges Bizet's opera *Carmen*, to cue the spectator to the parallels between Carmen and Amalia as free-spirited women in full control of their sexuality. Indeed, the lyrics to "La Habanera" provide a plausible description of Amalia's feelings at this juncture in the narrative:

> Love is a rebellious bird
> that nobody can tame,
> and you call him quite in vain
> if it suits him not to come. . . .
> Love is a gypsy's child,
> it has never, ever, known a law;
> love me not, then I love you;
> if I love you, you'd best beware!

Unaware of Amalia's presence, Dr. Jano approaches the crowd and stands behind a young woman. Amalia then surreptitiously eases herself in front of Dr. Jano, who proceeds to rub himself against her. The next shot is a profile of the two at waist level, and shows Amalia reaching back with her hand to touch Dr. Jano. Surprised, he jolts and turns to walk away, but not before Amalia locks eyes with him (fig. 10.4).

This last encounter shatters the entrenched filmic tradition that defines sexual desire through the male gaze. It also explicitly subverts the traditional masculine narrative trajectory, represented by Jano's relationship toward Helena, by privileging an alternative narrative of female desire centered on how Amalia desires Jano in ways that are not dependent on his narrative or his desires. In the end, when Amalia finally realizes that Jano rejects her (because she escapes his control), she sublimates her desire as a divine calling: Jano is a good man who has sinned and must be saved. Hence the film's title. However, because in the end Amalia sacrifices her own desires for the sake of Jano's male privileges, she embodies the contradictions and complexities of the dialectic between female desire and patriarchy: a wickedly innocent she-

FIGURE 10.4 Amalia (María Alche) controls the desiring gaze in *The Holy Girl* (Lucrecia Martel, Argentina, 2004)

wolf who simultaneously subverts and reproduces traditional gender and social relations.

The comparison to an animal is relevant because it points to the trilogy's links to fables, a short narrative form that, according to Annabel Patterson, "speaks to unequal power relations and prompts those without power to speak in metaphoric codes that can emancipate both the teller and the listener. Fables do not always end happily even when there is a resolution or a moral. They move readers and listeners to contemplate how they might act if they were in a similar situation. . . . The listener and reader of a fable are always given a choice, and human agency is thus respected. Fables tell us that we all have choices to make."[19]

Fables and fairy tales differ in form, especially in length and degree of realism, yet both share a preoccupation with moral choices, and this similarity leads us to the most important character in Martel's films: ourselves. Consider for example the marks on Vero's side window as she drives away from the scene of the accident in *The Headless Woman*. Are they human? Are they animal? In fact, they are both. Throughout the first shot of the sequence, they are clearly human. Then, after a very short second shot that shows viewers the scene of the accident through the car's rear window, a third shot once again frames Vero in profile, but the marks now look canine, not human (fig. 10.5). Could this change in the physiology of the marks indicate a change in Vero as well? Might Vero be like a Red Riding Hood who has just made the fateful

FIGURE 10.5 Vero's (María Onetto) mental confusion is visually suggested by the appearance of a canine footprint where there had just been a human handprint in *The Headless Woman* (Lucrecia Martel, Argentina, 2008)

decision to abandon the wolves she used to run with, to paraphrase the title of a popular book on the wild woman archetype?[20]

By privileging ambiguity (not only the marks on the car's side window, but also the fact that it is never clear whether Vero killed only a dog or a young man as well), and by having open endings that force us to ask ourselves what we would do in a similar situation, Martel implicates her viewers in the moral conundrums her characters face. Like fables, then, the films ask the most difficult of questions: how would we act in situations like these, where our baser instincts push us in one direction and our ethical selves in another? Should Dr. Jano, for example, be stripped of his medical license for being a sexual predator? Asked in this manner, the answer seems straightforward enough: yes. As we watch, however, we find ourselves torn between hoping for this execution of justice and hoping Jano will not be punished, for the sake of his family and his career.

Understandably, we repress the feelings of guilt that develop when we identify with characters whose behaviors are unethical and/or have ethically unacceptable consequences. But unlike most suspense films, where the danger is made explicit in the end and the spectator does not have to answer for his or her unethical wishes, Martel forces us to confront and examine our unethical wishes by evading narrative closure and thereby highlighting the idea, central to fables and fairy tales, that there is always a choice to be made, whether by the characters on the screen or by us in similar situations. In *The Holy Girl,* Dr. Jano may or may not be accused of child molestation, but more important is what the viewer wants for Dr. Jano and why.

The Salta Trilogy as an Allegory of the Precarious Transition to Democracy

While the action in Martel's Salta trilogy appears to develop in a temporal vacuum, as in a fairy tale, the machines in the films do suggest an approximate timeframe. The models of the phones, cars, and television sets in *The Swamp* suggest that the action takes place during the last years of the military dictatorship, in the late 1970s; in *The Holy Girl,* a coin-operated copying machine in a local shop suggests that the action is now set during Raúl Alfonsín's presidency, in the mid-1980s; and in *The Headless Woman,* the use of cell phones and color home videos anchors the action in the late 1990s, during Carlos Menem's presidency. This rough timeframe enables a complementary reading of the protagonists as metaphors of Argentina's civil society as it transitioned from being an infantilized social agent during the military dictatorship of the 1970s, to the equivalent of a brazen adolescent in the early years of fragile democracy in the 1980s, and finally to an accommodating accomplice of Menem's brand of populist neoliberalism in the 1990s.

The trilogy in this regard is a study of Martel's own generation. Born in 1966, Martel would have been Momi's age during Argentina's dictatorship, Amalia's age during the first years of democratic rule, and younger than Vero, but an adult nevertheless, during the height of neoliberalism and the Washington Consensus in the 1990s. In this multigenerational story, the double status of strong, intelligent, and socially privileged women as simultaneously courted and contained by patriarchy parallels the double status of Argentina's civil society as simultaneously courted and contained by the patriarchal state. More specifically, the fictional protagonists' unresolved dialectic between female desire and patriarchy is analogous to the unresolved dialectic between civil society's desire for freedom and the patriarchal state's containment of that freedom during key moments in Argentina's recent history.

For example, insofar as Momi represents the generation that grew up under the military dictatorship, her final statement to her sister Vero, to the effect that she did not see the image of the Virgin many claimed to have seen, represents her generation's potential to think for itself rather than accepting what the mass media, and the interests that lie behind the mass media, tell them to think and believe. Yet Momi's potential remains unrealized. Her moment of greatest awareness comes at a moment of personal crisis, when she must come to terms with a pregnant Isabel's decision to leave the household. At this critical juncture, when Momi should have given Isabel her full moral support, her choice to reproduce Mecha's racist and classist behavior toward a vulnerable Isabel indicates that her psychosexual development has stagnated, like everyone else's. This stagnation is further underscored by the closing shot of the two sisters lounging by the pool, much like their parents lounged, stagnant, in the opening sequence. *The Swamp* thus ends with Momi stuck in the equivalent of Freud's latent stage—sexually unfulfilled and unable to grow beyond her fixation on Isabel—a situation that parallels the predicament of Argentina's latent civil society during the last years of the dictatorship, when a clean cut with the military was as unlikely as Momi charting a radically different course from that of her family.

In *The Holy Girl,* by contrast, Amalia's boundless sexual desire is analogous to civil society's boundless political desire for freedom when democratic rule returned to Argentina in the 1980s. In this reading, Jano embodies the gender, class, and racial privileges so earnestly protected under the dictatorship, while Amalia embodies civil society's highest aspirations for freedom and even reconciliation. In the end, however, Amalia floats in the pool next to Josefina, who hypocritically tells Amalia that she will always protect her when in fact she has just betrayed her to save her own skin. Our knowledge of Josefina's duplicity facilitates a reading of this closing sequence as an indictment of the many times that civil society in Argentina has been betrayed by those who claim to be looking after society's interests, when in fact they are looking after their own.

Finally, in the closing sequence of *The Headless Woman,* the enclosed space of the hotel's activity room seems to give the film narrative closure, and in so doing points to a parallel with Menem's 1989 and 1990 presidential pardon of crimes committed by high officials in the military during the country's Dirty War in the 1970s, a pardon that Menem justified as a necessary condition for national reconciliation. The parallel, to be exact, is that like Menem, Vero justified the suppression of truths that threatened the Oedipal trajectory toward closure (over and above the ethical course of investigating committed crimes) in order to secure the class privileges that she clearly enjoys and that patriarchy protects. Yet the narrative closure in the film is only apparent because the tinted glass doors that lead to the hotel's activity room call attention to the fact that we can still see through the lies that sustain impunity for those who committed crimes against humanity during the Dirty War. Moreover, the fact that the doors are made of glass suggests that this impunity can always shatter, as it did in 2003, when the Argentinean Congress nullified the so-called impunity laws of 1986 and 1987, and again in 2010, when the Argentinean Supreme Court declared Menem's pardons unconstitutional. For many, the process of Argentina facing up to its criminal past culminated when a former junta director, the notorious General Jorge Rafael Videla, was sentenced to life in prison in 2010 and died there, to little fanfare, in 2013. What *The Headless Woman* suggests, however, is that Argentina's culture of impunity is very much alive, and will remain so as long as the dialectic between female desire and patriarchy is skewed in favor of the latter.

Because Martel cleverly uses suspense, a widely recognizable and popular narrative form, and because she subtly explores the ongoing conflict between female desire and patriarchy that transcends national contexts, her films have traveled well beyond Argentina, collecting nominations and awards from all the major festivals in Latin America and the North Atlantic, from Cannes to Sundance, Buenos Aires to Havana. At the same time, however, her work is finely tuned to the particular rhythms and values of provincial middle-class Argentina, a world whose economic stagnation and moral bankruptcy she dissects through narratives that play on viewers' sympathies by constantly shifting between favorable and unfavorable perspectives on her characters. This constant shifting of perspectives facilitates a critical reading where desire for freedom, whether sexual or political, is not an abstraction but rather something concretely anchored in a specific place with a century-long history of decadence, authoritarianism, and impunity. Provincial Argentina, to be more exact, is the specific context where, as the successive titles of the trilogy suggest, desire for freedom has been successively stagnated, sublimated, and truncated. Yet, as with every good fairy tale, the moral of Martel's trilogy is not limited to one place. It can be readily applied to other nations, Latin American and otherwise, whose civil societies still struggle to chart a new course where neither patriarchy nor impunity are justified as necessary conditions for social stability and national reconciliation.

The Milk of Sorrow (2009)

La teta asustada (*The Milk of Sorrow*; Claudia Llosa, Peru-Spain, 2009) is Peru's most awarded film of all time; it won, among many other prizes, best film awards at the Berlin, Havana, Lima, Guadalajara, and Bogotá film festivals. Like Martel's trilogy, it explores the legacy of Latin America's violent past, but it does so from the perspective of an indigenous woman without any of the class or race privileges that Martel's heroines enjoy. The film begins by narrating, rather than representing, the violence that took place during Peru's civil war in the 1980s, in an opening sequence that features what sounds like a lullaby against a black background. As the song progresses, however, and as we continue to read the subtitles of the lyrics in Quechua, we realize it is not a lullaby, and just as the lyrics are about to take a violent turn, the black screen fades into a close-up of the singer, a very old indigenous woman: "This woman who sings was grabbed, was raped that night. They didn't care about my unborn daughter. They raped me with their penises and hands with no pity for my daughter watching them from inside, and, not satisfied with that, they made me swallow the dead penis of my husband Josefo, his poor dead penis seasoned with gunpowder. With that pain I screamed, 'You better kill me and bury me with my Josefo. I know nothing here.'"

From the very beginning, then, the film calls attention to rape as both an individual and a collective experience: individual because it was this specific woman and her daughter Fausta (Magaly Solier) who suffered the rape, and collective because rape was a weapon of war used by both the Sendero Luminoso and the state armed forces to terrorize indigenous communities into supporting their side of the conflict.

When Fausta's mother dies shortly after this opening sequence, Fausta faints and is taken to a public hospital, where the staff learns that she keeps a potato inside her vagina. The doctor tries to convince Fausta's Uncle Lúcido (Marino Ballón) of the need to remove the tuber, and is exasperated by the uncle's explanation that Fausta suffers from the milk of sorrow, or the transmission of suffering from mother to offspring via breast milk. The ailment may sound like a fictional narrative device, but in fact director Claudia Llosa read about it in the anthropologist Kimberly Theidon's acclaimed book *Entre prójimos: el conflicto armado interno y la política de la reconciliación en el Perú* (*Intimate Enemies: Violence and Reconciliation in Peru*; 2004), where she coined the term "to convey how strong negative emotions can alter the body and how a mother could, via blood in utero or via breast milk, transmit this disease to her baby."[21]

Once home, Fausta explains the function of the potato in a song to her dead mother: "My uncle doesn't understand, mom. I saw it all from your belly. I felt the slashing of your belly. This is why I now wear this [potato] like a coat of arms, like a stopper. Because only revulsion stops revolting people." Presently, Fausta helps a group of women (and her transvestite cousin) apply warm oil to the body of the dead mother, then wrap it in what looks like a mummification ritual from pre-Columbian times. Unlike the ancient Incas, however, who mummified their dead for the afterlife, Fausta's aunt explains how she learned to do this for much more practical reasons: "How could we prove their existence? We didn't have a picture, or an ID card. We had no proof of being born, and much less of being killed." Having thus established the ethnic dimension of the mass rapes and killings in the country's recent history, the film proceeds to focus on Fausta's narrative trajectory of recovery from trauma. Her aunt tells her of a domestic job at the mansion of a rich criollo woman, but she must be willing to go and return on her own, something she never does out of fear of being raped. Fausta accepts only because it is the only way she will be able to pay for the transport of her mother's body back to her village in the Andes for a proper burial.

Much of the rest of the film focuses on two relationships Fausta develops in her new job: one with Aída (Susi Sánchez), the owner of the mansion and an acclaimed concert pianist who cannot find inspiration to write a new composition for her annual solo performance, and one with Noé (Efraín Solís), the mansion's gardener, who like Fausta speaks both Spanish and Quechua. When Fausta first meets Aída, Aída is drilling a hole to put up a picture on her bedroom wall. Aída asks Fausta to hold the electric drill, but when Fausta sees the picture—of a man in a military uniform—she feels nauseous and runs to the kitchen, where she begins to sing in Quechua, "Let's sing, let's sing. We must sing pretty things. To hide our fear, pretend it doesn't exist." Later, Aída asks Fausta to sing the song again, and when Fausta is unable to sing on demand, Aída offers her a deal: "If you sing, I'll give you a pearl. If you complete the necklace, it's yours."

In the end, Fausta keeps her end of the bargain, and Aída uses her melodies as the basis for her new piano composition. Aída, however, does not keep her end of the bargain. Instead, on the way back from the concert, when Fausta comments on how well the concert was received, Aída interprets the comment as a double threat: to her position as the servant's master, because Fausta spoke without being asked, and to her reputation as a composer, because Aída never acknowledged Fausta's contribution to her composition. Thus threatened, Aída tells her son to stop the car, and very subtly but surely orders Fausta to get out, right there, in the middle of the city, at night.

Fausta's relationship with Noé is more horizontal, but complicated by the fact that he is a man. After establishing an uneasy mutual trust, they have a decisive and symbolically rich conversation:

> *Fausta:* There are geraniums, camellias, daisies, cactus, sweet potatoes, everything but potatoes. Why?
>
> *Noé:* Why are you afraid to walk alone on the street? . . .
>
> *Fausta:* I'm not afraid because I want to.
>
> *Noé:* Only death is obligatory, the rest is because we want to.
>
> *Fausta:* And when they kill you or rape you, what? That's not obligatory! [Fausta turns and begins to walk away.]
>
> *Noé:* [Remorseful] Potatoes are cheap and flourish very little.

This conversation seals the relationship between them as one of solidarity between equals, and so it is fitting that when Fausta, despite her fears, returns to the mansion one last time to claim the pearls that Aída owes her, it is Noé who finds her in a faint by the front gate, and Noé the person she trusts to take her to the hospital to remove the potato from her vagina. With the potato and the fear it symbolizes finally removed from her body, Fausta is now able to complete her narrative trajectory of recovery. She uses the pearls to buy a truck, and on the way to the highlands, asks the driver to stop so that she can show her mother the Pacific Ocean, where, as a minor character had informed her earlier in the film, dead people can "unburden their sufferings and wash away their sorrows." The film ends with a beautifully evocative image. Having returned from the Andes, someone knocks on the door of the house where she lives with her extended family. Nobody is there when she opens the door, but then she looks down, and leans to enjoy the smell of the small white blossoms of a potted potato plant Noé has left for her.

As this summary of the film makes clear, the narrative does not center so much on the systematic rape of indigenous women per se, as on the ensuing trauma, and more specifically, on how the past could be remembered in ways that aid rather than hinder the victims' recovery. Broadly speaking, Fausta's traumatic memory evolves from something that thoroughly limits her to something she can overcome through resilience. Furthermore, because this trajectory is framed by a narrative conflict between Fausta and Aída, Fausta's individual trajectory bespeaks a broader cultural conflict between two competing memories of Peru's past: a memory rooted in what Aníbal Quijano calls the private-individual and aligned with the values of liberalism, and a memory rooted in indigenous practices of the private-social, a term Quijano uses to refer to the kind of communal ownership and decision making that combines a private that is not individual, with a social that is not of the state.[22]

For instance, when Aída finds her childhood doll buried in the garden, her recollection of the story of the buried doll is a memory that is hers only. It is not the kind of memory that is shared by other people of her generation, or even by women of her social class. Instead, Aída's private-individual memory reflects the class privileges that private property ownership can buy, including impunity for crimes that range from white-collar stealing, as when she appropriates Fausta's melody without compensating her, to the more heinous crimes of conquest and pillage that Aída's ancestors clearly practiced, and which are symbolically represented via the colonial artifacts and architecture of her mansion, as well as in the casting of her servants as either indigenous or Afro-Peruvians. By contrast, Fausta's memory is like the memory of Sebastián at the end of *La nación clandestina* (The Clandestine Nation; Jorge Sanjinés, Bolivia, 1989), meaning it is the memory of a collective-individual who participates in the kind of private-social ownership that defines *ayllus*. In fact, Fausta's extended family is structured like an *ayllu*, living as they do on a clearly demarcated plot of land of generous proportions, and with every member contributing to a wedding service business that functions like a family-run cooperative. This *ayllu*-inspired social structure, where ownership is both private and social (though not of the state), is therefore aligned with Fausta's own memory of rape, which is likewise a combination of experiences that are both private and social (though again, not of the state).

The distinction between private-individual and private-social memories is analogous to the distinction that Maurice Halbwachs, the father of memory studies, makes between history and memory. History, he argues, "gives the impression that everything . . . is transformed from one period to another [so that] two successive periods are like two tree stumps that touch at their extremities but do not form one plant because they are not otherwise connected." Society's collective memory, on the other hand, "is like a thread that is made from a series of . . . fibers intertwined at regular intervals; or, rather, it resembles the cloth made from weaving these threads together."[23] For example, when Aída unearths the buried doll and shares her private-individual memory with Fausta, they stand next to each other like two tree stumps that touch at

FIGURE 10.6 Bodies that do not touch function as a metaphor of private-individual memory and identity in *The Milk of Sorrow* (Claudia Llosa, Peru-Spain, 2009)

their extremities but do not form one plant because they are not otherwise connected (fig. 10.6). By contrast, when Fausta's aunt explains why she learned to preserve the bodies of the dead, the explanation is like one of many threads of a collective memory: each thread is distinct, yet they are interwoven into a recognizable pattern of systematic rape and murder. This idea is visually underscored through a carefully constructed mise-en-scène: clearly discernible individuals are gathered all around the dead body of Fausta's mother, yet their hands and arms are all connected, like buried threads or rhizomes, to the dead body (and the living memory) of the rape victim (fig. 10.7).

Each of these two memories—Aída's private-individual memory and Fausta's private-social memory—are in turn linked to different conceptions of time: one linear, the other cyclical. On the one hand, Aída is defined literally as the most recent member in a lineage of private individuals that decorates her bedroom wall, and her annual piano performances, she says, will go on until she can no longer compose, at which time she will play a funerary march that will symbolically mark the end of a linear musical career. By contrast, Fausta's time is cyclical, like a plant's life cycle. Hence the fable-like symbolism of plants in the film, most notably in the closing shot where Fausta is identified with a blooming potato plant that represents both her final blossoming as an

FIGURE 10.7 Hands and arms, connected like rhizomes under the thin surface of the cotton sheet, function as a metaphor of private-social memory and identity in *The Milk of Sorrow*

individual, and also the post–civil war blossoming of an indigenous community embodied most directly in Noé, whose choice of gift demonstrates that he now values the indigenous culture he once belittled.

Despite the anthropomorphization of plants (Noé at one point tells Fausta that "plants tell the truth; they're not like people") and the film's use of symbolically rich characters and situations, *The Milk of Sorrow* is not a fable. The film does not, for example, situate the action in an imprecise time and place, nor does it give viewers the sense that there is always a moral choice to be made, two conventions of fables that help them travel well across cultures. Instead, it situates the action at a very specific time and place, and in a dense cultural milieu with two competing memories of Latin America's violent past: a private-individual memory defined by privilege, and a private-social memory marked by ongoing struggles for justice. The subtle representation of this contested memory is at the heart of what makes the film exceptional beyond its clever use of suspense, its symbolically rich narrative, and its skillful use of independent cinema's production values such as naturalistic acting, flawless editing, and a professionally mixed soundtrack, all of which are necessary but not sufficient conditions for the film's having struck a nerve in Peru and on the international film circuit.

Specifically, what makes the film stand apart from many other films about memory and trauma is—to use an argument originally made by Julianne Burton-Carvajal in 1993—its positioning of spectators to readily identify with a protagonist whose rape is represented not only as a central part of a fictional narrative filled with *symbolic* meaning, but also as part of an *actual* system of social practices and cultural values that together foster and justify rape and other forms of collective torture and terror against women in general, and indigenous women in particular. In "Regarding Rape," Burton-Carvajal argues that Latin American cinema's representations of rape have seen an incremental if unsteady movement toward the alignment of spectatorial identification with a female subjectivity whose transformation is not simply symbolic.[24] A survey of Latin American cinema, she notes, "reveals a . . . number of (anti)foundational features in which an aberrant figure of coupling—prostitution, incest, sterilization, orphanhood, love triangle, [or] rape—substitutes for the mutually committed heterosexual pair (and the resultant patriarchal nuclear family) around whom the [nineteenth-century] literary foundational romances revolved."[25]

Burton-Carvajal goes on to discuss three Mexican and three Cuban features at some length. In *Doña Bárbara* (Fernando de Fuentes, Mexico, 1943) and in the first episode of *Lucía* (Humberto Solás, Cuba, 1968), she notes that the essence of key female characters is explained by a rape that is more symbolic than actual because the rapes are told in flashback or by a minor character, narrative strategies that reduce the referentiality of these rapes to any actual, systemic violence outside of the filmic space, and therefore make it difficult for us to empathize with the female character as a human being defined by something other than the rape. By contrast, in *La negra Angustias* (The Black Angustias; Matilde Landeta, Mexico, 1950) and *This Strange Passion* (Luis Buñuel, Mexico, 1953), "the victim throws off her attacker and, fortified by her own successful resistance, goes on to invert the established order that had shaped and sheltered her antagonists."[26] Likewise, *The Other Francisco* (Sergio Giral, Cuba, 1975) refuses "to symbolize the female" by showing in documentary style "the deplorable conditions which governed Afro-Cuban female sexuality under slavery," and *Hasta cierto punto* (*Up to a Point*; Tomás Gutiérrez Alea, Cuba, 1984) "deserves acknowledgement for confronting the issue of what Americans have called 'date rape.'"[27] Burton concludes that even though "the tendency to reduce and confine the female within a hackneyed symbology" persists in Latin American cinema's representations of rape, what is even more notable is the effort toward the alignment of spectatorial identification with female characters whose rape is not reduced to a mere symbolic event within a larger narrative, but rather linked to actual systems of violence outside of the filmic space. I would argue that this effort finds full expression in *The Milk of Sorrow*, a film that, paradoxically, does not visually represent rape. Instead, the film effectively weaves narrative and memory threads that are both individual and collective in order to create a denser examination of rape, not as an isolated act perpetrated by private individuals, but as part of an actual system of social practices and cultural values with historical, political, racial, ethnic, and gender dimensions that together foster and justify rape as a socially acceptable form of violence and repression. Significantly, as we have seen, this view of rape necessitates an understanding of trauma as a social phenomenon that includes private-individual memory but can never be reduced to it because it is always already linked to past and ongoing struggles for social, ethnic, and gender justice.

FROM NOSTALGIA TO SUSPENSE

Suspense, with its focus on the immediate, is especially well suited to exploring the political, economic, and social precariousness of the present historical moment. It has been used to good effect in the films by Lucrecia Martel and Claudia Llosa just discussed, as well as in a wide range of melorealist films of the last decade or so that attest to the remarkable creativity and sophistication of contemporary Latin American cinema: *Ratas, ratones, rateros* (Rats, Mice, Thieves; Sebastián Cordero, Ecuador, 1999), *Bolivia* (Adrián Caetano, Argentina–the Netherlands, 2001), *25 Watts* (Juan Pablo Rebella and Pablo Stoll, Uruguay–the Netherlands, 2001), *Historias mínimas* (*Intimate Stories*; Carlos Sorín, Argentina-Spain, 2002), *Japón* (Carlos Reygadas, Mexico-the Netherlands-Germany, 2002), *Ônibus 174* (*Bus 174*; José Padilha and Felipe Lacerda, Brazil, 2002), *Cidade de Deus* (*City of God*; Fernando Meirelles, Brazil-France, 2002), *Carándiru* (Héctor Babenco, Brazil-Argentina, 2003), *Suite Habana* (Fernando Pérez, Cuba-Spain, 2003), *Whisky* (Juan Pablo Rebella and Pablo Stoll, Uruguay-Argentina-Germany-Spain, 2004), *Sumas y restas* (*Additions and Subtractions*; Víctor Gaviria, Colombia-Spain, 2004), *Los muertos* (*The Dead Ones*; Lisandro Alonso, Argentina-France-the Netherlands-Switzerland, 2004), *El violín* (*The Violin*; Francisco Vargas, Mexico, 2005), *XXY* (Lucía

Puenzo, Argentina, 2007), *Hamaca paraguaya* (*Paraguayan Hammock*; Paz Encina, Paraguay-Germany-Denmark-Argentina-France-Spain, 2008), *Alamar* (Pedro González-Rubio, Mexico, 2009), *Gigante* (*Giant*; Adrián Biniez, Uruguay-Germany-the Netherlands, 2009), *O Som ao Redor* (*Neighboring Sounds*; Kleber Mendonça Filho, Brazil-the Netherlands, 2012), *Después de Lucía* (*After Lucia*; Michel Franco, Mexico, 2012), and *Pelo malo* (*Bad Hair*; Mariana Rondón, Venezuela-Peru-Argentina-Germany, 2013). Together, these films give ample evidence of a shift away from the pathos one sees in the social melodramas and nostalgic narratives of the 1990s, and toward the contained emotion and uncertainty that characterizes suspense.

What could be the meaning of this shift from nostalgia to suspense? Noël Carroll argues that in suspense films, morality is defined functionally by the circumstances at hand.[28] I take this to mean that in suspense films, what is ethical is not predicated by Kantian categories of good and evil, but rather that the same action can be good, evil, or even a combination of both, depending on the circumstances. The preference for suspense in Latin American cinema of the first decade of the twenty-first century is therefore consistent with the region's prevailing political economy of pragmatic reformism, relative to the second half of the twentieth century. It is, in other words, a political economy that speaks of a contingent and precarious present, rather than of a future utopia, as in the militant NLAC, or a glossy past, as in the nostalgic cinema of the 1990s.

Carroll also argues that in Hollywood films, "the audience is provided, often aggressively, with a stake in one of the alternatives by having its moral sensibility drawn to prefer one of the uncertain outcomes."[29] These outcomes, moreover, are clearly either/or: either "morally correct but improbable . . . or morally incorrect . . . but probable."[30] But in the Latin American suspense films I have discussed, and in many recent documentaries as well, audiences are provided with a stake in both of the ethical alternatives presented, as if both alternatives were simultaneously morally and immorally correct, but for different reasons. It is then up to the viewer to figure out not so much which is morally correct versus incorrect, but rather the extent to which each is moral and immoral, and why. Not surprisingly, given this preference for nuance over certainty, none of the dominant narratives of modernity—not liberalism, not socialism, not corporatism—can be said to be dominant in contemporary Latin America cinema. Instead, the more innovative films of the past two decades share with the neobaroque phase of the New Latin American Cinema not its aesthetics, but certainly its valorization of substantive reason, through narratives that glimpse askance at those privileged moments when reciprocity, solidarity, and sometimes even love cross boundaries of gender, race, class, nationality, sexuality, and ethnicity.

Conclusion

A Triangulated Cinema

In Latin America, films have variously privileged a local perspective, as in *Sangue Mineiro* (Mineiro Blood; Humberto Mauro, Brazil, 1929), a national one, as in *Lucía* (Humberto Solás, Cuba, 1968), or a transnational one, as in *Frida Still Life* (Paul Leduc, Mexico, 1983). All of these perspectives—the local, the national, and the transnational—have played an important role in what one might call the cinematic invention of Latin America. The idea of the Americas as an invention is of course much older than cinema. It dates back to the early sixteenth century, to a widely read and translated book about Columbus's voyages of discovery in the Caribbean: *Historia de la invención de las Indias* (*History of the Invention of the Indies*; 1528), by Fernán Pérez de Oliva. For its author, "invention" meant "'to discover, to find,' [as] a kind of creative act."[1] Almost five centuries later, Enrique Dussel used "invention" in a radically different way in *The Invention of the Americas* (1995), a scathing critique of the Eurocentric discourses of modernity that have emerged since those fateful voyages. Dussel's "invention" is the opposite of Pérez de Oliva's "invention": not to discover as an act of creativity, but to hide as an act of destructive concealment.[2] These two meanings may seem incompatible, yet throughout this book I have combined them. In the tradition of Pérez de Oliva's use of the word, I have celebrated those filmmakers who have succeeded in creating cinematic worlds. At the same time, however, I have taken a critical view of these cinematic inventions, and in the tradition of Dussel, I have sought to describe and examine what such inventions reveal as much as what they conceal about Latin America and its multiple modernities.

Perhaps the major takeaway from the diachronic examination of these shifting inventions is that, from the silent period to the digital age, Latin American narrative cinema has always been part and parcel of global cinematic flows and global cultural processes. It is a cinema, as Guattari and Deleuze would argue,[3] that is reciprocally caught up in, and forms a rhizome with, cinemas in other parts of the world, especially Europe and Hollywood. Organic metaphors aside, Latin American narrative cinema is, as we have seen, a triangulated practice whereby filmmakers oftentimes adapt European and Hollywood influences to their own needs by inflecting them with local documentary filmmaking practices. The weight of any of these referents on a specific filmmaker's triangulation varies according to specifics such as the filmmaker's interests and objectives, historical circumstances, the country or region of production, and audiences' knowledge of said referents, among others. But what is relatively constant is the presence of all three referents throughout the history of Latin American cinema.

As we have seen, conventional silent cinema incorporates practices associated with three modes of representation: Hollywood (action-filled sequences and psychologically driven narratives), Europe (the melodramatic excess of Italian superproductions and the gravity of French *films d'art*), and homegrown documentary practices (multiple visual and social perspectives, and a strong interest in local customs and manners). These influences are evident between films—*La Revolución de Mayo* (The May Revolution; Mario Gallo, Argentina, 1910) is clearly inspired by French filmed theater, *Wara Wara* (José María Velasco Maidana, Bolivia, 1930) by Italian superspectacles, and *El tren fantasma* (The Ghost Train; Gabriel García Moreno, Mexico, 1927) by Hollywood action films—and just as often within films. *Nobleza gaucha* (Gaucho Nobility; Eduardo Martínez de la Pera, Ernesto Gunche, and Humberto Cairo, Argentina, 1915), *El automóvil gris* (The Gray Automobile; Enrique Rosas, Joaquín Coss, and Juan Canals de Homs, Mexico, 1919), *Sangue Mineiro, Tepeyac* (José Manuel Ramos, Carlos E. González, and Fernando Sáyago, Mexico, 1917), and especially *El último malón* (The Last Indian Uprising; Alcides Greco, Argentina, 1916) combine elements from Hollywood and European genres with homegrown documentary modes of representation.

Just as sound was beginning to transform cinema, a handful of highly experimental silent films sought to transform the cinematic experience through an intense dialogue with the Soviet and Western European avant-gardes, but whereas *São Paulo, A Sinfonia da Metrópole* (São Paulo, a Metropolitan Symphony; Rodolfo Rex Lustig and Adalberto Kemeny, Brazil, 1929) and *Ganga Bruta* (Raw Gangue; Humberto Mauro, Brazil, 1933) use formal experimentation in support of conventional values, *¡Que viva México!* (Sergei Eisenstein, Mexico–United States, 1931) and *Limite* (Limit; Mário Peixoto, Brazil, 1929) use formal experimentation to represent radically alternative social relations and values. Other than *¡Que viva México!*, whose cinematography would help define the Mexican school of cinema in the 1940s, the legacy of this first avant-garde on subsequent filmmaking is limited, and almost nonexistent when compared with the legacy of conventional films such as *Tepeyac* and *Nobleza gaucha*.

The limited availability of private capital after the Wall Street crash of 1929, coupled with the sharp increase in costs associated with the coming of sound, forced Latin American filmmakers to seek financial support from newly constituted corporatist states, who in turn saw this as an opportunity to exert more control over representations on the big screen by supporting certain studios over others as studios struggled to shift from artisanal to industrial modes of production. This was also the time of Hollywood's experiment with "Hispanic films," or Spanish-language films produced by Hollywood studios in California and in France, such as *The Day You Love Me* (John Reinhardt, United States, 1935), a vehicle for Carlos Gardel that helped to consolidate his status as Latin America's biggest popular star. After Hispanic films proved to be financially unsustainable, many of the Latin American actors, directors, and technicians who had been working in them returned to their respective countries and brought with them an intimate knowledge of Hollywood practices that became instrumental in the creation of a vernacular Hollywood style in Latin American cinema. It is a style defined by high production values, driven by the studio imperatives of genre and stardom, and marked by the ideology of a resurgent corporatism throughout the region. *Out on the Big Ranch* (Fernando de Fuentes, Mexico, 1936), a musical comedy featuring a relatively well-known singer at the time, epitomizes this shift to a Latin American Hollywood vernacular with corporatist sympathies.

The two hubs of production during the studio era were Buenos Aires and Mexico City. Buenos Aires took an early lead in the 1930s with comedies such as *The Three Amateurs* (Enrique T. Susini, Argentina, 1933) and melodramas such as *Closed Door* (Luis Saslavsky, Argentina,

1939), but after the United States, as part of its Good Neighbor Policy, simultaneously propped up Mexico's film industry and isolated Argentina's, Mexico City decisively overtook Buenos Aires as the center of gravity in Latin American cinema, and in the second half of the 1940s Mexican films even competed head to head with Hollywood in the region. This commercial success went hand in hand with the development of a distinctive film style that came to be known as the Mexican school of cinema, with films such as *María Candelaria* (Emilio Fernández, Mexico, 1943) and *Río Escondido* (Emilio Fernández, Mexico, 1947) that combined star power, nationalist narratives, and highly polished cinematography into a marketable product. At the time, films were Mexico's second-largest export (after oil), and its remarkable distribution network included every other Latin American country, Western Europe (especially Spain), and North America (especially Mexican and Mexican-American communities in the United States). As a result, Mexican films of the second half of the 1930s and into the 1950s became part of popular culture throughout Latin America. As a cohesive force in Latin American identity formation, Mexican cinema was even more pronounced than the Hispanic films a decade earlier, for even though Hispanic films decisively influenced modes of production and representation throughout the region, they were only produced for a few short years, whereas Mexican films and Mexican coproductions with other Latin American countries were widely seen throughout the region for more than two decades. Argentinean studio cinema, for its part, enjoyed an increase in production under the protection of the first Peronist government, and even tried to compete with Hollywood and Mexican cinema with transnational products such as *God Bless You* (Luis César Amadori, Argentina, 1948).

After the "golden" 1930s and 1940s, Latin American film studios faced two challenges: a renewed Hollywood offensive backed by the U.S. State Department, and declining audience interest in narrative and audiovisual conventions that had in many ways become fossilized. In this context, the decision by some studios to churn out low-budget, soft-porn comedies (*pornochanchadas* in Brazil, *cine de ficheras* in Mexico) ensured they could at least make a profit by purposely giving up on the high production values that had been the shared goal of most Latin American filmmakers since the 1910s. Other responses to the new cinematic landscape of the 1950s included the continued use of studio modes of production and representation to address new social realities, as in *Aventurera* (The Adventuress; Alberto Gout, Mexico, 1950), and independent productions that oscillated between neorealism and art cinema. These independent productions—which range in style and thematics from the neorealist *Rio, Zona Norte* (Rio, North Zone; Nelson Pereira dos Santos, Brazil, 1957) to the auteurism of *This Strange Passion* (Luis Buñuel, Mexico, 1953) and *The Hand in the Trap* (Leopoldo Torre Nilsson, Argentina, 1961), to the combination of both in *Los olvidados* (The Forgotten Ones; Luis Buñuel, Mexico, 1950)—were closely linked to a new cinephilic culture that included film clubs, film journals, university programs, and film festivals. Concurrently, as a direct response to *pornochanchadas* in Brazil, one finds the anachronism called Vera Cruz, a state-of-the-art studio founded by industrialists in São Paulo with the explicit intent of creating a Hollywood-style film industry in Brazil. The experiment failed financially, in large measure because it focused on production while ignoring distribution and exhibition. *O Cangaceiro* (The Backlands Bandit; Victor Lima Barreto, 1953), for example, became the first Brazilian film to earn a prize at Cannes, but because Vera Cruz sold its international distribution rights, that success did not translate into more money for the studio. Ironically, the very success of the film galvanized a group of young filmmakers into countering the film's sanitized version of Brazil's northeast with what turned out to be the first films of Cinema Novo and thus the first films of what would become the New Latin American Cinema: *Black God, White Devil* (Glauber Rocha, Brazil, 1963), *Barren Lives* (Nelson Pereira dos Santos, Brazil, 1963), and *The Guns* (Ruy Guerra, Brazil, 1964).

The New Latin American Cinema was part of a global phenomenon that included New Cinemas in Africa, Europe, Asia, and North America. The difference between this round of triangulation and previous ones is that the dialogue was now reciprocated. Instead of being mostly a North-to-South flow of films and influences, films and influences between Latin America and the rest of the world also flowed, for the first time, South to North, and South to South. What most caught the imagination of audiences, critics, and filmmakers in the global North and the global South about the NLAC in the 1960s was its unprecedented and very effective combination of what Robert Stam calls the two avant-gardes: a political avant-garde identified with socialist revolution (the two models were Cuba and Chile), and an aesthetic avant-garde that experimented with ways to use documentary modes of representation to advance the cause of socialist revolution. This political function of the documentary finds full expression in the weekly

newsreels of Santiago Álvarez and in two documentaries of epic proportions that read like virtual political acts: *The Hour of the Furnaces*
(Fernando Solanas and Octavio Getino, Argentina, 1968) and *The Battle of Chile* (Patricio Guzmán, Chile-Cuba, 1975–79). It also finds its
way into narrative filmmaking via the incorporation of documentary
footage and documentary modes of representation in films as varied
as *Black God, White Devil, Memories of Underdevelopment* (Tomás
Gutiérrez Alea, Cuba, 1968), *Lucía*, and *One Way or Another* (Sara
Gómez, Cuba, 1974).

Already in these last three films, however, the clear teleological narratives and exemplary characters of the militant phase of the NLAC are
giving way to alternative temporalities and multidimensional characters. Revolution is still the central theme of these and subsequent films,
but after the authoritarian turn of the 1970s, when it became clear that
the socialist revolution that many anticipated or imagined in the 1960s
would not materialize, filmmakers begin to explore the constructed
nature of reality and of power itself. They do this primarily by decon-
structing vertical power structures through carefully constructed neobaroque mise-en-scènes and fragmentary narratives whose very forms
question the monologism and populism of authoritarian states on both
ends of the political spectrum. Thus, neobaroque films such as *Macunaíma* (Joaquim Pedro de Andrade, Brazil, 1969), *The Last Supper*
(Tomás Gutiérrez Alea, Cuba, 1976), *Frida Still Life* (Paul Leduc, Mexico, 1983), and *La nación clandestina* (The Clandestine Nation; Jorge
Sanjinés, Bolivia, 1989) present alternatives to heteronormativity, white
supremacy, and the idea of the modern nation as a homogeneous entity,
via correspondingly alternative modes of representation that very
clearly and deliberately set them apart from the Hollywood blockbusters and homegrown telenovelas that dominated the Latin American
audiovisual landscape at the time.

In terms of triangulation, filmmakers during the neobaroque phase
of the NLAC calculated their sightlines in part to take advantage of the
worldwide art-house cinema network of the 1970s and 1980s. Contemporary social dramas such as *El pez que fuma* (The Smoking Fish;
Román Chalbaud, Venezuela, 1977), *Tiempo de revancha* (Time for
Revenge; Adolfo Aristaraín, Argentina, 1981), *La ciudad y los perros*
(The City and the Dogs; Francisco Lombardi, Peru, 1985), *La historia
oficial* (The Official Story; Luis Puenzo, Argentina, 1985), and *La boca
del lobo* (The Lion's Den; Francisco Lombardi, Peru, 1988) also participated in this network, but their realist, televisual aesthetics anchor

them to the global resurgence of realist melodramas that took place in the 1980s, more than to a neobaroque praxis. In Latin America, these realist melodramas have evolved into a full-fledged melorealist cinema centered on affect and emotion, but without the excess normally associated with the telenovelas that had overtaken even Hollywood cinema as the region's most popular audiovisual narrative fare. The style of the melorealist cinema of the past two decades is correspondingly more restrained than the style of telenovelas, with realism achieved through the use of natural acting and lighting, restrained dialogue, on-location shooting, and the judicious use of nondiegetic sound.

Clearly, it is impossible to predict which specific directions Latin American cinema will take in the coming years and decades. What we can say with some certainty, however, is that Latin American narrative cinema will continue to be a triangulated practice even as it becomes more heterogeneous than ever before in its forms and themes. This increased heterogeneity responds to two related phenomena. First, there has been a historical accumulation of themes and styles within the medium of narrative cinema itself; and second, there has also been an ever more complex engagement between narrative cinema and other media over time. This engagement has included still photography since cinema's earliest years, theater and literature since the 1910s, radio since the 1920s, television since the 1950s, and digital media since the 1990s. It is therefore helpful to consider some of the parallelisms between contemporary cinema and earlier cinematic periods in order to find clues as to where Latin American cinema might be headed in the near future.

Thanks to digital technology, contemporary cinema shares with silent cinema of the 1920s the possibility of making artisanal narrative films with very limited resources. In the 1920s most of these artisanal films were made by privileged members of society, and with the exception of Mário Peixoto, they used the medium to celebrate the Euro-liberal values of capitalism, white supremacy, androcentrism, and heteronormativity. Today, artisanal films are being made by all sectors of society, from the most privileged to the most marginalized, and the values expressed are correspondingly much more diverse than in the 1920s. Despite this democratization, however, the limits of distribution and exhibition today are all too similar to those faced by artisanal filmmakers during the silent period. And because posting narrative films for free online is an unsustainable strategy, it is unlikely that artisanal filmmaking with high production values will flourish in the coming decades.

Parallelisms with the NLAC are less evident, but can nevertheless be found in contemporary narrative cinema's productive dialogue with cutting-edge documentary practices in films such as *Santiago* (João Moreira Salles, Brazil, 2007) and *Playing* (Eduardo Coutinho, Brazil, 2007). As Ana M. López has demonstrated, these documentaries shift "the ground of documentary spectatorship from 'knowledge' and 'consciousness' to emotion and affect . . . [in order to] question the very possibility of any 'documentary' certainty outside of the affective."[5] Conversely, many contemporary narrative films—from *¡Y tu mamá también!* (Alfonso Cuarón, Mexico-Spain, 2001) to *Central Station* (Walter Salles, Brazil-France, 1998) and *City of God* (Fernando Meirelles, Brazil-France, 2002)—question the very possibility of any emotion or affect outside of the social by anchoring fictional narratives to concrete social reality via the incorporation of documentarist second and third planes in the mise-en-scène.

The parallels with studio cinema are more pronounced. In the 1930s, a brief transition to sound was followed by a period of consolidation of technological changes, leading to a dramatic increase in production under the protection of corporatist states in the 1940s. Similarly, in the 1990s, a brief transition period (this time to digital technology) was followed by a period of consolidation of technological changes, and then in the 2000s by a dramatic increase in production under the protection of neocorporatist states. One question that arises from this particular parallelism is how long contemporary Latin American cinema will be able to sustain the qualitative and quantitative successes of the past two decades. Will it rely so much on formulas, as studio cinema of the 1950s did, that quantity of production is sustained, but at the expense of quality and innovation? This is certainly possible, and the nostalgic films of the 1990s, from *Danzón* (María Novaro, Mexico-Spain, 1991) to *Like Water for Chocolate* (Alfonso Arau, Mexico, 1992), pointed in this direction. But more recent contemporary cinema shares with cinema of the 1950s not the fossilized practices of an industry in decline, but its very productive cross-fertilization between realism and art cinema, and the supportive energy of a vibrant cinephilic culture that includes film festivals, journals (print and digital), websites, blogs, books, film schools, film archives, academic programs, academic congresses, and research associations, both national and pan–Latin American.[4] Consider the many parallels between Leopoldo Torre Nilsson's gothic trilogy and Lucrecia Martel's Salta trilogy, or the reemergence of a critical neorealism in films such as *Bolivia* (Adrián Caetano, Argentina–the

Netherlands, 2001), *Crane World* (Pablo Trapero, Argentina, 1999), and *Duck Season* (Mexico, 2004). Neorealist and art films like these would not be possible without today's cinephilic culture, but it remains to be seen if that culture is strong enough to sustain comparable productions in the long term.

Clearly, the legacy of past periods on today's narrative cinema is very much alive, if not always visible on the surface. Latin American narrative cinema will continue to evolve as a triangulated practice in dialogue with Hollywood and European cinemas, and quite possibly with Asian cinemas as well, as commercial and cultural exchanges between Latin America and China continue to grow at unprecedented rates. And regardless of which specific forms these triangulated practices take—something that new technologies, state policies, and regional integration initiatives will continue to impact in direct ways—Latin American cinema will speak in a language that is familiar because it is always already global, yet made unfamiliar because of the region's radically heterogeneous culture and its ongoing experience of modernity in the plural.

Appendix

Discourses of Modernity in Latin America

The corporatist idea of society as an organism whose parts are social actors organized hierarchically predates modernity. In *I Corinthians* 12:12–31, for example, Saint Paul describes the body politic as composed of members of unequal importance:

> For the body is not one member, but many. . . .
>
> If the whole body were an eye, where were the hearing? If the whole were hearing, where were the smelling? . . .
>
> And the eye cannot say unto the hand, I have no need of thee: nor again the head to the feet, I have no need of you. . . .
>
> And whether one member suffers, all the members suffer with it; or one member be honored, all the members rejoice with it.

Throughout the European Middle Ages, guilds, confraternities, universities, brotherhoods, and sisterhoods were established as members of a body politic that the Church sanctioned and coordinated in a hierarchical way. The Spanish and Portuguese brought these practices to their American colonies, and corporatism, in the form of Thomism, quickly became the dominant ideology throughout the region, taught at universities and seminaries, and spread far and wide by priests, teachers, and bureaucrats through churches, schools, and public offices.[1] Corporatism suffered a heavy blow after independence, when the triumphant criollo elites sought to differentiate themselves from their former masters by adapting liberalism to their own needs. But corporatism never died, and began a slow comeback with the publication in 1891 of the encyclical *De Rerum Novarum*. Subtitled "Rights and Duties of Capital and Labor," it was the Catholic Church's response to what it saw as the misery and wretchedness generated by unfettered capitalism.

Specifically, the Church proposed joining forces with like-minded states to help them create state-dependent workers' unions that could counterbalance both the confrontational practices of socialist and anarchist unions, and the exploitative excesses of capitalism. The objective was to create a body politic where labor and capital worked in harmony, mediated by a benevolent Church that functioned as an interpreter between workers and capitalists, and as a guardian of their distinct duties and obligations.[2] Given Latin America's strong Catholic tradition and the thoroughness with which Thomism permeated colonial life, it is not surprising that corporatism reemerged, after the Wall Street crash of 1929, in the form of state corporatism, and subsequently crystallized under Lázaro Cárdenas in Mexico, Gétulio Vargas in Brazil, and Juan Perón in Argentina. It is also not surprising that under the protection and outright financial support of these and similar governments, a studio cinema with a corporatist discourse flourished, where the state (or a character who is its surrogate) serves as a benevolent patriarch that mediates between social actors to reduce social conflict and increase the common good.

LIBERALISM

Liberalism is a much more recent discourse in Latin America than corporatism. It only goes back to the eighteenth century, but it has shared with state corporatism pride of place as one of the three dominant ideologies in Latin America since independence. In effect, the nineteenth century in Latin America is widely understood as a period of power struggles between conservatives, who advocated for the continuity of colonial corporatism (i.e., mercantilism, collective land tenure by institutions such as the Church and indigenous communities, and clearly demarcated social classes and groups), and liberals, who advocated for a *relatively* more open society based on free trade, privately owned land, and a somewhat more flexible social hierarchy. When Positivism appeared in the second half of the nineteenth century, it reinforced the economic agenda of liberalism by advancing private capitalism to levels never before seen in Latin America, most famously by accelerating the sale of indigenous and Church lands to wealthy locals and foreign interests.

Positivism in Latin America is Darwinist, and more specifically Spencerian: it views society as the collection of competing individuals, where the corporatist link between individuals and the common good has been severed, and where the fittest (i.e., white property owners) will survive. Because of this, Latin American Positivism is best understood as the combination of economic liberalism with political authoritarianism, a combination that applies to liberal regimes such as those of Domingo Faustino Sarmiento, Porfirio Díaz, and Brazil's First Republic in the late nineteenth and early twentieth centuries, as well as to neoliberal/neopositivist regimes such as those of Augusto Pinochet, Carlos Menem, and Carlos Salinas in the late twentieth century. In cinema, the discourse of Positivist-inflected liberalism is most evident during these and similar regimes: first during the silent period, in films such as *El último malón* (The Last Indian Uprising; Alcides Greco, Argentina, 1916) and *El automóvil gris* (The Gray Automobile; Enrique Rosas, Joaquín Coss, and Juan Canals de Homs, Mexico,

1919), and again in more recent cinema, in films such as *Como agua para chocolate* (*Like Water for Chocolate*; Alfonso Arau, Mexico, 1992) and *Amores perros* (Love's a Bitch; Alejandro González Iñárritu, Mexico, 2000).

SOCIALISM

Of the three dominant discourses of modernity in Latin America, socialism is the most recent, and the one that has least achieved and maintained power. Its origins in the region date back to the founding of Argentina's Socialist Party in 1896, and, broadly speaking, it advocates for direct state control of the means of production and distribution as the most efficient way to achieve social justice.[3] Michael Löwy has identified three distinct periods in the history of Latin American Marxism:

1. a revolutionary period in the 1920s, through 1935, whose most profound theoretical expression is the work of José Carlos Mariátegui and whose most important practical manifestation was the Salvadoran insurrection of 1932;

2. the Stalinist period, from the middle of the 1930s to 1959, during which the Soviet interpretation of Marxism was hegemonic, as was Joseph Stalin's theory of revolution by stages; and

3. the new revolutionary period after the Cuban Revolution, when different factions of socialists came to agree on the desirability of the Cuban model, the necessity of armed struggle, and the exemplary conduct of Che Guevara.[4]

Löwy wrote this in 1980, well before the end of the Soviet Union inaugurated a period of crisis for Marxism as one of the dominant political discourses in Latin America. Nevertheless, the periodization is useful because it highlights Latin America's tradition of heterodox Marxism (exemplified here in the figure of Mariátegui), and also because it highlights the centrality of the Cuban Revolution in the development of a uniquely Latin American socialism. In cinema, the discourse of socialist modernity was widespread in the 1960s, during the militant phase of the New Latin American cinema. During this period, characters are often social actors defined primarily by their class, and the idea of a dialectical historical process defined by historical materialism and class struggle is oftentimes integrated into the fabric of the films through visual montage and narrative discontinuity.

NEOBAROQUE

In contrast to the instrumentalist reason that grounds the corporatist, liberal, and socialist discourses of modernity, the neobaroque discourse of modernity is grounded on the combination of what Aníbal Quijano calls the original Andean rationality of reciprocity and solidarity, and what he calls historical reason, or the original Enlightenment reason of individual freedom and democracy "before it was marginalized and subordinated" by European empires and more recently by "actually existing socialism."[5] Quijano himself does not use the term "neobaroque," but his theorization of the tensile nature of Latin American subjectivity echoes arguments made by a long line of critics who use "neobaroque" to refer to the twentieth-century recovery of baroque representational strategies that had been widespread during the colonial period, not to reaffirm the official baroque of Church and empire, but rather to find radically different alternatives to the dominant discourses of modernity and their master narratives through the reconfiguration of fragments of liberatory rationalities into a tensile whole.[6] "One of the most insistent expressions of the tensile character of Latin American subjectivity," Quijano writes,

> is a permanent note of dualism in our intellectual manner, our sensibility, our imaginary. This dualism cannot be simplistically explained by the opposition between the modern and the nonmodern, as the apologists of "modernization" continue to attempt to do. Rather, it derived from the rich, varied, and dense condition of the elements that nourish this subjectivity . . .: from the original Andean rationality, a sense of reciprocity and solidarity; from the original modern rationality [of the Enlightenment], when rationality was still associated with social liberation, a sense of individual liberty and of democracy as a collective decision-making process founded on the free choice of its constituent individuals.[7]

A crucial distinction emerges from the difference between instrumental and liberatory rationalities, for whereas liberalism and socialism value economic efficiency over and above reciprocity, and corporatism values the hierarchic harmonization of social actors over and above solidarity, the neobaroque discourse of modernity values precisely the excess of reciprocity and solidarity, and the kind of democracy and individual liberty that can sustain this excess, through a correspondingly dynamic, multitemporal, pluriform aesthetics that does not justify sacrificing individuals or groups in the name of a future utopia.

For these reasons, the neobaroque discourse of modernity rejects the rigid and stable identities associated with patriarchy's androcentrism and heteronormativity, and the racism and teleology that have been central to Eurocentric understandings of modernity.[8] For example, while liberalism has historically privileged white, heterosexual, male property owners; socialism has historically privileged an avant-garde of white, heterosexual, working-class men from urban areas; and corporatism has historically privileged institutions such as the Church and the military (both of which have historically been embodied in white, male, heterosexual, patrimonial figures); the neobaroque discourse of modernity is neither ethnocentric, androcentric, nor heteronormative, and understands subjects as collective individuals. And these are not private individuals devoid of collective responsibilities (as in liberalism), nor social subjects devoid of individual rights (as in socialism), but rather subjects who can articulate private and collective subjectivities (and a whole range of additional binarisms) as complementary opposites that are in horizontal yet tensile relationships to one another.

Notes

The first time I mention a film title in the introduction, in a chapter, or in the conclusion, I do so in the original language, followed by its English translation, then the director, country, and year of release. If the film has been distributed in English and there exists consensus regarding the title used for said distribution, I italicize the English title upon first mention and then use it thereafter. If there is no "official" English version, then I offer my own translation but do not italicize it, and I subsequently use the original title.

Aside from the aforementioned cases of the film titles, all translations to English from Portuguese and Spanish sources are my own.

INTRODUCTION

1. Paulo Antonio Paranaguá, *Tradición y modernidad en el cine de América Latina* (Madrid: Fondo de Cultura Económica de España, 2003), 12–13.

2. Other important differences include the fact that my study is a narrative history whereas *Tradición y modernidad en el cine de América Latina* is a collection of relatively independent essays, and the fact that I cover the New Latin American Cinema, the first avant-garde, and contemporary cinema much more thoroughly. For a more detailed discussion of the Paranaguá's contributions to the historiography of Latin American cinema, see my review "Paranaguá, Paulo Antonio. *Tradición y modernidad en el cine de América Latina*," *Chasqui: Revista de Literatura Latinoamericana* 33 (May 2004): 172–74.

3. Telenovelas, the most popular form of mass entertainment in the region today, date to the 1950s, half a century after the appearance of narrative cinema and a full generation after the episodic narrative structure, melodramatic impulse, and stock themes of the telenovelas had already been firmly established in the studio cinema of the 1930s.

4. To make the book more readable and accessible I have limited my bibliographical references to the research that directly informs the arguments and analyses that I develop throughout. A comprehensive review of the literature on Latin American cinema, or of the individual films I discuss, is beyond the scope of this book.

5. The figure of 80 percent is a conservative estimate, based on incomplete yet fairly consistent data. See for example table 3 (National Film Production in Argentina, Bolivia, Brazil, Chile, and Mexico, 1930–1981) in Jorge A. Schnitman, *Film Industries in Latin America: Dependency and Development* (Norwood, NJ: Ablex, 1984), 116–17; and figure 10 (National First-Time Release Films in Latin America, 2005–2011) in "Emerging Markets and the Digitalization of the Film Industry: An Analysis of the 2012 UIS International Survey of Feature Film Statistics," UNESCO Institute of Statistics, August 2013, http://www.uis.unesco.org /FactSheets/Pages/default.aspx, 31. Paranaguá characterizes the production of the three groups of producers as "significant," "intermittent," and "vegetative," respectively, and places Chile and Bolivia in the third group. Paulo Antonio Paranaguá, *Tradición y modernidad en el cine de América Latina*, 23.

6. For a theoretical discussion of affect and emotion, and readings of recent Latin American films based on these concepts, see Laura Podalsky, *The Politics of Affect and Emotion in Contemporary Latin American Cinema: Argentina, Brazil, Cuba, and Mexico* (New York: Palgrave Macmillan, 2011).

7. John Beverly and José Oviedo, *The Postmodernism Debate in Latin America* (Durham, NC: Duke University Press, 1995), 2.

8. Monika Kaup, "Neobaroque: Latin America's Alternative Modernity," *Comparative Literature* 58, no. 2 (Spring 2006): 128–52.

9. François Lyotard, *The Postmodern Condition: A Report on Knowledge*, trans. Geoff Bennington and Brian Massumi (Manchester, England: University of Manchester Press, 1999), xxiv.

10. S.N. Eisenstadt, *Comparative Civilizations and Multiple Modernities, Part II* (Leiden, the Netherlands: Koninklijke Brill, 2003), 521–22.

11. I owe the concept of "corporatist syndicalism" to Maricruz Castro Ricalde, "El sindicalismo no corporativo: un *Distinto amanecer* para la nación," paper presented at the annual meeting of the Latin American Studies Association, San Juan, Puerto Rico, May 26–30, 2015.

12. As Aníbal Quijano writes in "Modernity, Identity, and Utopia in Latin America," *boundary 2* 20, no. 3 (1993):

In Latin America, what is a sequence in other countries is a simultaneity. It is also a sequence. But in the first place, it is a simultaneity. . . . Forms of . . . capitalism, . . . still tied to national imperialisms, and transnational capitalism today are all active, manifested in a pyramid structure of levels of domination rather than stages in a sequence. But neither could one completely deny their disposition as stages. Time in this history is simultaneity and sequence at the same time. . . . It is a question of a different history of time, and of a time different from history. This is what a lineal perspective and, worse, a unilineal perspective of time, or a unidirectional perspective of history (such as the "master narrative" of the dominant version of European–North American rationalism) cannot manage to incorporate into its own ways of production or giving "reason" meaning within its cognitive matrix. (149–50)

13. Aníbal Quijano, "Coloniality of Power, Eurocentrism, and Latin America," *Nepantla: Views from the South* 1, no. 3 (2000): 542.

14. Néstor García Canclini, for example, evocatively describes how economic migrants strategically enter and exit different kinds of overlapping modernities in Mexico City. See Néstor García Canclini, *Hybrid Cultures: Strategies for Entering and Leaving Modernity* (Minneapolis: University of Minnesota Press, 2005), 3–4.

15. A productive way to visualize this simultaneity is spatially, as the Cuban poet, narrator, and essayist José Lezama Lima does in his theorization of Latin American culture as one whose "effort to reach a unifying form creates a tension, a plutonism that burns the fragments, metamorphosing them and impelling them toward their end." José Lezama Lima, "Baroque Curiosity," trans. María Pérez and Anke Birkenmaier, in *Baroque New Worlds: Representation, Transculturation, Counterconquest*, eds. Lois Parkinson Zamora and Monika Kaup (Durham, NC: Duke University Press, 2010), 213. Lezama Lima's use of the geological term "plutonism" to anchor his theory of Latin American culture suggests that whenever a new cultural practice is imposed, adopted, or adapted in Latin America, it does not displace preexisting understandings or practices of modern or premodern worldviews and social relations. Rather, newer and older cultural models and practices coexist beneath the visible surface, like so many successive geological layers, and sometimes, under plutonic magmatic pressure, they fuse and subsequently fragment in creative and oftentimes violent ways. In this view, contemporary Latin American culture is but a thin veneer below which lie layer upon layer of accumulated cultures and worldviews that, because they are not dead but in creative tension with one another, can rise to the surface given the right circumstances. My theorization of multiple modernities in Latin American cinema therefore combines Lezama Lima's spatial understanding of Latin American culture as tensile layers with Quijano's temporal understanding of Latin American history as both sequence and simultaneity, to show how Latin American cinema represents a multiplicity of modern discourses over time and across space.

1. CONVENTIONAL SILENT CINEMA

1. For a summary of the various theories put forth to explain the etymologies of *crioulo* and *criollo*, see Eva Martha Eckkrammer, "On the Perception of 'Creole' Language and Identity in the Netherlands Antilles," in *A Pepper-Pot of Cultures: Aspects of Creolization in the Caribbean*, eds. Gordon Collier and Ulrich Fleishman (New York: Editions Rodopi, 2003), 85–108.

2. See José Juan Arrom, "Criollo: definición y matices de un concepto," *Hispania* 34, no. 2 (1951): 172–76.

3. In this chapter I focus on *criollo* as it was used in Spanish America during the silent cinema period. For a thorough discussion of the academic theorization of the French term *creole* and its variants, see Stephan Malmié, "Creolization and Its Discontents," *Annual Review of Anthropology* 35 (October 2006): 433–56.

4. Ana M. López, "Early Cinema and Modernity in Latin America," *Cinema Journal* 40, no. 1 (2000): 49–50.

5. Nitrate film, the film stock used during the silent period and much of the studio period until acetate film replaced it, is highly combustible. In 1957, many films burned in a fire at the Cinemateca Brasileira in São Paulo. In 1982, a fire destroyed many of the holdings of the Cineteca Nacional in Mexico. *La profecía del lago* (The Prophecy of the Lake; José María Velasco Maidana, Bolivia, 1925) was ordered burned by municipal authorities in La Paz. Many of José Agustín Ferreyra's films were burned to make combs as part of a creditor's attempts to collect part of a debt.

6. Consider these three examples: (1) a few reels believed to be part of *La profecía del lago* were found among the belongings of the director's first wife in 1988, (2) an incomplete copy of *Garras de oro* (Claws of Gold; P.P. Jambrina, Colombia, 1925) was found in 1986, and (3) a copy of *Wara Wara* (José María Velasco Maidana, Bolivia, 1930) was discovered in a trunk in 1995.

7. Compare this periodization of Latin American silent cinema with, for example, Kristin Thompson, "From Primitive to Classical," in *The Classical Hollywood Cinema: Film Style and Mode of Production to 1960*, eds. D. Bordwell, J. Staiger, and K. Thompson (New York: Columbia University Press, 1985), 157–73; and Roberta Pearson, "Early Cinema" and "Transitional Cinema," in *The Oxford History of World Cinema*, ed. G. Nowell-Smith (New York: Oxford University Press, 1996), 13–42.

8. Paulo Antonio Paranaguá, *Tradición y modernidad en el cine de América Latina* (Madrid: Fondo de Cultura Económica de España, 2003), 94.

9. The distinction between actualities and attractions is not always clear-cut. One way of distinguishing them is to highlight, as Tom Gunning does, the intention, in attractions, to impress by manipulating film's ability to create illusion. Gunning, who coined the term "cinema of attractions" based on Sergei Eisenstein's concept of the attraction, defines an attraction "less as a way of telling stories than as a way of presenting a series of views to an audience, fascinating because of their *illusory* power . . . and exoticism" (my emphasis). Tom Gunning, "The Cinema of Attractions: Early Film, Its Spectator and the Avant-Garde," in *Early Cinema: Space, Frame, Narrative,* ed. Thomas Elsaesser (London: British Film Institute, 1990), 56–57.

10. Paulo Antonio Paranaguá, *Tradición y modernidad en el cine de América Latina*, 32.

11. Giorgio Bertellini, "Introduction: Traveling Lightness," in *Italian Silent Cinema: A Reader*, ed. Giorgio Bertellini (London: John Libbey, 2003), 4.

12. Paulo Antonio Paranaguá, "Brésil," in *Les Cinémas de l'Amérique Latine*, eds. Guy Hennebelle and Alfonso Gumucio Dagron (Paris: Nouvelles Editions Pierre L'herminier, 1981), 98.

13. Ana M. López, "Early Cinema and Modernity in Latin America," 68.

14. Jorge A. Schnitman, *Film Industries in Latin America: Dependency and Development* (Norwood, NJ: Ablex, 1984), 19. The most prominent distributors/exhibitors during the second half of the silent period were Max Glücksmann in the Southern Cone, Francisco Serrador Carbonell in Brazil, and in Mexico, William O. Jenkins in partnership with Gabriel Alarcón and Manuel Espinosa Iglesias. This means that in the three major markets in Latin America, exhibition and a good part of distribution were in the hands of foreign-born

entrepreneurs. Carbonell, born in Valencia, Spain, arrived in Brazil in 1887 at the age of fourteen. Glücksmann, born in Chernowitz, then part of the Austro-Hungarian Empire, arrived in Buenos Aires in 1890 at the age of fifteen. Jenkins, born in Tennessee, arrived in Mexico in 1905 at the age of twenty-seven.

15. Paulo Antonio Paranaguá, *Tradición y modernidad en el cine de América Latina,* 35.

16. Ibid., 39.

17. For a discussion of how similar dynamics were represented in nineteenth-century Latin American novels, see Doris Sommer, *Foundational Fictions* (Berkeley: University of California Press, 1991), 6.

18. Alfonso Gumucio Dagron, "*Warawara,*" in *South American Cinema: A Critical Filmography, 1915–1994,* eds. Timothy Barnard and Peter Rist (Austin: University of Texas Press, 1996), 85–86.

19. Paulo Antonio Paranaguá, *Tradición y modernidad en el cine de América Latina,* 46–47.

20. The film reputedly earned a return of 600,000 pesos on an investment of only 20,000, thanks in part to sales outside Argentina.

21. Timothy Barnard, "*Nobleza gaucha,*" in *South American Cinema: A Critical Filmography, 1915–1994,* 7. The sequences where the landlord falsely accuses the gaucho and the final chase on horseback are missing in the copy I have seen. I owe this part of the synopsis to Barnard's review.

22. Paulo Antonio Paranaguá, *Tradición y modernidad en el cine de América Latina,* 43.

23. Hipólito Yrigoyen was elected president in 1916, only a year after the release of *Nobleza gaucha.* In 1919, the country's powerful unions called for a general strike to protest rising prices and stagnant wages. Yrigoyen and his Radical Party sided with the conservatives to repress not only the demonstrations, but the whole syndicalist and anarchist movement.

24. Timothy Barnard, "*Nobleza gaucha,*" 7.

25. Charles Ramírez Berg, "*El automóvil gris* and Mexican Classicism," in *Visible Nations: Latin American Cinema and Video,* ed. Chon A. Noriega (Minneapolis: University of Minnesota Press, 2000), 7–8.

26. Ibid., 9.

27. Ibid., 4.

28. Ramírez Berg points out that *El automóvil gris* "contains an early expression of twin themes—the corruption of Revolutionary ideals and the accompanying remorse over the loss of the unique opportunity the Revolution afforded—that would haunt the nation's cinema for the next seven decades." Ibid., 4.

29. Ana M. López makes the case that "two basic melodramatic tendencies developed between 1930 and 1960: family melodramas focused on the problems of love, sexuality, and parenting, and epic melodramas that reworked national history, especially the events of the Mexican revolution." Ana M. López, "Tears and Desire: Women and Melodrama in the 'Old' Mexican Cinema," in *Mediating Two Worlds: Cinematic Encounters in the Americas,* eds. John King, Ana M. López, and Manuel Alvarado (London: BFI Publishing, 1993), 150.

30. Just as Hollywood would portray Native Americans as the bad guys in countless Westerns, even though it was the settlers who were actually stealing the

Indians' lands, in the case of Mexicans, negative representations in a Eurocentric industry such as Hollywood had long-lasting effects that persist to this day.

31. Neither the bandit nor his more degenerate version, the "greaser," disappeared from Hollywood productions. In 1934, for example, *Viva Villa!* (William Wellman, Jack Conway, and Howard Hawks) depicted the Mexican revolutionary as a mixture of clown and greaser, while the 1935 film *Bordertown* (Archie Mayo) served as a warning to Latinos who wanted to succeed in the Anglo world not to even try. For a detailed discussion of the evolution of Latino stereotypes in Hollywood cinema, see Allen L. Woll, *The Latin Image in American Film* (Los Angeles: UCLA Latin American Center Publications, 1980).

32. Mario Behring and Adhémar Gonzaga, quoted in Paulo Antonio Paranaguá, "Brésil," 115.

33. Robert Stam, "Cross-Cultural Dialogisms: Race and Multiculturalism in Brazilian Cinema," in *Mediating Two Worlds,* 177.

34. See Gregorio C. Rocha, "*La venganza de Pancho Villa:* A Lost and Found Border Film," in *F is for Phony: Fake Documentary and Truth's Undoing,* eds. Alexandra Juhasz and Jesse Lerner (Minneapolis: University of Minnesota Press, 2006), 50–58.

35. Jorge Miguel Couselo, *José Agustín Ferreyra, un cine por instinto* (Buenos Aires: Grupo Editor Altamira, 2001), 56.

36. Ibid., 50.

37. Sheila Schvarzman, *Humberto Mauro e as imagens do Brasil* (São Paulo: Fundação Editora da UNESP, 2003), 15–16.

38. Robert Stam, "From Hybridity to the Aesthetics of Garbage," *Social Identities: Journal for the Study of Race, Nation and Culture* 3, no. 2 (1997): 275, doi: 10.1080/13504639752104.

39. Ibid.

2. AVANT-GARDE SILENT CINEMA

1. See Vicky Unruh, *Latin American Vanguards: The Art of Contentious Encounters* (Berkeley: University of California Press, 1994); and Jorge Schwartz, *Las vanguardias latinoamericanas: textos programáticos y críticos* (Mexico City: Fondo de Cultura Económica, 2002).

2. We know of at least two avant-garde films that have been lost: *Disparos en el Istmo de Tehuantepec* (Gunshots on the Isthmus of Tehuantepec; Manuel Álvarez Bravo, Mexico, 1935) and *777* (Emilio Amero, Mexico–United States, 1929). Others may very well surface in the future.

3. Comte's full motto is *L'Amour pour principe, l'Ordre pour base, et le Progrès pour but* (Love as the principle, Order as the basis, and Progress as the goal). Brazil's flag has a banner over an orb that reads "ORDEM E PROGRESSO" (Order and Progress).

4. Glauber Rocha, *Revisão Crítica do Cinema Brasileiro* (São Paulo: Cosac Naify, 2003), 45–53.

5. *Webster's New Collegiate Dictionary,* 9th ed., s.v. "gangue."

6. Sergei Eisenstein, *¡Que viva México!* script, trans. José Emilio Pacheco and S. Barros Sierra (Mexico City: Ediciones Era, 1964), 75.

7. Ibid., 45–46.

8. Ibid., 48.

9. Ibid., 51–52.

10. Sergei Eisenstein, *Film Form,* trans. Jay Leyda (New York: Hancourt, 1977), 234.

11. Ibid., 239.

12. Grigory Alexandrov, ed., *¡Que viva México!* (New York: Kino on Video, 2001); and Sergei Eisenstein, *¡Que viva México!* script.

13. Sergei Eisenstein, *¡Que viva México!* script, 54.

14. Ibid.

15. Sergei Eisenstein, "Notes for a Film of *Capital,*" trans. M. Sliwowski, J. Leyda, and A. Michelson, *October* 2 (Summer 1976): 8.

16. See Sergei Eisenstein, "First Outline of *¡Que viva México!*," in *The Film Sense,* trans. Jay Leyda (New York: Hancourt, 1975), 251–56.

17. See Francisco Pineda, "Operaciones del poder sobre la imagen de Zapata, 1921–1935," *Entretextos. Revista Electrónica Semestral de Estudios Semióticos de la Cultura* (2011), http://www.ugr.es/~mcaceres/entretextos /entre17–18/pineda.html.

18. Quoted in Aurelio de los Reyes, *Medio siglo de cine mexicano (1896– 1947)* (Mexico City: Editorial Trillas, 1987), 106–7.

19. Sergei Eisenstein, *¡Que viva México!* script, 55–56.

20. Sergei Eisenstein, *Nonindifferent Nature,* trans. H. Marshall (New York: Cambridge University Press, 1987), 378.

21. Glauber Rocha, *Revisão Crítica do Cinema Brasileiro,* 62.

22. See Bruce Williams, "Straight from Brazil? National and Sexual Disavowal in Mário Peixoto's *Limite,*" *Luso-Brazilian Review* 38, no. 1 (2001): 31–40.

23. Gilles Deleuze, *Cinema 2: The Time-Image,* trans. Hugh Tomlinson and Robert Galeta (Minneapolis: University of Minnesota Press, 1989), 272.

24. Ibid., 149.

25. Mário Peixoto, "Um filme da América do Sul," in *Mário Peixoto: Escritos sobre cinema,* ed. Saulo Pereira de Mello (Rio de Janeiro: Aeroplano, 2000), 85–93.

26. See Lois Parkinson Zamora and Monika Kaup, "Baroque, New World, Neobaroque: Categories and Concepts," in *Baroque New Worlds: Representation, Transculturation, Counterconquest,* eds. Lois Parkinson Zamora and Monika Kaup (Durham, NC: Duke University Press, 2010), 12.

27. For a discussion of rhizomatic space, see Gilles Deleuze and Félix Guattari, *A Thousand Plateaus: Capitalism and Schizophrenia,* trans. Brian Massumi (Minneapolis: University of Minnesota Press, 2014), 3–25.

28. Marjorie Perloff, *The Futurist Moment: Avant-Garde, Avant Guerre, and the Language of Rupture* (University of Chicago Press, 2003), xxii–xxiii.

3. TRANSITION TO SOUND

1. Sources: Paulo Antonio Paranaguá, *Tradición y modernidad en el cine de América Latina* (Madrid: Fondo de Cultura Económica de España, 2003),

99–105; and Tomás Pérez Turrent, "The Studios," in *Mexican Cinema,* ed. Paulo Antonio Paranaguá, trans. Ana M. López (London: BFI, 1995), 133–44.

2. From Jorge A. Schnitman, *Film Industries in Latin America: Dependency and Development* (Norwood, NJ: ABLEX Publishing Corporation, 1984), 116–17.

3. David Bordwell, Janet Staiger, and Kristin Thompson, *The Classical Hollywood Cinema: Film Style and Mode of Production to 1960* (New York: Columbia University Press, 1985), 3–7.

4. Santos Zunzunegui, *El extraño viaje. El celuloide atrapado por la cola, o la crítica norteamericana ante el cine español* (Valencia, Spain: Ediciones Episteme, 1999), 55–56.

5. Miriam Hansen, "Fallen Women, Rising Stars, New Horizons: Shanghai Silent Film as Vernacular Modernism," *Film Quarterly* 54, no. 1 (2000): 13.

6. Paulo Antonio Paranaguá, "América Latina busca su imagen," in *Historia general del cine,* vol. 10, eds. Gustavo Domínguez and Jenaro Talens (Madrid: Cátedra, 1996), 234.

7. Silvia Oroz, *Melodrama: O cinema de lágrimas da América Latina* (Rio de Janeiro: Funarte, 1999), 53.

8. See Lisa Jarvinen, *The Rise of Spanish-Language Filmmaking: Out of Hollywood's Shadow, 1929–1939* (New Brunswick, NJ: Rutgers University Press, 2012), which discusses not only "Hispanic films" but also other strategies, such as dubbing and subtitling, that emerged in Hollywood, Mexico, Spain, and Argentina in response to the coming of sound.

9. Paulo Antonio Paranaguá, "América Latina busca su imagen," 217–19.

10. Aaron Copland, "Mexican Composer," *New York Times,* May 9, 1937, http://www.nytimes.com/books/99/03/14/specials/copland-mexican.html.

11. John Mraz, "La trilogía revolucionaria de Fernando de Fuentes," in *El cine mexicano a través de la crítica,* eds. Gustavo García and David R. Maciel (Mexico City: UNAM/Instituto Mexicano de Cinematografía/Universidad Autónoma de Ciudad Juárez, 2001), 81.

12. Fernando de Fuentes, cited in John Mraz, "La trilogía revolucionaria de Fernando de Fuentes," 88.

4. BIRTH AND GROWTH OF AN INDUSTRY

1. César Maranghello, "*Besos brujos,*" in *Tierra en trance. El cine latinoamericano en 100 películas,* eds. Alberto Elena and Marina Díaz López (Madrid: Alianza Editorial, 1999), 47.

2. Lázaro Cárdenas, cited in Tzvi Medin, *Ideología y praxis política de Lázaro Cárdenas* (Mexico City: Siglo XXI Editores, 1992), 170.

3. By "foundational fictions" I mean what Doris Sommer, referring to nineteenth-century Latin American literary romances, called "idealized allegories ostensibly grounded in 'natural' heterosexual love and in the marriages that provided a figure for apparently nonviolent consolidation during internecine conflicts." Doris Sommer, *Foundational Fictions: The National Romances of Latin America* (Berkeley: University of California Press, 1991), 5.

4. Jorge Luis Borges, "Prisioneros de la tierra," in *Borges in/and/on Film*, ed. Edgardo Cozarinsky, trans. Gloria Waldman and Ronald Christ (New York: Luman Books, 1988), 53–54.

5. Teresa de Lauretis, "Desire in Narrative," in *Critical Visions in Film Theory: Classic and Contemporary Readings*, eds. Timothy Corrigan, Patricia White, and Meta Mazaj (Boston: Bedford/St. Martin's, 2001), 584.

6. John King, *Magical Reels: A History of Cinema in Latin America* (London: Verso, 2000), 57.

7. Jorge A. Schnitman, *Film Industries in Latin America: Dependency and Development* (Norwood, NJ: Ablex, 1984), 32–33.

8. Seth Fein, "From Collaboration to Containment: Hollywood and the International Political Economy of Mexican Cinema After the Second World War," in *Mexico's Cinema: A Century of Films and Filmmakers*, eds. Joanne Hershfield and David R. Maciel (Lanham, MD: SR Books, 2005), 139.

9. Welles, who enthusiastically accepted the commission, arrived in Rio a few days after he finished filming *The Magnificent Ambersons* in early 1942, a decision he would later regret when he realized that he had in effect lost control of the final cut, and with it what could have been a masterpiece to rival *Citizen Kane*. Other catastrophes were to follow. RKO, which was coproducing the film with Nelson Rockefeller's Office of the Coordinator of Inter-American Affairs (OCIAA), pulled the plug on the whole project in mid-1942 after several of the key backers of the project at RKO departed or resigned. Without this backing, Welles became an easy target for unfounded attacks, ranging from mismanagement of funds to being a Communist sympathizer. In the end, a project that started out as a commercial production in 1941 with three U.S. episodes and one Mexican episode, then morphed into a transnational Goodwill coproduction with one Mexican episode ("Bonito") and two Brazilian episodes ("Carnival" and "Four Men on a Raft"), came to naught.

Given the project's censorship for so many decades, it is impossible to speak of Welles's influence on the development of Mexican and Brazilian cinema in the same way that we can speak of Sergei Eisenstein's influence on Mexican cinema. What we *can* talk about, as Catherine Benamou correctly notes, are discursive linkages "suggestive of a broader, regional 'cinematic unconscious' rather than connections based on empirical contact and exchange during production." Catherine Benamou, *It's All True: Orson Welles's Pan-American Odyssey* (Berkeley: University of California Press, 2007), 293. Thus, the treatment of blacks in "Carnival" and Welles's decision to cast Grande Otelo as the protagonist in that episode suggests a connection to *Rio, Zona Norte* (Rio, North Zone; Nelson Pereira dos Santos, Brazil, 1957), discussed in chapter 6; while Welles's sympathetic treatment of fishermen in northeastern Brazil and their struggle for social and economic justice brings to mind Alberto Cavalcanti's *O Canto do Mar* (*Song of the Sea*; Brazil, 1954) and Glauber Rocha's first feature, *Barravento* (The Turning Wind; Brazil, 1962).

In 1993, Richard Wilson, Myron Meisel, and Bill Krohn released a documentary titled *It's All True: Based on an Unfinished Film by Orson Welles*. It traces the project's trajectory via revealing interviews with Welles, fragments of "Bonito" and "Carnival," and a reconstruction "Four Men on a Raft," an episode he filmed with rented cameras and a skeleton crew after RKO had abandoned the project. This last episode re-creates the real-life epic journey of four fishermen who in late 1941 traveled more than six thousand miles from Fortaleza to Rio on a sailing raft to petition President Vargas for state welfare protection for fishermen and their families (the same story as Cavalcanti's *O Canto do Mar*). Judging from these fragments and partial reconstructions, it is clear that Welles was characteristically ahead of his time, especially in his sympathetic treatment of Afro-Brazilians as protagonists in "Carnival" (something that put him in conflict with his RKO bosses and the Brazilian authorities) as well as in the combination, in "Four Men on a Raft," of a neorealist sensibility (before neorealism) with Eisensteinian montage-within-shots to represent the racially mixed fishermen and their community with dignity and respect.

10. Jorge A. Schnitman, *Film Industries in Latin America: Dependency and Development* (Norwood, NJ: Ablex, 1984), 34.

11. Paulo Antonio Paranaguá, "América Latina busca su imagen," in *Historia general del cine*, vol. 10, eds. Gustavo Domínguez and Jenaro Talens (Madrid: Cátedra, 1996), 237.

12. Julia Tuñón, "Emilio Fernández: A Look Behind the Bars," in *Mexican Cinema*, ed. Paulo Antonio Paranaguá, trans. Ana M. López (London: BFI, 1995), 186.

13. Zuzana Pick, "Gabriel Figueroa: la mística de México en *El fugitivo* (John Ford, 1947)," *El ojo que piensa* 3, no. 6 (2012), http://www.elojoquepiensa .net/06/index.php/modules-menu/gabriel-figueroa-la-mistica-de-mexico-en-el-fugitivo-john-ford-1947.

14. Joanne Hershfield, "Race and Ethnicity in the Classical Cinema," in *Mexico's Cinema: A Century of Films and Filmmakers*, eds. Joanne Hershfield and David R. Maciel (Lanham, MD: SR Books, 2005), 84–85.

15. Paulo Antonio Paranaguá, *Tradición y modernidad en el cine de América Latina* (Madrid: Fondo de Cultura Económica de España, 2003), 107.

16. Dirección General de Servicios de Documentación, Información y Análisis de la Cámara de Diputados de México, "La constitución política y sus reformas: febrero 1917-marzo 2013," 39–40, http://www.diputados.gob.mx/sedia /biblio/doclegis/cuad_cons_mar13.pdf.

17. See Tzvi Medin, *El sexenio alemanista* (Mexico City: Era, 1990).

18. Alemán's reductions in land redistribution responded to a policy shift calculated to promote the development of an agricultural bourgeoisie, while his neutralization of workers' unions was calculated to promote the development of an industrial oligarchy not unlike the one Japan had nurtured through similar corporatist policies. See ibid., 32.

19. Clara Kriger, *Cine y peronismo* (Buenos Aires: Siglo Veintiuno Editores, 2009), 163.

20. Ibid., 145–46.

21. Ibid., 153.

22. Two other well-known films that fall into this category include *Jalisco canta en Sevilla* (Jalisco Sings in Seville; Fernando de Fuentes, Mexico-Spain, 1949), and *La Balandra "Isabel" llegó esta tarde* (The Yacht *Isabel* Arrived This Afternoon; Carlos Hugo Christensen, Venezuela, 1950).

5. CRISIS AND DECLINE OF STUDIO CINEMA

1. Seth Fein, "From Collaboration to Containment: Hollywood and the International Political Economy of Mexican Cinema After the Second World War," in *Mexico's Cinema: A Century of Film and Filmmakers*, eds. Joanne Hershfield and David R. Maciel (Lanham, MD: SR Books, 2005), 139–41.

2. Ibid., 152–55.

3. Ibid., 155.

4. Armando Bó's 1956 film *El trueno entre las hojas* (Thunder in the Leaves; Argentina) included the first fully nude scene in Latin American narrative cinema and launched Isabel Sarli's career.

5. João Luiz Vieira, "From *High Noon* to *Jaws*: Carnival and Parody in Brazilian Cinema," in *Brazilian Cinema*, eds. Randal Johnson and Robert Stam (New York: Columbia University Press, 1995), 262.

6. Jean-Claude Bernardet, *Trajetória Crítica* (São Paulo: Polis, 1978), 210–11.

7. Carlos Monsiváis, "Cantinflas and Tin Tan: Mexico's Greatest Comedians," in *Mexico's Cinema: A Century of Film and Filmmakers*, 76–77.

8. Ana M. López, "Tears and Desire: Women and Melodrama in the 'Old' Mexican Cinema," in *Mediating Two Worlds: Cinematic Encounters in the Americas*, eds. John King, Ana M. López, and Manuel Alvarado (London: BFI Publishing, 1993), 158. López points out that Sevilla's gendered performativity is not so much a parody as the provocative affirmation of a sexualized gender identity, yet it is also possible to see the two—parody and the excessively provocative affirmation of gender identity—as being perfectly compatible in this case.

9. According to Emilio García Riera, the number of films about life in the cabarets and *arrabales* (working-class barrios) went from three in 1946 to thirteen in 1947, twenty-five in 1948, forty-seven in 1949, and fifty in 1950. The numbers include both *cabareteras* and *arrabaleras;* the author does not differentiate between the two, as oftentimes films about *arrabales* incorporate life in the cabarets. Emilio García Riera, *Breve historia del cine mexicano* (Mexico City: Instituto Mexicano de Cinematografía, 1998), 154.

10. Ibid., 153–55.

11. In calling Elena spirited, I am following Gilberto Pérez, "Melodrama of the Spirited Woman: *Aventurera*," in *Latin American Melodrama*, ed. Darlene J. Sadlier (Chicago and Urbana: University of Illinois Press, 2009), 19–32, where he writes:

> Plato distinguished three parts of the human soul: the part that reasons, the part that desires, and the part that gets angry, the spirited part. Anger is in rather low repute nowadays, an emotion often thought to call for therapy, "anger management," but Plato valued it almost as highly as reason: it is the emotion that makes warriors, and the rulers of the Republic are to be warriors as well as philosophers, outstanding not only for their love of wisdom but also for their spiritedness. Elena may not be a philosopher but she is certainly a warrior, and *Aventurera* celebrates her invincible spiritedness.

12. Paulo Antonio Paranaguá, "Orígenes, evolución y problemas," in *Cine documental en América Latina*, ed. Paulo Antonio Paranaguá (Madrid: Cátedra, 2003), 34–35.

13. One year before, in 1935, the Cárdenas government tried to establish an Instituto Nacional Cinematográfico, "before it was undone, to a large extent, by a Hollywood boycott." Seth Fein, "From Collaboration to Containment," 147.

14. Fernão Pessoa Ramos, "Humberto Mauro," in *Cine documental en América Latina,* 128–29.

15. Sheila Schvarzman, *Humberto Mauro e as imagens do Brasil* (São Paulo: Editora UNESP, 2003), 303.

16. Carlos Roberto de Souza, "Humberto Mauro," in *Le Cinéma Brésilien,* ed. Paulo Antonio Paranaguá (Paris: Editions du Centre Pompidou, 1987), 140.

17. Fernão Pessoa Ramos, "Humberto Mauro," 135.

18. Sources: Paulo Antonio Paranaguá, *Tradición y modernidad en el cine de América Latina* (Madrid: Fondo de Cultura Económica de España, 2003), 105; Julianne Burton, "Film and Revolution in Cuba: The First Twenty Five Years," in *New Latin American Cinema, Volume 2: Studies of National Cinemas,* ed. Michael T. Martin (Detroit: Wayne State University Press, 1997), 126; "Memory of the World Register: Original Negatives of the Noticiero ICAIC Latinoamericano," http://www.unesco.org/new/fileadmin/MULTIMEDIA/HQ/CI/CI /pdf/mow/nomination_forms/cuba_noticiero_icaic.pdf; and Damian Fagon, "Villa del Cine: Venezuela Beyond Hollywood," *[CIMA]* (May 2013), http:// www.cimamag.com/venezuela-beyond-hollywood.

19. See for example Sergio de la Mora, *Cinemachismo: Masculinities and Sexuality in Mexican Film* (Austin: University of Texas Press, 2006); and Isabel Arredondo, *Motherhood in Mexican Cinema, 1941–1991: The Transformation of Femininity on Screen* (Jefferson, NC: McFarland, 2014).

6. NEOREALISM AND ART CINEMA

1. Sourced from Paulo Antonio Paranaguá, "América Latina busca su imagen," in *Historia general del cine,* vol. 10, eds. Gustavo Domínguez and Jenaro Talens (Madrid: Cátedra, 1996), 234; and Julianne Burton, "Reframing the Fifties," *Nuevo Texto Crítico* 21/22 (1998): 7–8.

2. See David Bordwell, "The Art Cinema as a Mode of Film Practice," in *Film Theory and Criticism,* eds. Leo Braudy and Marshall Cohen (New York: Oxford University Press, 2004), 774–82.

3. See Barry Keith Grant, ed., *Auteurs and Authorship: A Reader* (Oxford: Blackwell Publishing, 2008).

4. Paulo Antonio Paranaguá, "Of Periodizations and Paradigms: The Fifties in Comparative Perspective," *Nuevo Texto Crítico* 21/22 (1998): 41.

5. In his influential essay "Some Ideas on the Cinema," for example, Zavattini writes:

> Neorealism can and must face poverty. . . . The theme of poverty, of rich and poor, is something one can dedicate one's whole life to. We have just begun. We must have the courage to explore all the details. If the rich turn up their noses especially at *Miracolo a Milano,* we can only ask them to be a little patient. *Miracolo a Milano* is only a fable. [Its] fundamental emotion . . . is not one of escape (the flight at the end), but of indignation, a desire for solidarity with certain people, a refusal of it with others. The film's

structure is intended to suggest that there is a great gathering of the humble ones against the others. But the humble ones have no tanks, or they would have been ready to defend their land and their huts.

Zavattini's emphasis here is clearly on neorealism's social function, which he believes is to activate viewers' solidarity with the poor as a first step toward eliminating their oppression. Cesare Zavattini, "Some Ideas on the Cinema," in *Critical Visions in Film Theory: Classic and Contemporary Readings,* eds. Timothy Corrigan, Patricia White, and Meta Mazaj (Boston: Bedford/St. Martin's, 2001), 918–19.

6. In "The Evolution of the Language of Cinema," for example, Bazin argues that "neorealism tends to give back to the cinema a sense of the ambiguity of reality. The preoccupation of Rossellini when dealing with the face of the child in *Allemania Anno Zero* is the exact opposite of that of Kuleshov with the close-up of Mozhukhin. Rossellini is concerned to preserve its mystery." André Bazin, "The Evolution of the Language of Cinema," in *Critical Visions in Film Theory: Classic and Contemporary Readings,* 323.

7. Here I am thinking of Bazin's rhetorical question: "Then as to the style itself, is [neorealism] not essentially a form of self-effacement before reality?" Ibid., 318.

8. The comedy was titled *El gran calavera* (*The Great Madcap*; Mexico, 1949). See Emilio García Riera, cited in Agustín Sánchez Vidal, *Luis Buñuel: obra cinematográfica* (Madrid: Ediciones JC, 1984), 119.

9. Julianne Burton, "Toward a History of Social Documentary in Latin America," in *The Social Documentary in Latin America,* ed. Julianne Burton (Pittsburgh: University of Pittsburgh Press, 1990), 4.

10. Luis Buñuel, "Cinema, Instrument of Poetry," in *The European Cinema Reader,* ed. Catherine Fowler (London: Routledge, 2002), 47.

11. Luis Buñuel, José de la Colina, and Tomás Pérez Turrent, *Prohibido asomarse al interior* (Mexico City: Consejo Nacional para la Cultura y las Artes, 1996), 90–91.

12. Luis Buñuel, cited in Emilio García Riera, *Historia documental del cine mexicano* (Mexico City: Ediciones Era, 1972), 157.

13. Luis Buñuel, cited in Agustín Sánchez Vidal, *Luis Buñuel: obra cinematográfica,* 119.

14. Octavio Paz, cited in Emilio García Riera, *Historia documental del cine mexicano,* 164.

15. Ibid., 166–67.

16. I owe this reading to Paulo Antonio Paranaguá, *Luis Buñuel. Él* (Barcelona: Ediciones Paidós, 2001), 57–58.

17. A third Mexican film by Buñuel that deserves mention is *El ángel exterminador* (*The Exterminating Angel*; 1962), where surrealism takes over completely. In so doing, it looks back to his earlier *L'Age d'or* (*The Golden Age*; France, 1930) and forward toward the anarchist films he would direct in France in the 1970s.

18. Breixo Viejo, "O Cangaceiro," in *The Cinema of Latin America,* eds. Alberto Elena and Marina Díaz López (London: Wallflower Press, 2003), 65–66.

19. Quoted in ibid., 66.

20. Alberto Cavalcanti, *Filme e Realidade* (Rio de Janeiro: Livraria-Editora da Casa do Estudante do Brasil, 1957), 268.

21. Glauber Rocha, *Revisão Crítica do Cinema Brasileiro* (Rio de Janeiro: Editora Cosac Naify, 2003), 73–74.

22. Heliodoro San Miguel, "*Rio, 40 Graus*," in *The Cinema of Latin America*, 76.

23. Mariarosaria Fabris, *Nelson Pereira dos Santos: Um Olhar Neo-Realista?* (São Paulo: Editora da Universidade de São Paulo, 1994), 196.

24. Robert Stam, "Visual Style and Racial Politics in Three Brazilian Features," *Nuevo Texto Crítico* 21/22 (1998): 117–18.

25. Nelson Pereira dos Santos, cited in Darlene J. Sadlier, *Nelson Pereira dos Santos* (Chicago and Urbana: University of Illinois Press, 2009), 21.

26. Paranaguá calls Torre Nilsson "the first intellectual and modern auteur in a national cinema where, up to that point, instinctive and bohemian directors had prevailed, and where formal concerns seemed merely calligraphic (Luis Saslavsky)." Paulo Antonio Paranaguá, "América Latina busca su imagen," 295.

27. Gonzalo Aguilar, "Leopoldo Torre Nilsson: un cineasta entre escritores," in *Leopoldo Torre Nilsson: una estética de la decadencia*, ed. M. del C. Veites (Buenos Aires: Grupo Editorial Altamira, 2002), 17.

28. Susan Martin-Márquez, "Coloniality and the Trappings of Modernity in *Viridiana* and *The Hand in the Trap*," *Cinema Journal* 51, no. 1 (2011): 113.

29. Leopoldo Torre Nilsson, "Entrevista con Torre Nilsson," in *Leopoldo Torre Nilsson: una estética de la decadencia*, 104.

30. Edmund Stephen Urbanski, "La pampa y los porteños en la reciente interpretación argentina," in *Actas del III Congreso de la Asociación Internacional de Hispanistas* (1968) (Mexico City: El Colegio de México, 1970), 881, http://cvc.cervantes.es/literatura/aih/pdf/03/aih_03_1_096.pdf.

31. Susan Martin-Márquez, citing Gonzalo Aguilar, notes that "filmmakers and essayists associated with the militant 'Third Cinema' movement (Fernando Solanas, Octavio Getino, and Juan José Hernández Arregui, among others) accused cultural producers such as Torre Nilsson of complicity with neoimperialist power structures." Susan Martin-Márquez, "Coloniality and the Trappings of Modernity in *Viridiana* and *The Hand in the Trap*," 113.

32. Paulo Antonio Paranaguá, "Of Periodizations and Paradigms," 41.

33. Ibid., 42.

34. Nelson Pereira dos Santos, cited in Darlene J. Sadlier, *Nelson Pereira dos Santos*, 21; Silvia Oroz, *Tomás Gutiérrez Alea: los filmes que no filmé* (Havana: UNEAC, 1989), 50; and Leopoldo Torre Nilsson, "Entrevista con Torre Nilsson," 104.

7. NEW LATIN AMERICAN CINEMA'S MILITANT PHASE

1. Fernando Birri, *Fernando Birri: el alquimista poético-político* (Madrid: Cátedra/Filmoteca Española, 1996), 326. There are two versions of the film: a

1958 version lasting fifty-nine minutes, and a 1960 version lasting thirty-three minutes. The 1960 version is the standard version screened today.

2. Ana M. López, "An 'Other' History: The New Latin American Cinema," in *Resisting Images: Essays on Cinema and History*, eds. Robert Sklar and Charles Musser (Philadelphia: Temple University Press, 1990), 312.

3. Julianne Burton-Carvajal, "*Araya* Across Time and Space: Competing Canons of National and International Film History," *Nuevo Texto Crítico* 11, nos. 21–22 (1998): 217–18.

4. Zuzana M. Pick, *The New Latin American Cinema: A Continental Project* (Austin: University of Texas Press, 1993), 42.

5. John Mraz, "Santiago Álvarez: From Dramatic Form to Direct Cinema," in *The Social Documentary in Latin America*, ed. Julianne Burton (Pittsburgh: University of Pittsburgh Press, 1990), 136.

6. Nicole Brenez, "Light My Fire: *The Hour of the Furnaces*," *Sight and Sound* (April 2012), accessed December 1, 2012, http://www.bfi.org.uk /news-opinion/sight-sound-magazine/features/greatest-films-all-time-essays /light-my-fire-hour-furnaces.

7. Ivana Bentes, "*Deus e o Diabo na Terra do Sol*," in *The Cinema of Latin America*, eds. Alberto Elena and Marina Díaz López (London: Wallflower Press, 2003), 90.

8. Glauber Rocha, "An Esthetic of Hunger," in *New Latin American Cinema*, vol. 1, ed. Michael T. Martin (Detroit: Wayne State University Press, 1997), 60.

9. In his essay "*Black God, White Devil*: The Representation of History," in *Brazilian Cinema*, eds. Randal Johnson and Robert Stam (New York: Columbia University Press, 1995), Ismail Xavier rightly observes that

> the film neither idealizes nor downgrades popular culture. Rather than dismiss popular forms in the name of ideological correctness, Rocha uses them even as he questions the traditional character of their representation. Cinema Novo confronted this task— of reelaborating popular traditions as the springboard for a transformation-oriented critique of social reality—in diverse ways. *Black God, White Devil* is a key film because it incorporates within its very structure the contradictions of this project. It avoids any romantic endorsement of the "popular" as the source of all wisdom, even as it discredits the ethnocentric reductionism that sees in popular culture nothing more than meaningless superstition and backward irrationality, superseded by bourgeois progress and rationalism. Adopting the didactic formula, *Black God, White Devil* decenters the focus of its "models for action" school, challenges us with an aggressive fistful of interrogations. Rather than offer, in a single diapason, an insipidly schematic lesson about class struggle, it encourages reflection on the peasantry and its forms of consciousness, and more important, on the very movement of History itself. (147–48)

10. Ernesto "Che" Guevara, "Mensaje a los pueblos del mundo a través de la *Tricontinental*," accessed December 1, 2012, http://www.marxists.org /espanol/guevara/04_67.htm. This text was first published on April 16, 1967, as a special supplement of the Havana-based journal *Tricontinental*. The title of the journal references an international conference of socialists from three continents (Africa, Asia, and Latin America) that took place in Havana in 1966.

11. José Martí, "Carta a José Dolores Poyo de 5 de diciembre de 1891," in *Obras completas,* vol. 1 (Havana: Editorial Nacional de Cuba, 1963), 275.

12. Robert Stam, "*The Hour of the Furnaces* and the Two Avant-Gardes," in *The Social Documentary in Latin America,* 257.

13. Paulo Antonio Paranaguá, "América Latina busca su imagen," in *Historia general del cine,* vol. 10, eds. Gustavo Domínguez and Jenaro Talens (Madrid: Cátedra, 1996), 339.

14. Robert Stam, "*The Hour of the Furnaces* and the Two Avant-Gardes," 264–65.

15. Cited in Jorge Ruffinelli, *Patricio Guzmán* (Madrid: Cátedra, 2001), 184.

16. Guzmán himself noted that "Had we edited the film in Amsterdam, Paris, or Venezuela, the results would have been much more inferior. Because [it] is also a product of the influence that the Cuban Revolution has had on us." Ibid., 133.

17. Santiago Álvarez had helped edit *The Hour of the Furnaces,* and thus established a precedent of pan–Latin American collaboration that García Espinosa followed in *The Battle of Chile.*

18. Combative, that is, compared to Chilean filmmakers exiled elsewhere, such as Raúl Ruiz in France or Alejandro Jodorowsky in Mexico. These two are the best known, but far from the only ones. Richard Peña defines this exilic cinema as unique in the history of world cinema in the sense that its output was larger than that produced in Chile, and also in the sense that it was defined by its exilic condition. See Jorge Ruffinelli, *Patricio Guzmán,* 194.

19. In 1996, Guzmán returned to Chile to screen *The Battle of Chile,* which had been censored under Augusto Pinochet. *Chile, la memoria obstinada* (Chile, the Obstinate Memory, 1997), a medium-length documentary of this experience, includes a final sequence of adolescent students overcome by emotion as they watch *The Battle of Chile,* clear evidence of the film's having achieved its goal of winning over the hearts and minds of depoliticized Chileans, albeit twenty-some years later.

20. Patricio Guzmán, "Politics and the Documentary in People's Chile" (interview with Julianne Burton), in *Cinema and Social Change in Latin America: Conversations with Filmmakers,* ed. Julianne Burton (Austin: University of Texas Press, 1986), 50–51.

21. Ibid., 51.

22. Ana M. López, "*The Battle of Chile:* Documentary, Political Process, and Representation," in *The Social Documentary in Latin America,* 277–78.

23. Jorge Ruffinelli, *Patricio Guzmán,* 139.

24. Cited in ibid., 152.

25. Ibid., 157.

26. For a detailed discussion of Alea's ouvre, see Paul A. Schroeder [Rodríguez], *Tomás Guitérrez Alea: The Dialectics of a Filmmaker* (New York: Routledge, 2002).

27. See Julianne Burton, *Cinema and Social Change in Latin America: Conversations with Filmmakers,* 130.

28. Ernesto "Che" Guevara, "Socialism and Man in Cuba," accessed December 1, 2012, http://www.marxists.org/archive/guevara/1965/03/man-socialism

.htm. This essay was first published in *Marcha*, an Uruguayan journal with a continental readership, on March 12, 1965.

29. In a political context that saw the emergence of détente as the official policy of the Soviet Union, the Cuban heresy "centered on the advocacy of guerrilla warfare in Latin America and elsewhere as a means of creating revolutionary conditions" (Michael Chanan, "Cuba and Civil Society," *Nepantla: Views from South* 2, no. 2 [2001]: 392); while in philosophy, "the Cuban heresy adopted Gramsci unselfconsciously, even when he remained very problematic in the USSR and in Eastern Europe" (Fernando Martínez Heredia, "Gramsci in 1960s Cuba," *Nepantla: Views from South* 2, no. 2 [2001]: 373).

30. Peter Brooks, *The Melodramatic Imagination: Balzac, Henry James, Melodrama, and the Mode of Excess* (New Haven, CT: Yale University Press, 1976), 14–15.

31. This attitude was expressed not only within Cuba, where critics unanimously praised the third episode at the expense of the first two and even at the expense of the overall interconnectedness of the film. In the *New York Times*, Nora Sayle wrote that "the first part is too overacted. Women yell and play, making these scenes look like a parody of virginity. The operatic music vibrates each time that the lovers' glances meet, and the apologetic battle scenes look like they were taken from a Western; it's strange that a Cuban filmmaker would use such a worn-out capitalist model." Quoted in "En pantalla: la *Lucía* de Solás," in *A solas con Solás*, ed. Rufo Caballero (Havana: Letras Cubanas, 1999), 240. In another article, published in the Uruguayan journal *Marcha*, Roberto Meyer criticized the first episode for being "too closed in its exploration of private passions that only by chance are connected to history, [and] too subject to stylistic searches that range from poetic realism to expressionism. Roberto Meyer, "*Lucía*: fastos cubanos," in *A solas con Solás*, 244.

32. Eduardo López Morales, "Sí, es posible descubrir de nuevo a *Lucía*," in *A solas con Solás*, 210.

33. Ibid.

34. In this regard, Renée Méndez Capote has contextualized the second episode by noting, "Under pressure from the economic collapse, men began to lose the moral authority that came with their role as providers. Women began to be faced with the necessity of assuming their share of the home's economic survival, and when, following Machado's fall, public jobs and positions in private offices were opened to them, they threw themselves at this new opportunity like swallows who migrate in search of better climes. The miserable wages continued, and men had no choice but to bow their heads and let their daughters, mothers, wives and fiancées work outside the house." Renée Méndez Capote, "*Lucía 1932*," in *A solas con Solás*, 223.

35. Paul Schrader, "Notes on Film Noir," in *Film Genre Reader II*, ed. Barry Keith Grant (Austin: University of Texas Press, 1997), 221.

36. Alfredo Guevara, "El cine cubano 1963," *Cine Cubano* 3, nos. 14–15 (1963): 1.

37. Rufo Caballero and Joel del Río, "No hay cine adulto sin herejía sistemática," *Temas* (Havana) 3 (1995): 114.

38. Quoted in Julio García Espinosa, "Por un cine imperfecto," in *Hojas de cine: Testimonios y documentos del Nuevo Cine Latinoamericano,* vol. 3, ed. Fundación Mexicana de Cineastas (Mexico City: Secretaría de Educación Pública/UNAM, 1988), 74.

39. Ernesto "Che" Guevara, "Socialism and Man in Cuba."

8. NEW LATIN AMERICAN CINEMA'S NEOBAROQUE PHASE

1. Olinda Celestino and Albert Meyers, *Las cofradías en el Perú: región central* (Frankfurt: Vervuert, 1981), 127.

2. Ibid.

3. In *The Andean Hybrid Baroque: Convergent Cultures in the Churches of Colonial Peru* (Notre Dame, IN: Notre Dame University Press, 2010), Gauvin Alexander Bailey succinctly summarizes the situation facing confraternities at this juncture, caught as they were between a Church they had successfully refashioned in their image and a Bourbon state seeking to impose enlightened despotism:

> The Great Rebellion of Túpac Amaru II (1742–81) and Tupaj Katari (1750–81) was one of the most decisive episodes in the history of the Altiplano, from its beginning in the town of Tinta in 1781 to its eruption over the entire southern highlands during the next two years. The political activism and earlier revolts that led to the Great Rebellion began as early as the 1720s, incited by the repressive measures of the Bourbon government [including . . .] the Crown's sale of products to Native Americans at artificially high prices, . . . the expulsion of the Society of Jesus in 1767, the curtailing of Native American confraternities, a draconian restriction of popular devotion and policing of parishes, and the introduction in 1770 of the hated *arancel,* an ecclesiastical schedule of fees that sought to control and homogenize the costs of masses and other church ceremonies. Specifically, [this last set of] reforms had to do with reducing the role of Andean participation in Christian ritual. . . . When the Bourbons imposed unpopular reforms Andeans did not seek a return to the pre-Hispanic past as much as they sought a reinstitution of the pragmatic compromise Andean elites had enjoyed for generations under the Habsburgs and the indigenized Church. In the words of O'Phelan, "To return to the past was, perhaps, not to go back to the Inca Empire, but to return to a much closer past, the period of concessions and recognitions on the part of the politics of the Habsburgs, to return to the 'equilibrium' of the colonial pact." (9–12)

4. I have not yet found direct evidence of a link between the facade of San Lorenzo de Potosí and a confraternity. However, we do know that this church was reserved for indigenous people, and that at the center of the facade's composition is an image of San Miguel Arcángel, a popular figure among indigenous groups at the time. We also know that in contemporary Lima, an Amerindian confraternity of San Miguel Arcángel "provided Andean masons with professional representation" (Gauvin Alexander Bailey, *Art of Colonial Latin America* [New York: Phaidon, 2005], 198). It is therefore not implausible that at San Lorenzo de Potosí there was a confraternity of indigenous masons, and that this confraternity commissioned one of its own members, José Kondori, to sculpt the church's famous facade.

5. See Juan Haro, "Un escultor singular: Antonio Francisco Lisboa, 'O Aleijadinho,'" *Revista de Cultura Brasileña* (Madrid) 50 (1979): 91–107.

6. For a detailed discussion of these differences, see Paul A. Schroeder Rodríguez, "After New Latin American Cinema," *Cinema Journal* 51, no. 2 (2012): 87–112.

7. Ángel Guido in his *Redescubrimiento de América en el arte* (1936), Pedro Henríquez Ureña in "Barroco en América" (1940), and Mariano Picón Salas in *De la Conquista a la Independencia* (1944), where he coins the term "Barroco de Indias" (Baroque of the Indies). For a helpful introduction in English to these and other foundational texts in the theorization of a Latin American neobaroque, see Loise Parkinson Zamora and Monika Kaup, "Baroque, New World Baroque, Neobaroque: Categories and Concepts," in *Baroque New Worlds: Representation, Transculturation, Counterconquest*, eds. Lois Parkinson Zamora and Monika Kaup (Durham, NC: Duke University Press, 2010), 1–35.

8. José Lezama Lima, "La expresión americana," in *El reino de la imagen*, ed. Julio Ramos (Caracas: Biblioteca Ayacucho, 1981), 385.

9. Severo Sarduy, *Barroco* (Buenos Aires: Editorial Sudamericana, 1974), 103–4.

10. For example, while a work of the Spanish Baroque, for instance Narciso Tomé's *Transparente* in the Cathedral of Toledo (1721–32), naturalizes existing social relations by entrancing parishioners into accepting the central figures of Saint Idelfonso and Saint Eugene, archbishops of Toledo during the seventh century, as intermediaries between them and the heavens above, the New World Baroque, for instance José Kondori's facade of the Church of San Lorenzo in Potosí, makes us identify not with the Spaniards or their saints, but with the conquered native populations as represented by the Inca angel-warrior standing directly above the entrance door and flanked by the mermaids of Inca lore on either side.

A similar argument can be made in the case of Aleijadinho's work at the Sanctuary of Bom Jesus do Congonhas, Brazil. Take for example the Station that represents the Last Supper. The grouping makes viewers feel as if they are being invited to sit down at the table with Jesus and his disciples, not only because these are life-size statues sitting around a circular table (which in itself places everyone at the same level), but also because their expressions are quotidian, from the loving gesture of Judas to the startled surprise of one of the disciples who seems to be responding to our presence. The approachability of this Jesus and his disciples stands in stark contrast to the unapproachability of Jesus in many European representations of the Last Supper, whether Leonardo da Vinci's Milan fresco, whose location above eye level and geometrically closed composition sets viewers outside and below the represented sacred space, or Tintoretto's mannerist masterpiece of 1594, whose high drama and dynamic perspectives distance us from Jesus and his disciples.

11. André Breton and Leon Trotsky, "Towards a Free Revolutionary Art," accessed December 3, 2013, http://www.generation-online.org/c/fcsurrealism1 .htm. The manifesto was written by Breton and Trotsky, but subsequently published under the names of Breton and Diego Rivera in *Partisan Review* in 1938 because Trotsky thought it would carry more weight if it came from artists.

12. Manuel Moreno Fraginals, *El ingenio: el complejo económico social cubano del azúcar, Tomo I (1760–1860)* (Havana: Comisión Nacional Cubana de la UNESCO, 1964), 49. The date of 1727 does not come from Moreno Fraginals, but from Agnes Lugo-Ortiz, "Between Violence and Redemption: Slave Portraiture in Early Plantation Cuba," in *Slave Portraiture in the Atlantic World*, eds. Agnes Lugo-Ortiz and Angela Rosenthal (New York: Cambridge University Press, 2013), 201.

13. The intertextuality with Buñuel's *Viridiana* is also evident. In Buñuel's film, beggars from the town where Viridiana's uncle lives break into his estate and stage a riotous feast. The feast ends in a frenzied orgy accompanied by the strains of Handel's *Messiah*. When Viridiana returns from town, she is all but raped by a leper, and her spiritual pride is shattered forever. Blasphemous and ironic, Buñuel's masterpiece is the ultimate insult to Christian hypocrisy, and while Alea never reached such extremes, the intertextuality clearly points to their common practice of using religious history to highlight practices and aspects of consciousness unchanged since the eighteenth century or earlier. K. Jaehne, "*The Last Supper,*" *Film Quarterly* 33, no. 1 (1979): 48.

14. Antonio Nicolás Duque de Estrada, *Explicación de la doctrina cristiana acomodada a la capacidad de los negros bozales*, quoted in Manuel Moreno Fraginals, *El ingenio*, 49. In the film, the Count tells Sebastián: "You see, Sebastian, where pride has led you! [Turning to the other slaves] Negro doesn't learn, he is stubborn. Overseer, say what he say, Negro must close his mouth and obey. Negro don't answer back to overseer. Don Manuel is the overseer and you don't complain when he orders you to work. Negro suffers because he is ignorant. Then don Manuel is right to get rough. Negro takes off to the hills, overseer catches him and then has to punish him real hard, so that Negro does not do it again."

15. Dennis West, "Esclavitud y cine en Cuba: El caso de *La última cena*," *The Western Journal of Black Studies* 3, no. 2 (1979): 132.

16. The original goes as follows:

> Olofi jizo lo mundo, lo jizo completo: jizo día, jizo noche; jizo cosa buena, jizo la cosa mala; también jizo lo cosa linda y lo cosa fea también jizo. Olofi jizo bien to lo cosa que jay en lo mundo: jizo Verdad y jizo también Mentira. La verdad le salió bonita. Lo Mentira no le salió bueno: era fea y flaca-flaca, como si tuviera enfermedá. A Olofi le dá lástima y le dá uno machete afilao pa defenderse. Pasó lo tiempo y la gente quería andar siempre con la Verdad, pero nadie, nadie, quería andar con lo Mentira. . . . Un día Verdad y Mentira se encontrá en lo camino y como son enemigo se peleá. Lo Verdad es más fuerte que lo Mentira; pero lo Mentira tenía lo machete afilao que Olofi le da. Cuando lo Verdad se descuidá, lo Mentira ¡saz! y corta lo cabeza de lo Verdad. Lo Verdad ya no tiene ojo y se pone a buscar su cabeza tocando con la mano . . . [Sebastián tantea la mesa con los ojos cerrados] Buscando y buscando de pronto si tropezá con la cabeza de lo Mentira y . . . ¡ran! arranca cabeza de lo Mentira y se la pone donde iba la suya mismita [Sebastián agarra la cabeza del puerco que está sobre la mesa con un gesto violento, y se la pone delante de su rostro.] Y desde entonce anda por lo mundo, engañando a todo lo gente el cuerpo de lo Verdad con la cabeza de lo Mentira.

17. Alejo Carpentier, *El reino de este mundo* (San Juan: Editorial de la Universidad de Puerto Rico, 1998), 4–7.

18. Manuel Moreno Fraginals, *El ingenio,* 34.

19. Carmelo Mesa-Lago, *Cuba in the 1970s: Pragmatism and Institutionalization* (Albuquerque: University of New Mexico Press, 1978), 26.

20. Louis A. Pérez, *Cuba: Between Reform and Revolution* (New York: Oxford UP, 1995), 337–39.

21. Ibid., 339.

22. Ibid., 340.

23. Ernesto Guevara, "El hombre nuevo," in *Los dispositivos en la flor,* ed. Edmundo Desnoes (Hanover, NH: Ediciones del Norte, 1981), 525–32.

24. A notable previous attempt is *Kukuli* (Luis Figueroa, Eulogio Nishiyama, and César Villanueva, Peru, 1961), a beautifully shot experimental film that has several distinctions, including being the first color film in Peru, the first to be shot in its entirety in Cuzco, the fact that it uses the Quechua language almost exclusively, and the fact that it is based on a myth.

25. Freya Schiwy, *Indianizing Film: Decolonization, the Andes, and the Question of Technology* (New Brunswick, NJ: Rutgers University Press, 2009), 28.

26. The German scientist Ernst Haeckel coined the phrase "ontogeny recapitulates phylogeny." While the idea has been scientifically discredited, I find it useful for a culturalist reading of *La nación clandestina.*

27. Aníbal Quijano, "Modernity, Identity, and Utopia," *boundary 2* 20, no. 3 (1993): 147.

28. Jorge Sanjinés, "El plano secuencia integral," *Cine Cubano* 125 (1989): 69–70.

29. José Carlos Avellar, *A Ponte Clandestina: O diálogo silencioso entre os cineastas latinoamericanos nos anos 1950 e 60* (São Paulo: University of São Paulo, 1995), 7.

30. Michael Chanan, ed., *Twenty-Five Years of New Latin American Cinema* (London: British Film Institute, 1983); Fundación Mexicana de Cineastas, ed., *Hojas de cine. Testimonios y documentos del Nuevo Cine Latinoamericano,* 3 vols. (Mexico City: Secretaría de Educación Pública/UNAM, 1988); and Michael T. Martin, ed., *New Latin American Cinema,* 2 vols. (Detroit: Wayne State University Press, 1997).

31. Raúl Ruiz, *Poetics of Cinema,* trans. Brian Holmes (Paris: Dis Voir, 1995).

32. Glauber Rocha, "Eztetyka do Sonho," in *Glauber Rocha: del hambre al sueño,* eds. Eduardo F. Costantini Jr., Ana Goldman, and Adrián Cangi (Buenos Aires: Fundación Eduardo F. Costantini/MALBA, 2004), 47.

33. Glauber Rocha, jacket cover for *A Idade da Terra* (*The Age of the Earth*; 1980), directed by Glauber Rocha, released on DVD in 2008 by the São Paulo–based Versátil Home Video.

34. Fernando Birri, "Cinema and Underdevelopment," in *New Latin American Cinema,* vol. 1, ed. Michael T. Martin (Detroit: Wayne State University Press, 1997), 87, 94.

35. Hermann Herlinghaus, "La película *Org* (1969/1978) de Fernando Birri," *Revista de Crítica Literaria Latinoamericana* 73 (2011): 121–22.

36. For an analysis of Wilhelm Reich's theory of orgon as it applies to *Org,* see Paul A. Schroeder Rodríguez, "La fase neobarroca del Nuevo Cine Latinoamericano," *Revista de Crítica Literaria Latinoamericana* 73 (2011): 27.

37. Fernando Birri, "Fernando Birri: un constructor de utopías" (interview with Mariluce Moura), *Pesquisa* 127 (2006), n.p., http://revistapesquisa.fapesp.br/es/2006/09/01/fernando-birri/.

38. Ibid.

39. Fernando Birri, in *Fernando Birri: el alquimista poético-político* (Madrid: Cátedra / Filmoteca Española, 1996), 19.

40. Severo Sarduy, *Barroco* (Buenos Aires: Sudamericana, 1974), 14.

41. Ibid., 13.

42. Jorge Sanjinés, "Antecedentes históricos del cine social en Bolivia," in *Hojas de cine. Testimonios y documentos del Nuevo Cine Latinoamericano,* vol. 1, ed. Fundación Mexicana de Cineastas (Mexico City: Secretaría de Educación Pública / UNAM, 1988), 105–6.

43. Jorge Sanjinés, "Problemas de forma y de contenido en el cine revolucionario," in *Hojas de cine* vol. 1, 119.

44. Oswald de Andrade, "Cannibalist Manifesto," trans. Leslie Bary, *Latin American Literary Review* 19, no. 38 (1991): 43.

45. Quoted in Andrea Giunta, "Strategies of Modernity in Latin America," in *Beyond the Fantastic: Contemporary Art Criticism from Latin America,* ed. Gerardo Mosquera (London: Institute of Visual Arts, 1995), 59–60.

46. Daniel Sauvaget, "Arturo Ripstein: un barroco social," in *Los grandes directores de cine,* eds. Jean A. Gili et al. (Barcelona: Ediciones Robinbook, 2008), 305–6.

47. See Isabel Arredondo, "Un cine para 'vísceras pensantes': Bolívar, Sinfonía Tropikal de Diego Rísquez," *Revista de Crítica Literaria Latinoamericana* 37, no. 73 (2011): 149–72.

48. Monika Kaup, "Antidictatorship Neobaroque Cinema: Raúl Ruiz's *Mémoire des apparences* and María Luisa Bemberg's *Yo, la peor de todas,*" in *Neobaroque in the Americas: Alternative Modernities in Literature, Visual Art, and Film* (Richmond: University of Virginia Press, 2012), 183–242.

49. Ibid.

50. This view was popularized by Teshome Gabriel in *Third Cinema in the Third World: The Aesthetics of Liberation* (Ann Arbor, MI: UMI Research Press, 1982), and ironically reproduced in Jim Pines and Paul Willemen, *Questions of Third Cinema* (London: BFI Publishing, 1989), which ostensibly set out to rebut the homogenization of the Third World and its cinemas.

9. COLLAPSE AND REBIRTH OF AN INDUSTRY

1. Fernando Birri, *Fernando Birri: el alquimista poético-político* (Madrid: Cátedra / Filmoteca Española, 1996), 25.

2. Sources: Luisela Alvaray, "National, Regional, and Global: New Waves of Latin American Cinema," *Cinema Journal* 47, no. 3 (2008): 48–65; Tamara L. Falicov, *The Cinematic Tango: Contemporary Argentine Film* (New York:

Wallflower Press, 2007); and Carolina Rocha, "Contemporary Argentine Cinema During Neoliberalism," *Hispania* 92, no. 4 (2009): 841–51.

3. Néstor García Canclini, "Will There Be a Latin American Cinema in the Year 2000? Visual Culture in a Postnational Era," in *Framing Latin American Cinema: Contemporary Critical Perspectives,* ed. Ann Marie Stock (Minneapolis: University of Minnesota Press, 1997), 246–58.

4. See for example Tamara Falicov, "Programa Ibermedia: Co-Production and the Cultural Politics of Constructing an Ibero-American Audiovisual Space," *Spectator* 27, no. 2 (2007): 21–30; and Luisela Alvaray, "National, Regional, and Global."

5. See for example Lúcia Nagib, ed., *The New Brazilian Cinema* (New York and London: I. B. Tauris and Co., 2003); Carlos Bolado, "New Mexican Cinema: A Marketing Idea" (in which Richard K. Curry, José Miguel Muñiz, and Mikel Angel Zárate interview Bolado), *Cine y . . . Revista de estudios interdisciplinarios sobre el cine en español / Journal of Interdisciplinary Studies on Film in Spanish* 1, no. 1 (2008): 98–119; and Horacio Bernades, Diego Lerer, and Sergio Wolf, eds., *El nuevo cine argentino: temas, autores y estilos de una renovación* (Buenos Aires: Tatanka-Fipresci, 2002). Brazilian critics speak of a *Retomada* and not of a *Cinema Novo,* so the use of "new" in English-language publications on recent Brazilian cinema may be a case of marketing strategies in the world of publishing getting in the way of more rigorous scholarship. In Mexico and Argentina, however, critics and promoters continually use "nuevo" to speak of these countries' recent return to the global cinematic landscape.

6. Patricia Aufderheide, "New Latin American Cinema Reconsidered," in *The Daily Planet: A Critic on the Capitalist Culture Beat* (Minneapolis: University of Minnesota Press, 2000), 243–44.

7. Quoted in ibid., 245.

8. Paul Leduc, "Nuevo cine latinoamericano y reconversión industrial (una tesis reaccionaria)," in *El Nuevo Cine Latinoamericano en el mundo de hoy: Memorias del IX festival internacional del Nuevo Cine Latinoamericano* (Mexico City: UNAM, 1988), 19–21.

9. Paul Leduc, quoted in Patricia Aufderheide, "New Latin American Cinema Reconsidered," 248.

10. See Beatriz Bermúdez Rothe, *Pueblos indígenas de América Latina y el Caribe: catálogo de cine y video* (Caracas: Biblioteca Nacional, 1995); and Freya Schiwy, *Indianizing Film: Decolonization, the Andes, and the Question of Technology* (New Brunswick, NJ: Rutgers University Press, 2009). On the web, see Native Networks (nativenetworks.si.edu) and Coordinadora Latinoamericana de Cine y Comunicación de los Pueblos Indígenas (clacpi.org).

11. Jorge Ruffinelli, "El nuevo nuevo cine latinoamericano," *Nuevo cine latinoamericano* (Havana) 2 (2001): 36–37.

12. Damián J. Fernández, *Cuba and the Politics of Passion* (Austin: University of Texas Press, 2000), 149.

13. The shift toward *petit histoires* is especially pronounced in a number of documentaries that do call attention to their own filmmaking—as happens in *La televisión y yo* (Television and Me; Andrés di Tella, Argentina, 2002), *Los rubios* (The Blondes; Albertina Carri, Argentina, 2003), *Santiago* (João Moreira

Salles, Brazil, 2007), and *Jogo de Cena* (Playing; Eduardo Coutinho, Brazil, 2007)—yet from decisively subjective perspectives. This mode of documentary filmmaking is closer to what Bill Nichols calls the reflexive and performative modes of documentary than to the participatory and observational modes that prevailed during the NLAC. See Bill Nichols, *Introduction to Documentary* (Bloomington: Indiana University Press, 2010), 172–211.

14. For a sociological discussion of the glocal, including the epistemology and ideological connotations of the term, see Roland Robertson, "Glocalization: Time-Space and Homogeneity-Heterogeneity," in *Global Modernities*, eds. Mike Featherstone, Scott Lash, and Roland Robertson (London: Sage Publications, 1995), 25–44.

15. Fredric Jameson, *Postmodernism, or the Cultural Logic of Late Capitalism* (Durham, NC: Duke University Press, 1990), 118.

16. Cited in Tzvi Medin, *Cuba: The Shaping of Revolutionary Consciousness*, trans. Martha Grenzback (Boulder: L. Rienner Publishers, 1990), 82.

17. Ibid., 23–25.

18. Indeed, after Castro's initial statements to the effect that no matter what happened in Europe after the fall of the Berlin Wall, the Revolution would continue its Marxist-Leninist course, references to Leninism were eliminated from the Cuban constitution in 1992, and Castro's speeches after 1992 have concentrated on patriotism and anti-imperialism, two pillars of Martían discourse. See Oscar Quiros, "Critical Mass of Cuban Cinema: Art as the Vanguard of Society," *Screen* 37, no. 3 (1996): 292.

19. As Lúcia Nagib perceptively points out, "The lack of an oppressive power [in *Central do Brasil*] allows the action to be transferred from the collective to the individual realm" with the result that society's ills are "not investigated, since class conflict, as well as a hypothetical, if at all existing, ruling class, remains outside the filmic space." Lúcia Nagib, *Brazil on Screen: Cinema Novo, New Cinema, Utopia* (London: I.B. Tauris, 2007), 41.

20. Cited in Paul Julian Smith, *Amores perros* (London: BFI, 2003), 11.

10. LATIN AMERICAN CINEMA IN THE TWENTY-FIRST CENTURY

1. Anna Marie de la Fuente, "Latin Biz Thrives as Local Pic Funds Mature," *Variety*, February 7–13, 2011, A4.

2. Courtney Brannon Donoghue, "Sony and Local-Language Productions: Conglomerate Hollywood's Strategy of Flexible Localization for the Global Film Market," *Cinema Journal* 53, no. 4 (2014): 3–27.

3. "Emerging Markets and the Digitalization of the Film Industry: An Analysis of the 2012 UIS International Survey of Feature Film Statistics," UNESCO Institute of Statistics, August 2013, http://www.uis.unesco.org /culture/Documents/IP14-2013-cinema-survey-analysis-en.pdf, 29.

4. Paulo Antonio Paranaguá, *Tradición y modernidad en el cine de América Latina* (Madrid: Fondo de Cultura Económica de España, 2003), 247–50.

5. In a recent survey, three feature films by the Argentinean director Lucrecia Martel made it onto a list of the ten best Latin American films of the first decade of this century. Martel was the only director to have more than one film on this

list, and was also the only woman on it, yet none of this was highlighted in the survey's press release, a tacit acknowledgment that in Latin America today, the fact that the leading filmmaker is a woman is not something out of the ordinary. "The Ten Best Latin American Films of the Decade," *IFC Center,* Independent Film Channel, accessed February 12, 2013, http://www.ifccenter.com/series /the-ten-best-latin-american-films-of-the-decade.

6. Lucrecia Martel, cited in David Oubiña, *Estudio crítico sobre* La Ciénaga (Buenos Aires: Picnic Editorial, 2007), 15.

7. Lucrecia Martel, interview by Haden Guest, *BOMB* 106 (Winter 2009): n.p., accessed May 24, 2013, http://bombmagazine.org/article/3231/.

8. Teresa de Lauretis, "Desire in Narrative," in *Critical Visions in Film Theory: Classic and Contemporary Readings,* eds. Timothy Corrigan, Patricia White, and Meta Mazaj (Boston and New York: Bedford/St. Martin's, 2011), 590.

9. Gonzalo Aguilar, *Otros mundos: un ensayo sobre el nuevo cine argentino,* 2nd ed. (Buenos Aires: Santiago Arcos, 2010), 101.

10. Teresa de Lauretis, "Desire in Narrative," 584.

11. Freud was clear about the distinction between fear and anxiety. Anxiety, he wrote, "has a quality of *indefiniteness and lack of object.* In precise speech we use the word 'fear' rather than 'anxiety' if [the danger] has found an object." Sigmund Freud, *Inhibitions, Symptoms and Anxiety,* trans. Alex Strachey (New York: W.W. Norton & Co., 1959), 90–91.

12. Michel Chion, *Audio-Vision: Sound on Screen,* trans. Claudia Gorbman (New York: Columbia University Press, 1994), 123–26.

13. Ibid., 132.

14. Lucrecia Martel, "El sonido en la escritura y la puesta en escena," *Casamérica* (Casa de América, Spain) (October 2009), n.p., accessed February 12, 2013, http://www.casamerica.es/temastv/el-sonido-en-la-escritura.

15. Lucrecia Martel, interview by Haden Guest.

16. Jack Zipes, *The Irresistible Fairy Tale: The Cultural and Social History of a Genre* (Princeton, NJ: Princeton University Press, 2012): 138.

17. Ibid., 143.

18. Ibid., 147.

19. Annabel Patterson, as summarized by Jack Zipes, ibid., 13.

20. Clarissa Pinkola Estés, *Women Who Run with the Wolves: Myths and Stories of the Wild Woman Archetype* (New York: Ballantine Books, 1992).

21. Kimberly Theidon, "The Milk of Sorrow: A Theory on the Violence of Memory," *Canadian Woman Studies* 27, no. 1 (2009): 9.

22. Aníbal Quijano, "Modernity, Identity, and Utopia in Latin America," *boundary 2* 20, no. 3 (1993): 147–77.

23. Maurice Halbwachs, extract from *The Collective Memory,* in *The Collective Memory Reader,* eds. Jeffrey K. Olick, Vered Vinitzky-Seroussi, and Daniel Levy (New York: Oxford University Press, 2011), 143.

24. Julianne Burton-Carvajal, "Regarding Rape: Fictions of Origin and Film Spectatorship," in *Mediating Two Worlds: Cinematic Encounters in the Americas,* eds. John King, Ana M. López, and Manuel Alvarado (London: BFI Publishing, 1993), 267–68.

25. Ibid., 260.

26. Ibid., 262.

27. Ibid., 267.

28. Noël Carroll, *Theorizing the Moving Image* (Cambridge, England: Cambridge University Press, 1996), 112.

29. Nöel Carroll, *Beyond Aesthetics: Philosophical Essays* (Cambridge, England: Cambridge University Press, 2001), 259.

30. Ibid., 260.

CONCLUSION: A TRIANGULATED CINEMA

1. Rolena Adorno, *Colonial Latin American Literature: A Very Short Introduction* (London: Oxford University Press, 2011), 17.

2. "By invention," Enrique Dussel writes, "I mean . . . Columbus's construing of the islands he encountered as Asian. The Asiatic being of these islands existed only in the aesthetic and contemplative fantasy of the great navigators of the Mediterranean. . . . This Indian was not discovered as Other, but subsumed under [the category of] Asiatic and . . . so denied as Other, or *covered over (en-cubierto)*." Enrique Dussel, *The Invention of the Americas: Eclipse of the "Other" and the Myth of Modernity*, trans. Michael D. Barber (New York: Continuum, 1995), 28, 32.

3. Gilles Deleuze and Félix Guattari, *A Thousand Plateaus: Capitalism and Schizophrenia*, trans. Brian Massumi (Minneapolis: University of Minnesota Press, 1987), 3–25.

4. This cinephilic culture awaits a thorough study whose point of departure might very well be the study of national research associations such as SOCINE (Sociedade Brasileira de Estudos de Cinema e Audiovisual), Sepancine (Asociación Mexicana de Teoría y Análisis Cinematográfico), and AESECA (Asociación Argentina de Estudios de Cine y Audiovisual), and at a transnational level, RICILA (Red de Investigadores sobre Cine Latinoamericano).

5. Ana M. López, "A Poetics of the Trace," in *New Documentaries in Latin America,* eds. Vinicius Navarro and Juan Carlos Rodríguez (New York: Palgrave Macmillan, 2014), 27.

APPENDIX: DISCOURSES OF MODERNITY IN LATIN AMERICA

1. Louisa Hoberman writes in "Hispanic American Political Theory as a Distinct Tradition," *Journal of the History of Ideas* 41, no. 2 (1980):

> Thomism was [the Church's] conception of the polity as the location of man's effort to make a virtuous and happy life for himself on earth and to progress to a greater comprehension of Divine Truth. . . . Unity presupposed a polity whose component parts complemented one another. It also implied a hierarchical distribution of power, for the natural and human world was composed of superior and inferior entities. At the top of the human hierarchy was the government, civil and ecclesiastical, preferably headed by a king. . . . The claims of the state in the colonial period were identified with the interests of the individual subjects. Subject and state complemented one another. When sixteenth-century Thomists wrote that as a member of an organized

community, the individual was subordinate to a higher end and unity, they meant that subject and ruler were comprehended in the same moral enterprise, not that the interests of one were subordinate to the interests of the other. (202–4)

2. *De Rerum Novarum* neatly summarizes this position:

The great mistake made in regard to the matter now under consideration is to take up with the notion that class is naturally hostile to class, and that the wealthy and the working men are intended by nature to live in mutual conflict. So irrational and so false is this view that the direct contrary is the truth. Just as the symmetry of the human frame is the result of the suitable arrangement of the different parts of the body, so in a State is it ordained by nature that these two classes should dwell in harmony and agreement, so as to maintain the balance of the body politic. Each needs the other: capital cannot do without labor, nor labor without capital. Mutual agreement results in the beauty of good order, while perpetual conflict necessarily produces confusion and savage barbarity. Now, in preventing such strife as this, and in uprooting it, the efficacy of Christian institutions is marvelous and manifold. First of all, there is no intermediary more powerful than religion (whereof the Church is the interpreter and guardian) in drawing the rich and the working class together, by reminding each of its duties to the other, and especially of the obligations of justice. (Papal Encyclicals Online, accessed March 20, 2013, http://www.papalencyclicals.net/Leo13/l13rerum .htm)

3. Even though the founder of that party, Juan B. Justo, was the first to translate Marx's *Capital* into Spanish, his social democratic platform owes more "to social-Darwinism and to Spencer—or to Sarmiento and his school of thought in Argentina—than to Marx." Michael Löwy, "Trayectoria de la Segunda Internacional Socialista en América Latina," *Cuadernos Políticos* (Mexico City) 29 (1981): 36.

4. Michael Löwy, *Marxism in Latin America from 1909 to the Present*, trans. Humanities Press International (Atlantic Highlands, NJ: Humanities Press International, 1992), xiii.

5. Aníbal Quijano, "Modernity, Identity, and Utopia," *boundary 2* 20, no. 3 (1993): 147.

6. For an introduction to this long line of Latin American critics, see Monika Kaup, "Neobaroque: Latin America's Alternative Modernity," *Comparative Literature* 58, no. 2 (Spring 2006): 128–52.

7. Aníbal Quijano, "Modernity, Identity, and Utopia," 149–54.

8. Quijano calls the practice of these Eurocentric "myths" in everyday social relations the "coloniality of power." Aníbal Quijano, "Coloniality of Power, Eurocentrism, and Latin America," *Nepantla: Views from the South* 1, no. 3 (2000): 542.

Index